IN SEARCH OF KNOWLEDGE MANAGEMENT: PURSUING PRIMARY PRINCIPLES

IN SEARCH OF KNOWLEDGE MANAGEMENT: PURSUING PRIMARY PRINCIPLES

EDITED BY

ANNIE GREEN

George Washington University, Washington, DC, USA

MICHAEL STANKOSKY

George Washington University, Washington, DC, USA

LINDA VANDERGRIFF

The Aerospace Corporation, Chantilly, VA, USA

United Kingdom • North America • Japan
India • Malaysia • China

Emerald Group Publishing Limited
Howard House, Wagon Lane, Bingley BD16 1WA, UK

First edition 2010

British Library Cataloguing in Publication Data
A catalogue record for this book is available from the British Library

ISBN: 978-1-84950-673-1

Awarded in recognition of
Emerald's production
department's adherence to
quality systems and processes
when preparing scholarly
journals for print

INVESTOR IN PEOPLE

To ("Aunty") Cecelia Mullis
She lit up any room she entered.

To Freddie Lee Green and Malqueen Green Grant
In your memory I achieve
My achievements make you immortal — never to be forgotten

To Beatrice Ellen (Nelle) Kenwright Dawbarn
Her love of learning and service is part of the rich legacy she gave to all.

Contents

SECTION III: LEARNING APPLICATIONS

SECTION IV: TECHNOLOGY APPLICATIONS

SECTION V: RESEARCH IN KNOWLEDGE MANAGEMENT

SECTION VI: KNOWLEDGE MANAGEMENT CASE STUDIES

List of Contributors

Vittal S. Anantatmula
College of Business, Western Carolina University, Cullowhee, NC, USA

Aurilla Aurélie Bechina Arntzen
College Unversity i Buskerud, HIBU, Faculty of Technology, Kongsberg , Norway

Anthony P. Burgess
The United States Military Academy at West Point, New York

Francesco A. Calabrese
Managing Director, GWC Institute for Knowledge & Innovation, DC, USA

Alfredo Federico Revilak De La Vega
Institute for Knowledge and Innovation (IKI), The George Washington University, Washington, DC, USA

Massimo Franco
SEGES Department, University of Molise, Campobasso, Italy

Rudy Garrity
The George Washington University, Washington, DC, USA

Juan Pablo Giraldo
IBM Global Business Services, Herndon, VA, USA

Jeffery Grabowski
VP Technology & Innovation, Xerox Global Services, Webster, NY, USA

Annie Green
Institute of Knowledge and Innovation (IKI), George Washington University, DC, USA

Linda Larson Kemp
The Institute for Knowledge and Innovation, The George Washington University, Washington, DC, USA

Valentina Maksimova
Moscow State University of Economics, Statistics and Informatics (MESI), Moscow, Russia

Stefania Mariano
NYIT – School of Management, Adliya, Kingdom of Bahrain

Gabriele McLaughlin	The Institute for Knowledge and Innovation & School of Engineering and Applied Science, The George Washington University, Washington, DC, USA
J. Steven Newman	ARES Corporation, VP Technology Applications, Arlington, VA, USA
Kevin J. O'Sullivan	Department of Management and Marketing, School of Management, New York Institute of Technology, New York, NY, USA
Elsa Rhoads	The George Washington University, Washington, DC, USA
Vincent M. Ribière	The Institute for Knowledge and Innovation, Bangkok University, Bangkok, Thailand
Juan A. Román	Johns Hopkins University, Carey Business School, Baltimore, MD, USA
Aleša Saša Sitar	Faculty of Economics, Ljubljana, Slovenia
Yury Telnov	Moscow State University of Economics, Statistics and Informatics (MESI), Moscow, Russia
Vladimir Tikhomirov	Moscow State University of Economics, Statistics and Informatics (MESI), Moscow, Russia
Natalia Tikhomirova	Moscow State University of Economics, Statistics and Informatics (MESI), Moscow, Russia
Philippe van Berten	University of Pittsburgh, 300 Campus Drive, Bradford, PA, USA
Linda J. Vandergriff	The Aerospace Corporation, Chantilly, VA, USA
Stephen M. Wander	Retired, NASA, Lecturer at School of Engineering and Applied Sciences, The George Washington University, Washington, DC, USA

Acknowledgments

One of the privileges of being at a University is listening to the eternal sounds of learning and knowledge creation. They are consistent, never ending, the closest thing to defining infinity. One of my themes is that codification, collaboration, convergence, and coherence lead to success. Since I joined the faculty of engineering management and systems engineering at George Washington University in 1998, I have found success through the incredible group of practitioners and scholars who have come together in the hot pursuit of knowledge management (KM). They pursue it not only for their own personal goals, but also because they recognize how critical it is to the world community that we do this, and get it right. The names of the authors in this book are but a sampling of those; others span many professions and continents. The list is legion. However, I do want to recognize in a special way the contributions from Russia. Dr. Vladimir Tikhomirov and Dr. Natalya Tikhomirova, President and Rector, respectively, from the Moscow State University of Statistics, Economics, and Informatics, and their colleagues, provide unique perspectives into knowledge management and institutions of higher learning. I have had the privilege of working with this group, and their insights, energy, and dedication to knowledge management are truly inspirational.

This book is clearly codified today because of my colleague-editors, Dr. Annie Green and Dr. Linda Vandergriff. The amount of work and persistence to guide this to fruition is hard to quantify; it is an incredible accomplishment! Special recognition must also be given to Dr. Francesco Calabrese, another contributing author. Francesco has been the managing director of the Institute for Knowledge and Innovation, and his personal time and energy spent in both the intellectual and business sides of the institute have gotten us where we are today. Many minted doctors owe a lot to him. I owe him a great deal. His "Introduction" chapter tells our story, and you will see, he is the right person to tell it.

Diane Heath, commissioning editor at Emerald Group Publishing Limited, deserves special mention. Diane recruited me as an editor for *VINE: The Journal of Information and Knowledge Management Systems*, from which I recently resigned after three years. With Diane's vision, we expanded the journal from a library science publication, to the issues of information and knowledge management in enterprise-wide, global settings. She recently was transferred to the book publishing section at Emerald, and it was she who gave me the encouragement and support to do this.

I would like to recognize my co-directors of the Institute for Knowledge and Innovation: Dr. Diana Burley, Graduate School of Education and Human Development, and Dr. Richard Donnelly, School of Business, George Washington University. I, from the School of Engineering and Applied Science, make this triumvirate unique in a university setting, demonstrating that we can break down walls. My co-founder and past co-director, Professor Emeritus William Halal deserves special mention for his pioneering efforts in this enterprise. Bill is not resting on his laurels, but is ever present in his new ideas and writings on technology forecasting. Dr. Art Murray is also another pioneer, who made a big difference in the early days, and still does, with our new umbrella research activity: "the enterprise of the future." He is also the ultimate KM practitioner.

I want to recognize my chair, Dr. Tom Mazzuchi. Tom has been an incredible support at the University, constantly providing me with the right touch of counsel and freedom on how to get things done in a large complex that our university is. When I write my book on political engineering, Tom will be one of my models.

Finally, it should be noted that the opinions and theories presented in this book are those of the individual authors and do not represent an official position of any of the associated institutions or organizations.

Michael Stankosky

Foreword

Knowledge management is about leveraging an organization's relevant
knowledge assets to improve efficiency, effectiveness, and innovation.

What a journey it has been! I never heard of the concept of knowledge management
(KM) until I joined the Faculty of Engineering Management and Systems
Engineering at the George Washington University (GWU) in August 1998. I, like
many still today, was suspicious of the idea that anyone could manage knowledge.
Even the definition of what knowledge is was never a fixed one in my mind. This was
the "Information Age," and what was this peculiar intruder, dubbed KM? It
sounded like another of those management fads that come and go every so many
years. Why and what should I be doing, occupying myself with another fad?

Such was my mindset when I first came across the term while exploring the latest
in artificial intelligence, one of the several courses I inherited from my predecessor.
Search engines were in their infancy way back then, and Google was not even an
idea, let alone the verb that it is today. However, what were apparent were the
prolific writings, applications, and technologies on KM that were sprinkled all over
the landscape. What struck me the most, and still has the most profound influence in
my decision to undertake creating a discipline of KM was the simple fact that
knowledge, by any definition, was what Peter Drucker (considered as the father of
management art and science) termed the "factors of production" in the latter part of
the 20th century. He also coined the term "knowledge worker." Another writer,
Thomas A. Stewart, in his book *Intellectual Capital*, stressed the point that
knowledge is the new wealth of organizations. In his later book, *The Wealth of
Knowledge*, he is emphatic about the primacy of knowledge in our global economy.
Today, in this 21st century, *knowledge* is the undisputed currency of the day. It is
truly, as Drucker described it, the principal raw material driving the wealth of people,
organizations, and nations. Thus, knowledge, in the parlance of capitalists, is *capital*,
a *strategic asset*, an *indispensible* resource, critical to the effectiveness, efficiency, and
innovation of the 21st century global economy. Again, Thomas Stewart eloquently
points this out in both his books mentioned above. Rough figures indicate that
knowledge assets account for over 70% of the U.S. and European Union GDPs.
Wow! This fact alone inspired me to tackle the monumental task of trying to
determine exactly what is KM, with all its shades and nuances.

This led me to resist the legion of definitions on KM, which do not point out this singular aspect of knowledge. Most treat knowledge and KM as a technology, a process, a community, an initiative, a whatever ..., but few, if any, treat it as strategic asset inputs. My first instinct was to derive a definition from these facts, since a definition is a true starting point for research, and for creating an academic discipline. Additionally, there was a need to create a framework to bind the many discussions and treatises on KM. A definition and framework would also be necessary to attract the many researchers and students who would see much confusion in their own explorations. Eventually, our goal was to create primary or first principles of KM — the underpinnings for a theory. Without these, practices become games of chance; experiments that follow the whims of those on the scene. Imagine physics without the first principles of Newton and Einstein, derived from their research. I could only envision chaos and disaster in the Industrial and Nuclear Ages. Remember, theory makes perfect; practice makes permanent.

Our foundational definition became, after much reflection and research: *leveraging relevant knowledge assets to enhance organizational effectiveness, efficiency, and innovation.*

A short explanation of this definition is appropriate here, especially since it frames the rest of my discussion. *Leveraging* is a powerful verb, and it basically indicates that knowledge shared realizes a potential far greater than it being hoarded. One plus one thus becomes more than two (i.e., an organizational multiplier). *Relevant* is a most important qualifier, for organizations should only concern themselves with knowledge that meets their objectives. Thus, the true metric for knowledge payoff is its ability to produce the product and/or service as delineated by the organization (*effectiveness*). After effectiveness, *efficiency and innovation* normally follows the continued leveraging of the organizational knowledge assets.

Dr. Francesco Calabrese discusses our foundational framework (*four pillars: leadership, organization, learning, and technology*) in the "Introduction" chapter, and also describes the 10-year journey taken on our road to discovery and validation. This *four-pillar* construct frames the research and applications in the various chapters that follow. They also were the basis for GWU's KM curriculum.

One principle discovered: these *four pillars* must all be present and operate in a balanced harmony for any KM asset and initiative to be leveraged and successful. No one pillar is more important than the other; all four are vital.

Two events are noteworthy of highlighting in our search of knowledge management. The first one was the need to have KM education and research credit-bearing, leading to the master's and doctorate degrees. Few come to school to learn; they come for a degree, which is the primary certificate for hire and advancement in our knowledge economy. The doctorate became the critical degree, because course content in the master's degree flows from research in the doctorate. Since I could not find any university at that time which had degrees around KM, I applied for such at GWU, and received approval, following the rigorous process of course and degree certification.

The second event was to create a global community of practitioners and scholars to challenge and advance the basic KM premises that Dr. Calabrese describes in the "Introduction" chapter. Our legitimization came from creating an institute at GWU, which has evolved into its current incarnation as The Institute for Knowledge and Innovation (see www.gwu.edu/~iki). This institute has become an international community for advancing the practice and research for KM. While it is housed at GWU, it is a truly international group, who are dedicated to seeing KM become a truly global academic discipline and a professional organization. At one period of time, we had over 45 doctoral researchers and 12 adjunct faculty. You will meet some of them in the following chapters. One thing is evident: collaboration, diversity of backgrounds, and focus bring a richness of ideas and practices that remain the hallmark of innovation.

This book is a second installment that records and characterizes our community's KM practice and research. The first was published in 2005, under the title *Creating the Discipline of Knowledge Management: The Latest in University Research*. A third book, led by Dr. Annie Green, is already underway.

We are still a long way from realizing our goal of a unified KM global definition and framework, with its accompanying primary principles and professional society. The journey must continue! KM is not a fad. The knowledge economy is bustling all around us, and is like a fast moving train. Someone recently asked me if the current economic depression was caused by the lack of KM understanding. It gave me much pause ... still does. My answer was more another question. Why is it that, if knowledge is the primary raw material for our global economy, is it not properly valued and accounted for in our macro and micro economic models? Why is it that I have not met a CEO who has a complete inventory of their knowledge assets, given that they are the majority of their strategic capital assets? Someone said that you cannot mange what you cannot measure. I go a bit further, and say you cannot measure what you cannot name. You cannot do risk management if you cannot value; and you cannot value what you cannot name. How can you do risk management if you have no name for the asset, and corresponding value?

When someone asks me to justify a KM initiative, I worry. It is like asking to justify why we use rubber to make a tire. So, the search of KM continues. When I look at the number of global conferences, myriad papers, and books on KM, and the legion of KM practitioners and scholars, it gives me hope. Hopefully, we will all connect, collaborate, converge, and find our way to a global KM definition and framework. So, why KM; it's all about KM!

Michael Stankosky
Professor of Engineering Management and Systems Engineering
Lead Professor, Knowledge Management
Co-founder and co-director, Institute for Knowledge and Innovation
George Washington University, Washington, DC

FURTHER READING

Drucker, P. F. (2001). *Management challenges for the 21st century*. New York: Harper Collins.

Stankosky, M. (2005). *Creating the discipline of knowledge management: The latest in university research*. Burlington, MA: Elsevier.

Stewart, T. A. (1997). *Intellectual capital: The new wealth of organizations*. New York: Currency Doubleday.

Stewart, T. A. (2001). *The wealth of knowledge: Intellectual capital and the twenty-first century organization*. New York: Currency Doubleday.

Introduction: GWU-KM: A Decade of Leadership in Creating the Discipline of Knowledge Management

Francesco A. Calabrese

The George Washington University's knowledge management (GWU-KM) journey is completing the first decade on its orbit of "Theory to Practice — a Continuum." Progress continues in a series of spiral "events," often beginning with the challenge of converting theory (research) into practice (application). Yet just as often the resulting application leads to lessons learned, spawning the need to extend the original or add new research in GWU's continuing quest to evolve the discipline of knowledge management (KM) toward a universally accepted set of theorems; replicable practices; and a common language created by a real and virtual global community of interest/practice.

In this GWU Volume II, *In Search of Knowledge Management*, the authors and editors have elected to present the main body of chapter contents in the sequence of Applications, Research and Case Studies. This Introduction chapter positions those contents against the backdrop of major milestone developments, which have defined the continually expanding spirals, extending the GWU-KM evolution into a global influence.

1. The Formative Years

A decade ago, the combination of a directed research project and its following dissertation, introduced a graphic icon labeled the "four-pillar framework" as a means of presenting a short-hand statement for the GWU's definition of a KM system for the 21st century.

The "elevator statement" describing that Framework remains valid today. "With **Leadership** commitment supporting **Organizational** collaborative practices, processes and forums, and appropriate

Technology enabling tools one can grow a **Learning Enterprise/ Environment** to perpetuate a sustainable knowledge-enabled culture." (Calabrese, 2000)

Follow me on a quick "graphic tour" of evolution by systems thinking scholars and experienced practitioners who have populated this GWU's KM journey of exploration and discovery.

2. The Verification Period

Concurrent with the evolution of our KM "model" reflected in Figures 1–4, research effort was also devoted by others to testing, tempering, extending, challenging, proving/disproving, etc. the merits and utility or perishability of our theories and early applications. During the ensuing years, GWU's KM Community met all challenges. Adhering to its mantra of "Theory to Practice — A Continuum," the community's leadership and members spawned the creation of a body of knowledge usages, forums, and influences through

- the dissertations and research papers of some 25 graduated doctoral candidates (2000–2008);
- the creation and active engagement (1999–2008) of a community of interest of more than 70 members whose participant core has expanded into a global network of scholars and practitioners;

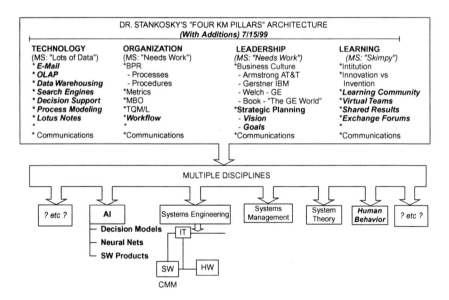

Figure 1: The original version (Calabrese, 1999, Directed Research): A thought depiction of the four pillars captured on the "cave wall" in a systems engineering style.

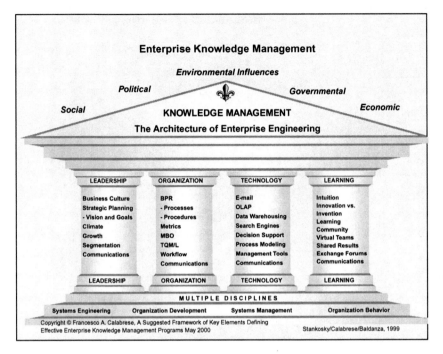

Figure 2: The "validated, generic" version (Calabrese, May 2000): A more descriptive depiction, augmented by an integrating foundation of some 40 disciplines and within a spectrum of environmental stakeholder influences.

- the chartering of the Institute of Knowledge Management in 2001, now titled the "Institute of Knowledge and Innovation";
- the consolidation in 2005 of early writings into an initial book *Creating the Discipline of Knowledge Management*;
- the stream of continuing knowledge "nuggets" through the Emerald Group's VINE Journal editorially guided for the past four years (2005–2008) by Dr. Michael A. Stankosky, GWU's Lead Professor for Knowledge and Information Management;
- the establishment of iKi South East Asia (iKi-SEA) by Dr. Vincent Ribière, an early GWU D.Sc. knowledge graduate with the support of the faculty and the senior leadership of Bangkok University (2008); and most recently
- the completion of this year's book on *In Search of Knowledge Management* (Vol. II) under the stimulating intellects of Dr. Annie Green and Dr. Linda Vandergriff with Dr. Stankosky's guidance.

Throughout this verification period, the GWU community has challenged itself on multiple occasions concerning the continuing relevance of the "four pillar" contents to encompass the meaning(s) of KM research and practices within the vastly expanding KM universe. As indicated at the outset, this framework appears to

RESEARCH MAP Supporting the Four Pillars

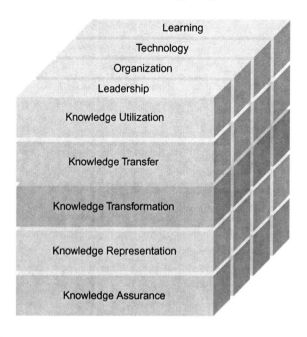

Figure 3: The pillars and "knowledge research" version (Murray, Calabrese et al., 2000): Recognizing the critical need to cross matrix the four-pillar architecture and system with the research elements of the knowledge domain.

remain cogent at the core of each pillar, and holistically within the "system of systems" represented by the four pillars in balance and harmony. Admittedly, there has been a stream of changing "labels" describing the pillars and reflecting the exponential infusion of globally dispersed thought leaders enriching the body of

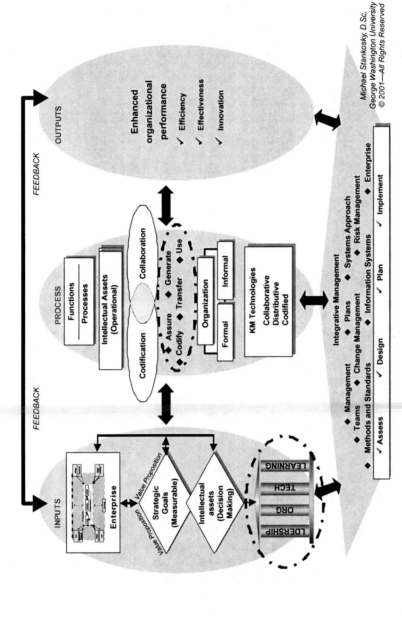

Figure 4: The "engineering and integration" version (Stankosky, 2001): Embedding the four-pillar mental model and research domain within the global reality of organizational existences.

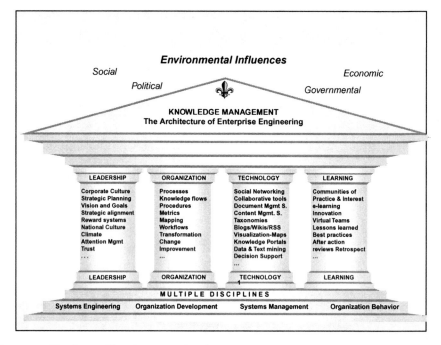

Figure 5: The four pillar framework: circa 2009 (Green, Vandergriff, & Stankosky, 2009).

knowledge through books, articles, cyber linkages, web and portal sites, and ongoing applications and implementations. One current version drawn from the graphic on the cover of Volume II is shown in Figure 5.

Augmentation of representative "labels" even beyond those reflected in Figure 5 are presented in Table 1 spanning KM titled attributes, methods, concepts, practices, and tools. Readers are invited and encouraged to further augment the listings from their own "knowledge repositories."

3. Threshold to Future Research and Applications

Concurrent with the "graphic evolution" presented, GWU-IKI has been sponsoring an initiative to extend our research and applications into a knowledge-based *Enterprise of the Future (EoF)* guided by Dr. Arthur J. Murray, IKI's first Managing Director and Senior Fellow. "IKI, EoF Focus Areas" is reasonably self-descriptive of the expanding vision spawned within the framework of the four pillars (Figure 6). The research, applications, and future publications from this initiative are expected to further enhance the global body of knowledge in the 21st century.

Table 1: Representative current additional pillar "descriptors".

Leadership	Organization	Technology	Learning
• Enlightened	• Agile	• SOA	• Peer-to-Peer
• Catalytic	• Adaptive	• Pod Casts	• Storytelling
• Participative	• Complex	• Blogs	• Lifelong Learning
• Motivational	• Crowd Sourcing	• Wikis	• COIs
• Nonautocratic	• Social Networking	• Twitter	• CoPs
• Humble	• B2 B (Business 2)	• Portals	• Lessons Learned
• Inclusive	• P2 P (Peer 2)	• Social SW	• Sharing
• Coaching	• Performance	• Web 2.0	• Trust
• Mentoring	measures	• Cloud computing	• Virtual worlds
• Visionary		• MyFace	• Thought power
		• SharePoint	
		• Adobe Connect	
		• GotoMeeting	
		• Mind Maps	
		• The Brain	

Note: Again, attributes of leaders, forms of organization, enabling technology capabilities and learning mechanisms can all be accommodated and logically related to the named "pillars of the framework" (Calabrese, 2009).

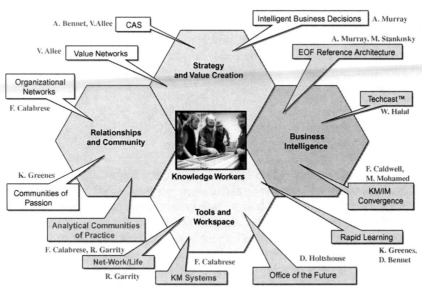

Figure 6: IKI-EoF research and application focus areas (Murray, Greenes, & IKI KM Community, 2006/2007).

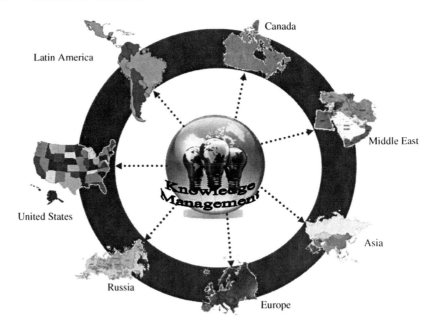

Figure 7: GWU's nodes for a global KM network (Stankosky, IKI KM Community, 2008).

4. Potential for a Global KM Society

We are in a globally engaged "knowledge era." Not surprisingly our lead visionary, Dr. Stankosky, has conceived and is collaborating with peers and institutions worldwide on the notion of a "global knowledge management society" (see Figure 7). A "discipline," after all, must create standards and criteria for levels of excellence and practices, which are understood and consistently applied to demonstrate the governance that can lead to universally acceptable certification of new and revised concepts, researchers, and practitioners.

5. Summary

We have journeyed through only a few of the multiple "landmarks" created and built upon by hundreds of scholar practitioners in the GWU KM classrooms, laboratories, study halls, offices, and private homes in the past decade. The majority earned certificates and/or master's degrees, and a significant percentage achieved entry into the "academy of scholars" at the doctoral level. But *all* contributed and were enriched in the arena of intellectual challenges transitioning as pioneers across the threshold of the 21st century and the explosive global outpouring of literature and programs, which has been documented by the 1998–1999 "hockey stick" chart of the growth curve (Despres & Chauvel, 1999).

At the GWU, we have maintained a steady pace of accomplishments in creating the discipline of knowledge management. We have also applied the principles of Lessons Learned/After Action Reviews to strengthen insights into both enterprise applications and research areas of the future, and to encourage the creation of global awareness forums to speed the collaboration between the earth's multibillion minds. We trust that a microcosm of these endeavors emerges for the readers of our Volumes I and II.

SECTION I

LEADERSHIP APPLICATIONS

Management is doing things right, Leadership is doing the right thing.
Benis & Namus (1985)

The KM Leadership pillar focuses on doing the right thing to empower the Intellectual Capital of an organization. Calabrese (2000) validated this pillar and further defined subelements as timely strategic planning, vision sharing, goal and objective, executive commitments, setting incentives and metrics for knowledge management use, and defining KM roles and responsibilities. Leadership role is to find, enable, and communicate a coherent vision or mental model of the environment and of where the Enterprise wants to go. This is often called providing "coherence" to the endeavor. The following chapters focus on Leadership related applications.

References

Benis, W., & Namus, B. (1985). *Leaders: The strategies for taking charge*. New York: Harper & Row.

Calabrese, F. A. (2000). *A suggested framework of key elements defining effective enterprise knowledge management programs*. D.Sc. dissertation, George Washington University, Washington, DC.

Chapter 1

Leadership Role in Making Effective Use of Knowledge Management

Vittal S. Anantatmula

Abstract

The challenge facing knowledge management (KM) professionals is how to leverage knowledge for improving the organization's competitive advantage. KM systems improve communication, and collaboration to enhance employee skills with a focus on improving their productivity and performance. From a leadership perspective, it is critical to ensure that KM investments result in promoting collaborative culture at individual and organizational levels to encourage knowledge sharing for better decision-making and innovation. Ultimately, the purpose of KM is to leverage knowledge in order to improve organizational performance internally and externally. This chapter aims to address KM challenges from a leadership perspective.

1.1. Introduction

Technology developments and a number of other factors have converged since early 1990s to create a shrinking world and an expanding global economy. The business world is experiencing a transition from the Industrial to Intelligence Age (Tyson, 1997). Many companies joined the global economy, intensifying the global competition in the market for intellectual capital and market share. Specifically, advances in communication and information technology (IT) have revolutionized the way business is managed and led. The global competition is compelling organizations to develop products and services faster, cheaper, and better in order to attain and sustain competitive advantage in the marketplace. Organizations strive to meet this

In Search of Knowledge Management: Pursuing Primary Principles
Copyright © 2010 by Emerald Group Publishing Limited
All rights of reproduction in any form reserved
ISBN: 978-1-84950-673-1

challenge by improving their efficiency, effectiveness, and innovation with respect to intellectual capital.

New business trends are in place to utilize continuous advances in IT and communication technologies. These technologies are adopted to meet growing new business needs effectively and efficiently. They have also provided opportunities to manage knowledge at the individual and various organizational levels. Companies participating in the global economy exhibit two distinct operational characteristics: outsourcing and geographically dispersed virtual teams. But for the technological advances, outsourcing and virtual global teams would not have become feasible. These two features also have an impact on how organizations view manage and share knowledge.

1.2.   Outsourcing and Geographically Dispersed Virtual Teams

Global economy is compelling organizations to establish operating divisions and factories close to marketplaces and other strategic locations where people of requisite experience and resources are available at a lower cost. Consequently, virtual teams are integral to many organizations in the current economy.

Outsourcing is a common business practice as it helps acquire quality services and expertise at a lower cost. For instance, quite often you will end up talking to a service representative in India when you call for a product helpline concerning an appliance manufactured by General Electric. Many organizations employ outsourcing as a strategy to reduce costs without sacrificing quality.

Often you will find that major software development projects use geographically dispersed virtual project teams. A case in point is Infosys Technologies Limited — one of the leading software consultants in the world — has a conference room in Bangalore, India that can hold a virtual meeting of the key players from its entire global supply chain on a super size screen to integrate project functions and work as an effective project team (Friedman, 2005). These virtual teams span various time zones, different languages and cultures, and possess a wide range of competencies, and skills. Needless to say, outsourcing and consequent virtual global teams are challenging the traditional organizational structures. The benefits of these virtual project teams to an organization include the following:

- Increases access to a diverse pool of intellectual capital at lower costs;
- Promotes innovation and responsiveness because of the diversity of intellectual capital;
- Supports 24×7 operations because of the team's geographical distribution;
- Lowers risk of geographical related disruptions.

From the organizational standpoint, outsourcing and virtual global teams present important challenges such as

- adopting outsourcing and global virtual teams seamlessly into business operations;
- leading outsourcing and virtual global teams effectively;

- safeguarding individual and organizational knowledge; and
- accommodating diverse cultural, knowledge, and legal sensitivities.

It is critically important for organizations to address these challenges to sustain their competitive advantage.

Both these distinct features — outsourcing and virtual global teams — have one feature in common: the knowledge of the organization is no longer confined within the organization. The challenging task that faces organizations is how do they manage knowledge resources to gain and sustain their competitive advantage?

1.3. Justification for KM

In the current economy, top management priorities — in the context of projects — are building virtual teams with a minimum of face time, clearly defining work, measuring cybernetic worker productivity, and managing employee communications across time zones (Nidiffer & Dolan, 2005). While it is obvious that technology plays a critical role in supporting a management's efforts to meet these priorities, effective knowledge management (KM) also plays a supportive role in achieving these priorities.

However, KM is often perceived as merely IT by many organizations and is often associated with technological solutions such as intranets and databases (Marr, 2003). Many organizations have employed KM initiatives relying primarily on IT tools (Greenhalgh, Robert, MacFarlane, Bate, & Kyriakidou, 2004) and as a result, may not achieve desired results.

Several studies focused on linking IT and/or KM methods and models to improved organizational performance (Marchand, Kettinger, & Rollins, 2000; Jennex & Olfman, 2002; Ahn & Chang, 2002; King, 2002). However, we find research studies often contradict this notion. Marchand et al. (2000) observed that even after spending several billions of dollars on IT, it is difficult to reliably map the investment to improved business performance. Likewise, a weak relationship between IT and business presents a challenge for business organizations, specifically in KM area (Martin, Hatzakis, Lycett, & Macredie, 2004), to make a continuing business case for necessary investments.

Martin et al. (2004) contend that the IT–business gap is traced to a lack of knowledge of each other's issues and communication norms. Without a clear IT business performance vision, untargeted knowledge sharing practices lead to poor coordination of work practices, project management deficiencies, and defective information systems. In this context, KM is seen as a bridge between IT and business. Thus, KM can be seen as a holistic way to manage the complex relationship between business and IT (Martin et al., 2004). Martin et al. (2004) contend that effective KM promotes one vision and improved communication will have a direct impact on the ability of firms to bridge the gap between IT and end-users, thereby impacting organizational performance.

In addition to KM's role in improving communication as identified by Martin et al. (2004), another research has shown that KM leads to enhanced collaboration as well (Anantatmula, 2005). Further, enhanced collaboration leverages employee skills in the context of decision-making to improve productivity and quality. KM, therefore, improves decision-making and productivity internally, and customer satisfaction externally.

Improved KM is often associated with change, which habitually faces resistance. This resistance is often manifested in reluctance to modify actions at the individual level, and adjusting working culture at the organization level. From this perspective, leadership assumes importance and is a determinant of success, as it provides vision of the value of change, adopts the change incentives to adopt the needed change, and the ability to cope with change. Therefore, we can argue that leadership assumes importance in utilizing new knowledge in the organization. However, this is not the only reason why leadership is important for KM. Leadership skills become important in developing a KM initiative and implementing KM systems in organization because they are new by definition; employees are required to adapt to the changes in behavior and practices. It is worthwhile exploring the literature on the subject prior to developing a detailed sketch of leadership in making effective use of KM.

1.4. Leadership and Management

Making effective use of knowledge requires intervention of leadership and management because it is associated with incentivizing vision and planned change in direction. The roles of both the leader and the manager are important at different stages of KM life cycle. Leadership plays a critical role in developing and implementing KM systems or initiatives. Once KM processes are developed, the manager's role assumes greater importance in maintaining their effectiveness and efficiency. Promoting innovation using KM process requires collaborative culture and participation in decision-making. Leadership promotes innovation by creating a vision and strategic direction. Therefore, leadership has a critical role in developing and managing KM systems.

Developing and implementing KM systems are akin to projects. Both are time-bound endeavors with schedule, budget, scope, and quality constraints. We can, therefore, use project management literature in addition to KM literature to understand leadership role for developing and implementing KM initiatives. On the other hand, KM leadership role in promoting innovation using KM systems requires a review of the KM literature.

1.5. Leadership in the Context of KM

Leadership skills required for KM initiatives and processes are no different from what a traditional leader must possess. A good leader as one who focuses on *doing the right things*, compared to a project manager who focuses on *doing the things right* (Verma, 1996). Leadership is viewed as the ability to influence the behavior of others to align their goals with that of the leader (Liu & Fang, 2006). For this to happen, leaders must not only confident, but also inspire confidence in the people they interact with (Prabhakar, 2005). However, one must understand that leaders must understand the type of leadership that must be employed because they are perceived as role models.

As is true with any leadership in different situations and organizations, good project leaders need to get things done through others while creating a vision of the destination, a compelling reason to get there, a realistic timetable, and a capacity to attract a willing team (Selg, 2007). Further, senior managers who sponsor projects should have qualities such as political awareness, willingness and ability to facilitate connections for the project manager, courage, support the vision, partnering, and communication (Helm & Remington, 2005). At the project level, a project manager's inherent traits and their applicability to leadership have been cited as contributing to a project's success (Gehring, 2007).

The ability of the project leader to project the vision of the project with all the stakeholders in developing, communicating, and delivering the message in a way that ensures continued support is a contributing leadership factor that plays a large role in project success or failure (Christensen & Walker, 2004). Further, the project leader should ensure that the project team is "creating purposeful, strategic action that will augment the organization's business strategy" (Norrie & Walker, 2004, p. 48) and it can be applied to KM initiatives. These two observations, albeit true in the context of projects, are relevant and applicable in KM initiatives as well.

A research study investigating KM process for software engineering (Ward & Aurum, 2004) identified leadership as the most important one among the four enablers of KM — leadership, technology, culture, and measurement. Likewise, KM model developed by Baldanza and Stankosky (2000) identified leadership is one of the important pillars of the four-pillar KM model of leadership, organization, technology, and learning.

Other studies have also highlighted the importance of leadership in the context of KM. Leadership is considered an important KM enabler (Okunoye & Karsten, 2002; Koh, Ryan, & Prybutok, 2005). Several KM success factors can be viewed as facilitating factors for a KM initiative and they include leadership, investing in people, and developing supporting organizational conditions like technical infra-structure and secured knowledge structure (Chourides, Longbottom, & Murphy, 2003; Jennex & Olfman, 2002).

Innovation is one of the important outcomes of making effective use of KM systems. Knowledge creation and knowledge sharing through collaboration are not enough. KM leadership must translate them into action by incentivizing people to participate in decision-making. Collaborative decision-making often leads to innovation. In addition to identifying the measures of success, the inclusion of the appropriate decision makers are a critical aspect of leadership that must not be underestimated (Schwarber, 2005).

1.6. KM and Organizational Performance

IT and KM contribute to organizational performance and business results. However, it is people who make use of these systems and thus, it is imperative to understand the extent to which these systems help people in their day-to-day functions. Earlier discussions suggested that KM acts as a bridge between IT and end-users. Thus, the real impact of KM is on people and organizational performance.

In a research study, KM success of 147 organizations in 21 countries identified improved communication, enhanced collaboration, improved employee skills, better decision-making, and improved productivity as the most useful outcomes (Anantatmula, 2005). Using interpretive structural modeling (ISM) to develop relations among these outcomes, Anantatmula and Kanungo (2006) showed that enhanced collaboration leverages employee skills in the context of decision-making to influence productivity and quality.

In principle, KM criteria must be guided by an organization's goals, and bottomline results such as business performance and profitability. However, the research findings discussed above revealed that KM efforts result in soft measures, which are not directly tied to end results. These results also imply that KM outcomes are difficult to measure. Further, all of them are people-related factors, which emphasize the importance of KM leadership's people-related role in directing KM efforts successfully.

1.7. Leadership Role in KM Effectiveness

The discussions so far have set the stage to discuss leadership and management roles in successful KM implementation. Two recent studies have examined the role of leadership in making an effective use of KM. The first study is focused on identifying and modeling enablers for successful implementation of KM (Anantatmula & Kanungo, 2007). The second one is an explorative study of the role of leadership and management in the success of KM (Anantatmula, 2007).

1.8. Study 1: Modeling Enablers for KM Success

This study identified and modeled enablers for successful implementation of KM. Anantatmula and Kanungo (2007), using literature review, identified 13 factors, which could influence KM success. They are strategic focus, leadership, top management support, culture, top management involvement, measurement of results, technology infrastructure, standard KM practices, content quality, collaboration and formalization, communication, and budgetary support. Although the study of literature helped to identify important factors of KM success, understanding how these factors interact and influence each other is considered important to develop methods and strategies for successful KM implementation. With the use of a

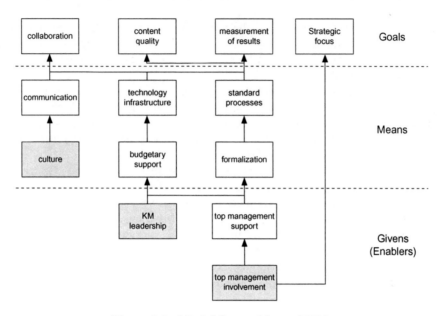

Figure 1.1: Model for enablers of KM.

research study, data was collected to develop interrelations among all the important enablers (Figure 1.1).

The model in Figure 1.1 shows that top management involvement, KM leadership, and the culture of the organization are the main driving factors based on which we can build a successful KM effort. With the top management involvement, KM initiatives will gain support and active participation of the senior executives of the organization. Top management involvement also ensures that KM initiatives would have strategic focus.

Figure 1.1 model shows that competent leadership of KM initiative combined with the support from the top management leads to budgetary support for KM initiatives. Budgetary support would assist in developing technology infrastructure for sharing and archiving knowledge.

The authors of the model (Figure 1.1) contend that it can also be interpreted in terms of givens, means, and goals in a KM effort. The elements at the bottom (starting points) can be considered as the set of givens. These *givens*, from a management standpoint, can be considered to be aspects that are present or absent in an organization. It is generally difficult to cultivate the enabler quickly.

In our model, KM leadership, top management support, and top management involvement are considered to be a set of givens. In other words, leadership, top management involvement, and culture are independent variables. However, effective KM leadership can influence the other two independent variables, albeit indirectly, to a certain extent. Capable KM leadership can garner the support of the top management and influence the culture.

Goals tend to be the elements at the top of the model, which are collaboration, content quality, measurement of results, and strategic focus. In other words, they are the end results of the KM effort. Clearly, leadership plays an important role in successfully meeting these goals.

Means, the authors argue, are the elements that can be controlled, manipulated, or developed to form the link between the *givens* and the *goals*. Communication, technology infrastructure, standardized processes, culture, budgetary support, and formalization of the KM effort are all aspects that can be changed, increased, or decreased in order to accomplish the *goals*.

These enablers can act as barriers too. For instance, strong and effective KM leadership leads to budgetary support and formalization of the KM effort. However, weaknesses in KM leadership or competing resource demands will dilute the support for budgetary support and the realization of KM processes.

This study stresses the importance of selecting a competent and committed KM leadership. This KM leadership plays a critical role in projecting KM values, securing funds and management support for building technology infrastructure, and aligning technology solutions with organizational culture to accomplish KM goals and objectives.

1.9. Study 2: Role of Management and Leadership in KM Success

Leadership involves the motivation of an organization's people to achieve desired goals. Therefore, in this research effort, eight people-related success factors and their interrelations are used to sketch the role of leadership in making effective use of KM systems and managing KM initiatives. These eight people-related factors briefly described in Table 1.1.

Using these success factors and ISM to obtain input from KM professionals, management and leadership model is developed (Figure 1.2). The resultant model represents the mental models of those who participated in the study. Therefore, these results are subject to interpretation and hence the name interpretive structural model (ISM). These arrows represent *leads to* and these relations are tenable.

As can be seen in the figure, organizational support and IT infrastructure are the independent variables; they are required to be present for a successful KM system. An effective KM facilitates trust among the participating and contributing employees. It will also establish a system to manage its outcomes.

Because of the entwined roles of leadership and management, the distinction between them is not always obvious. Classical functions such as planning, organizing, and controlling are considered within the boundaries of management. Management is also concerned with decision-making — specifically related to processes and functions — to improve operational efficiency and effectiveness. Leadership, on the other hand, has its efforts directed toward convincing people about the need to change, aligning them to a new direction, and motivating people to work together to achieve KM objectives under difficult and demanding work

Table 1.1: Contributors to KM systems.

Success factor	Description
Create clarity	Clarity in defining goals and outlining likely outcomes is important during the early stages of KM initiative. Otherwise, some of the important requirements of the KM system may not be identified. As a consequence, the KM system will be perceived as a failure and incorporating these requirements at a later stage may not help.
Define roles and processes	In general, many employees, in addition to their primary responsibilities and functions, participate in KM efforts for knowledge creation and sharing. Therefore, formal definition and approval of roles and processes is very important. Clear assignments of roles and responsibilities without ambiguity or overlapping responsibilities are important for conflict resolution and productivity.
Communicate expectations	Defining and establishing expectations from all the stakeholders is imperative for KM success and if we fail to do so, KM efforts will eventually result in both perceived and actual incidences of not delivering expected results. Objective and formally defined processes in developing knowledge repositories and effective dissemination of these processes and results are some of the means to communicate what is expected of all stakeholders.
Employ consistent processes	Organizations tend to manage KM with no formal processes. Mandating consistent and formal processes would encourage greater participation and contribution. Participation in knowledge development and sharing the new knowledge within the group and throughout the organization are the tenets of KM systems and consistent process is the means to implement these policies.
Establish trust	Trust is critical for knowledge sharing and teamwork. An environment of trust is influenced by the organizational culture, which can promote transparency, openness in communication, and collaboration. Needless to say, clear definition of roles and responsibilities promote team effectiveness.
Facilitate organizational support	A significant success factor to implement KM systems is to gain support and participation from key personnel representing all the functions in the organization and top management. Obtaining organizational support is one of the challenges. Functional managers generally control resources and their collaboration to KM efforts is a prerequisite to successful implementation of KM. Failure to facilitate organizational support would lead to ineffective use of KM systems and ultimate failure.

Table 1.1: (*Continued*)

Success factor	Description
Manage outcomes	KM efforts require resources and therefore, management would expect results that would indicate better business performance. As is true with projects, most perceptions of failure and success of KM systems are based on unspoken and personal indices. As a result, different people assess the same project differently (Rad, 2002). Therefore, there is a need for a set of performance indices that formalize the process and make explicit what is implicit in these seemingly subjective evaluations. Such an organized performance evaluation system would promote excellence.
Facilitate IT support	IT systems support electronic storage in miniscule size, and efficient and fast retrieval of large amounts of data. Thus, IT serves KM systems well in effective communication and developing KM tools such as electronic yellow pages, knowledge repositories, Intranet, and virtual communities of practice. Organizations should — when developing IT systems — focus on specific business needs.

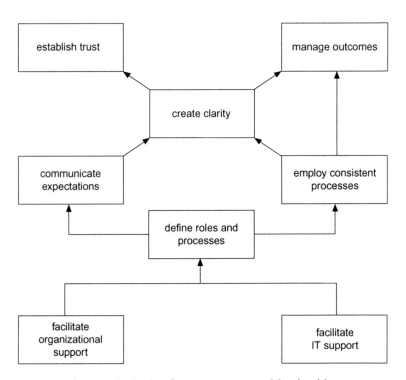

Figure 1.2: Role of management and leadership.

environments. Leadership is concerned with motivation and support to people in order to realize their potential and achieve challenging and difficult goals. Among the leadership styles, situational leaders focus on various tasks and relationship behaviors (Hersey & Blanchard, 1996) and transformational leaders may inspire followers, meet their developmental needs, and encourage new approaches and more effort toward problem-solving (Selzer & Bass, 1990).

As is true with many projects, KM has the characteristics of uniqueness, complexity, and unfamiliarity when it is initiated in an organization. Thus, these KM development and deployment efforts are often associated with significant changes in the working culture. As a consequence, leadership is a determinant of success as it provides vision and ability to cope with change (Kotter, 1999). Additionally, the role of management and leadership in creating and transferring knowledge within an organization is more challenging because of the dynamic nature of the organization structure and culture as a result of virtual teams and outsourcing.

1.10. KM Project Management

KM is aimed at making use of people in enhancing the knowledge base of the organization. To provide clarity and purpose, the roles of individuals participating in the KM initiative and processes associated with KM must be clearly defined first. Without such formal definition and approval of roles, KM would lack support from top management and functional managers. Defining the roles and processes would logically lead to developing formal processes that would facilitate an understanding of the organizational requirements needed to internally and externally support KM.

KM system cannot be left to only voluntary participation. KM must incentivize people to interact within and across disciplines and functions; each person brings specific expertise and experience. Defining each member's role would help in creating and sharing of knowledge. Consistent processes help managing a diverse group of people from different functions and divisions. By defining the roles and process, and by identifying the organizational support needs, managers can successfully lead teams and effectively accomplish the expected outcomes. It would also help managers define and manage KM goals and outcomes.

In the context of virtual teams and outsourcing, management should make a prudent and informed choice to identify areas of knowledge that can be shared among all the groups. To facilitate effective communication in a virtual team, extensive use of technology tools such as Intranet, video conferencing, electronic yellow pages, and electronic bulletin boards of virtual communities of practice is desirable. For effective use of these tools and knowledge transfer, management should encourage free flow of information and archive all the relevant and useful information. Usually, outsourcing is a choice for hiring expertise or quality of work at a lower cost for organizations. These tasks could be either familiar or unfamiliar to the parent organization and in either case, outsourcing provides an opportunity to learn and enhance organizational knowledge.

1.11. KM Project Leadership

By defining processes and roles, and communicating what is expected of all the member of the KM community, one can establish both predictability and openness. Both predictability and openness, in turn, can be used to develop expectations and manage outcomes. Trust and open communication are essential to nurture human relationships; predictability and openness are important factors in establishing trust (Gray & Larson, 2005). Establishing trust in virtual teams — where face-to-face interaction is limited or nonexistent — is a challenging task. Effective and frequent communication using technology can be a solution. With virtual teams, organizations usually employ electronic medium for written communication and group meetings (video conferencing).

By communicating clearly and effectively, managers can establish an environment of openness and transparency. It can lead to a work environment where team members willingly share information, experiences, and knowledge. These factors also instill trust — among all the participants — in their leader. Trust, in turn, encourages participants to collaborate, network, and innovate. Ring (1996) analyzed trust at the interpersonal level and found it as a precursor to forming ongoing networks. Although it should evolve mutually, trust is more important for leaders as they try motivating participating employees to accomplish a vision and to realize goals. And by establishing trust, leaders can also mitigate conflicts, a deterrent to knowledge creation and transfer.

Because people are motivated by challenges and opportunities to further their career goals, participants are almost always interested in accomplishing personal and professional goals in addition to completing their routine responsibilities. Therefore, it is imperative that KM leadership should understand and support the personal aspirations of the people and align them with the objectives of the organization.

As a prerequisite to successful implementation of KM in organizations, leadership of the organization is responsible for practicing strategic planning and systems thinking approaches, making best use of resources, fostering a culture that encourages open dialogue and team learning, and finally, for encouraging and rewarding risk-taking, learning, and knowledge sharing.

1.12. KM Organizational Support

Research has shown that top management involvement, KM leadership, and the culture of the organization are important driving factors based on which a successful KM system can be built (Anantatmula & Kanungo, 2007). With the involvement of top management, KM initiatives will gain support and active participation of the senior executives of the organization. Top management involvement would also ensure that KM initiatives will have strategic focus. The research has also indicated that competent leadership of KM initiative combined with the support from the top management would lead to budgetary support for KM initiatives.

Organization culture that encourages open and transparent communication among the employees of the organization would lead to increased collaboration and knowledge sharing at hierarchical levels of the organization, which leads to knowledge sharing. Increased communication with the aid of standard processes, and technology infrastructure make it easy and enhance collaboration.

The organization should have a structure, which facilitates personal interactions and supports communities of practice to capture tacit and explicit knowledge within the organization and this structure should be extended to virtual teams and outsourcing personnel in applicable areas through appropriate communication tools. Likewise, technology (both IT and KM) infrastructure should promote efficient capture of explicit knowledge and support knowledge sharing within and outside the organization by developing processes and systems that are easy to use.

The organization should identify means and provide opportunities for individual learning and link it to organizational learning and business performance. Such organizations should develop metrics to measure the results of learning and challenge people to perform better by setting tougher targets.

1.13. Conclusion

Intense competition and consequent need to sustain competitive advantage, frequently changing consumer needs, and greater opportunities in the marketplace due to globalization are some of the driving forces that have led to increased interest in studying how knowledge is used, applied, and leveraged. Further, it has led to placing greater emphasis on understanding and developing better frameworks for assessing KM effectiveness, thereby determining its impact on bottomline business results (Lim & Ahmed, 2000).

The selection of a competent and committed leader is critical for KM initiatives as the leader plays a critical role in securing funds and building technology infrastructure to accomplish KM goals and objectives. Capable leaders garner the support of the top management and influence the collaborative culture.

KM initiative — during its implementation stage — has to deal with complexity and changes under multiple constraints. It is characterized by newness, time and budget constraints, uncertainty, uniqueness, complexity, and demanding expectations. Therefore, leadership assumes greater importance during the implementation stage. Once the KM system is in place, it becomes process-oriented and well-defined, the emphasis shifts to routine project management functions. However, even at this stage, leadership plays a critical role in promoting collaboration in decision-making and developing innovative solutions.

Good leadership ensures developed technology systems meet specific business and project needs cognizant of the organizational culture.

References

Ahn, J., & Chang, S. (2002). *Valuation of knowledge: A business performance-oriented methodology*. HICSS35. New York, NY: IEEE Computer Society.

Anantatmula, V. (2005). Outcomes of knowledge management initiatives. *International Journal of Knowledge Management, 1*(2), 50–67.

Anantatmula, V. (2007). Linking KM effectiveness attributes to organizational performance. *The VINE: Journal of Information and Knowledge Management Systems, 37*(2), 133–149.

Anantatmula, V., & Kanungo, S. (2006). Structuring the underlying relations among the knowledge management outcomes. *Journal of Knowledge Management, 10*(4), 25–42.

Anantatmula, V., & Kanungo, S. (2007). *Modeling enablers for successful KM implementation*. HICSS40, 0-7695-2755-8/07. New York, NY: IEEE Computer Society.

Baldanza, C., & Stankosky, M. (2000). *Knowledge management: An evolutionary architecture toward enterprise engineering* (pp. 13.2-1–13.2-8). INCOSE, Seattle, WA, pp. 13.2-1–13.2-8.

Chourides, P., Longbottom, D., & Murphy, W. (2003). Excellence in knowledge management: An empirical study to identify critical factors and performance measures. *Measuring Business Excellence, 7*(2), 29–45.

Christensen, D., & Walker, D. H. (2004). Understanding the role of vision in project success. *Project Management Journal, 35*(3), 39–52.

Friedman, T. (2005). *The world is flat: A brief history of the twenty-first century*. New York: Farrar, Straus and Giroux.

Gehring, D. (2007). Applying traits theory of leadership to project management. *Project Management Journal, 38*(1), 44–54.

Gray, C. F., & Larson, E. W. (2005). *Project management: The managerial process*. New York: McGraw-Hill.

Greenhalgh, T., Robert, G., MacFarlane, F., Bate, P., & Kyriakidou, O. (2004). Diffusion of innovations in service organizations: Systematic review and recommendations. *The Milbank Quarterly, 82*(4), 581–629.

Helm, J., & Remington, K. (2005). Effective project sponsorship: An evaluation of the role of the executive sponsor in complex infrastructure projects by senior project managers. *Project Management Journal, 36*(3), 51–61.

Hersey, P., & Blanchard, K. (1996). Great ideas revisited: Revisiting the life-cycle theory of leadership. *Training & Development, 50*(1), 43–47.

Jennex, M. E., & Olfman, L. (2002). Organizational memory/knowledge effects on productivity, a longitudinal study. In: *Proceedings of the 35th Hawaii international conference on system sciences*. HICSS35, IEEE Computer Society.

King, W. R. (2002). IT capabilities, business processes, and impact on the bottom line. *Information Systems Management (Boston), 19*(2), 85–87.

Koh, E. C., Ryan, S., & Prybutok, V. R. (2005). Creating value through managing knowledge in an E-government to constituency (G2C) environment. *The Journal of Computer Information Systems, 45*(4), 32–41.

Kotter, J. P. (1999). *John P. Kotter on what leaders really do*. Boston, MA: Harvard Business School Press.

Lim, K. K., & Ahmed, P. K. (2000). *Enabling knowledge management: A measurement perspective, CMIT 2000*. New York: IEEE Computer Society.

Liu, A., & Fang, Z. (2006). A power-based leadership approach to project management. *Construction Management and Economics, 24*, 497–507.

Marchand, D. A., Kettinger, W. J., & Rollins, J. D. (2000). Information orientation: People, technology and the bottom line. *Sloan Management Review*, *41*(4), 69–80.

Marr, B. (2003). Known quantities. *Financial Management Journal*, *3/4*, 26–27.

Martin, V. A., Hatzakis, T., Lycett, M., & Macredie, R. (2004). Building the business/IT relationship through knowledge management. *Journal of Information Technology Cases and Applications*, *6*, 2.

Nidiffer, K., & Dolan, D. (2005). Evolving distributed project management. *IEEE Software* (September/October), 63–72.

Norrie, J., & Walker, D. (2004). A balanced scorecard approach to project management leadership. *Project Management Journal*, *35*(4), 47–56.

Okunoye, A., & Karsten, H. I. T. I. (2002). *ITI as enabler of knowledge management: Empirical perspective from research organisations in SubSaharan Africa, HICSS32*. New York: IEEE Computer Society.

Prabhakar, G. (2005). Switch leadership in projects: An empirical study reflecting the importance of transformational leadership on project success across twenty-eight nations. *Project Management Journal*, *36*(4), 53–60.

Rad, P. F. (2002). A model to quantify the success of projects. *AACE Transactions*, CS51.

Ring, P. S. (1996). Fragile and resilient trust and their roles in economic exchange. *Business and Society*, *35*(2), 148–175.

Schwarber, P. (2005). Leaders and the decision-making process. *Management Decision*, *43*(7 and 8), 1086–1092.

Selg, R. A. (2007). Successfully managing one-of-a-kind projects. *AACE International Transactions*, 5.1–5.4.

Selzer, J., & Bass, B. (1990). Transformational leadership: Beyond initiation and consideration. *Journal of Management*, *16*(4), 693–703.

Tyson, K. W. (1997). *Competition in the 21st century*. Delray Beach, FL: St. Lucie Press.

Verma, V. (1996). *Human resource skills for the project manager* (Vol. 2). Newton Square, PA: Project Management Institute.

Ward, J., & Aurum, A. (2004). *Knowledge management in software engineering – Describing the process*. ASWEC 2004. New York, NY: IEEE Computer Society.

Chapter 2

Understanding the Intelligence Age Knowledge Management Context

Linda J. Vandergriff

Abstract

An effective 21st century enterprise provides customer-focused services and products. Unfortunately, organizations and their leaders are struggling with management and workforces tooled for the controllable Industrial Age. At the dawn of the Intelligence Age, it is essential to re-examine the underlying assumptions about the operating context that drive the infrastructure investments. Without such an examination, the piecemeal investment choices will provide incompatible or wrong capabilities with substantial chance of missing needed capabilities (Farr & Buede, 2003; Lissack, 2000; Sull, 1999). This chapter examines the dynamic Intelligence Age context and discusses the needs for an informed decision support cycle and its associated ubiquitous knowledge management (KM) services and capabilities.

2.1. Introduction

For enterprises of the 21st century to be successful, they must provide the demanded services and products with improved productivity and customer-focused delivery. Organizations and their leaders struggling with management and workforces tooled for the controllable manufacturing era, are trying to re-tool for the dynamic

In Search of Knowledge Management: Pursuing Primary Principles
Copyright © 2010 by Emerald Group Publishing Limited
All rights of reproduction in any form reserved
ISBN: 978-1-84950-673-1

Intelligence Age[1] context (Farr & Buede, 2003; Lissack, 2000; Sull, 1999). Application vendors promise off-the-rack solutions. Business re-engineering consultants claim gains from their recommended improved processes and increased procedure efficiency. The results are billions, if not trillions, of dollars of information technology (IT) solution investments spent to harness the promise of improved performance without the expected return on investment (KPMG, 2000). However, just using technology and optimization will not transform these earth-bound caterpillars into the desired agile enterprises butterflies. The metamorphosis into agile enterprises requires leadership with a vision that provides the infrastructure to empower the enterprise's intellectual capital.

Drucker and many other management experts assert it will require a profound change in basic organizational paradigms to realize effective 21st century enterprises. In part, the problem lies with the ever-increasing rate of change and the reality that it is difficult, if not impossible, to reliably predict the long-term future. In this context, an enterprise has several possible approaches. One is to try to minimize the impact of change (e.g., become robust and absorb the change). Another is for an organization to allow quick adaptation (e.g., become adaptable). A third is to delay commitment (e.g., become agile to maneuver and leverage opportunities). This chapter focuses on agile enterprise decision support that requires organizations to leverage their intellectual capital to drive profitable decision-making and implementation.

What is an agile enterprise? The Intelligent Enterprise Working Group (IEWG) of the International Council on Systems Engineering (INCOSE) (Ring, 2004) proposed the definition used for this chapter. They defined an enterprise "as two or more individuals applying resources through actions to achieve mutual purpose." Thus, an organization like General Electric (GE) is an enterprise, as well as, the GE Capital Services Group's finance department. The working group goes on to define agile or intelligent enterprises as ones that "exhibit the ability to self-adapt (e.g., display agility) to changes in its context (e.g., fitness landscape), its internal capabilities, and its stakeholder interest (e.g., value) while honoring principles of systems and society (e.g., coherence)."

In the Intelligence Age, enterprises are struggling with decision-making and implementation support designed for the Industrial Age. Lissack (2000) identified the current business metaphor as a 17th century invention that represents the world as a machine with linear mechanistic behaviors that result from simple cause and effects. In this model, the organization consists of separate parts (e.g., division of labor) that do separate functions (e.g., sequential flow processes) with little interaction except for control and reporting communications. It includes a hierarchical worldview where top management is in control and makes decisions, and production line workers implement them (Apte, Beath, & Goh, 1999).

---

1. Term coined by Kirk Tyson (1997) refers to a more inclusive concept than the IT-dominated Information Age term coined by AT&T marketing.

In short, Industrial Age business models fail, in large part, because several built in assumptions[2] are no longer applicable. This realization requires significant re-examination of the business models (paradigms). Today's enterprises need to incorporate several Intelligence Age context observations:

- Context is shifting from a world of long lead-time, controllable, predictable, stable, incremental, and linear changes to one of rapid discontinuous change reflected in complexity theory models of chaos and nonlinearity. In other words, change is occurring at an ever-increasing rate[3] (Toffler, 1970; Malhotra, 1998; Bixler, 2000).
- Enterprises and their context co-evolve, thus each enterprise must continually tailor its own leading indicators to provide situational awareness and real-time adjustments (Darling & Semich, 1996; Caldwell, 1996; Boyd, 1987).
- Revenue-generating capital is no longer only physical, but is dominated by unique intellectual capital assets (e.g., knowledge workers, patents, customer relations).
- Globalization[4] requires access to and ability to capture a shared set of rules for economic, security, behavior, and technology by individuals, companies, and nations to guide interaction (Barnett, 2004; Kemp, Moerman, & Prieto, 2001; Tyson, 1997).
- In the new economy, new sources of wealth generation exist and are increasingly reliant on the free flow of Intelligence, Wisdom, Knowledge, Information, Data and Measurement (IWKIDM[5])-based products and services (Vandergriff, 2006; Allee, 1998).

---

2. Industrial Age assumptions about Newtonian mechanistic world model with linear relationships, independence of the systems/enterprise and its context, slowly changing predictable context, predominance of physical capital, interchangeability of assets, and efficiency metrics lead to bad decisions.

3. Hock, founder of Visa International, identified this as the "collapse of float." Before the world was so connected, concepts and things took time to travel. The knowledge about how to smelt iron took almost a century to cover the European continent, ushering in the Iron Age. Today, intelligence is available in minutes, if not seconds. Thus, information float has virtually disappeared. Technology floats are minimal, with new technology adoption happening in months or days. With collapse of cultural floats, popular trends sweep across the world almost instantaneously (Hoffman, 2002).

4. The third wave of globalization replaces concepts of a first, second, and third world with a new model involving the globalized functional core and the nonintegrating gap. The core is developing integrated rule sets for economic, security, behavior, and technology by individuals, companies, and nation states to guide interaction. The participants in the core tend to settle disputes with other members of the core with lawyers and diplomats. The nonintegrating gap entities tend to resolve the disputes between themselves and with the core entities through violent intervention by terrorists and soldiers.

5. Describes the Intelligence Pyramid, where Intelligence is the translation in to the user's frame of reference of the various levels wisdom, knowledge, information, data, and measurement about the world. Based on this author's dissertation work (Vandergriff, 2006), the following WKIDM levels of abstraction are defined. "Measurement" is defined as physical readings of phenomena from scientific instruments (e.g., photons) or event/object observations by individuals or groups. "Data" is the symbols, numbers, textual clauses, and other descriptive phrases or displays of measurements (e.g., evidence). "Information" is built from the organization of data sets through quantitative and/or qualitative analysis that relate those data sets, and can range from math equations, paragraphs, graphical illustrations, or images. "Knowledge" is created by applying experience to available measurements, data, and information. "Wisdom" results from the application of cognitive capability and judgment.

- Obsolescence drives need for innovation, adaptation, and vision, in contrast with traditional emphasis on optimization (Kemp et al., 2001; Malhotra, 1998)
- Innovation and creativity are the currency of this new knowledge economy, because they are requisites for maintaining an organization's capacity for creating new, and updating old, knowledge. In addition, ongoing and continuous learning ensure that expertise and core competencies continue (Stewart, 2001; Bixler, 2000; Malhotra, 1998).
- The Intelligence Age's arrival introduced a new type of worker. This worker is not an interchangeable assembly-line worker, but rather represents a highly qualified individual that makes and implements decisions under nonroutine, unstructured, and uncertain environments (Purington, Butler, & Gale, 2003; Knight, Murray, & Willmott, 1993; Alshibl, 1990).
- Drucker and others have observed that today's global economy is in transition to being knowledge-based and technology-enabled. Intellectual capital and the resultant knowledge economy has been cited, along with globalization and networking, as the driving forces of business and national competitiveness in the foreseeable future (Stankosky, 2004; Skyrme, 1997).
- Increasing communications availability and the complex interdependencies of organizational relationships have allowed and, indeed, required more contact. This increased demand for intelligence that affects their interest, or enterprise "transparency," has moved beyond just immediate buyers and suppliers to an ever-expanding web of stakeholders. In this environment, a much more sophisticated stakeholder has arisen, one who has challenging demands regarding time, cost, flexibility, quality, and visibility into the corporate governance, processes, products, and services of the enterprise (Allee, 2004; Bixler, 2000; van der Spek & Spijkervet, 1997).

This demand for more "intelligent" enterprises requires the utilization of all the intellectual assets of the organization. To meet this need, all the knowledge management (KM) and business intelligence solutions must align with a new business model that exploits in-depth analytical capability to sense the organizational business internal and external context and turn it into actionable intelligence.[6] It is critical that organizations have the ability to make and implement fast reliable decisions at all levels of the organization to cope effectively with the dynamic business context.

The literature identified several key contributors to organizational agility.

- An informed decision cycle provides the ability to cope with a dynamic context (Deming, 1994, 1986; Boyd, 1987).

---

6. "Intelligence" as used here, is defined as the result of the translation of wisdom, knowledge, information, data, or measurements into the user's frame of reference to support decision-making or decision implementation (Vandergriff, 2008).

- Success depends upon integrated decision-making and implementation facilitated by ubiquitous KM (Nutt, 1999; Simon, 1993).
- Control limits responsiveness and reduces competitive advantage, while coherent leadership guides the decision-making and implementation with a common set of values and goals (Barry, 2004; Farr & Buede, 2003; Pepper, 2003; Bixler, 2000; Lissack & Roos, 2000).
- Organizational and individual knowledge worker competencies combine to provide the emergent competencies of the enterprise. This requires significant amounts of decision-making and implementation activities to occur either in collaboration with the knowledge worker or autonomously at the knowledge worker level (Bixler, 2000).
- Knowledge workers provide the value directly to the customer. The value not only depends on the technical features (e.g., information provided, questions answered), but also on the lean process related features (e.g., speed, innovation, quality, accuracy, delivery, presentation) (Delic, Douillet, & Dayal, 2001; Hope & Fraser, 1997).
- An empowered workforce receives authority to represent the enterprise, takes initiative to ensure timely informed decisions, and ensures effective implementation. Collaboration with a diverse set of individuals often provides the best-fit solutions (Lynn & Akgün, 2003; Zemke, Raines, & Filipczak, 2000; Whitaker, 1995).
- Flexible, but known, processes free the knowledge worker to spend more time on the harder effort of thinking (Mascitelli, 2002; Alshibl, 1990). The processes tend to be minimalist, focusing on simple clear principles and rules. They adapt for competitive advantage and allow effective development of "standard" and tailorable "specialized" processes (Hedberg, Nystrom, & Starbuck, 1976; Pasternack & Viscio, 1998; Mascitelli, 2002; Drucker, 1994).
- Synergistic technologies provide a free flow of intelligence. Technologies are used to provide timely, and view-appropriate access to the intellectual assets to inform the decision cycle (Skyrme, 2003; Delic et al., 2001; Nichols, 2001; Briggs, De Vreede, Nunamaker, & Sprague, 2001; Allee, 1999; Baek, 1998; Davenport & Prusak, 1998; Malhotra, 1998).

To realize agility, the chief knowledge officer (CKO) and supporting system engineers must provide leadership and account for these fundamental changes in the operating context, organizational culture, and operational business model. The main emphasis is the development and maintenance of the enterprise's infrastructure.

2.2. Decision Support

Many researchers propose that effective problem-solving, decision-making, and implementation make an enterprise successful (Anantatmula, 2004; Wiig, 2004; Mohamed, Stankosky, & Murray, 2004; Power, 2003; Drucker, 1994). Thus, a key component of enterprise infrastructure is decision support. Understanding what is involved in decision support is difficult because of the many stakeholder viewpoints and implementations that have evolved over time (Beverage, 1981). The "big tent" of decision support systems (DSS) definition used here is based on several other DSS researchers (Power, 2003; Sprague & Carlson, 1982; Alter, 1980; Sprague, 1980).

> DSS is a specific class of computerized information system that supports decision-making and implementation activities. These DSS are interactive computer-facilitated systems and subsystems intended to aid decision-makers and implementers to identify problems, develop alternative solutions, make decision, track/manage implementation, and integrate lessons learned for future decision support.

The literature suggests that the "perfect" decision support would provide for an informed decision cycle that operated faster than the changes in the context. An informed decision cycle provides ability to adapt and take advantage of the dynamics of the context and the empowered enterprise capabilities. Increased speed in the new economy results in a compression of opportunity windows and less time to integrate competencies. It is now not good enough to just have the best mousetrap; it must also be the first to market (APQC, 1999).

An informed decision cycle provides the ability to sense and respond. It allows an organization to take advantage of the dynamics of the fitness landscape[7] and the empowered competencies. Rylander and Peppard (2003) propose using a yacht racing metaphor for knowledge-intense organizations operating in dynamic contexts. Winning involves not only competition with other crews, but also with the weather and sea. Each member of the crew senses the changing environment and responds. This response is in real-time by the individual members of the crew, each incentivized by the desire to win. Success relies upon awareness of the goals and environment and knowledge/skill of the whole crew in collaboration; such is the informed decision cycle in an agile enterprise.

In this construct, the primary decision support activities are

- decision-making aided by appropriate KM and computerized assistance with problem definition, alternative generation, decision analysis, and decision communication and
- decision implementation informed by effective decision coordination, execution planning, and change feedback in an co-evolving context and enterprise

In the face of "hyperturbulence" (D'Aveni, 1994) or "permanent white water" (Vaill, 1996), the informed decision cycle relies on real-time knowledge worker

---

7. A concept from Complexity Theory describing evolutionary "fitness" of the system to the context it resides.

participation to be successful. Thus, an enterprise needs to be decentralized, with empowered decision-making and implementing at all levels according to the knowledge worker's roles and responsibilities. In this paradigm, assumptions about the independent nature of decision-making and decision implementation are violated for agile knowledge-based enterprises due to their complex nature. Thus, isolated decision support and program management implementation underperform or fail. Vahidov and Kersten (2004) identify that this lack of "situated decision support" leads to bottlenecks and inefficiencies in the informed decision cycle.

Agile knowledge-based enterprises drive a need for a more aware, inclusive, and responsive decision support. This requires CKO leadership to focus on the ubiquitous KM supporting the decision-making and decision implementation cycle. Goldman, Nagel, and Preiss (1995) however observe that organizations are responding to these needs in a piecemeal fashion. Although significant research exists on agile manufacturing, decision-making tools, KM, decision analysis, and other decision support applications, Vahidov and Kersten (2004) assert that researchers and developers lack a unified decision support approach with a decision support theory, framework, or architectures. Without an overarching decision support framework for identification and evaluation of needed capabilities, investment choices can provide incompatible or wrong capabilities with substantial chance of missing needed capabilities. All of these situations lessen the return on investment expected from a unified approach.

To enable the informed decision cycle, KM must be provided seamlessly throughout the enterprise's infrastructure. Today's organizations are using the term KM to discuss the management of the whole IWKIDM chain that informs the decision-maker and implementer. For each IWKIDM category, different techniques are needed to elicit, capture, share, and distribute. Data can be measured, gathered, and stored. Information can be created through analysis and processing. Knowledge becomes less automatable, as it is combining a human element of experience with information about the world, enterprise, or challenge. Expert systems have tried with varying levels of success to automate the combination of knowledge with judgment to result in wisdom. The translation of any of these into user-understandable intelligence is very case-specific and thus rarely automated except in very fixed prearranged formats. User actionable intelligence, however, is the most important, with all entities in the WKIDM pyramid translated into the user frame of reference (Vandergriff, 2008).

Researchers have proposed that IWKIDM quality has five properties: accuracy (i.e., reflects real world), completeness (i.e., all relevant pieces present), consistency (i.e., same model from all viewpoints), timeliness (i.e., meets uses needs at operational tempo), and assured access (i.e., to the right user at the right time) (Ballou & Pazer, 1985; Engkavanish, 1999; Tayi & Ballou, 1998; Boyd, 1987).

The informed decision cycle needs to access both explicit "codified" and tacit "personal" knowledge as defined by Polanyi (1958, 1966). KM research uses different approaches to capture and share explicit and tacit knowledge. Both are valuable to the decision-maker, thus decision support must provide access to explicit, as well as, tacit knowledge (DeTienne Bell, & Jackson, 2001).

Explicit knowledge consists of refined knowledge mainly consisting of facts, concepts, and models of relationships between entities, which can be captured in books and training. IT structures capture and share explicit intellectual assets such as products (e.g., reports and graphs) and process (e.g., best practice, procedures).

Tacit knowledge is contextual in nature and represents a knowledge worker's "know how" or experience (Wiig, 1993). Sharing tacit knowledge requires different approaches from those used by traditional IT (Malhotra, 1998). Dixon (2000) stressed that tacit knowledge transfers most effectively between people. For any given situation, those knowledge workers share their knowledge with those who need it.

Thus, the informed decision cycle requires the KM functions of knowledge use, transfer, codification, generation, and assurance. Therefore, in addition to the decision-making and decision implementation capabilities, research has identified the associated KM capabilities for decision support for agile enterprises.

The 21st century agile enterprise and its decision cycle have an evolving context with very different constraints and drivers than that of its Industrial Age ancestor. Research summarized in a following chapter used this understanding to develop and validate a comprehensive recommended set of decision-making and decision implementation capabilities with extensive support by integrating KM capabilities. In addition, the research performed a user evaluation of perceived desirability of the proposed capabilities. This evaluation reflects a different prioritization than current decision support research proposes. These results reflect the expanding scope of decision support that challenges current technologies and methods.

In the Intelligence Age, KM services and capabilities contribute to the enterprise's intellectual capital success. Key is the ubiquitous informed decision cycle that helps react to the "hyperturbulence" context. To realize an effective return on investment, the CKO and the system engineering staff needs to understand the Intelligence Age context and demands for KM capabilities and services. Informed with this knowledge, the team must provide leadership to ensure corporate commitment and strategic planning for the agile enterprise infrastructure look forward to provide adequate KM in a timely and effective manner. Without such leadership, the piecemeal investment choices will provide incompatible or wrong capabilities with substantial chance of missing needed capabilities.

2.3. Conclusion

The human race has experienced several cultural ages, each marked by innovation and change. As the 21st century arrives, the closing of the Industrial Age gives rise to the beginning of the Intelligence Age. The need for ubiquitous knowledge management is driven by the Intelligence Age context most Enterprises find themselves in. As the transition from Industrial Age business models give way to the new Intelligence Age business models, the focus shifts from physical capital dominated assembly line efficiencies to the intellectual capital dominated empowered unique asset effectiveness. This requires an informed decision cycle that uses situational awareness, not backward looking indicators, to enable empowered agents to take advantage of opportunities and mitigate risks introduced by the hyperturbulent environment.

References

Allee, V. (1998). *The knowledge economy.* Retrieved from Verna Allee Web site http://www.vernaallee.com/

Allee, V. (1999, December). New tools for the new economy. *Perspectives in on Business and Global Change, 13*(4), World Business Academy. Verna Allee Value Net Works™. Available at http://www.vernaallee.com/library%20articles/New%20Tools%20for%20a%20New%20Economy.pdf. Accessed on September 9, 2005.

Allee, V. (2004). 360-Degree transparency and the sustainable economy. *Transformation, 18*(2). World Business Academy.

Alshibl, G. A. (1990). *A study of the impact of using automated information systems on middle mangers in large industrial organizations.* D.Sc. dissertation, George Washington University, Washington, DC.

Alter, S. (1980). *Decision support systems: Current practice and continuing challenges.* Reading, MA: Addison-Wesley.

Anantatmula, V. (2004). *Criteria for measuring knowledge management efforts in organizations.* D.Sc. dissertation, George Washington University, Washington, DC.

APQC. (1999). Knowledge management. *APQC Benchmarking Study Best Practice Report.* American Productivity and Quality Center Consortium, Houston, TX.

Apte, U. M., Beath, C. M., & Goh, C.-H. (1999). An analysis of the production line versus the case manager approach to information intensive services. *Decision Sciences, 30*(4), 1105–1129.

Baek, S. I. (1998). *Knowledge management for multimedia systems design — Toward intelligent web-based collaboration.* D.Sc. dissertation, George Washington University, Washington, DC.

Ballou, D. P., & Pazer, H. L. (1985). Modeling data and process quality in multi-input and multi-output information systems. *Management Sciences, 31,* 150–162. (quoted by Engkavanish, 1999).

Barnett, T. P. M. (2004). *The Pentagon's new map: War and peace in the twenty-first century.* New York: G.P. Putnam's Sons.

Barry, M. (Ed.). (2004). The agile organization. *eINFORM, 4*(1). Available at http://monkey.biz / Content / Default / Support / Resources /IDC_TheAgileOrganization_1710.pdf. Accessed on September 9, 2005.

Beverage, R. (1981). *A structured methodology to ascertain requirements for computer based decision support systems.* D.Sc. dissertation, George Washington University, Washington, DC.

Bixler, C. H. (2000). *Creating a dynamic knowledge management maturity continuum for increased enterprise performance and innovation.* D.Sc. dissertation, George Washington University, Washington, DC.

Boyd, J. R. (1987, August). *A discourse on winning and losing.* Unpublished briefing.

Briggs, R. O., Vreede, G. J. de, Nunamaker, J. F., Jr., & Sprague, R. (2001). Special Issue: Enhancing organizations' intellectual bandwith: The quest for fast and effective value creation. *Journal of Management Information Systems, 17*(3), 3–8 [Editorial].

Caldwell, B. (1996). Wal-Mart ups the pace. *Information Week*, December 9.

Darling, C. B., & Semich, J. W. (1996). Extreme integration. *Datamation, 42*(17).

D'Aveni, R. A. (1994). *Hypercompetition: Managing the dynamics of strategic maneuvering.* New York: The Free Press.

Davenport, T. H., & Prusak, L. (1998). *Working knowledge: How organizations manage what they know.* Harvard, MA: Harvard Business School Press.

Delic, K. A., Douillet, L., & Dayal, U. (2001). Toward an architecture for real-time decision support systems: Challenges and solutions. In: *Database Engineering and Applications, 2001 International Symposium,* 16–18 July, pp. 303–311.

Deming, W. E. (1986). *Out of the crisis.* Cambridge, MA: MIT Center for Advanced Engineering Study.

Deming, W. E. (1994). *The new economics for industry government, education.* Cambridge, MA: MIT Center for Advanced Engineering Study.

DeTienne Bell, K., & Jackson, L. A. (2001). Knowledge management: Understanding theory and developing strategy. *Competitiveness Review, 11*(1), 1–10.

Dixon, N. (2000). *Common knowledge.* Boston, MA: Harvard Business School Press.

Drucker, P. F. (1994). The theory of business. *Harvard Business Review, 72*(5), 95–104.

Engkavanish, S. (1999). *Analysis of the effectiveness of communication and information sharing in virtual project organizations.* D.Sc. dissertation, George Washington University, Washington, DC, USA.

Farr, J. V., & Buede, D. M. (2003). System engineering and engineering management: Keys to the efficient development of products and services. *Engineering Management Journal, 15*(3), 3–9.

Goldman, S. L., Nagel, R. N., & Preiss, K. (1995). *Agile competitors and virtual organizations: Strategies for enriching the customer.* New York: Van Nostrand Reinhold.

Hedberg, B., Nystrom, P. C., & Starbuck, W. H. (1976). Camping on seesaws: Prescriptions for a self-designing organization. *Administrative Science Quarterly, 21*(1), 41–65.

Hoffman, M. (2002). Transformation by design: An interview with Dee Hock. *Enlightenment Magazine*, WIE Issue 22, Fall–Winter.

Hope, J., & Fraser, R. (1997). Beyond budgeting, breaking through the barrier to the third wave. *Management Accounting, 75*(11), 20–23.

Kemp, J. L. C., Moerman, P. A., & Prieto, J. (2001). On the nature of knowledge-intensive organizations: Strategy and organization in the new economy. In: K.- D. Thoben, F. Weber & K. S. Pawar, (Eds), *The 7th international conference on concurrent enterprising.* 27–29 June, Bremen, Germany: ICE.

Knight, D., Murray, F., & Willmott, H. (1993). Networking as knowledge work: A study of strategic interoganizational development in the financial services industry. *Journal of Management Studies, 30*(6), 975–995.

KPMG. (2000). *Knowledge management research report.* London: KMPG Consulting.

Lissack, M. R. (2000). *Complexity metaphors and the management of a knowledge based enterprise; an exploration of discovery.* Doctorate in Business Administration dissertation, Henley Management College, Oxfordshire, UK.

Lissack, M. R., & Roos, J. (2000). *The next common sense, the e-manager's guide to mastering complexity.* London: Nicholas Brealey Publishing.

Lynn, G. S., & Akgün, A. E. (2003). Launch your new products/services better, faster. *Research Technology Management, 46*(3), 21–26.

Malhotra, Y. (1998). Tools @ work: Deciphering the knowledge management hype. *Journal for Quality and Participation, 21*(4), 58–60.

Mascitelli, R. (2002). *Building a project-driven enterprise: How to slash waste and boost profits through lean project management.* Northridge, CA: Technology Perspectives.

Mohamed, M., Stankosky, M., & Murray, A. (2004). Applying KM principles to enhance cross-functional team performance. *Journal of Knowledge Management, 8*(3), 127–142.

Nichols, D. H. (2001). *A framework for information technology strategies integrated with business strategies that contribute to successful business performance within organizations.* D.Sc. dissertation, George Washington University, Washington, DC.

Nutt, P. C. (1999). Surprising but true: Half of organizational decisions fail. *The Academy of Management Executive, 13*(4), 75–90.

Pasternack, B. A., & Viscio, A. J. (1998). *The centerless corporation: A new model for transforming your organization for growth and prosperity.* New York: Simon & Schuster.

Pepper, A. (2003). Leading professionals: A science, a philosophy and a way of working. *Journal of Change Management, 3*(4), 349–360.

Polanyi, M. (1958). *Personal knowledge.* Chicago, IL: University of Chicago Press.

Polanyi, M. (1966). *The tacit dimension.* London: Routledge & Kegan Paul.

Power, D. J. (2003). What are the characteristics of a decision support system? *DSS News e-Newsletter, 4*(7).

Purington, C., Butler, C., & Gale, S. F. (2003). *Built to learn: The inside story of how Rockwell Collins became a true learning organization.* New York: AMACOM.

Ring, J. (2004). Intelligent enterprises. *INCOSE Insight, 6*(2), January.

Rylander, A., & Peppard, J. (2003). From implementing strategy to embodying strategy: Linking strategy, identity and intellectual capital. *Journal of Intellectual Capital, 4*(3), 316–331.

Simon, H. A. (1993). Strategic and organizational evolution. *Strategic Management Journal, 14*(Winter Special Edition), 131–142.

Skyrme, D. J. (1997). The global knowledge economy: And its implications for markets. *Insight,* (21), David Skyrme Associates. Available at http://www.skyrme.com/insights/21gke.htm

Skyrme, D. J. (2003). Knowledge management: Making sense of an oxymoron. *Insight Update,* (22), David Skyrme Associates. Available at http://www.skyrme.com/insights/22km.htm. Accessed on September 7, 2005.

Sprague, R. H., Jr. (1980). A framework for research on decision support systems. In: G. Fick & R. H. Sprague, (Eds), *Decision support systems: Issues and challenges. Proceedings of an International Task Force Meeting.* New York: Pergamon Press.

Sprague, R. H., Jr., & Carlson, E. D. (1982). *Building effective decision support systems.* Englewood Cliffs, NJ: Prentice Hall.

Stankosky, M. A. (2004). Tackling a unified KM framework. *KMWorld e-Magazine, 31*(1).

Stewart, T. A. (2001). *The wealth of knowledge: Intellectual capital and the twenty-first century organization.* New York: Doubleday.

Sull, D. N. (1999). Why good companies go bad. *Harvard Business Review, 77*(4), 42–50.

Tayi, G. K., & Ballou, D. P. (1998). Examining data quality — Introduction. *Communications of the ACM, 41*(2), 54–57.

Toffler, A. (1970). *Future shock.* New York: Bantam Books.

Tyson, K. W. (1997). *Competition in the 21st century.* Delray Beach, FL: St. Lucie Press.

Vahidov, R., & Kersten, G. E. (2004). Decision station: Situating decision support system. *Decision Support Systems, 38*(2), 283–303.

Vaill, P. R. (1996). *Learning as a way of being: Strategies for survival in a world of permanent white water.* San Francisco, CA: Jossey-Bass.

Vandergriff, L. J. (2006). *Unified approach to decision support for agile knowledge-based enterprises*. D.Sc. dissertation, George Washington University, Washington, DC.

Vandergriff, L. J. (2008). Welcome to the intelligence age: An examination of intelligence as a complex venture emergent behavior. *VINE: The Journal of Information and Knowledge Management Systems, 38*(4).

Van der Spek, R., & Spijkervet, A. (1997). *Knowledge management, dealing intelligently with knowledge*. Utrecht Knowledge Management Network. Kennisecantrum CIBIT, The Netherlands (quoted by Bixler, 2000).

Whitaker, R. (1995). Self-organization, autopoiesis, and enterprises. Hypertext paper on the Association for Computing Machinery Special Interest Group on Supporting Group Work (SIGGROUP) (December). Available at http://www.acm.org/sigois/auto/Main.html. Accessed on September 9, 2005.

Wiig, K. M. (1993). *Knowledge management foundations: Thinking about thinking — How organizations create, represent and use knowledge*. Arlington, TX: Schema Press.

Wiig, K. M. (2004). People-focused KM: How effective decision-making leads to enterprise success. KM Europe 2004 Presentation.

Zemke, R., Raines, C., & Filipczak, B. (2000). *Generations at work: Managing the clash of veterans, boomers, xers, and nexters in your workplace*. New York: American Management Association.

SECTION II

ORGANIZATION APPLICATIONS

> Organizations to stay successful must be adaptable and willing to change to stay current. Norm Augustine (2003)

The KM organization pillar focuses on understanding and structuring the culture to best apply intellectual capital to provide the demanded serves and products with improved productivity and customer-focused delivery. Calabrese (2000) validated this pillar and further defined subelements as the culture of the organization, reflecting the business processes and procedures, workflow, structure, and shared values with respect to knowledge use. The membership/hierarchical organization model had significant capability for a tangible asset; however, it tends to hamper knowledge sharing and organizational operation (Mohamed, Stankosky, & Murray, 2004). In response to this new challenge, more agile organization structures are appearing. These flatter organizations minimize cross-functional boundaries and empower knowledge sharing. Thus, flatter organizations with KM are proposed to improve decision-making efficiency and organizational effectiveness (Calabrese, 2000; Halal, 1998; Gustafon & Kliener, 1994). The following chapters focus on organization-related applications.

References

Augustine, N. (2003). Things have improved ... In spite of my contributions. Unpublished speech presented on 7 May.

Calabrese, F. A. (2000). *A suggested framework of key elements defining effective enterprise knowledge management programs.* D.Sc. dissertation, George Washington University, Washington, DC.

Gustafon, K., & Kliener, B. H. (1994). New developments in team building. *Industrial and Commercial Training, 26*, 17–22.

Halal, W. E. (1998). Organizational intelligence: What is it, and how can managers use it to improve performance. *Knowledge Management Review, 1*, 20–25.

Mohamed, M., Stankosky, M., & Murray, A. (2004). Applying KM principles to enhance cross-functional team performance. *Journal of Knowledge Management, 8*(3), 127–142.

Chapter 3

The Critical Role of Culture in Knowledge Management

Vincent M. Ribière and Aleša Saša Sitar

Abstract

This chapter presents the various aspects of organizational culture and how they relate to knowledge management (KM) and its success. After a brief description of the concept of culture, the link between KM success and culture is explained. The core cultural attributes necessary to reach an "ideal" culture are presented as well as various approaches to assess your current culture. Finally, the role of leaders in cultural changes is emphasized and the concept of culture is broadened by including other dimensions of culture like national culture.

3.1. Introduction

The latest researches show that softer management issues like corporate culture[1] are in the focus of management today (Hardy, 2008). In fact, corporate culture has been addressed as the biggest impediment to knowledge activities (Barth, 2000a; Chua & Lam, 2005; Knowledge Management Review, 2001; KPMG Consulting, 2000; Microsoft, 1999; Pauleen & Mason, 2002) as well as the most significant input to effective knowledge management (KM) (King, 2007). Cultural barriers are inhibiting individuals and teams to participate in knowledge-sharing activities rather maintaining status quo (Husted & Michailova, 2002), in use of information technology to support knowledge codification, storage and transfer (Leidner, 1998), among others.

---

1. In this chapter the terms *corporate culture* and *organizational culture* will be used interchangeably.

In Search of Knowledge Management: Pursuing Primary Principles
Copyright © 2010 by Emerald Group Publishing Limited
All rights of reproduction in any form reserved
ISBN: 978-1-84950-673-1

Positive culture can be the difference between successful companies and those that fail. And there are only 10% of companies that are successful at creating a high-performance culture (HR Focus, 2007). Some companies will need to evolve their command and control type of culture to more open types of cultures that will facilitate knowledge flows.

Most authors in the knowledge management literature suggest that corporate culture should be changed in order to support knowledge management activities. On the other hand, there are some authors claiming that culture is too enduring therefore knowledge management initiative should be adjusted to it (Hislop, 2005; McDermott & O'Dell, 2001). Though culture change is a long-term, complex process, in this chapter, we agree with the first group and arguing that this might be the only way. Organizational culture and its impact on people, teams, communities, organizations, and enterprises is a very complex and broad topic. In this chapter, we will try to provide you with the key issues and concepts related to this topic.

3.2.   Organizational Culture: What Is It About?

Organizational culture can be described, summing up definitions from different authors (Daft, 1998; John, 1998; Schein, 1994), as a set of assumptions, values, norms, guiding beliefs, invented, discovered, or developed by a certain group of people, who have been working together for a considerable period of time. Throughout this period, they have developed certain behavior to deal with and solve their problems as well as a collective identity and know how to work together effectively.

Culture guides employees' day-to-day working relationships and determines how people communicate within the organization, what behavior is acceptable, and how power and status are allocated. Because their behavior resulted in success for the company, the behavior is taught to new members of the group. Besides internal integration of employees, culture also helps the organization adapt itself to the external environment. As culture helps guide the daily activities of workers to meet certain goals, it can help the organization to rapidly respond to customer needs or moves of competitors.

Culture presents itself at three levels (see Figure 3.1): observable artifacts, espoused values, and basic underlying assumptions (1992). The three layers are not independent of each other, but they mutually influence each other. Observable artifacts represent the visible part of the culture and include symbols, ceremonies, stories, slogans, physical layouts, dress codes, manners in which people address each other, as well as company records, products, and annual reports (Daft, 1998; John, 1998; Robey, 1991). They are the most visible, particularly to newcomers. Two companies might have similar observable artifacts but their underlying culture might be totally different. So it is important to study and understand the two underlying layers of culture.

The second level, values, include espoused and documented values, norms, beliefs, attitudes, feelings, ideologies, charters, and philosophies, which are at the first sight

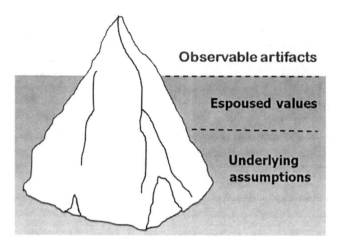

Figure 3.1: Three levels of organizational culture, based on Schein (1992).

invisible, can be recognized through several survey instruments like interviews or questionnaires but also by understanding the history of the company and by organizing focus groups where employees can share their experiences. Values determine how members interpret the environment and bond members to the organization.

The most invisible level of culture, the third level, includes underlying and usually unconscious assumptions that determine employees' perceptions, thought processes, feelings, and behavior and are commonly taken for granted. They develop when values become a part of members' mindset and affect their interpretation of a situation. They are usually directly affected by the history of the company, different leaders, and various events/challenges that the company had to face (good or bad). Table 3.1 illustrates the culture attributes of two imaginary companies.

Figure 3.2 illustrates the influence of the three layers of organizational culture on the daily behavioral patterns of employees. Beliefs, values, and artifacts affect the practices, norms, and tools favored and used by employees to do their job and ultimately their daily behavioral patterns. Understanding the reasons why employees are not willing to share knowledge or do not want to use previously codified organizational knowledge could be explained by going back to the cultural roots of the problem.

3.3. Culture: The Missing Link to KM Success

What's happened here is 90% culture change. You need to change the way you relate one another. If you don't do that, you won't succeed.
Robert H. Buckman, CEO of Buckman Labs (2004)

Table 3.1: Two examples of organizational culture (Tuggle, 2002).

	Company "A"	Company "B"
Visible artifacts	• Coats and ties; everyone "dressy" • Offices with doors mostly closed	• Khakis and short sleeved shirts • Cubicles; frequent interruptions
Espoused values	• Keep costs under control • Maximize shareholder value	• Expect a lot of dead ends before you find a winning idea • Have fun; work smart
Underlying beliefs	• Only provide information on a "need to know" basis • Juniors defer to seniors	• When the team wins, everyone wins • Good ideas trump seniority

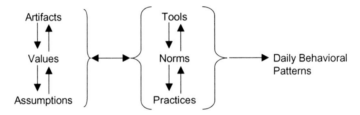

Figure 3.2: Organizational factors influencing daily behavioral patterns (Tuggle, 2002).

Organizational culture is an important barrier to KM success and is an important precondition for KM success (Tuggle & Shaw, 2000). Cultural barriers have been recognized to make it difficult to realize the full potential of KM (King, 2007). Buckman Laboratories is one of the best success stories in terms of changing its culture to become a knowledge-driven organization. Buckman describes four core basic virtues that shape the culture of Buckman labs (Buckman, 2004):

- *Justice:* Acting honestly and fairly, keeping promises
- *Temperance:* Acting with self-discipline, avoiding overt self-service
- *Prudence:* Displaying practical wisdom and the ability to choose well in any situation
- *Fortitude:* Showing strength of mind and character and the courage to persevere in the face of adversity

A knowledge culture is a way of organizational life that enables and motivates people to create, share, and utilize knowledge (Oliver & Kandadi, 2006). It has been named differently by different authors like a knowledge-flow friendly culture (Hardy, 2008) or a learning culture, corporate culture for learning (Sitar, 2004). Culture influences knowledge-related activities by determining which knowledge is appropriate to share, with whom, and when (King, 2007). In KM culture, knowledge and its creator/user is valued, rewarded, and nurtured (Neuhauser, Bender, & Stormberg, 2000). In a knowledge culture, each individual recognizes and accepts knowledge sharing as a desirable behavior. Debowski (2006) presents some of the values that may be found in effective knowledge cultures (Figure 3.3).

Corporate culture is a set of values, norms, symbols, and guiding principles that enable and encourage people to be involved in knowledge activities of knowledge generation, codification, storage, sharing, and uses behavior. Culture (King, 2007):

- shapes assumptions about which knowledge is important,
- mediates the relationship between organizational and individual knowledge,

Figure 3.3: Implicit values of collaborative knowledge cultures (Debowski, 2006).

- creates a context for social interaction,
- shapes processes for the creation and adoption of new knowledge,
- encourages knowledge creation by influencing employees to be involved in organizational learning activities,
- encourages employees to use information technology to codify and store knowledge in knowledge management systems,
- encourages knowledge sharing by making it the norm of acceptable behavior, and
- stimulates knowledge use by influencing employees to constantly innovate and implement knowledge gained.

Therefore, corporate culture is needed to encourage all phases of the knowledge management cycle and focus on tacit as well as explicit knowledge. Explicit knowledge can be easily documented and shared, whereas tacit knowledge is acquired through experience, and more difficult to express and document. Since tacit knowledge resides in employees, culture should support its creation and sharing through interaction, whereas for explicit knowledge, culture should encourage employees to codify it, enter it into knowledge management systems, and take part in activities of its transfer.

3.4. The "Ideal" KM Culture

Various researches have been conducted to better understand what motivates people to share or not to share information. Most research focuses on knowledge sharing at the individual level, but Sun and Scott (2005) also investigated the barriers to knowledge transfer at the team, organizational, and interorganizational level.

Davenport and Prusak (1998) identified some of the key reasons why someone will be willing to share knowledge. The main factors were reciprocity, reputation, altruism, and trust. Some people will be willing to share their knowledge expecting to receive some in return (reciprocity). The exchange does not have to happen simultaneously but no new knowledge will be shared if the initial recipient does not demonstrate his/her willingness to return the "favor." After many knowledge exchanges, trust will be established and both parties will stop "counting." Some people will share knowledge just because they like be known/recognized being knowledgeable or to be considered has expert. Altruism is associated with people who share their knowledge just because it is good for the company and to help their colleagues. They do not expect anything in return. Finally, the concept of trust is probably the most important. Trust can be defined as the

> willingness to increase your vulnerability to another person whose behavior you cannot control, in a situation in which your potential benefit is much less than your potential loss if the other person abuses your vulnerability (Zand, 1997).

Numerous research papers have been published regarding the concept of trust (McKnight & Chervany, 2000). Trust can occur at different levels: personal, organizational, and institutional. McAllister (1995) describes two types of trust: cognitive and affective trust. Cognitive trust is based on beliefs about competence, integrity, responsibility, credibility, reliability, and dependability. It is more task-oriented. Affective trust relies on beliefs about reciprocated care and concern, benevolence, altruism, commitment, and mutual respect. It is more relationship-oriented (McAllister, 1995). Both types of trust might motivate people to share knowledge. Some people will share their knowledge with others because they are just close to them (friends) or because they like or appreciate these people (affective trust). Other will share their knowledge with people they do not know just because they believe that they are competent and that it will help them accomplish a task (cognitive trust). Ribière (2005; Ribière & Tuggle, 2005) studied the relationship between trust and KM initiative success. The level of organizational trust demonstrated to be related to KM initiative success. Park, Ribière, and Schulte (2004) looked at the critical attributes of organizational culture in promoting knowledge sharing and technology implementation successes. An adapted version of the organizational culture profile (OCP) designed by O'Reilly, Chatman, and Caldwell (1991) was used and its correlation with knowledge sharing was assessed and ranked (Table 3.2). The correlation score indicates to what extent the attribute contributes to a knowledge-sharing behavior. A team-oriented environment is very likely to promote knowledge sharing.

Another approach is to look at why people will hoard their knowledge. Garfield (2006) presents 10 main reasons (Table 3.3).

Building on previous research (Pirc, 2001), culture that supports KM should have the following general characteristics. It should have artifacts like open office landscape architecture that will support communication and knowledge sharing. A common sharing space or environment is critical for knowledge transfer and knowledge creation to take place. This was early on defined by Nonaka and Konno (1998) by the concept of "Ba" where this shared space can be

- physical (e.g., office, dispersed business space),
- virtual (e.g., e-mail, teleconference),
- mental (e.g., shared experiences, ideas, ideals), or
- any combination of these.

The ideal KM-friendly culture should also have a high degree of informality, a high degree of confrontation and conflict, no status symbols, a sense of high energy and emotional involvement, and a strong sense of community. Every employee should be treated as an individual, expressing excitement about the importance of his or her work, and award celebrations could be used in order to officially celebrate/ reward those employees who go above their call of duty. It will encourage *values* like hard work, innovation, positive thinking, optimistic attitude, importance of rapid solutions, maximum contribution, no punishment for making mistakes, and risk taking. The underlying assumption of a knowledge-driven organization will see every

Table 3.2: Correlations (ranked) between knowledge sharing and OCP cultural attributes (Park, Ribière, & Schulte, 2004).

OCP attributes	Correlation
Team-oriented work	0.72
Working closely with others	0.68
Sharing information freely	0.62
Trust	0.61
Supportive of employees	0.58
Take advantage of opportunity	0.52
Flexibility	0.46
Confront conflict directly	0.44
Autonomy	0.44
Having a good reputation	0.41
Fairness	0.38
Being innovative	0.37
Developing friends at work	0.35
Adaptability	0.31
Experimentation	0.31
Fitting in at work	0.29
Praised good performance	0.27
Being thoughtful	0.24
Problem-solving	0.20
Socially responsible	0.19
Informality	0.17
High expectation for performance	0.15
Respect for individual's right	0.15
Enthusiasm for the job	0.10
Tolerant of failure	0.06
Security of employment	0.01

Table 3.3: Reasons people do not share their knowledge (Garfield, 2006).

They do not know why they should do it	There is no positive consequence to them for doing so
They do not know how to do it	They are punished for doing it
They think that the recommended way will not work	They do not know what they are supposed to do
They think their way is better	They think they are doing it
They think that something else is more important	They are rewarded for not doing it

individual as a source of innovation and productivity, giving the company its only sustainable competitive advantage.

But since KM is a cycle/process, consisting of several phases, we should focus on characteristics of corporate culture that will support each of its different activities. We can agree that supporting knowledge creation activities through culture does not necessarily mean that we stimulate knowledge sharing as well. We can enforce employees to learn but also to keep their knowledge to themselves. Therefore, by progressing from one phase to the other, new characteristics should be added to the corporate culture (see Figure 3.4).

If we want corporate culture to encourage knowledge creation and individual learning, an organization should be driven by common values like innovativeness, resourcefulness, creativity, experimentation, learning, knowledge, etc. If corporate culture is to enhance knowledge codification and storage as well, it should encourage people to write down what they know, think of who else might be able to take advantage of their knowledge, make knowledge explicit for later reuse, expressing values of trust, maximum contribution, positive thinking, documentation, self-organization, etc.

Taking the next step, for corporate culture to support knowledge sharing, it should include such characteristics that will support values like trust, optimism, cooperativeness, reliability, interdependence, friendship, mutual support and understanding, help, loyalty, etc. And for supporting the last phase of the knowledge management cycle, knowledge use, organizational values like hard work and results, creativity, experimentation, innovation, importance of rapid solutions, maximum contribution, mistakes and risk taking, will support a corporate culture that allows mistakes and encourages risk taking and innovation.

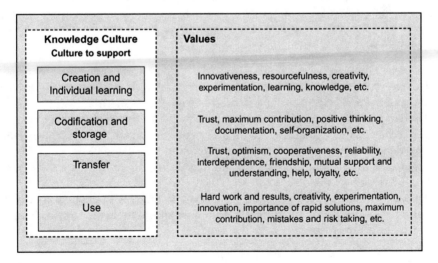

Figure 3.4: Various aspects of a knowledge culture and their associated supporting values.

Concluding from the above description, corporate culture should include all of the above listed values. There is very simple question puzzling researchers and practitioners all over the world: "Which comes first, the knowledge culture or the exchange of knowledge?" (Dixon, 2000). In fact, the KM culture and KM processes are a coevolutionary complex venture that has significant feedback and feed forward loops. Changing a corporate culture usually takes a lot of time, and therefore companies invest money into activities that will have an impact on organizational learning immediately. But, with such activities we are already starting off with bringing about a change in our corporate culture. So actually changes occur simultaneously. Fullan (2001) agrees with that, saying that knowledge activities are "as much a route to creating collaborative cultures as it is a product of the latter." Therefore, culture can be studied as an independent as well as a dependent variable (King, 2007).

3.5. Problems Related to Organizational Culture

Due to its intangibility, changing corporate culture is one of the most difficult tasks organizations are faced with. What we are changing is in fact the way people think and behave. Every day routines, the way things are done around here, how relationships are perceived are all demonstrations of our behavior and our underlying assumptions. Any attempt to change is going to be a difficult, slow, and complex task. Changing culture involves a slow, long-term process that will require a strong support of leaders, commitment, and enthusiasm of change agents, and champions and acceptance of all the employees (Debowski, 2006). Implementing knowledge management in an organization might require changing the culture to become more knowledge supportive but it can be slowed down by several setbacks:

(1) Existing culture is strong and not supportive of KM. Values employees share encourage knowledge hoarding instead of knowledge sharing.
(2) The company lacks management commitment to change. Changing corporate culture takes time and effort. And if a company is successful, then leaders believe that they have no real need to change anything (Hardy, 2008).
(3) Employees are reluctant to change and reject attempts to influence their existing way of working.
(4) The attempts to culture change are not synchronized with changes in structure and processes. Changes of culture should happen simultaneously with changes of structure and processes.

In the following sections, we will discuss in more details on how to overcome these cultural barriers to KM.

3.6. Assessing Your Organizational Culture

There is agreement among researchers concerning organization culture components and their definition. Unfortunately, this agreement is not so strong when we look at how to measure culture.

Rousseau states, "Quantitative assessment of culture is controversial" (Rousseau, 1990), and that only certain dimensions of culture may be appropriately studied using quantitative methods. Reigle and Westbrook (2000) noted that "currently there are inadequate means to measure organizational culture." Many typologies have been created to classify the character or the culture of an organization. Among the most popular are the following:

- The managerial grid by Blake and Mouton (1969, 1985) where two dimensions (*concern level for production* and *concern level for people*) are used to identify the culture type.
- The organizational culture profile (OCP) by O'Reilly et al. (1991) used to examine person-culture fit and its implications for work attitudes and behavior. The OCP is based on 54 items/attributes that are used to characterize both individuals and organizations.
- The organizational content and process typology by Schneider (1994) later on modified by Moore (2000) categorizes a company's culture in a matrix of four quadrants. The vertical axis considers an organization's attention focus, or its "content." The horizontal axis considers how an organization makes decisions, forms judgments, or its "process." The content axis is bounded by *actuality* and *possibility*; the process axis is bounded by *impersonal* and *personal*.
- The Organizational Culture Assessment Instrument (OCAI) by Cameron and Quinn (1999), which uses two main dimensions to define six key dimensions of organizational culture (dominant characteristics, organizational leadership, management of employees, organizational glue, strategic emphases, and criteria of success). One dimension differentiates effectiveness criteria that emphasize flexibility, discretion, and dynamism from criteria that emphasize stability, order, and control. The second dimension differentiates effectiveness criteria that emphasize an internal orientation, integration, and unity from criteria that emphasize an external orientation, differentiation and rivalry (Cameron & Quinn, 1999).
- The sociability, solidarity, and the double S Cube by Goffee and Jones (1998) employs two very old and well-established sociological concepts solidarity and sociability. Where solidarity is defined as "a measure of a community's ability to pursue shared objectives quickly and effectively, regardless of personal ties" and where sociability is defined as "the measure of emotional, non-instrumental relations (those in which people do not see others as a means of satisfying their own ends) among individuals who regard one another as friends" (Goffee & Jones, 1998). Goffee and Jones plotted the two dimensions against each other and defined four culture types: networked, fragmented, mercenary, and communal.

As Schein (2004) states, typologies are very useful to create culture categories that help to simplify and to better understand complexity but by this oversimplification the categories provided might be incorrect in terms of their relevance to what is being assessed/understood. So ones needs to be careful in using such typologies and the tools (questionnaires) associated with them. Schein (2004) presents different methods (quantitative and qualitative) and tools that can be used based on the level of researcher's involvement and bases on the level of the subject's involvement.

3.7. Culture Change

The process of developing a corporate culture supportive of knowledge management consists of three phases: cultural analysis, evaluation, and change. The first phase includes culture analysis, where a detailed analysis of existing behaviors, attitudes, and patterns must be conducted (culture diagnosis). The focus must be made on existing symbols, office layout, legends, stories, ceremonies, values, norms, the ways problems are solved, management orientation, and employee commitment. The identification of the existing culture, its strength, presence of subcultures, and the like is performed at this stage. In culture analysis, different diagnostic approaches (research methods) can be used. Among intensive techniques, we can find observations, interviews, study of different internal documents and guidelines, examination of case histories, focus groups, action research and others. Extensive techniques include surveys based on questionnaire, trend analysis, social network analysis, among others.

In the next phase, a culture evaluation must be performed in order to establish its current alignment with the KM strategy. The understanding of reasons associated with the following questions will have to be performed;

- Why or why not the knowledge is created, codified, stored, shared, and used?
- What barriers get in the way of knowledge activities?
- What gets shared, when and why?
- What are the effects of incentives and rewards on knowledge activities, collaboration, and teamwork?
- What are the informal rules and norms regarding knowledge activities?
- How do power and status affect sharing?
- What are the current levels of collaboration, teamwork, and sharing? (Neuhauser et al., 2000).

By answering these and other questions, one can identify if existing artifacts, values, and assumptions are in line with KM activities. The focus here is on the level of alignment and gap identification. The alignment with structure, systems, strategy, and processes should also be tested since changes should be made simultaneously.

In the last phase, the directions of culture change are recognized. Changing a corporate culture is a very delicate activity. Smith (2003) estimates that only 10–32% of cultural change initiatives are successful and that they often happen with other organizational changes. If you do it wrong or slip, you have missed your golden opportunity, thereby threatening all future change programs. Culture change should therefore be a well-planned intervention, based on a holistic approach combining management intentions and actions. It is advisable to use a project management approach. You should start by clarifying desired outcomes and change strategies before any activities are actually started, thereby providing clarity and direction of all the other activities. Pay special attention to informing people about progress. Regular, accurate communication throughout the project is vital to maintain commitment and decrease uncertainty if delays or obstacles are encountered. Though a culture change to support KM is an organization-wide project (as well as implementing KM), it is advisable to start with a pilot project to test for possible problems and create success stories and experts to learn from when the overall change is initiated. As with every project, there should always be room for changes and adjustments if needed, as additional insights are gathered throughout the project (Debowski, 2006). Knowledge champions, help desk, mentoring, communal learning will help employees cope with changes (Debowski, 2006).

Once the culture will be changed, it will have to be maintained. Maintaining the changed culture and growing it stronger will require socialization of new members, a reward and performance management systems, the development and mentoring new leaders, an ongoing development of knowledge-related competencies, an integration and a constant improvement of existing knowledge systems and services, the recognition of key knowledge workers, the celebration of major advancements and strategies, and ongoing sharing of expertise (Debowski, 2006).

3.8. How Leaders Support the Creation of Knowledge Culture

Knowledge managers from all over the world are claiming that not knowledge, but knowledge sharing is powerful in the 21st century workplace. Their authority is rooted in sharing what they know (Hardy, 2008). Knowledge leaders stimulate sharing and collaboration by demonstrating their value and worth through communication, celebration of successful projects, incentives, and rewards. They are realizing that commitment of their coworkers is to a great degree determined by their own behavior (Hardy, 2008). They see as one of their crucial tasks the creation of right working environment and establishment of culture of mutual trust and respect (Hardy, 2008).

Creating a trust-based culture, rewards and recognition, setting a good example, and spreading positive examples and success stories are all mentioned as managerial actions that will provide the right infrastructure to encourage and stimulate the desired knowledge-sharing behavior (Husted & Michailova, 2002). They present critical success factors for KM success.

In order to create such culture, managers play the vital part. Through their behavior they state what is important therefore in order to encourage organizational learning they are expected to show a convincing level of engagement in knowledge activities (Probst, Raub, & Romhardt, 2000). Through their actions, commitments, statements they shall support the knowledge culture, lead by example, involving into learning activities themselves. Knowledge, information, and learning shall be elements of the management vocabulary, showing the connection between KM and growth and profit, knowledge development, sharing, and distribution activities should be taken into account when rewarding employees and recruit such employees with skills to communicate and share their knowledge with all employees. They should use all of their leadership skills and tools like leadership style, communication, motivation, and staffing to support knowledge activities.

In order to create corporate culture for learning, the leadership behavior should focus on establishing and reinforcing habits of organizational learning by emphasizing knowledge as a core value and embody it in the organizations actions (Fuller, 2000). Leaders should foster right norms, behaviors, rules by personally leading the way (Balvanera & Koval, 2003; Garvin, 2000; Miller, 2002). Some companies say this can be done by linking knowledge sharing to rewards and compensation (Ward, 2002), but some state that the right words in the right time are enough (Seeley, 2002).

Often leaders neglect the fact that critical part of leader's job is cultural definition and development (Steere, 1996). They often even underestimate the influence culture has on business performance. In fact, a leader is responsible for communicating organizational values, specifying them through leading by example, reward the desired behavior. Stewart (2001) explains: "Leaders change culture by changing work, then providing ways to help people get the work done – cheerleading, counseling, training, equipment, financial incentives, and so on." In fact, the immediate supervisors are the key to instilling a knowledge-sharing culture (Seeley, 2002). What they say or do will give the strongest message to their employees. To support this Dayan (2003) wrote that employees, used to working a certain way, need to be convinced that the company is serious about the changes. Therefore, lower level leaders have to be involved in the changes.

If changes are difficult and in great extent influence the way people work, as changing corporate culture or implementing knowledge management initiatives, the change program often looks to employees "as if the executives were randomly changing their mind. This results in low work moral, frustration, people resisting or sabotaging new ways of work" (Miller, 2002). Ward (2002) explains the message of importance of knowledge management will not get across unless leaders "prioritize knowledge sharing through their words, actions and compensation structure." In fact, people learn what is important to leaders by the actions they see modeled by those leaders (Kinsey Goman, 2002). From all stated above, we can now conclude that not the corporate culture, but bad leadership (as part of management) is what is the problem in reality.

If managers are not committed to cultural change, nothing will happen. The worst happens, when managers say they want to change corporate culture, announce it openly, but then do just the opposite; reinforce the existing culture (Barth, 2000b). Culture changes only when leaders "walk the talk" (Schein, 1994). Through changing their own behavior and embedding new values and practices in organizational processes and routines, they start changing underlying assumptions of their employees.

Therefore, leaders first have to make sure they employ the right people; those that fit the desired culture, have the necessary learning ability and are aware that lifelong learning is part of their job. Using knowledge, not status, as source of their power, leaders communicate their commitment to knowledge and by rewarding participation in KM activities create the necessary commitment among employees. Adjusting motivation and rewards systems is vital, if we want employees to change their behavior. All these activities will help develop the learning supportive culture on individual and organizational level, encouraging knowledge creation, codification and storage, transfer, and use as well.

3.9. Relationship between National Culture and Organizational Culture

Culture or should we say cultures? Any individual is exposed to various levels of culture. Among them we could cite, family culture, professional culture, corporate culture, corporate subcultures or subunit, team culture, and national culture. All of them influence to a certain extent (based on the situation; Figure 3.5) the importance of knowledge and relationships (CEN, 2004).

We will mainly focus on the influence of national culture in this section but it is important to mention about subcultures and organizational climate. Organizations have subcultures (based on professions, departments, units) that inherit some values, beliefs, and artifacts from their parent culture (De Long & Fahey, 2000; Deal & Kennedy, 1982; Schein, 1992, 1999). This inheritance might be more or less influential depending if the parent culture is strong or weak (Deal & Kennedy, 1982) also described as integrated or fragmented (Martin, 2002). A strong culture is

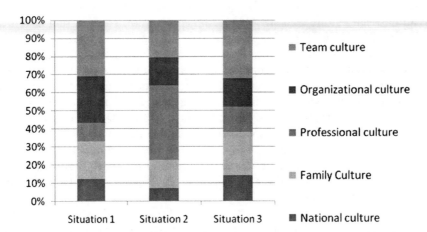

Figure 3.5: Cultural layers have different impacts, which depend on circumstances (CEN, 2004).

often the result of a strong leadership and its various subcultures are relatively homogeneous. In a weak culture, there will be much more variation between the subcultures and changes might more difficult to successfully implement.

In this chapter, we did not address the concept of organizational climate. Organizational climate is closely related to organizational culture. It is more related to a contextual work atmosphere during a certain period of time. It touches on issues like patterns of behavior, attitudes, and feelings. It is not as strong as culture (not as deeply rooted in beliefs and assumptions) and consequently it is easier to change and manipulate. Sometimes only a climate change might be required to facilitate knowledge sharing.

Since corporate culture is under strong influence of national culture, it is important to address its influence on KM as well. National culture develops in a certain society and relates to certain characteristics that are common to individuals in a nation. It is revealed in a pattern of behavior that is acquired early in life and through later experiences (King, 2007). National culture influences how people in a society think, feel, respond to problems, and collect information. It describes a unique way how a certain society responds to general issues like power distance, collectivism versus individualism, femininity versus masculinity, and uncertainty avoidance (Hofstede, 2001).

Most of the literature about creating a knowledge culture discusses the western approach, as majority of this chapter, but there are substantial differences in approaches suitable in other societies.

The influence of national culture on KM, particularly on knowledge-sharing behavior was recognized by Michailova and Husted (2003, 2004), King (2007), Al-Alawi, Al-Marzooqi, and Mohammed (2007), and Lai and Lee (2007). National characteristics of society can create an environment that is more or less hostile to knowledge sharing, thus demanding a different approach to the corporate culture change process.

Michailova and Husted (2003) studied the Russian society and recognized Russian national culture as a strong impediment to knowledge-sharing activities in companies. They have proposed a conscious managerial approach to corporate culture change by forcing the process on knowledge sharing, assigning employees to work on tasks that cannot be completed without more intensive knowledge sharing, constantly controlling their involvement, giving direct orders and instructions that do not allow to avoid knowledge sharing, punishing lack of initiative and involvement in knowledge sharing (Michailova & Husted, 2003). Though these interventions seem harsh, the authors argue that this is the only way to achieve a culture change to be less hostile to knowledge sharing. They also advise to be cautious, consistent, and spend a lot of time to understand the actual situation in a particular company.

Arabic and Muslim societies (Al-Alawi et al., 2007) are known for excessive formality, hierarchy, and bureaucracy in procedures but are adopting modern managerial styles and undergoing cultural transformation. In order to encourage culture change toward knowledge sharing, trustworthy relationships should be stimulated between coworkers through informal social events and discussions, office design should be improved to allow for open communication and sense of equality, job rotation, and effective rewards should be provided to employees to increase motivation and management commitment should be expressed through strong relationships with employees, the level of employee participation in decision-making should increase in order to reduce the hierarchical boundaries and enable easier flow of information. Though these guidelines are generally acceptable in Arabic societies, a case by case approach is still recommended in order to investigate the additional specific problems in every single organization.

Asian societies with collective cultures are perceived as the least problematic from the knowledge sharing point of view. They have a group-oriented mentality naturally inclined to share knowledge within a team, department, or organization (Lai & Lee, 2007; Ribiere & Sitar, 2003). Among other research on the impact of national culture, we can mention the work of Po-Jeng Wang (Schulte & Wang, 2005; Wang, 2004) who conducted a comparative analysis between Taiwan and the United States in term of KM factors, expectations, and practices.

3.10. Conclusion

As discussed, organizational culture and its impact on people, teams, communities, organizations, and enterprises is a very complex and broad topic. We tried to provide you with the key issues and concepts related to this topic, which are particularly important for effective knowledge management, but much more could be said about it. To summarize we state the following:

- Culture is part of a company's competitive asset.
- As Davenport and Prusak (1998) suggested, you should take a look at your culture before launching any KM initiative. Since the main reason for KM failure is related to cultural factors, assessing your culture(s) upfront will help determining the best KM approach and will decrease its risk of failure.
- There are different levels of culture (national, organizational, professional, familial, team) and all of them influence, one way or another, the behavior of employees and their willingness to facilitate/engage in knowledge flows.
- One needs to be careful in trying to assess the culture of its organizations. Various typologies and tools (survey) have been developed to categorize organizational cultures but they often oversimplify things and they might not provide a clear representation of what is really being assessed. A combination of various techniques is recommended.
- A knowledge culture is a culture where knowledge sharing takes place but also a culture that supports knowledge creation, codification, transfer, and use.
- Organizational trust is one of the main virtues required in a knowledge culture.
- KM approach needs to be tailored to leverage organizational culture.
- The concepts of knowledge culture and leadership are intertwined, particularly in period of cultural changes.

- After assessing their culture(s), organizations might have to change or evolve in order to become knowledge-friendly. This is not an impossible task. The determination, the degree of involvement, the strategy, the level of transparency, and the approach used will determine the chance of success. For some organizations, the cultural transformation will take longer than for others but at the end, organizational culture will become more knowledge-friendly.

We will end by a quote from Alison Tucker from Buckman labs (Buckman, 2004):

Communications is human nature; knowledge sharing is human nurture.

References

Al-Alawi, A. I., Al-Marzooqi, N. Y., & Mohammed, Y. F. (2007). Organizational culture and knowledge sharing: Critical success factors. *Journal of Knowledge Management, 11*(2), 22–42.

Balvanera, B., & Koval, O. (2003). Creating a collaborative culture at EBRD. *Knowledge Management Review, 6*(3), 28–31.

Barth, S. (2000a). KM horror stories. *Knowledge Management Magazine, 3*(October), 37–40.

Barth, S. (2000b). KM horror stories. *Knowledge Management Magazine, 3*(10), 36–40.

Blake, R. R., & Mouton, J. S. (1969). *Building a dynamic corporation through grid organizational development.* Reading, Mass: Addison-Wesley.

Blake, R. R., & Mouton, J. S. (1985). *The managerial grid III.* Houston: Gulf Publishing Company.

Buckman, R. H. (2004). *Building a knowledge-driven organization.* New York: McGraw-Hill.

Cameron, K. S., & Quinn, R. E. (1999). *Diagnosing and changing organizational culture.* Upper Saddle River, NJ: Addison-Wesley.

CEN, E. C. f. S. (2004). *European guide to good practice in knowledge management – Part 2: Organizational culture.* Brusselso. Document Number, CWA 14924-2.

Chua, A., & Lam, W. (2005). Why KM projects fail: A multi-case analysis. *Journal of Knowledge Management, 9*(3), 6–17.

Daft, R. L. (1998). *Organization theory and design* (6th ed.). Cincinnati, OH: South-Western College Publishing.

Davenport, T., & Prusak, L. (1998). *Working knowledge. How organizations manage what they know.* Boston, MA: Harvard Business School Press.

Dayan, R. (2003). KM and culture change at Israel aircraft industry. *KM review, 6*(2), 12–15.

De Long, D. W., & Fahey, L. (2000). Diagnosing cultural barriers to knowledge management. *Academy of Management Executive, 14*(4), 113–127.

Deal, T. E., & Kennedy, A. A. (1982). *Corporate cultures: The rites and rituals of corporate life.* Cambridge, MA: Perseus Books.

Debowski, S. (2006). Developing and sustaining a knowledge culture. In: *Knowledge Management.* Milton, Qld.: John Wiley & Sons Australia.

Dixon, N. M. (2000). *Common knowledge: How companies thrive by sharing what they know.* Boston, MA: Harvard Business School Press.

Fullan, M. (2001). *Leading in a culture of change.* San Francisco, CA: Jossey-Bass.

Fuller, S. (2000). Note on the discipline/note sociologique. *Canadian Journal of Sociology*, *25*(4), 507–516.

Garfield, S. (2006). 10 reasons why people don't share their knowledge. *Knowledge Management Review*, *9*, 10.

Garvin, D. A. (2000). *Learning in action: A guide to putting the learning organization to work*. Boston, MA: Harvard Business School Press.

Goffee, R., & Jones, G. (1998). *The character of a corporation. How your company's culture can make or break your business*. New York: HarperBusiness.

Hardy, B. (2008). Collaboration, culture and technology. *Knowledge Management Review*, *10*(6), 18–23.

Hislop, D. (2005). *Knowledge management in organizations*. Oxford: Oxford University Press.

Hofstede, G. (2001). *Culture's consequences: Comparing values, behaviors, institutions and organizations across nations* (2nd ed.). Thousand Oaks, CA: Sage Publications.

HR Focus. (2007). Why culture can mean life or death for your organization. *HR Focus*, *84*, 9.

Husted, K., & Michailova, S. (2002). Diagnosing and fighting knowledge-sharing hostility. *Organizational Dynamics*, *31*(1), 60–73.

John, C. (1998). Learning to trust and trusting to learn. *Management Learning*, *29*(3), 365–382.

King, W. R. (2007). A research agenda for the relationships between culture and knowledge management. *Knowledge and Process Management*, *14*(3), 226–236.

Kinsey Goman, C. (2002). What leaders can do to foster knowledge sharing. *Knowledge Management Review*, *5*(4), 10–11.

Knowledge Management Review. (2001). KM review survey reveals the challenges faced by practitioners. *Knowledge Management Review*, *4*(November/December), 8–9.

KPMG Consulting. (2000). *Knowledge management research report*.

Lai, M.-F., & Lee, G.-G. (2007). Risk-avoiding cultures toward achievement of knowledge sharing. *Business Process Management Journal*, *13*(4), 522–537.

Leidner, D. E. (1998). *Understanding information culture: Integrating knowledge management systems into organization: INSEADo*. Document Number, 98/58/TM.

Martin, J. (2002). *Organizational culture: Mapping the terrain*. Thousand Oaks, CA: Sage.

McAllister, D. J. (1995). Affect and cognition-based trust as foundations for interpersonal cooperation in organizations. *Academy of Management Journal*, *38*(1), 24–59.

McDermott, R., & O'Dell, C. (2001). Overcoming cultural barriers to sharing knowledge. *Journal of Knowledge Management*, *5*(1), 76–85.

McKnight, H. D., & Chervany, N. L. (2000). What is trust? A conceptual analysis and an interdisciplinary model. Paper presented at the Americas conference on information systems (AMCIS), Long Beach, CA, 10–13 August.

Michailova, S., & Husted, K. (2003). Knowledge-sharing hostility in Russian firms. *California Management Review*, *45*(3), 59–77.

Michailova, S., & Husted, K. (2004). Decision making in organisations hostile to knowledge sharing. *Journal for East European Management Studies*, *9*(1), 7–19.

Microsoft. (1999). *Practicing knowledge management*.

Miller, R. (2002). Motivating and managing knowledge workers: Building strategy and culture in knowledge organizations. *Knowledge Management Review*, *5*(1), 16–20.

Moore, G. A. (2000). *Living on the fault line. Managing for shareholder value in the age of the internet*. New York: Harper Business.

Neuhauser, P. C., Bender, R., & Stormberg, K. L. (2000). *Culture.com: Building corporate culture in the connected workplace*. Toronto, Canada: Wiley.

Nonaka, I., & Konno, N. (1998). The concept of Ba building a foundation for knowledge creation. *California Management Review, 40*(3), 40–54.

Oliver, S., & Kandadi, K. R. (2006). How to develop knowledge culture in organizations? A multiple case study of large distributed organizations. *Journal of Knowledge Management, 10*(4), 6–24.

O'Reilly, C. A. I., Chatman, J., & Caldwell, D. F. (1991). People and organizational culture: A profile comparison approach to assessing person-organization fit. *Academy of Management Journal, 34*(3), 487–516.

Park, H., Ribière, V., & Schulte, W. D. (2004). Critical attributes of organizational culture promoting knowledge sharing & technology implementation successes. *Journal of Knowledge Management, 8*(3), 106–117.

Pauleen, D., & Mason, D. (2002). *New Zealand knowledge management survey: Barriers and drivers of KM uptake.* Available at http://www.nzkm.net/mainsite/NewZealandKnowledge ManagementSurveyBarriersandDriv.html. Retrieved on January 10, 2004.

Pirc, A. S. (2001). How leaders can create knowledge supporting culture. Paper presented at the second European conference on knowledge management, Bled School of Management, Bled, Slovenia, 8–9 November.

Probst, G., Raub, S., & Romhardt, K. (2000). *Managing knowledge: Building blocks for success.* Chichester, UK: Wiley.

Reigle, R., & Westbrook, J. D. (2000). Organizational culture assessment. Paper presented at the national conference of the American Society for Engineering Management, Washington, DC, October.

Ribière, V. (2005). *The critical role of trust in knowledge management* [*Le rôle primordial de la confiance dans les démarches de gestion du savoir*]. Unpublished Ph.D. dissertation (Management Sciences), Université Paul Cézanne, Aix en Provence (France). Available at http://proquest.umi.com/pqdweb?did=1127190691&sid=3&Fmt=2&clientId=31812& RQT=309&VName=PQD&cfc=1

Ribière, V., & Tuggle, F. D. (2005). The role of organizational trust in knowledge management tools and technology use and success. *International Journal of Knowledge Management, 1*(1), 60–78.

Ribiere, V. M., & Sitar, A. S. (2003). Critical role of leadership in nurturing a knowledge-supporting culture. *Knowledge Management Research & Practice, 1*(1), 39–48.

Robey, D. (1991). *Designing organizations* (3rd ed.). Homewood, IL: Irwin.

Rousseau, D. (1990). Quantitative assessment of organizational culture: The case for multiple measures. In: B. Schneider (Ed.), *Frontiers in industrial and organizational psychology* (Vol. 3, pp. 153–193). San Francisco, CA: Jossey-Bass.

Schein, E. H. (1992). *Organizational culture and leadership* (2nd ed.). San Francisco: Jossey-Bass.

Schein, E. H. (1994). Organizational culture. In: B. A. Gold (Ed.), *Exploring organizational behavior* (pp. 302–316). Forth Worth, TX: The Dryden Press.

Schein, E. H. (1999). *The corporate culture survival guide.* San Francisco: Jossey-Bass.

Schein, E. H. (2004). *Organizational culture and leadership* (3rd ed.). San Francisco: Jossey-Bass.

Schneider, W. E. (1994). *The reengineering alternative. A plan for making your current culture work.* Burr Ridge, IL: IRWIN.

Schulte, W. D., & Wang, P. J. (2005). The state of knowledge management practice in Taiwan. In: M. A. Stankosky (Ed.), *Creating the discipline of knowledge management* (pp. 104–117). Burlington, MA: Elsevier/Butterworth-Heinemann.

Seeley, C. P. (2002). Asking smart questions to shape your knowledge culture. *Knowledge Management Review, 5*(1), 5.

Sitar, A. S. (2004). Corporate culture and its influence on organizational learning: Combining theory and practical experiences. Paper presented at the EGOS Colloquium. Available at http://egosnet.org/

Smith, M. E. (2003). Changing an organisation's culture: Correlates of success and failure. *Leadership and Organization Development Journal, 24*(5), 249–261.

Steere, W. C. (1996). Key leadership challenges for present and future executives. In: *The leader of the future* (pp. 265–272). New York: Jossey-Bass.

Stewart, T. A. (2001). *The wealth of knowledge: Intellectual capital and the twenty-first century organization*. New York: Currency Doubleday.

Sun, P. Y.-T., & Scott, J. L. (2005). An investigation of barriers to knowledge transfer. *Journal of Knowledge Management, 9*(2), 75–90.

Tuggle, F. D. (2002). *Lecture on the role of culture in knowledge management*. Unpublished work, American University.

Tuggle, F. D., & Shaw, N. C. (2000). The effect of organizational culture on the implementation of knowledge management. Paper presented at the Florida Artificial Intelligence Research Symposium (FLAIRS), Orlando, FL, May.

Wang, P. J. (2004). *An exploratory study of the effect of national culture on knowledge management factors, expectations and practices: A cross-cultural analysis of Taiwanese and U.S. perceptions*. Washington, DC: George Washington University.

Ward, S. (2002). Rewarding knowledge sharing at context integration. *Knowledge Management Review, 5*(1), 3.

Zand, D. E. (1997). *The leadership triad-knowledge, trust, and power*. New York, NY: Oxford University Press.

Chapter 4

Knowledge Management Practices in U.S. Federal Agencies: The Catalyst for E-Government Transformation

Elsa Rhoads

Abstract

After September 11, 2001, the United States recognized the need to reform and transform government's knowledge generation and sharing capabilities. First, there was a need to understand why we were caught unprotected and second, to provide recommendations for the transformation of our governance to improve our capabilities as a nation to respond to the threat of a terrorist act of this nature and to make sure that it could not happen again. This chapter discusses some of the knowledge management related organizational changes needed to prepare U.S. federal agencies for the twenty-first century.

4.1. Introduction

If federal agencies had aggregated their knowledge prior to 9/11, would the outcome of the terrorist plot have been different? Could 9/11 have been prevented if sharing knowledge within and between federal agencies had been the routine practice of government? Did organizational barriers prevent the transfer and acceptance of critical knowledge from one agency to another? What could be done to prevent the next possible incursion? Is the transformation to "e-government" promoted through knowledge management (KM) practices in U.S. Federal agencies the first step toward prevention?

In Search of Knowledge Management: Pursuing Primary Principles
Copyright © 2010 by Emerald Group Publishing Limited
All rights of reproduction in any form reserved
ISBN: 978-1-84950-673-1

Mark Forman (2002), formerly with the Office of Management and Budget (OMB) defined e-government as "The use of digital technologies to transform government operations in order to improve effectiveness, efficiency, and service delivery." The sharing and management of both intraagency and interagency knowledge via web-based electronic interdependencies mark the convergence of KM and e-government.

Many believe the outcome might have been different had the management of our knowledge and the practice of knowledge-sharing between our intelligence agencies been the norm. Certainly KM practitioners working in federal agencies to promote knowledge management recognized 9/11 as an example of what can happen when federal intelligence agencies are ill-prepared, or unable, or even unwilling to share their knowledge, due to ingrained cultural norms, technical interoperability, legal ramifications of sharing data, which may be suspect, but not provable in court, or ignorance of the value of the information the federal government possesses.

After a yearlong review of the situation, the members of the 9/11 Commission concluded, "The U.S. government has access to a vast amount of information. But it has a weak system for processing and using what it has. The systems of 'need to know' should be replaced by a system of 'need to share'" (United States, 2004).

The value and importance of the government's stewardship of its knowledge is now better recognized and appreciated. In fact, 9/11 is considered by many to have been a "wake-up call" to make changes in policy and processes. Members of the federal government are now ready to help promote an environment for sharing knowledge and to consider, with new appreciation, the importance of knowledge management or KM, as it is also termed.

KM programs concentrate on managing and distributing what the government knows within and among its agencies in order to take collaborative action. The basic tenet of KM is that the right knowledge needs to be made available to the right people at the right time for taking concerted action.

The most important role of the federal government is unarguably protecting its citizens from harm, and specifically from terrorist threats. As a result of 9/11, President George W. Bush, upon a recommendation of the 9/11 Commission, began rectifying the gap in sharing information and coordinating action by creating the Department of Homeland Security (DHS). Twenty-two different agencies with a total of 180,000 employees were reorganized into a single agency for the purpose of deterring and preventing terrorist attacks and protecting citizens and infrastructure from threats and hazards.

DHS established a standard that is being applied to all federal agencies. The intent of DHS is to make future disasters less likely by sharing knowledge horizontally (across federal agencies) and vertically (between federal, state and local entities). Real focus has been placed on improving communications within and among all federal agencies, sharing critical knowledge to achieve interoperability, and developing a coordinated method to provide services not solely to prevent national disasters, but to handle disaster recovery as well.

And then, "Katrina" occurred, a natural disaster of overwhelming proportions. As "9/11" is the shortcut name for the terrorist disaster, the word "Katrina" stands as the single name that reminds us of the raging hurricane that struck New Orleans,

Louisiana and other southern states with a vengeance not seen in the United States in recent history.

Was this a second "wake-up" call? Could the communication of our knowledge of "what we needed to know and when we needed to know it" been improved? Decisive management decisions between federal, multistate, and local agencies needed to be made quickly to address the challenging turmoil presented to the United States during the aftermath of recovery following this new and unexpected natural disaster. Would a more effective collaboration between these entities have made a difference?

Federal, state, and local agencies do not intentionally seek to avoid their obligation to transform the way they share knowledge and provide services to the public. The problem is one of a difficulty of execution.

1. Hierarchical "command-and-control" management styles and organizational structures make it difficult to share intraagency knowledge across department "silos" as well as to conduct cross-agency collaboration with other agencies. Unfortunately, sharing knowledge vertically, between federal, state, and local agencies can be negatively affected by these same management styles and organizational structures.
2. Information technology (IT) systems of government agencies face an ongoing presence of costly-to-maintain federal legacy systems that make it technically difficult to share information with other government entities. The difficulty is multiplied when considering the lack of complementary IT capabilities between federal, state, and local agencies and their respective communities.
3. The OMB in 2001 created a common Federal Enterprise Architecture Framework (FEAF) to remedy the cost of duplicate or similar information systems being developed by individual agencies. This effort has resulted in large-scale savings, due to collaboration between agencies to develop systems jointly for particular lines of business (LoBs) relative to the business services they provide to the public.
4. The government's intellectual capital is comprised not only of explicit (written down) employee knowledge, but also of the tacit (not written down) working knowledge in the minds of approximately 1,800,000 federal employees counted in workforce tables on OPM's website (FedScope, 2005). The best way to capture and track this valuable knowledge is still an evolutionary process being driven by individual agencies as they see fit.
5. The "brain-drain," so called because the baby boomer generation has reached retirement age and the cost and time required to hire, train and replace experienced workers is considerable. The effort of retaining the knowledge of the organization's intellectual capital before the employee leaves has not been recognized as a potential loss of critical business process information. The development of a proactive knowledge retention program is not uniformly performed.

There has been little comprehensive research into the value proposition of implementing KM programs and specific practices to achieve improvements in productivity within single federal agencies, or to define improvements in productivity resulting from the transfer of knowledge between agencies in service to the same public customer. Questions remain.

- Which federal agencies have implemented KM programs?
- Which types of KM practices have been implemented?
- Which practices have proven most effective?

This first empirical research of this kind was carried out in a doctoral dissertation entitled "Knowledge Management Practices in U.S. Federal Agencies: The Catalyst for E-Government Transformation" in 2006 (Rhoads, 2006). It was conducted through the auspices of the KM program provided under the School of Engineering and Applied Science (SEAS) and the Engineering Management and Systems Engineering (EMSE) department of The George Washington University in joint collaboration with the participation of the members of the KM Working Group (KMWG) then sponsored by the Federal CIO Council. The author was a founding member of the KMWG in 2000.

4.1.1.   Knowledge Management in the U.S. Federal Government

The federal government has been termed the "gearbox of society," meaning that both business and the general public continually interact with the government. Before e-government became a possible reality, interaction with the government was physical, time-consuming, and costly. It often meant phone calls and personal visits to agency locations to pick up the right forms to be filled in and mailed back. The private sector showed the way; and yet, transformation by the government came hard.

What is so different about the government that makes transformation more difficult to achieve than in the private sector?

- It is more complex.
- Governments do not have a profit motive or a stock price that creates a sense of urgency and that measures progress.
- Government decisions are generally open to public review and opposition political parties are quick to criticize.
- Legislatures may resist change and be at political odds with the executive branch of government, making it difficult to get laws enacted.
- Political terms limit the time in which to implement changes.
- Governments are also more limited in their ability to hire and fire workers.
- These real differences must be acknowledged and understood (Ramsey, 2004, p. 159).

Both Presidents William J. Clinton and George W. Bush embraced the transformation to e-government. The public demanded the same caliber of e-business services from the public sector that it received from the private sector.

The transformation to e-government is mandated at the highest level of the government, with agency performance tracked by the OMB, reporting to the president. E-government is also tracked by the Government Accountability Office (GAO), reporting to Congress.

In the Industrial Age, not so long ago, value was concentrated in land, buildings, physical equipment, and financial holdings, in other words physical capital. In what is called the Knowledge Age or knowledge economy, value is concentrated in human capital (employees) and their knowledge assets (what they know and produce), in other words intellectual capital. If invested properly, these knowledge assets grow and increase in value over time, and have the ability to adapt to the organization's changing requirements and environment. In government, where there is little competition from the marketplace, these diverse assets become an important source for innovation.

4.2. Public Sector Governance

"September 11, 2001, was a day of unprecedented shock and suffering in the history of the United States. The nation was unprepared. How did this happen, and how can we avoid such tragedy again?"

The 9/11 Commission Report stated, "… ways of doing business rooted in a different era are just not good enough. Americans should not settle for incremental, ad hoc adjustments to a system designed generations ago for a world that no longer exists" (2004, p. 399). "Information was not shared, sometimes inadvertently or because of legal misunderstandings. Analysis was not pooled. Effective operations were not launched." (2004, p. 353). The Commission believed that this was a symptom of the government's "… broader inability to adapt how it manages problems in the new challenges of the twenty-first century" (2004, p. 353).

Shortly after President Bush took office in 2001, he defined his agenda to achieve efficiencies of scale to enable government to improve its services to citizens. Bush established his President's Management Agenda (PMA), and in the agenda, he stated the goal that the federal government was to apply a "customer-centric, results-oriented, and market-driven approach" to operations. The aims of the PMA are the following (Bush, 2002, p. 7):

- Hierarchical, "command and control" bureaucracies will become flatter and more responsive;
- Emphasis on process will be replaced by a focus on results;
- Organizations burdened with overlapping functions, inefficiencies, and turf battles will function more harmoniously;
- Agencies will strengthen and make the most of the knowledge, skills, and abilities of their people in order to meet the needs and expectations of their ultimate clients — the American people.

The specific use of the discipline of KM for its transformational effect on organizations receives longstanding support from David M. Walker, the Comptroller General of the United States. Walker was appointed by President Clinton in 1998 to a 15-year tenure to represent the GAO as it "supports the Congress in meeting its constitutional responsibilities and to help improve the performance and ensure the accountability of the federal government for the benefit of the American people" as affirmed in GAO's Strategic Plan (2004, p. 4).

The physical reorganization or restructuring of federal agencies for the purpose of improved serviced transformations is difficult, notwithstanding the president's reorganization of the DHS. However, Hannah Sistare (2004) described the concept of achieving government reorganization for the twenty-first century through means of a "virtual reorganization," propelled by the vehicle of e-government. This has been increasingly possible, due to the growth of the Internet.

The 9/11 Commission provided a dramatic example of the promotion of recommendations for federal government reorganization from a commission. The work of other commissions has been equally important. The National Commission on the Public Service, in a report entitled "Revitalizing the Federal Government for the 21st Century," the second Volcker Commission 2003, declared that the necessity for reorganization was "... urgently needed to improve its capacity for coherent design and efficient implementation of public policy." This Commission called the structure of the federal government "outmoded" and stated that certain programs no longer have viable missions and that too many different agencies share responsibilities that could be combined. The commission concluded that decision-making is often entangled in "knots of conflict, clearance, coordination, and delay" (as quoted in Sistare, 2004, p. 8).

After the establishment of the federal portal named FirstGov.gov in 2000, David Barram, a former administrator of the General Services Administration (GSA), declared that *virtual reorganization*, which was brought about through e-government would "eventually make the physical reorganization of government unnecessary" (as quoted in Sistare, 2004, p. 27).

This first Web site provided by the federal government to the U.S. general public resulted in the "virtual reorganization of the government's cacophony of programs for the public" (Sistare, 2004). For the first time, the public could view federal agency programs by logically grouped topics, rather than by the agency responsible for creating them, making public accessibility to information more direct and efficient. The public did not need to know which agency created and managed the service. Thereafter, this topic-based versus an organizational-based approach was applied to individual agency Web sites.

KM programs, which promote the cross-agency transfer of knowledge, are implemented by U.S. federal agencies on a purely voluntary basis, since there is no mandate from the OMB, for example, to direct the agency-wide implementation of KM practices.

Leading by example, the General Accountability Office delineated the benefits for maximizing value and reducing risk through knowledge management. As a keynote speaker at an international forum on the subject of KM entitled

"Advancing Knowledge and the Knowledge Economy" under the auspices of the National Science Foundation (NSF), Comptroller General David M. Walker described the benefits of the implementation of KM programs.

- Helps leaders facilitate and manage change;
- Supports results-orientation and matrix management (with mechanisms to bring the right people with the right skills together to maximize value and manage risk involved with any undertaking);
- Aids coordination and integration across borders, sectors, agencies, units, levels, and boundaries;
- Helps managers plan their IT efforts to support employees' knowledge-sharing needs;
- Helps employees identify with their own organization's strategic plan; and
- Helps leaders and employees embrace needed cultural transformation (Walker, 2005).

The status quo is that KM is practiced by individual U.S. federal agencies on a voluntary basis. There is no government-wide assessment of the advancement of agency KM practices. However, many federal agencies choose to implement KM practices for the purpose of increasing productivity in business operations, or for the launch of new products or services, or to improve their own organization's internal efficiency and effectiveness (IEE), as specified in the PMA.

In 1995, the American Productivity and Quality Center (APQC) in Houston, led by Dr Carla O'Dell, President of APQC, held its first KM consortium study group to benchmark with both public and private sector organizations. Selected "best-of-breed" knowledge-centric organizations participated by relating their best practice experiences in the adoption of KM practices in their own organizations with the members of the consortium group. There were few training programs for KM practitioners in organizations that were early adopters of KM in the public sector. Many KM practitioners in federal agencies took their training through the APQC's ongoing benchmarking consortium studies.

In 2001, KM practitioners working in agencies of the federal government wrote individual chapters for a book entitled *Knowledge Management: The Catalyst for Electronic Government*. This book began the dialogue that linked the subjects of KM and e-government in the public sector. Dr Shereen Remez, then Chief Knowledge Officer (CKO) of the U.S. GSA, the first CKO appointed by a federal agency, authored a chapter called "KM and E-Gov: Can We Have One without the Other?"

In this chapter, Remez spoke for other KM practitioners in federal agencies when she wrote: "Convinced that both e-government and KM are here to stay, our thesis is that they are so intimately linked – as preconditions and enablers of each other – that we will have both, and not one without the other." She stated further "There's no retreat from putting the 'e' into government – and without KM, government isn't e-government" (Barquin, Bennet, & Remez, 2001, p. 207). She felt strongly that "KM, in the context of e-government ... is leveraging the collective knowledge of agencies to fulfill the mission of the overall federal enterprise" (Barquin et al., 2001, p. 210).

On the relationship between KM and technology, in her first book *If Only We Knew What We Know: The Transfer of Internal Knowledge and Best Practice*, O'Dell and Jackson Grayson (1998, p. 226) was reflective of the fact that "technology is a catalyst, but no panacea." Most of the KM thought leaders in the late 1990s pointed out that technology was only an "enabler" to the implementation of knowledge management. This was an effort to counteract the effect of technology consulting firms that sought to promote KM through the development of a KM system (KMS), often leaving out the elements of people and processes. Technology was the third element of this triad, not the only solution to a successful implementation of KM, nor the most important element.

O'Dell stated that "KM has come of age." Two important myths have been dispelled. The first myth is that "Culture change is more often a consequence of knowledge-sharing than an antecedent to it" (O'Dell & Jackson Grayson, 1998, p. 4). Her research in the many benchmarking studies conducted by the APQC through the years have proven that the KM implementation efforts, with the support and sponsorship of business leadership, have the influence to cultivate a knowledge-sharing culture, and that this can occur throughout the stages of implementation, while executive involvement lends credibility and motivates progress (O'Dell, 2004).

The second myth — that KM cannot be measured — has also been dispelled. While knowledge by itself is intangible and hard to measure, the impact of KM is easier to gauge when aligning with the organization's expected business outcomes and working backwards to correlate the organization's progress with KM deliverables (O'Dell, 2004).

Beginning in 2000, Dr Michael A. Stankosky inaugurated a regular column in the monthly publication *KMWorld* on the KM perspective from the academic viewpoint. Dr Charlie Bixler, from his purview as the first doctoral graduate of The George Washington University's KM program, an adjunct professor in the program, and a KM consultant to federal agencies also contributed a *KMWorld* column entitled "KM: A Source of Practical Solutions to Emerging Government Needs."

Table 4.1 identifies seven federal sector problems that the implementation of a KM program could resolve, according to Bixler.

Bixler affirms that KM is the key to solving these problems. The steps to accomplish this are to identify the problem and its causes, analyze the existing environment, understand the workflow and current business processes, and to devise processes that resolve problems and improve productivity. This translates into improved performance for the public (Bixler, 2002).

4.3. Knowledge Management and the OECD

Headquartered in Paris, the Organization of Economic Cooperation and Development (OECD) provides a forum where the governments of 30 industrialized

Table 4.1: Federal sector problems that KM could resolve.

Federal sector problems	Problem description
Retiring work force	Massive exodus of retirees leads to loss of tacit knowledge in key government mission areas. Debilitating at best and harmful at worst.
Problems with databases and information	Information overload is often redundant, and unstructured information leaves employees spending excessive time searching rather than analyzing information
Lack of intraagency and interagency collaboration	Stove-piped organizations deliver stove-piped databases, resulting in lackluster performance and substantial loss of time and money
Lack of a coordinated approach to KM	Leads to nonstandardization and the inability to promote interoperability within and between agencies
Untimely dissemination and reporting of critical knowledge	Not getting the right information to the right people at the right time and location can be critical, even life-threatening, for senior officials and frontline workers, warriors and agents
Not meeting constituent demands with grace, speed and agility	Lack of flexibility in information processing results in long lines for government services and unhappy customers
Inability to connect with the experts	Tremendous expertise and tacit knowledge is available, but a lack of connectivity makes it inaccessible

Source: Adapted from KMWorld, Bixler (2002, volume 11, issue 8).

countries, with democratic governments, work together to solve the common economic, social, and governance challenges of the member countries. The OECD was founded in 1947 to oversee the launch of the Marshall Plan for the reconstruction of Europe after the end of World War II. It has served as a forum for member countries to respond to new developments, particularly to the new "knowledge economy." The exchange of experiences and the identification and sharing of best practices provide incentives for adoption among member countries.

The OECD benefits from the breadth of its 30-country membership and 1000-member staff who have worked for over 40 years to provide databases of reliable sources for the sharing of comparable statistical, economic, and social data across these countries. KM and e-government are two of the areas of interest studied by the OECD.

OECD conducted the first international survey of KM practices "for ministries/departments/agencies of central government in OECD member countries" (GOV/PUMA/HRM, 2002) designed to review the actual KM practices implemented, as well as a self-assessed perception of the results of these practices. The survey compiled results by country and by ministry/sector, i.e., all seven ministries/sectors in a country and the same ministry/sector across all countries. Countries achieved more significant results than ministries/sectors. This finding led to the conclusion that there was a "need to think about KM from a 'whole of government' perspective rather than from the perspective of individual organizations within central government" (OECD, GOV/PUMA/HRM, 2003, p. 25).

This is a key difference from the perspective of how KM programs are implemented in the U.S. federal government. While they may be adopted within individual departments or agencies, they are not directed from a central government administration. The author organized the completion of the survey from U.S. Federal Agencies and was invited to the OECD in Paris for the deliberation of the participating countries.

4.4. PMA and Government Paperwork Elimination Act Execution

After he was elected to office, President Bush made a commitment to reform government in his PMA in fiscal year 2001–2002, which detailed his commitment. Table 4.2 shows the five areas selected for reform.

The Bush administration carried out the efforts of the Clinton administration with the prospect of reducing the amount of paperwork produced by the government, advocated by the adoption of the Government Paperwork Elimination Act (GPEA), and to reform the federal government by advocating the transformation to e-government.

This was a targeted, top-down implementation directed by the OMB, reporting directly to the President. The OMB prepared a key document, entitled "E-Government Strategy" to simplify and guide the implementation of the PMA, including the delivery of services to citizens through e-government.

Supported by the ongoing evolution of the Internet, and motivated by the success of electronic commerce in the private sector, resulting from the demand by American citizens, federal agencies were mandated to become citizen-centered by utilizing e-government web-based technology. President Bush stated in the PMA that "This administration's goal is to champion citizen-centered electronic government

Table 4.2: The president's management agenda performance requirements (fiscal year 2001).

Federal mandate to improve government performance				
Five government-wide areas for transformation				
Human capital	Competitive sourcing	Financial management	Electronic government	Budget/performance integration
Citizen-centered — not bureaucracy or agency-centered Results-oriented — measurable improvements for citizens Market-based — actively promoting innovation				

Source: PMA, FY2002.

that will result in a major improvement in the federal government's value to the citizen" (PMA, FY, 2002, p. 23).

Prior to the PMA of President Bush, the GPEA of 1998 mandated four types of transitions to e-government, categorized as e-government portfolios. In 2001, as part of its execution of the GPEA and the PMA, the OMB mandated 25 specific e-government, cross-agency initiatives for implementation by U.S. federal agencies. Table 4.3 lists the 25 initiatives within the portfolios to which they pertain. E-Authentication is a cross-cutting initiative.

Once fully implemented, the OMB mandates are expected to eliminate duplicate programming and software maintenance for the 19 agencies that were found to have overlapping LOBs, consisting of the same services delivered by different individual agencies. One of the outstanding successes was the outcome of the E-Payroll initiative, which resulted in a notable reduction from 14 government payroll systems to two payroll systems.

The most ambitious of the four portfolios is represented by governmental agencies working together government to government, or (G2G) to provide services to citizens. The OMB has motivated government agencies to adopt increasingly more sophisticated cross-agency applications for e-government. This will continue until all agencies reach the goal of collaboration to provide new or improved services to the public. Mark Forman's prescription for agency improvements by "an order of magnitude" is the equivalent of a 10-fold increase in the value of customer services (OMB, 2002).

Table 4.3: Summary of e-government GPEA portfolios.

Categories of the Government Paperwork Elimination Act (GPEA)	
Government to customer (G2C) • Recreation one-stop • GovBenefits.gov • Online access for loans • USA services • IRS free filing	Government to business (G2B) • E-rulemaking • Expanding electronic tax products for business • Federal asset sales • International trade process streamlining • One-stop business compliance
E-authentication — Cross-cutting initiative	
Government to government (G2G) • Geospatial information one-stop • E-grants • Disaster management • Consolidated health informatics • SAFECOM • E-vital	Internal efficiency & effectiveness (IEE) • E-training • Recruitment one-stop • Enterprise HR integration • E-clearance • E-payroll • E-travel • Integrated acquisition environment • E-records management

Source: E-Government Strategy (OMB, 2002, p. 10).

4.5.   Transformation to a Federal Enterprise Architecture

Enterprise architecture (EA) is a mandate for the ultimate transition to e-government. The federal enterprise architecture (FEA) defines the organization's processes from a business and operational perspective.

The E-Government Act of 2002 assigned OMB the responsibility for oversight relative to the mandate for a consistent implementation of a FEA plan in accordance with the government's recommendations both for internal agency business operations and for G2G interoperability.

OMB uses its authority to ensure an outcome of the best, most compatible IT systems, in order to make prudent investment funding for large IT systems. Agencies of the U.S. federal government are mandated to follow the FEA as a framework for compliance, gradually making the transition from older, less efficient, costly-to-maintain IT systems to newer more efficient systems — from the "as-is" to the "to-be" systems. Thereafter, OMB uses these individual enterprise architecture plans for evaluating and approving the IT funding requested by each agency.

The GAO also plays a key role in carrying out the FEA program, with the responsibility for evaluating each agency's progress in meeting the goals of the FEA every 2 years.

In Figure 4.1 Richard (Dick) Burk, Chief Architect of OMB's Office of E-Government and Information Technology, guides OMB's effort to establishing the FEAF. The OMB monitors agency commitment to the FEAF. Burk has stated that executing federal agency compliance to the FEA framework will result in "nothing less than the transformation of government" (Burk, 2005).

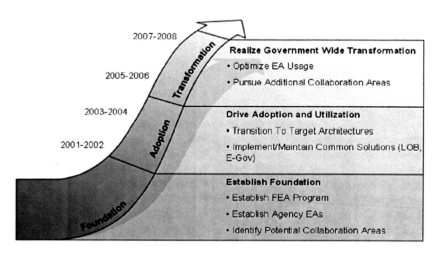

Figure 4.1: Phases in establishing a government-wide enterprise architecture (Available at http//:georgewbush-whitehouse.archives.gov/.../egov/.../2005_FEA_PMO_Action_Plan_FINAL.pdf).

The Figure 4.1 presents a phased approach to government-wide transformation. Agencies have been moving towards their targeted Enterprise Architecture Plan (EAP) and should be deriving positive outcomes toward achieving agency mission and goals through adherence to the standards of the FEAF.

In effect, OMB "manages" the major IT investments and strategic technological decisions of each agency through compliance mandates. This has resulted in the ability to achieve a reduction in the duplication of overlapping LOBs in different agencies; it has promoted the cross-agency effort for collaboration to bring these initiatives to fruition.

The "aha" or key understanding of this research was the realization that it need not take a physical reorganization of agencies (as in the creation of the DHS) to affect major coordinated improvements in public sector governance.

We have the opportunity to use federal mandates across agencies to effect a virtual reorganization if it will better serve the country.

References

Barquin, R. C., Bennet, A., & Remez, S. G. (Eds). (2001). *Knowledge management: The catalyst for electronic government.* Vienna, VA: Management Concepts.

Bixler, C. H. (2002). Knowledge management: A practical solution for merging global security requirements. *KM World, 11*(8), September.

Burk, R. D. (2005). EA for results: Nothing less than the transformation of government. Paper presented at the Enterprise Architecture Conference, Sponsored by The E-Gov Institute, Washington, DC, 21 September. Available at http//:georgewbush-whitehouse.archives.gov/.../egov/.../2005_FEA_PMO_Action_Plan_FINAL.pdf

Bush, G. W. (2002). United States office of management and budget, executive office of the president, the president's management agenda [Electronic version]. Available at http://www.whitehouse.gov/omb/budget/fy2002/mgmt.pdf. Retrieved on March 17, 2008.

FedScope. (2005). OPM. Available at http://www.fedscope.opm.gov/index.asp. Retrieved on January 2, 2005.

Forman, M. A. (2002). Simplifying and unifying knowledge management to drive better government performance. Paper presented at the Knowledge Management-E-Gov Institute.

GAO. (2004). *Strategic plan 2004–2009.* Document no. GAO-04-534. United States General Accounting Office. http://www.gao.gov/sp/d04534sp.pdf. Retrieved on November 6, 2009.

GOV/PUMA/HRM. (2002). Organisation for Economic Co-operation and Development (OECD). Survey on knowledge management practices for ministries/departments/agencies of central government in OECD member countries. Public Management Service-Public Management Committee-JT00119787-PUMA/HRM/(2002)1. Available at http://www.oecd.org/document/20/0,3343,en_2649_34139_1946900_1_1_1_1,00.html

GOV/PUMA/HRM. (2003). *Draft report for discussion: Conclusions from the results of the survey of knowledge management practices for ministries/departments/agencies of central government in OECD member countries.* Document No. JT00138295. Public Governance and Territorial Development Directorate/Public Management Committee/Human Resources Management Working Party.

O'Dell, C. (2004). *The executive's role in knowledge management.* Houston, TX: APQC.

O'Dell, C., & Jackson Grayson, C. Jr. (1998). *If only we knew what we know: The transfer of internal knowledge and best practice.* New York: The Free Press.

OMB. (2002). E-government strategy: Implementing the President's management agenda for E-government. http://www.whitehouse,agency/OMB

Ramsey, T. (Ed.) (2004). *On demand government: Continuing the e-government journey.* Big Sandy, TX: MC Press.

Rhoads, E. P. (2006). *Knowledge management practices in U.S. federal agencies: The Catalyst for E-government transformation.* D.Sc. dissertation, The George Washington University, Washington, DC.

Sistare, H. (2004). *Government reorganization: Strategies and tools to get it done.* Washington, DC: IBM Center for The Business of Government.

United States. (2004). The 9/11 commission report: Executive summary. New York: W. W. Norton & Company (p. 24). Available at http://www.911commission.gov/report/911 Report_Exec.pdf. Retrieved on Novermber 6, 2009.

Walker, D. M. (2005). Advancing knowledge and the knowledge economy. Paper presented at the National Science Foundation's International Conference. http://www.gao.gov/cghome/2005/ke01112005/ke01112005.pdf. Retrieved in November, 2009.

Addendum

David M. Walker

Many who worked in the field of knowledge management in the federal sector for a decade were disappointed in the resignation of David M. Walker, the Comptroller General of the United States and head of the Government Accountability Office (GAO). After completing only the first 10 years of his appointment by President Clinton for a 15-year tenure, beginning in 1998. Walker joined the Peter G. Peterson Foundation as president and CEO in March 2008, presumably to do what he was not able to do under the GAO.

His work in the federal government as its chief auditor provided the background for his series of "wake-up tours" around the country to warn the public about the worsening fiscal condition of the United States. As a follow-up, under the auspices of the Peterson Foundation, a film entitled "I.O.U.S.A" was introduced in selected theaters across the country in August 2008 to bring home the attention of the public the consequences of major fiscal and other sustainability challenges facing the country.

Richard (Dick) Burk

Richard (Dick) Burk retired in October 2007, a statistic of the "baby boomer" retirement situation affecting the government. After nearly 40 years of government service, in the Department of Housing and Urban Development (HUD) and following that, a challenging and meaningful role as chief architect in the Office of Management and Budget (OMB), whose task is to measure the performance of Information Technology (IT) in U.S. federal agencies for the improvement of government services to the public.

Trained in public service, with a tour in the Peace Corps, and a master's degree in public administration, his was a government career, well-executed.

Federal KMWG and NASA Wiki

One of the constants concerning the adoption of KM programs in U.S. federal agencies has been The Knowledge Management Working Group (KMWG). Originally chartered under the auspices of the Federal CIO Council in 2000, it is now an independent organization, called the Federal Knowledge Management Working Group.

Jeanne M. Holm, co-chair of the Federal KMWG and chief knowledge architect at of the Jet Propulsion Lab at the National Aeronautics and Space Agency (NASA) arranged for the Federal KMWG to establish a wiki on a NASA Web site. The wiki is read-only to the pubic, but provides full collaboration for members. Membership is open. The mission of the Federal KMWG is stated as follows:

> *Mission*: Inform and support federal government departments, agencies, organizations and their constituencies in the research, development, identification and implementation of knowledge management (KM) activities, practices and lessons learned, and technologies.
>
> *To accomplish this mission*, the Federal KMWG will mobilize and leverage thought leaders and KM practitioners from government, quasi-government, academia, non-government, nonprofit, and the private sector around the globe. (2008).

Advocates of KM support policies and practices for sharing knowledge that has applicability to federal agencies. Click the following link to reach the site: http://km.gov.

The George Washington University

The George Washington University is one of the first major universities if not *the* first university to offer a concentrated knowledge management program leading to a Doctor of Science (DSc) degree from the Engineering Management and Systems Engineering (EMSE) Department in the university's School of Engineering and Applied Science (SEAS).

The university has graduated almost 40 DSc degrees in the past decade. Many of these scholars have joined other universities as professors, here in the United States as well across the world.

In just one decade, the presence of The George Washington University's location in Washington, DC has had an unmistakably significant influence in the establishment of KM programs in U.S. federal agencies as well as to prepare KM consultants to serve the private sector well. Exporting the knowledge in how to organize and teach this science makes a genuine contribution, which affects the quality and productivity of both public and private sector organizations in other countries and improves the lives of their citizens.

Chapter 5

The Function of Knowledge Management Systems in Large-Scale Organizational Design [☆]

Kevin J. O'Sullivan, Juan Pablo Giraldo and Juan A. Román

Abstract

Research conducted by Eccles and Nolan [Eccles, R. & Nolan, R. (1993). A framework for the design of the emerging global organizational structure. In: S. Bradley, J. Hausman, & R. Nolan (Eds), *Globalization, technology, and competition*. Boston, MA: Harvard Business School Press.] focused on creating an "organizational design" to manage a large-scale company. They recognized that understanding of designing effective large-scale organizations is in an embryonic stage. However, their efforts are intended to build a framework that analyzes and critiques traditional managerial approaches. Their criticism focuses on three points. First, traditional approaches are based on the assumption that senior management could design the total organizational structure. Second, traditional approaches implicitly embody restrictions on the flow of and access to knowledge. Third, traditional approaches are based on a sharp, formal articulation of objectives and strategies. In their research, they propose two levels of design in order to manage a large-scale company. The first level deals with the responsibility of senior management for putting in place key infrastructures of assets, resources, and management practices that will be utilized by individuals (knowledge workers) throughout the company to

[☆] The views expressed by the authors in the article do not necessarily represent the views of the National Aeronautics and Space Administration.

perform a "self-design" level (second level). At this level, individuals use the infrastructure to build relationships to accomplish what needs to be done.

In this chapter, we shall examine the current literature and a relevant case study to establish the functionality of knowledge management (KM) systems in the design of large-scale organizations to create competitive advantage by enhancing the knowledge worker's capabilities.

5.1. Introduction

Many authors have speculated that organizational culture achieved prominence in the late 1970s and 1980s, primarily driven by falling performance levels of big businesses in United States and Europe, and the Japanese management methods and practices, which were gaining popularity (Pettigrew, 2000). Kotter and Heskett (1992) concluded, after conducting four cultural studies, that the culture of the company has a powerful effect on the performance and long-term effectiveness of the organization. They also point out that although we usually talk about organizational culture in the singular form, all organizations have multiple cultures that are associated with different functional groupings or geographic locations.

Goffee and Gareth (1996) assert that the culture of an organization is perhaps the single most powerful force for the cohesion in the modern organization and unless you are very near the top of the organization, its overarching values, beliefs, and behavioral norms are pretty much out of your hands. When a new employee starts working for a company, he or she joins its culture because is something that is deeply embedded in the fabric of an organization and is not easily changed.

There are many definitions of organizational culture. Some of them are based on an anthropological foundation and others are based on sociological foundations. Also, they vary in terms of the required depth or levels that need to be unfurled in order to uncover the true culture of an organization. McDermott, Carlin, and Womack (1999) in the American Productivity and Quality Center (APQC) organizational culture study, define it as:

> The environment that influences behavior; decision making; and the organization's approach to markets, customers, and suppliers. It is the combination of shared history, expectations, unwritten rules, and social mores that affects behavior throughout the organization. Culture is underlying beliefs that while never actually articulated, are always present to color the perception of actions and communications. These beliefs are transmitted through everyday language and actions.

For an organization to achieve the necessary level of adjustment to attain its optimum performance, it requires the understanding and awareness of the culture composition. The "culture types" operating within an organization's boundaries comprise its overall organizational culture. Understanding the organizational culture is of paramount importance when designing and implementing effective processes, tools, and technologies across them. In addition, a cultural analysis is also necessary to grasp how implementing knowledge management (KM) efforts influence the organization, and at the same time, are influenced by the organization. The implementation of a KM system (KMS) at the organization-wide level cuts across many different cultures. The interaction of these different culture types impinge on KMS implementation, acceptance, and overall success.

McDermott et al. (1999) revealed that no matter how strong the commitment and approach to KM, the organizational culture is stronger. In order to have successful KMSs, they recommend the creation of a KM strategy that fits the culture and to link KM to the core culture values, which are widely held throughout the organization (McDermott et al., 1999; McDermott and O'Dell, 2000).

5.2. KM Factors: Technology Roles

5.2.1. *Maintain and Keep Track of Operational Data of Large-Scale Transactions*

A very high number of references describe large investments and efforts of large-scale organizations that have been made to develop databases and to keep track of multinational operational data. These developments and efforts are directed to *gather* data through the use of standardized platforms such as Intranets and Extranets that use markup languages such as XML as a middleware component to access global databases (Glushko, Tenenbaum, & Meltzer, 1999) and *data warehousing* (Taylor, 2000).

The concept of *portals*, explored by Nielsen (1999) and Messmer (1999), introduces the creation of "communities" for sharing and disseminating information and knowledge. Portal products have basically two dimensions: diversity of content usually powered by *content management* technologies (Taylor, 2000), and user community.

5.2.2. *Analyze the Large-Scale Environment*

Karakaya and Kaynak (1995) identified the use of databases to identify potential opportunities and new markets by providing marketing, management, finance, accounting, and taxation. In their research, they described a large international business databases as a source of primary and secondary research to complement the functional orientation of most practitioners in large-scale organizations. Examples of the business applications include competitor analysis, sales profiles, geographic configuration, trends and strategies, employment profiles, governance, strategic change, financial performance, financial risk, accounting standards, income tax rates, and intangible asset values.

5.2.3.   Support the Decision-Making Process of Large-Scale Decisions

Two main topics are studied in this domain. The first one covers all *decision support systems* that include analytical models to aid the decision-making process. The second one addresses a gamut of technologies that are oriented to enhance the decision-making process of large-scale organizations.

During the 1990s, a large body of literature has emphasized the use of models to aid the decision-making process (Dyer & Forman, 1991; Turban & Aronson, 1998). One of the main roles of decision support systems is to make use of decision analysis frameworks that are capable of: supporting decision involving several alternatives, addressing competing criteria or factors, and incorporating subjective and objective factors. In other words, the role of decision support systems is to provide a framework for all that fits the analysis of many marketing problem-solving/ opportunity assessment situations by involving both quantitative and qualitative factors (Dyer & Forman, 1991).

5.2.4.   Enhance Collaboration and Group Decision Making Among Global Players

Technology impacts the way workers execute their work and also changes the way in which organizations work (Turban & Aronson, 1998; Marquardt & Kearsley, 1999). Collaborative computing software supports groups whose members are in different locations. People can work at home not only as individuals but also as participating team members supported by group collaboration and decision support systems.

5.3.   KM Factors: Investment

One of the major strategic commitments for firms is to make investments in networking infrastructure to gain competitive advantage in the industry they operate (Bradley, 1993). In this research, it is pointed that the problem stems not from lack of creative ideas about how to use technology, but rather from inadequate understanding and analysis of the logic that underlies the sustainability of competitive advantage. Bradley's research focuses on the decisions to *invest* in networking infrastructure with a view toward improving management's understanding of the likely competitive advantage to be gained and the financial returns to be obtained. To illustrate how the technology is being implemented and the nature of the competitive advantage sought, a classification of strategic applications of technology networking is presented.

Clemons (1993) studied large-scale implications of increased cooperation through technology. He concluded that technology is likely to produce significant changes in the relative importance of cooperation and coordination. First, technology improves coordination and monitoring performance across the boundaries of firms. Second, investments in information technology are flexible, not restricted to a single use with a single partner, and thus do not increase strategic vulnerability.

From our research, we have found that there are four critical actions that support investment in technologies for KM. First, KM technologies are linked to corporate strategy. Second, technologies for KM are supported by leaders/champions within the organization. Third, organizations have personnel who are responsible for coaching employees on the use of these technologies. Fourth, organizations provide incentives (e.g., user value, recognition, awards, monetary rewards) to use these technologies.

5.4. KM Factors: Technologies

Before trying to capture the relationship between knowledge and technology, the terms data, information, and knowledge must be clarified (Spiegler, 2003). Two opposing views of this relationship are that knowledge is needed before data collection and it indeed determines what data are stored (Tuomi, 2000) and that a recursive and spiral model linking data, information, and knowledge exists, as Spiegler (2000) suggests and illustrated in Figure 5.1.

The CODASYL (Conference on Data Systems Language) report of 1971 defines the distinction between data, information, and knowledge as follows:

- *Data* are symbols inscribed by human hands or instruments.
- *Information* is a judgment by an individual or groups, which given data resolve a question, disclose, or reveal distinctions or enable a new action.
- *Knowledge* is the capacity for effective action in a domain of human actions.

Both models are effective in describing the role of technology in generating knowledge, however, there can be a distinction drawn between technologies that generate knowledge and KM technologies.

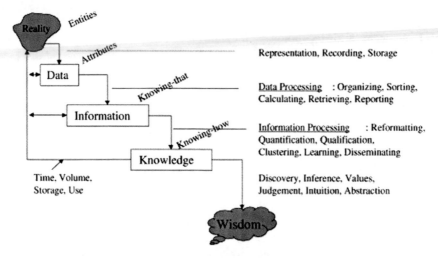

Figure 5.1: Data, information, and knowledge (Spiegler, 2003).

With the one exception of KM technology performance statistics, one can see the impact of KM everywhere (Malhorta, 2003). This seems like a contradiction of sorts given the pervasive role of information and communication technologies in most KM applications (Malhorta, 2004).

There are technologies associated with each of the aspects put forward by Nonaka. In his paper on "The concept of Ba; Building a foundation for knowledge creation" (Nonaka & Konno, 1998), he states that although individuals experience each of these processes from a KM and therefore an organizational perspective, the greatest value occurs from their combination. New knowledge is created, disseminated, and internalized by other individual, who can therefore act upon it and thus form new experiences and tacit knowledge that can in turn be shared with others and so on (Nonaka & Konno, 1998).

Marwick's (2001) research adds specific KM technologies to the Nonaka model. In his article "KM Technologies" he outlines seven categories of KM technologies used in the processes of socialization, externalization, combination, and internalization:

- Expertise locators
- Groupware
- Speech recognition
- Search engines
- Document management and taxonomies
- Portals and metadata
- Summarization agents

Another approach to classifying KM technologies is advocated by Davenport and Prusak (1998) in *Working Knowledge*. Their approach is to evaluate KM technologies from the perspective of time to solution and level of knowledge required allowing us to plot different technologies along a continuum. In categorizing the technology that they deem KM technologies they have created seven broad categories of technologies:

- Neural networks
- Groupware
- Web-based technologies
- Expert systems
- Case-based reasoning
- Constraint-based reasoning
- Knowledge artifacts

Another model for defining KM technologies was postulated by Jackson (2001) based upon a study of the types of software that could be included under the term KM technologies (Fayyad, Piatetsky-Shapiro, Smyth, & Uthurusamy, 1996; Lethbridge, 1994) and concluded that there were five broad categories of KM technologies involved in the KM process: synthesis, dissemination, communication, gathering, and storage.

A sixth category, systems for managing intellectual property, can be added as an adjunct category, although they are not specifically KM tools, they help codify the intellectual assets of an organization and are certainly part of the domain of the knowledge manager (Edvinsson, 1999; Leonard, 1995).

KPMG in 2000 developed a KM technology classification system that codified the approach taken by Nonaka. In creating the classification system, they created eight categories of KM technologies:

- Internet-based tools
- Intranet-based tools
- Extranet-based tools
- Data warehousing
- Document management/content management
- Decision support systems
- Knowledge agents
- Groupware

The approach taken with this model of KM technologies spans those alluded to earlier in this section and uses the KPMG Consulting (2000) amalgam as the basis for the research construct. As such, we will consider the eight major categories of KM technologies:

- Internet
- Intranet
- Extranet
- Data warehousing
- Document management/content management
- Decision support systems
- Knowledge agents
- Groupware

5.5. KM Factors: Organizational Learning

The concept of organizational learning or learning organizations has been evolving for more than two decades (Daft & Weick, 1984; Fiol, Marjorie, & Marjorie, 1985; Senge, 1990; Schwandt, 1997; Argyris, 1996; Garvin, 1998). Marquardt and Kearsley (1999) stress the criticality of this issue for large-scale organizations. First, change is more rapid and ever more intense. Second, global competition forces companies to face the knowledge resources of the world's best companies.

Pucik (1991) analyzed competitive advantage and organizational learning from a technology transfer perspective. He concludes that organizational learning is not a random process, but a carefully planned and executed set of policies and practices designed to enlarge the knowledge base of the organization. Also, organizational learning is a strategic requirement for firms engaged in competitive collaboration, when technology is transferred between competitors. Finally, he introduced a set of obstacles to organizational learning in strategic alliances.

5.6. Organizational Learning and Organizations as Dynamic Social Systems

Schwandt's (1996) approach provides a counter-argument to present strategic management practices that deal *only with performance* changes that demand all organizations activities "add value" to their end products, as opposed to an approach that deals with *performance and collective learning*. He focuses on explaining an alternate explanation of change by thinking of organizations as *dynamic social systems* being formed, reformed, and consuming energy in states of punctuated equilibrium with periodic movements between order and disorder as shown in Table 5.1. He defines the collective (organization) as an amalgamation of actors, objects, and norms and is characterized by social phenomena that are more than the sum of individual behaviors and attitudes of the individual actors.

Each of these interdependent relationships among the subsystems is maintained through sets of "interchange media." The media are complex patterns made up of organizational variables traditionally used in singular cause–effect relationships. Each subsystem in the performing subsystem maintains a critical dependency on each of the other subsystems for process inputs where the output function of one subsystem becomes an input for each of the other subsystems. Interdependence of all the learning and performing subsystems are depicted in Figure 5.2.

5.7. KM Strategic Approach to Knowledge Flow

Two main strategies or approaches emerge in the literature when considering the flow of knowledge throughout an organization. Different authors identify them differently; however, the purpose and essence are the same. For example, Denning (2000) categorizes the two approaches as the "Connecting and Collecting Dimensions", Weidner (2002) names them "Connect and Collect", and Hansen, Nohria, and Tierney (1999) describe them as "Codification" and "Personalization". These two approaches represent the knowledge utilization throughout the organization. At the core of these conceptualizations is the notion that organizations are comprised of knowledge-producing and knowledge-exchanging subsystems (Schulz, 2001). Therefore, the acquisition and sharing of knowledge are primary mechanisms in knowledge-based organizations.

The "codification" approach is generally defined as the formalization of tacit knowledge that is typically difficult to express or explain by developing processes that

Table 5.1: Dynamic social system subsystems Schwandt's (1996).

Subsystem	Description
Environmental interface	Functions as the portal for information entering the organizational learning system. It consists of a collection of independent activities and actions that responds to signals from both inside and outside of the organization determining the information it seeks and disperses. The processes used by the subsystem range from those designed to purposefully gather information based on internal criteria (e.g., market surveys) to those which passively receive information such as regulations and economic indicators imposed upon the organization from the external environment.
Action-reflection	Creates valued knowledge from new information. This subsystem consists of a set of activities and actions the collective uses to accomplish the goals of the learning system and to understand the meaning of an action so judgments can be made concerning the action. The organization can reflect on its actions from three perspectives: the processes used in the action, the content or results of the action, and/or the underlying premises of the action.
Dissemination and diffusion	Exists to transfer information and knowledge within the organization, thus integrating the learning system. Characterized by its ability to match transfer mechanisms with the requirements of the other learning subsystems. Dissemination processes are those that are more purposefully directed and governed by formal procedures and policies. Diffusion techniques represent more informal processes such as rumors and informal communications. Both modes include acts of communication, networking, management coordination and other acts and roles supporting the movement of information and knowledge.
Meaning and memory	Provides the foundation from which the other subsystems draw guidance and control. It maintains the mechanisms that create the criteria for the judgment, selection, focus, and control of the organizational learning system. They are those acts directed at sustaining and creating the cultural beliefs, values, assumptions and artifacts of the organization.
Acquisition of resources	Provides the organizational performance system with the adaptation function. It is responsible for screening, obtaining, and putting in service organizational resources in an effort to respond to the needs of the internal collective as they perform goal attainment actions.

Table 5.1: (*Continued*)

Subsystem	Description
Production/service	Provides the organizational performance system with the goal attainment function. This subsystem is complex because it incorporates all of those actions and processes that the organization must perform to produce a product or reach a goal.
Management and control	Provides the organizational performance system with the integration function. Includes management of control processes, job design, training, organizational development, and operational and strategic planning.
Reinforcement	Provides the organizational performance system with pattern maintenance/latency function. It is comprised of those elements that contribute to maintenance and management of tensions regarding the standards, norms and values that the organization uses to reinforce its performance.

acquire it or by developing mechanisms that allow this knowledge to become explicit and then, become documented. The codification strategy is based on a people-to-document approach and it uses information systems to carefully codify knowledge and store it in a location that can be accessed and reused by everyone in the organization. An electronic document system that supports the life cycle (codifies, stores, disseminates, and reuses) of the knowledge-objects is one example of a codification approach. The knowledge-object can be key pieces of a document, an analysis, or something similar.

On the other hand, the "personalization" approach is the sharing of tacit knowledge by direct contact from person-to-person; therefore, allowing the flow of knowledge that probably could not be codified. It is focused on dialogue among individuals, teams, and groups of employees in formal and informal settings. The personalization approach can help them achieve deeper insight by engaging in an open dialogue. The knowledge is kept close to whoever developed it and it uses information systems to help communicate that knowledge but not for storing it. An example of the personalization approach can consist of a network of people within their organization resulting in a network of colleagues. Using information systems such as an expert locator or directory of expertise, people can benefit from their experiences. Electronic document systems are also used, but their purpose is finding documents to help users get up to speed in a particular subject matter, and identifying who has done previous work on the topic in order to approach them directly.

Many organizations have found that both codification and personalization approaches are needed for an effective KM effort. However, the emphasis of one

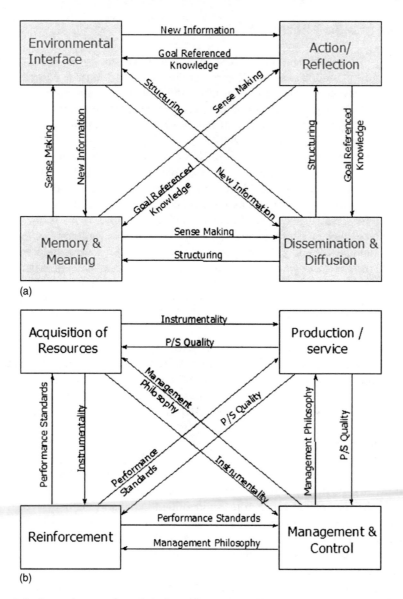

Figure 5.2: Learning–performing interchange media: (a) Schwandt (1996) and (b) Johnson (2000).

approach over the other or a balanced approach depends on the large-scale organization's overall strategy. The correct balance can be influenced by the way the organization serves its clients or stakeholders, the economics of its business (e.g., for-profit, nonprofit, government), and the human capital it possesses.

5.8. KM Critical Success Factors

According to Berkman (2001), KM has fallen victim to a mixture of bad implementation practices and software vendors eager to turn a complex process into a pure technology play. However, more and more companies are now starting to realize that "KM deployment is not an overnight installation but a complex shift in business strategy and process, one that requires thorough planning and must involve end users" (Dyer & McDonough, 2001).

For the successful implementation of KM efforts, just like for any other business efforts, there are a few areas in which reasonable results ensure successful performance. They are areas where things must go right for the endeavor to flourish. These areas are defined as critical success factors. Critical success factors are useful for structuring environmental analysis because there is an important connection between environmental analysis and the factors leading to organizational success (Digman, 1990). The analysis and evaluation of success factors provides important insight through identification of the core areas that are critical in KM implementations. Therefore, KM efforts need to identify and evaluate these core areas to gauge its potential for success. The findings from leading KM practitioners, researchers, and recent studies are the major sources that can be used to identify the critical success factors for KM.

After conducting an empirical study of factors affecting successful implementation of KM utilizing 217 responses from different sectors, Choi (2000) concluded that top management leadership, fewer organizational constraints, and information systems infrastructure were the top three critical success factors for KM to succeed. Kemp, Nenneth, Nidiffer, Rose, and Stankosky (2001) presented a collection of success factors based on the experience of implementing KM at the Software Productivity Consortium. They identified clear goals, strong sponsorship, realistic expectations, an interactive approach, a system approach, a flexible framework, an evolutionary process, integrated measurement, a capability model, and technical maturity as critical factors for their program success and key to any KM implementation effort. Another collection of success factors are identified by Chait (2000), derived from the experiences assessing, planning, pilot testing, and implementing the successful KMS for Arthur D. Little consulting firm. Chait identified three factors and four domains that are key in the successful implementation of any KMS. They are ensuring vision and alignment, managing four domains, and creating an effective plan. The four domains included content, culture, process, and infrastructure. He stressed that information technology supporting the KMS is only one element in a broad effort to maximize the potential of the knowledge resources.

However, after careful analysis and applicability towards our objectives, we believe the critical success factors for KM implementation identified by Davenport, De Long, and Beers (1998) are the most appropriate. They address the practical realities of KM projects, are considered comprehensive in their scope, and are the most applicable for large-scale organizations. These critical success factors were derived from a study based on 31 KM projects in 24 different companies. They were found to be the major factors that contributed to their success. According to

Davenport et al. "Success and failure are ambiguous terms ... but we identify eight key characteristics that we judged successful." In addition, the Davenport et al. success factors can be easily implemented in a survey format as key operational variables providing the best way to evaluate the potential for success of different KM efforts for large-scale organizational design.

5.9. Case Study: Large-Scale Organizational Design with Knowledge Management at NASA

Starting in 2000, the term "human capital crisis" started to emerge in reports about the federal workforce, in congressional testimony, and in the vocabulary of agency human resources directors (Friel, 2003). A major challenge identified by the Office of Personnel Management (OPM) and General Accounting Office (GAO) is the need for the government sector to manage its human capital more effectively. David Walker, Comptroller General of the United States, and other government experts have forecasted a train wreck unless something is done to recruit, retain, and retrain parts of our federal workforce to have the necessary set of skills to run the government of the 21st century (Byrd, 2001). Walker (2001) affirms "People are assets whose value can be enhanced through investment". It was, in part, a reaction to the reduction in the federal government workforce by approximately 325,000 employees between fiscal years 1993 and 2002, which brought it to the lowest level since 1950. This downsizing was accomplished through across-the-board reductions and hiring freezes. A consequence of these actions was the increase in the average age of the federal workforce to 46 years and with a skill set that is further out of balance with the current needs. Additionally, the potential exodus of baby boomers from the government workforce exacerbated this problem. As of fiscal year (FY) 2002, approximately 71% of the government permanent employees will be eligible for either regular or early retirement by 2010. Of those eligible, 40% are expected to do so (The President's Management Agenda, Fiscal Year, 2002).

In 2001, the GAO realized the potential adverse effect of the retirement problem within the government and added human capital to the government-wide risk category. Soon after that, it ranked at the top 10 of most serious management challenges for nine major federal agencies (The President's Management Agenda, Fiscal Year, 2002). The key problems in the government sector [a large-scale organization] that the human capital effort seeks to address are: (1) an aging workforce in which many with the most valuable skills and experience will retire in the next half decade; (2) the federal government not being competitive in the current job markets, which will increase the difficulty in attracting, hiring, and retaining a talented workforce; (3) the downsizing of the 1990s slowed the infusion of new employees to the government workforce and decreased investment in training; and (4) performance management focusing on results (Hyde, 2002). Some federal officials are dealing with these problems by analyzing workforce demographics and skill sets, tying those assessments to agency goals, changing the government culture by emphasizing on results, developing managers' leadership skills, and revamping human resources processes that will attract and retain employees.

One of the agencies most impacted by the human capital crisis and that is taking significant steps forward in this area is the National Aeronautics and Space Administration (NASA). The federal administration has a current workforce of approximately 19,000 civil servants employees and a direct private sector employment that exceeds 100,000 work years of effort annually. It experienced a 26% reduction from FY 1993 to FY 2000. In addition, approximately 15% of NASA's scientist and engineers are eligible to retire in 2003 and this number is expected to increase to almost 25% by 2008. Compounding this problem is the aging workforce, with employees over 60 years of age outnumbering those under 30 by nearly 3 to 1. In addition, NASA is facing recruitment and retention problems, with almost 8% departure rate for science and engineering employees within the 25–39 years age group (NASA Strategic Human Capital Plan, 2003). This represents a significant knowledge loss that needs to be actively managed.

In contrast, others such as Friel and Hyde claim that a review of workforce statistics, recent agency experiences, and observations by human resource directors indicates there is no reason for a "crisis" but for a concern. Actual retirement rates government-wide are expected to average between 2% and 4% a year for most agencies (Hyde, 2002; Friel, 2003). However, they recognize that NASA and other agencies that have specialized workforce, such as the National Institutes of Health (NIH) and certain occupations, are at greater threat. The projected retirement between 1999 and 2006 for government employees in the following at-risk areas are: program management (30%), meteorological technician (29%), criminal investigators (27%), mine safety (25%), and physics (23%) (Friel, 2003).

One of the key areas stated in President George W. Bush's management agenda is the adoption of information technology systems to capture some of the knowledge and skills of retiring employees. Furthermore, it encourages the use of KM as part of the effective strategy to generate, capture and disseminate knowledge that is relevant to the organization's mission (The President's Management Agenda, Fiscal Year, 2002). Moreover, the GAO has developed Human Capital Standards for Success with the purpose of assessing the status and impact across the federal government. It integrates recommended elements from the Office of Management and Budget (OMB) and the OPM consisting of six dimensions: strategic alignment, workforce planning and developing, leadership and knowledge management, performance culture, talent, and accountability (NASA Strategic Human Capital Plan, 2003).

Thus, the House of Representatives and Senate legislated to create a Chief Human Capital Officer (CHCO) position in every major agency, under the provision of the Homeland Security Act of 2002, Sec. 1304, "Strategic Human Capital Management" (Homeland Security Act, 2002). The CHCO position is comparable to a chief information officer (CIO) and chief financial officer (CFO). The responsibilities of a CHCO include developing and advocating a culture of continuous learning, identifying best practices and benchmarking studies, applying methods of measuring intellectual capital, and the development and implementation of a KM strategy supported by appropriate investment in training and technology (Homeland Security

Act, 2002). It is worth noting that these responsibilities have common characteristics and, in some areas, they overlap with the traditional responsibilities of a chief knowledge officer. KM as a concept and as an approach to human capital is rapidly becoming central to government performance and productivity. KM can leverage the existing human capital and intellectual assets within the overall government sector to help generate, capture, organize, and share knowledge that is relevant the organizations' mission, while improving their efficiency, effectiveness, and innovation.

KM programs and systems can establish new ways to manage critical knowledge and expertise obtained from individuals near retirement to help present and future employees. Nonetheless, technology alone will not harvest the full benefits. In order to realize this vision, large-scale organizations such as the U.S. federal government has to successfully implement a functional KM environment. Soliman and Spooner (2000) believe that intellectual assets and resources can be utilized much more efficiently and effectively if organizations apply KM for leveraging their human resources. Since there are many disciplines and a mix of skills required to successfully implement the government human capital strategy, KM is a key element of the overarching program. Therefore, there is a need to strategically position and integrate KM and human capital efforts throughout the government to find new and better ways to create, store, transfer, and leverage knowledge to build a government that can meet the future challenges.

5.10. Conclusions

Successful KMSs for large-scale organizations include the following attributes:

- Putting in place key infrastructures of assets, resources, and management practices that will be utilized by knowledge workers throughout the company to perform a "self-design" level.
- Adopt technologies to maintain and keep track of operational data of large-scale transaction, to analyze the large-scale environment, to support the decision-making process of large-scale decisions and to enhance collaboration and group decision making among global players.
- Invest in technology infrastructures with a view toward improving management's understanding of the competitive advantage that will be gained and financial returns that will be obtained.
- Design large-scale organizations as dynamic social systems that balance performance with collective learning.
- Codification and personalization are two main strategies when considering the flow of knowledge throughout a large-scale enterprise.
- Codification and personalization approaches are needed for an effective KM effort; however, the emphasis of one approach over the other or a balanced approach depends on the organization overall strategy.

- The selection and evaluation of key critical success factors provide the best way to evaluate the success of different KM efforts for large-scale organizational design.
- Need to strategically integrate KM and human capital efforts to find new and better ways to create, store, transfer, and leverage knowledge for the effective design of large-scale organizations so they can meet the future challenges that are threatening their survival.

References

Argyris, C. (1996). Toward a comprehensive theory of management. In: B. Moingeon & A. Edmondson (Eds), *Organizational learning and competitive advantage*. Thousand Oaks, CA: Sage.

Berkman, E. (2001). When bad things happen to good ideas. *Darwin Magazine* (online document). Available at http://www.darwinmag.com/read/040101/badthings.html. Accessed on March 5, 2006.

Bradley, S. (1993). The role of IT networking in sustaining competitive advantage. In: S. Bradley, J. Hausman & R. Nolan (Eds), *Globalization, technology, and competition*. Boston, MA: Harvard Business School Press.

Byrd, R. J. (2001). *Time to team up. Government Executive Magazine* (online document). Available at http://www.govexec.com. Accessed on March 5, 2006.

Chait, L. P. (2000). Creating a successful KM system. *IEEE Engineering Management Review*, 28(2), 92–95.

Choi, Y. S. (2000). *An empirical study of factors affecting successful implementation of knowledge management*. Doctoral dissertation, University of Nebraska, Lincoln, NE.

Clemons, E. (1993). Information technology and the boundary of the firm: Who wins, who loses, who has to change. In: S. Bradley, J. Hausman & R. Nolan (Eds), *Globalization, technology, and competition*. Boston, MA: Harvard Business School Press.

Daft, R., & Weick, K. (1984). Toward a model of organizations as interpretation systems. *Academy of Management Review*, 9(2), 284–295.

Davenport, T. H., De Long, D. W., & Beers, M. C. (1998). Successful knowledge management projects. *Sloan Management Review*, 39(2), 43–58.

Davenport, T. H., & Prusak, L. (1998). *Working knowledge: How organizations manage what they know*. Boston, MA: Harvard Business School Press.

Denning, S. (2000). *The springboard: How storytelling ignites action in knowledge-era organizations*. Boston, MA: Butterwoth Heinemann.

Digman, L. A. (1990). *Strategic management: Concepts, decisions, cases* (2nd ed.). Homewood, IL: BPI/Irwin.

Dyer, R., & Forman, E. (1991). *An analytic approach to marketing decisions*. Englewood Cliffs, NJ: Prentice Hall PTR.

Dyer, G., & McDonough, B. (2001). The state of KM. *Knowledge Management Magazine*, May p.23.

Edvinsson, L. (1999). In: Edvinsson, L. & Malone, M. S. (Eds), *El capital intelectual/cómo identificar y calcular el valor de los recursos intangibles de su empresa*. Barcelona: Gestión 2000, DL 1999, 255pp. ISBN: 8480883081.

Fayyad, U. M., Piatetsky-Shapiro, G., Smyth, P., & Uthurusamy, R. (Eds). (1996). *Advances in knowledge discovery and data mining*. Menlo Park, CA: AAAI Press. ISBN: 0262560976.

Fiol, C., Marjorie, L., & Marjorie, M. (1985). Organizational learning. *Academy of Management Review, 10*(4), 803–813.

Friel, B. (2003). The human capital crisis. *Government Executive Magazine* (May), 20–27.

Garvin, D. (1998). Building a learning organization. In: *Harvard business review on knowledge management*. Boston, MA: Harvard Business School Press.

Glushko, R., Tenenbaum, J., & Meltzer, B. (1999). An XML framework for agent-based E-commerce. *Communications of the ACM, 42*(3), 106–114.

Goffee, R., & Gareth, J. (1996). What holds the modern company together? *Harvard Business Review, 74*(6), 133–148.

Hansen, M. T., Nohria, N., & Tierney, T. (1999). What's your strategy for managing knowledge? *Harvard Business Review, 77*(2), 106–116.

Homeland Security Act. (2002). 107, H.R. 5005.

Hyde, A. C. (2002). Strategic human capital management. *The Public Manager, 31*(1), 64–67.

Jackson, C. (2001). *Process to product: Creating tools for knowledge management* (online document). Available at http://www.brint.com. Accessed on March 5, 2006.

Johnson, C. (2000). *A theoretical model of organizational learning and performing action systems: The development and initial validation of the duality of a Parsonian action frame of reference through confirmatory factor analysis*. Ph.D. Dissertation, The George Washington University.

Karakaya, F., & Kaynak, E. (1995). *How to utilize new information technology in the global marketplace*. New York: International Business Press.

Kemp, L. L., Nenneth, E., Nidiffer, L. C., Rose, R. S., & Stankosky, M. (2001). Knowledge management: Insight from the trenches. *IEEE Software, 18*(6), 66–68.

Kotter, J. P., & Heskett, J. L. (1992). *Corporate culture and performance*. New York: Maxwell Macmillan International.

KPMG Consulting. (2000). *Knowledge management research report*. KPMG.

Leonard, D. (1995). *Wellsprings of knowledge*. Boston, MA: Harvard Business School Press.

Lethbridge, T. (1994). *Practical techniques for organizing and measuring knowledge*. Doctoral thesis, University of Ottawa, Canada.

Malhorta, Y. (2003). *Measuring knowledge assets of a nation: Knowledge systems for development*. Invited research paper sponsored by the Untied Nations Department of Economic and Social Affairs. Keynote presentation at the Ad Hoc Group of Experts meeting at the United Nations Headquarters, New York City.

Malhorta, Y. (2004). Integrating knowledge management technologies in organizational business processes: Getting real time enterprises to deliver real business performance. *Journal of Knowledge Management, 9*(1), 7–29.

Marquardt, M., & Kearsley, G. (1999). *Technology-based learning*. Boca Raton, FL: CRC Press.

Marwick, A. D. (2001). Knowledge management technology. *IBM Systems Journal, 40*(4), 814–830.

McDermott, R., Carlin, S., & Womack, A. (1999). *Creating a knowledge-sharing culture*. Houston, TX: American Productivity & Quality Center.

McDermott, R., & O'Dell, C. (2000). *Overcoming the 'cultural barriers' to sharing knowledge* (online document). Available at http://www.apqc.org. Accessed on March 5, 2006.

Messmer, E. (1999). E-commerce portals open for business (to business). *Network World*, *16*(18), 40–45.

NASA. (2003). *NASA 2003 strategic human capital plan*. Washington, DC: National Aeronautics and Space Administration.

Nielsen, J. (1999). *Intranet portals: The corporate information infrastructure* (online document). Available at http://www.useit.com/alertbox/990404.html. Accessed March 5, 2006.

Nonaka, I., & Konno, N. (1998). The concept of Ba: Building a foundation for knowledge creation. *California Management Review*, *40*(3), 40–54.

Pettigrew, A. M. (2000). Foreword. In: N. M. Ashkanasy, C. P. M. Wilderom & M. F. Peterson (Eds), *Handbook of organizational culture & climate*. London: Sage.

Pucik, V. (1991). Technology transfer in strategic alliances: Competitive collaboration and organizational learning. In: T. Agmon & M. Von Glinow (Eds), *Technology transfer in international business*. New York: Oxford University Press.

Schulz, M. (2001). The uncertain relevance of newness: Organizational learning and knowledge flows. *Academy of Management Journal*, *44*(4), 661–682.

Schwandt, D. R. (1996). Organizational learning: A theory of action perspective. Paper presented at the Goldman & Associate executive human resources conference, Jacksonville, FL.

Senge, P. (1990). *The fifth discipline – The art and practice of the learning organization*. New York: Currency Doubleday.

Soliman, F., & Spooner, K. (2000). Strategies for implementing knowledge management: Role of human resources management. *Journal of Knowledge Management*, *4*(4), 337–345.

Spiegler, I. (2000). Knowledge management: A new idea or a recycled concept. *Communication of the AIS*, *14*(3), 1–24.

Spiegler, I. (2003). Technology and knowledge: Bridging the "generation" gap. *Information and Management*, *40*(6), 533–539.

Taylor, B. (2000). Directory to customer and knowledge management solutions – A special supplement for summer and fall 2002. *KMWorld Magazine*, May 15.

The President's Management Agenda, Fiscal Year. (2002). Washington, DC: Executive Office of the President.

Tuomi, I. (2000). Data is more than knowledge: Implications of the reverse knowledge hierarchy for knowledge management and organizational memory. *Journal of Management Information Systems*, *16*(3), 103–117.

Turban, E., & Aronson, J. (1998). *Decision support systems and intelligent systems*. Upper Saddle, NJ: Prentice Hall PTR.

Walker, D. M. (2001). E-government in the information age. *The Long View*, July 11, p.16, Washington, DC.

Weidner, D. (2002). Using connect and collect to achieve the KM endgame. *IT Professional*, *4*(1), 18–24.

SECTION III

LEARNING APPLICATIONS

The real voyage of discovery consists not in making new landscapes
but in having new eyes." Marcel Prousti

The KM learning pillar focuses on allowing an organization to maintain its dynamic
assured knowledge base. Calabrese (2000) validated this pillar and further defined
subelements as the various continuous learning practices for tacit and explicit
knowledge such as mentoring, virtual teams, exchange forums, distance learning,
Communities of Practice, and the sharing of innovations, lessons learned, and best
practices. An organization can develop and maintain a competitive advantage
through becoming learning and innovative. (Mohamed, Stankosky, & Murray, 2004;
Park, 2002; Garvin, 1993). KM supports and simplifies the perpetual cycle of
observing, knowing/orienting, deciding, and implementing that is constantly learning
within one cycle in preparation for the next. The following chapters focus on
learning-related applications.

References

Calabrese, F. A. (2000). *A suggested framework of key elements defining effective enterprise
knowledge management programs.* D.Sc. dissertation, George Washington University,
Washington, DC.
Garvin, D. A. (1993). Building a learning organization. *Harvard Business Review* (July–August),
78–91.
Mohamed, M., Stankosky, M., & Murray, A. (2004). Applying KM principles to enhance
cross-functional team performance. *Journal of Knowledge Management, 8*(3), 127–142.
Park, H. (2002). *Assessing the success of knowledge management technology implementation as a
function of organizational culture.* D.Sc. dissertation, George Washington University,
Washington, DC.

Chapter 6

Innovation on the Frontline: Structured Approach to Knowledge Creation Through Open Innovation with Customers

Jeffery Grabowski and Gabriele McLaughlin

Abstract

Innovation remains a top priority for corporate leaders worldwide. The innovation focus can range from the ad hoc to the deliberate, from the employee suggestion box to a formal research and development program, and from small incremental improvements to game-changing discoveries that reset the competitive gauge. There is no monolithic model that manages all instances of innovation equally well and companies often look for plausible surrogates to reign in the innovation inflation. This chapter describes a structured approach to client-centric services innovation that emerged when one team moved their innovation processes closer to their customers. The resulting services innovation framework describes in detail what it takes to successfully move innovation to the frontlines.

6.1. Introduction

Innovation remains a top priority for corporate leaders worldwide. Companies are struggling to find the right approach to innovation and innovation management to ensure continued growth and sustainable organizational performance (The McKinsey Quarterly, 2007).

A recent report to the Secretary of Commerce (Advisory Committee on Measuring Innovation on the 21st Century Economy, 2008) on innovation measurement defines

In Search of Knowledge Management: Pursuing Primary Principles
ISBN: 978-1-84950-673-1

innovation as "the design, invention, development, and/or implementation of new or altered products, services, processes, systems, organizational structures, or business models for the purpose of creating new value for customers and financial returns for the firms."

On the basis of this definition, innovation trajectories can range from the ad hoc to the deliberate, from the employee suggestion box to a formal research & development program, and from small incremental improvements to game-changing discoveries that reset the competitive gauge.

There is no monolithic model that manages all instances of innovation equally well, and companies often look for plausible surrogates to reign in the innovation inflation. Management practices such as risk management, program management, strategic planning, and knowledge management are often applied in an attempt to put method to the madness. If overprescribed, these practices can seriously dent the innovation pipeline by demanding a perfect set of decision parameters too early in the innovation process. If underprescribed, resources are wasted without adequate innovation to provide meaningful return on investment.

One way to balance the need for future-proofing innovation is to link innovation to emerging customer needs. Close to the customer, the theory asserts, innovations can be vetted and validated more realistically. The value propositions and value chains can be crafted with line of sight to those who will have to adopt and absorb them. Another argument for customer-centric innovation is the need for ever faster innovation conversion cycles, and the realization that innovations without adoption and commercialization constitute a lost opportunity and forfeited market share.

The concept of customer-led innovation was initially adopted and fine-tuned in product engineering and development organizations. The old *modus operandi* of "we build it and the customer will come" was abolished in favor of giving future buyers a chance to state their needs and opinions to influence the innovation thrust. In our company (Xerox Corporation), customer-led innovation is a well-documented best practice and has been propagated across the enterprise (Advisory Committee on Measuring Innovation on the 21st Century Economy, 2008).

This chapter documents how a small team of dedicated practitioners successfully changed the way emerging technologies are vetted and validated within Xerox Global Services, a subsidiary of Xerox Corporation. The Emerging Technology team (commonly referred to as ET) customized the corporate best practice to develop an agile, open, and customer-centric approach to facilitate the seamless and speedy integration of emerging technologies with emerging business needs. The sheer number of possible alternatives forced the team to adopt a validation prioritization model that focuses on breakthrough innovation rather than incremental process enhancements. Over a period of 5 years, the model evolved into the *services innovation framework* that is being described here.

In this model, the ET team vets and validates promising emerging technologies and research prototypes on the frontlines, that is, in "live" business settings. What may start out as solving a difficult business problem or as realizing a client's vision frequently facilitates and accelerates the adoption of new technologies into

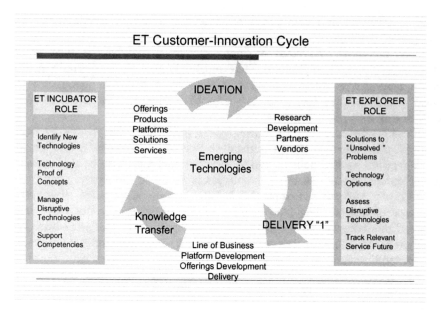

Figure 6.1: ET customer innovation cycle.

platforms, offerings, and services, and informs future research themes and funding decisions (Figure 6.1).

6.2. The ET Team

It takes a special kind of practitioner to go so deep into "foreign" territory and operate without the customary safety nets.

The ET core team is quite small, on average 12–14 employees. The sizing is deliberate. Additional resources are brought in from research and development on an as needed basis.

The team consists of highly skilled, seasoned professionals from a broad spectrum of backgrounds (computer science, engineering, information management, psychology, social sciences, and program management). Several team members span multiple disciplines. There are two levels of technical competence required. Practitioners involved in the engagement stage who must conduct vision workshops with the customer require a broad understanding of systems architecture, information technology (IT) infrastructure, and enterprise content management. This must be coupled with a deep understanding of the functional capabilities of the advocated emerging technologies. Practitioners involved in the proof of concept stage require experience in rapid, iterative prototype development. Specific software skills (e.g., .net vs. JAVA) are not as important because these are typically dictated by the customer environment. Most of the development at this level is limited to scripting and configuration, some user interface development, but no heavy process coding.

One of the most important attributes for team members is their ability to successfully deal with ambiguity. They must navigate unclear requirements and funding constraints, while innovating and solving difficult document-intensive process problems that the customer may have already attempted to solve by themselves or with other partners.

In those instances where a solution works technically, but cannot be deployed effectively in the customer's environment or delivered economically in a repeatable, scalable service-oriented delivery model, practitioners must also be able to deal with negative outcomes and quickly self-motivate to go on to the next project.

In addition, each team member has specific industry experience. This configuration is not accidental. The high velocity of ET projects does not leave time for "learning" the industry. The practitioners must reliably establish a trustworthy level of thought leadership within their target industry. And while industry expertise is a key entry requirement for each practitioner, the team, in the aggregate, continuously facilitates cross-industry pollination through the way they work together. In the innovation business, this level of diversity is highly desirable to avoid the pitfalls of group think and promote the emergence of innovations.

The practitioners are conceptual thinkers and visionaries with a practical bend. They must quickly vet and abandon ideas that do not deliver on their productivity or transformation promise in favor of those that do.

The small size of the team mandates that each practitioner must often stand on his/her own feet and know when to engage other team members for their expertise. This simultaneous need for independence and interdependence requires each practitioner to be a consummate team player.

Resilience is another unifying characteristic. No one is easily intimidated by an "impossible" request and everyone can effectively navigate different engagement levels, business environments, and business models.

The high-performance attributes in Figure 6.2 have emerged over a period of 5 years as critical success factors for consistent team performance. It is noteworthy that each attribute is anchored by a set of opposites. Understanding where a practitioner ranks on the spectrum becomes a useful representation of developmental needs that can then guide the annual personal develop plan and career planning for each practitioner.

It is important to note that the majority of the team members have self-selected into this environment because they find the opportunity challenging and exciting.

6.3. The Process

A key mandate for the ET team is to accelerate the rate and speed of conversion of innovation into products and services. This process is very structured in the product

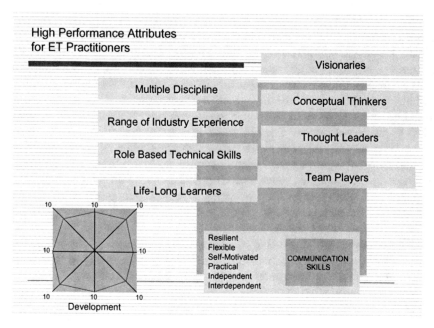

Figure 6.2: High-performance attributes for ET practitioners.

world (time-to-market, platform roadmaps, program and project management) and often imposes significant formalities and timelines.

The innovation process in the services world on the contrary often emerges in real time and can seem opportunistic and ad hoc. This emergence would be stifled by a traditional product development lifecycle approach. Yet, some kind of structure is clearly needed to ensure that ideas and insights lead to demonstrable innovations along the way.

The ET team initially used a modified time-to-market structure for their projects (as a subset of the offerings development process), but found that this approach was not flexible enough. It did not adequately reflect the client-centric nature of the team's work nor did it provide the necessary decision support tools to make fast and deliberate decisions about the prioritization of emerging technologies, activities, and resources.

The team temporarily regrouped under a delivery model and used a typical IT project approach for a while, and quickly discovered that this was creating administrative overlays and barriers that hampered the client-centric innovation process. Too many of the process steps in IT project model were outside the span of control of the ET team and the constant demand for project meetings and project communications exceeded resource availability.

The team learned a few things along the way and started to compile these observations and lessons into a *services innovation framework* for customer-centric innovation to enable successful outcomes and consistency. It turned out that the real needs for a structured approach existed at the front end of the innovation process. The most important lessons learned are described in the following text.

Customer-centric innovation first and foremost requires *solid customer relationships* in terms of value, collaborative temperament, and cultural fit. Both parties must have the capacity to deal with ambiguity and risk, and the innovation promise must be greater than the risk of failure.

It is important to have an existing *funnel of "ready" technologies*. In some cases, the ET team strings two or more of these new technologies together to solve the tricky problems. The objective is to create higher service agility and more service flexibility through new capability and technology mash ups. In addition, it is imperative to operate under a cost and complexity-out paradigm (Nanette, 2007) as an integral part of the innovation process. This approach can lead to new service models for both the customer and Xerox as the example below demonstrates.

A large, decentralized financial services enterprise was struggling to manage its new client administration process. It faced the challenge of taking new client applications and supporting documentation at branch offices and the requirement to have the applications reviewed, processed, and approved centrally. This customer spent significant sums routing new client documentation in overnight mail in order to speed the process of approving new client accounts. After reviewing the process, the proposal was to deploy multifunction printer/scanners to print key documents populated with new client information, to have the client sign them in branch, and to scan and route the client application to the central office for processing. The result was significant cost savings for the customer, with now best in class turnaround for new client enrollment. The result for Xerox was a very satisfied client, but additionally a new competitive capability that could be standardized and offered to other customers with similar decentralized operations.

In addition, there must be a strategic fit and alignment of intentions internally and externally for the technologies we can deploy and the problems customers are trying to solve, as well as the services to be created and leveraged. Without this strategic alignment, there is a risk of many "one-offs" that will not translate into replicable new services. To this end, the new capability must be either a broad, new horizontal service that can be applied in multiple customer or industry scenarios or a deep, vertically specific application that can be scaled and leveraged to solve a very specific industry challenge.

Both parties must commit to the "rapid" validation process. The ET team typically structures validation projects and proof-of-concepts into short (1–3 months) efforts with frequent decision gates. For them, competitive advantage is a point in time not a perpetual condition, and time is indeed money when it comes to services innovation. The ET team develops a "conceptual pursuit model" (CPM) for each opportunity that outlines in detail the anticipated outcomes, proposed approaches, activities, decision points, decision criteria, and frequency of go/no go decisions. The CPM is then managed by a program manager with a dashboard-type single page program plan. This leaves critical resources focused on the innovation process.

Customer-centric innovation requires financial cosponsorship. Both parties must have the proverbial "skin in the game." This commitment is often reflected in the way resources are aligned and committed in support of the innovation project. Without a substantial financial commitment on both sides, projects can easily be derailed by day-to-day operational emergencies. The CPM mentioned above discloses early what level of commitment the team needs from customer resources.

There is a real need for enlightened and pragmatic contracting support. In the early days, many of the validation projects were frequently derailed for weeks and months by the legal parsing. The fine-parsing of legal language can grow exponentially when the contract matter revolves around ideas, IP, innovation, and technical information. Even with substantially standardized engagement language, there are no "routine" experiences. In contracting terms, each innovation project remains a challenge, but with each project, the team is getting closer to a replicable matrix of terms and conditions by type of engagement.

6.4. Conclusions

The services innovation framework is still evolving (Figure 6.3). It is tested with each new engagement and updated in real time based on new insights. It came out of the need for putting method to the madness and to find a better balance between process and pragmatism, between organic discovery and the proactive generation of opportunities, and between incremental improvements and the deliberate pursuit of breakthrough innovation that occurs at the intersection of emerging customer needs and emerging technologies.

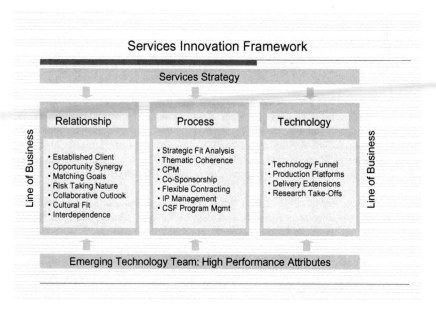

Figure 6.3: Services innovation framework.

The services innovation framework acknowledges that customer-centric innovation is foremost a joint discovery process that is best served with a stage-gated approach toward breakthrough innovation. "Good, better, breakthrough" is the motto of the ET team. There is no safety in the status quo. Higher risk will yield higher rewards if the project is selected with care and executed and conducted with the Hippocratic oath in mind. "First do no harm" becomes particularly important when innovation projects touch "live" processes where proof of concept explorations strain to become "alpha" production systems without the safeguard of a structured release process.

The push for speed and agility is driven by the need to continuously accelerate the value chain expansion. Customer-centric innovation must lead to competitive advantage for the customer and for Xerox in order to prevail.

For long term, the ET team is looking to codify and operationalize the framework. Particularly, the people side of the equation must be formalized to ensure a steady future supply of the right kind of talent. This is a vital prerequisite for scalability.

In addition, the team is collaborating with the researchers to develop an algorithm for opportunity selection and valuation in an effort to capture and apply the tacit knowledge that is currently in the practitioner's head.

This case study was first presented to a live audience in November 2007 and summarized in a subsequent newsletter (Center for Innovation Management Studies, 2008). There appears to be great interest in supplementing this practice-driven approach with additional research to determine, if it is scalable and repeatable and can successfully be transferred from the development organization to a delivery model, but in the current business climate funding constraints may be the single largest barrier.

References

Advisory Committee on Measuring Innovation on the 21st Century Economy. (2008). *Innovation Measurement: Tracking the state of innovation in the American economy: A report to the Secretary of Commerce.* Available at http://www.innovationmetrics.gov/Innovation%20Measurement%2001-08%20rev%20040908.pdf. Retrieved on January 2008.

Center for Innovation Management Studies (CIMS). (2008). What Xerox is learning about service innovation. *Newsletter,* Winter 2007–2008, NC State University College of Management.

Nanette, B. (2007). Xerox' new design team: Customers; its dual-engine printer was a close collaboration with users from idea to sketches to final testing. *Business Week, 4033,* 72. Available at http://www.businessweek.com/magazine/content/07_19/b4033087.htm. Retrieved on May 7, 2007.

The McKinsey Quarterly. (2007). *How companies approach innovation. A McKinsey Global Survey.* Available at http://www.mckinseyquarterly.com/How_companies_approach_innovation_A_McKinsey_Global_Survey_2069. Retrieved on January 2008.

Chapter 7

Situational Learning: Predicate to Knowledge Management

Rudy Garrity

Abstract

There is no knowledge creation and sharing — and no need for knowledge management (KM) if learning has not already occurred or is not in the process of occurring. KM is important in understanding our personal and organizational effectiveness and development. However, we need to appreciate that we are first and foremost awash in a sea of information relating to the situations we experience. Some of these situations are routine and need little attention, whereas others may be significantly life and/or career changing. What is important to understand is that every situation we encounter requires some amount of information gathering and analysis followed by decision making concerning what to do with that knowledge and if further action is appropriate. Every situation is a potential learning opportunity. The situational learning we acquire contributes to our store of knowledge we deem to be reliable and useful. This chapter summarizes the many perspectives in a model of situational learning that serve as a predicate for KM.

7.1. Introduction

Learning is a vital function for humans and it relies heavily on discovery, creation, and acquisition of different types of measurements, data, information, knowledge,

Table 7.1: Situational learning foundational anchors summary.

Learning and the dialogue of learning	Time, change, complexity perspectives
Fifth discipline	Attaining temporal balance
Critical thinking	Handling discontinuous change
Learning-to-learn	Wicked problems and social complexity
Interpersonal dialogue	

Reasoning, learning, and action	Learning systems: cycles of learning
Motives and conditions for learning	Learning cycles
Orientations to learning	Situation handling
Ten philosophical mistakes	Action learning
	Adaptive learning

and wisdom[1] through individual and corporate experiences. It leads to the development of new and/or expended capabilities, preferences, values, and understanding (i.e., intellectual capital). The situational learning discussed in this chapter occurs through a sequential series of lifelong learning cycles in which aspiration, reasoning, action, and evaluation enable people in their roles as individuals, organization members, and community citizens to work toward their goals. These goals can be summarized in three categories: self-fulfillment, high performance, and the common good.

Learning is essential for human and social system development. Learning results from resolving (albeit temporarily) the dynamic tension among societal forces by individuals, organizations, and communities.

An ideal learning objective is to achieve *systems optimization* at the metasystem level. People in their roles as individuals, participants in organizations, and members of communities balance their respective developmental imperatives with consideration of the needs and interests of others. Improving on social system *information processing* (cognitive and emotional), *decision-making* (reasoning and judgment), and *action* (evaluation and feedback) provide a well-spring of new learning for the individual, the organization, and the community.

This chapter provides a number of perspectives to illuminate the foundational anchors for effective situational learning and its role in enabling knowledge management (KM). These anchors are summarized in Table 7.1.

---

1. *Elements of the Intelligence Pyramid.*

7.2. Learning and the Dialogue of Learning

The first situational learning foundational anchor is based on an understanding of the concepts of thinking and learning in the complex real world. In addition, this anchor addresses the dialogue of learning. For the purpose of this chapter, thinking is generally described as a mental process that manipulates inputs and current knowledge to form or refine concepts and engage in problem solving. Learning is a mental process that acquires different types of knowledge to develop new capacities, skills, values, understanding, or preferences. The dialogue of learning addresses the various forms of conscious and unconscious learning such as habituation, conditioning, rote, experiential, formal education, and informal interactions.

7.2.1. Fifth Discipline

Situational learning is an activity informed by Peter Senge's (1990) five disciplines of the learning organization. All of these disciplines (theories and methods) are essential contributors to the use of critical thinking and interpersonal dialogue by individuals, organizations, and communities. The key learning-related disciplines can be summarized as:

1. Developing personal mastery. "Personal Mastery is the discipline of continually clarifying and deepening our personal vision, of focusing our energies, of developing patience, and of seeing reality objectively. As such it is an essential cornerstone of the learning organization — the learning organization's spiritual foundation" (Senge, 1990).
2. Understanding mental models. "Mental models are deeply ingrained assumptions, generalizations, or even pictures that influence how we understand the world and how we take action. Very often, we are not consciously aware of our mental models or the effects they have on our behavior" (Senge, 1990).
3. Building shared vision. "The practice of shared vision involves the skills of unearthing shared 'pictures of the future' that foster genuine commitment and enrollment rather than compliance" (Senge, 1990).
4. Ensuring team learning. "Team learning is vital because teams, not individuals, are the fundamental learning unit in modern organizations. This where 'the rubber meets the road'; unless teams can learn, the organization cannot learn" (Senge, 1990).
5. Performing systems thinking. "Systems thinking is a conceptual framework, a body of knowledge and tools that has been develop over the last fifty years, to make full patterns clearer, and to help us see how to change them effectively." It focuses on inferring how local changes influence the overall neighboring state (i.e., it rejects Descartes' scientific reductionism). In other words, it addresses problems in context rather than isolation because this is the best approach to complexity (Senge, 1990).

These disciplines are important because they promote core situational learning capabilities: developing reflective conversation, fostering aspiration, and coping with complexity.

7.2.2. Critical Thinking

M. Neil Browne and Stuart Keeley, authors of *Asking the Right Questions: A Guide to Critical Thinking* (2001), define their use of critical thinking by saying that "Critical thinking consists of an awareness of a set of interrelated critical questions, plus the ability and willingness to ask and answer them at appropriate times." The critical thinking approach thus applies a process of discernment, analysis, and evaluation to reconcile scientific evidence (e.g., information gathered by all the senses) and common sense (e.g., credibility, accuracy, logic, significance, and fairness).

Browne and Keeley (2001) based on their approach to critical thinking postulate two approaches to learning; the *sponge approach* and the *panning-for-gold approach*. In the sponge approach, the learner spends much time reading and listening carefully to information in the manner the writer or speaker chooses to present it. Absorption is the passive technique that leverages explicit knowledge.[2] In the panning for gold approach, the learner is an active participant in *dialogue* seeking out the nuggets of both explicit and tacit knowledge he or she has decided to obtain. *Interactive involvement* is the technique used by the proactive panning-for-gold learner.

Interactive involvement means careful pursuit of essential information for reasoning and decision-making and engaging others through questioning that clarifies the information and/or motives of writers and speakers. This approach provides not only the information but also the context necessary for successful critical thinking. The type of inquiries and direct questioning that gets to the essential information for contemplation are listed below:

1. Require facts and valid reasoning, reduce ambiguity, and challenge loaded language
2. Request clarification and stronger reasons to support another's perspective
3. Inquire as to the quality and appropriateness of research, observations, and conclusions
4. Build the impression that collaboration and inclusion are being pursued
5. Convey a willingness to learn and accept new conclusions
6. Present oneself as willing to suspend preconditions in the search for better information
7. Voice critical questions with curiosity and a willingness to listen
8. Constrain inappropriate emotions and concentrate on effective reasoning

---

2. Explicit and tacit knowledge terms used in this chapter are based on Polanyi (1967, 1962) definitions.

9. Encourage others to join in mutual examination of assumptions and factual information
10. Restate what has been heard to assure others of being heard and respected

Browne and Keeley (2001) understand that the use of interactive involvement critical thinking skills can be intimidating to those unaware of the usefulness of asking pertinent questions seeking better information and clarity of thinking. To alleviate possible resistance, they advocate a few guidelines for use during dialogue:

1. Be certain to demonstrate that you really want to grasp what is being said. Ask questions that indicate your willingness to grasp and accept new conclusions.
2. Restate what you heard or read, and ask whether your understanding of the argument is consistent with what was written or spoken.
3. Voice your critical questions as if you were curious. Nothing is more deadly to the effective use of critical thing than an attitude of "Aha, I caught you making an error."
4. Convey the impression that you and the other person are collaborators, working toward the same objective — improved conditions.
5. Avoid critical thinking jargon that the other person would not understand.

Critical thinking addresses real world complex learning situations. In a reflective way, it solves the problem of judging what to believe or what to do. It does this by giving consideration to the available evidence, the judgment's context, the relevant criteria, the applicable judgment techniques, as well as appropriate theoretical constructs for understanding the nature of the problem and the question at hand.

7.2.3. *Learning-to-Learn*

In *Workplace Basics: The Essential Skills Employers Want*, Carnevale, Gainer, and Meltzer (1990) attribute the view that "Learning how to learn involves possessing, or acquiring, the knowledge and skill to learn effectively in whatever learning situation one encounters" to Robert M. Smith (1982) of Northern Illinois University. They add that individuals need to acquire learning-to-learn skills because the real world situations which they encounter are likely to be unpredictable and fraught with changing task demands. This constantly changing environment requires that they become *adaptive learners and leaders*. Some of the earliest contributors to this theme were

1. Benjamin Franklin who founded a discussion club, the Junto, that had rules to forestall dogmatism, minimize conflict, and foster productive inquiry.
2. Arnold Toynbee who advocated that learners turn themselves into "self-teachers."
3. John Dewey who suggested that schools be evaluated in terms of their success in causing students to desire "continual growth" and in providing them with the capability to do so.

The challenge in assisting individuals to acquire the learning-to-learn skill is to first help them identify their own developmental needs and to take responsibility for their learning and its progress. Next, the task is to enlighten them with the knowledge, resources, and techniques that make the learning process accessible and successful. Learning-to-learn training designs strive to help trainers use, and learners take personal advantage of the learning theory components summarized in Table 7.2.

7.2.4.   *Interpersonal Dialogue*

A short definition of dialogue as used in this text is: *Dialogue is thinking and conversation using information inquiry and advocacy at a common time and place.* And, the view here is that situational learning is enabled whenever communications is based more on dialogue and less on debate or argument. In *Dialogue and the Art of Thinking Together*, William Issacs (1999) asks:

- How can we learn, as individuals, to take actions that might be conducive to evoke dialogue?
- How can we create dialogue in settings where people may not have initially been willing to engage in it?
- How can we prevent retrenchment?

He offers that "dialogue is a conversation with a center, not sides," and that dialogue builds interpersonal relationships and trust that leads to more effective communication and results in social situations. Specifically, the objectives of dialogue are to:

1. produce coherent actions,
2. create fluid structures of interaction, and
3. provide a wholesome space for dialogue.

Issacs (1999) proposes four characteristics that distinguish dialogue from other forms of communication. These are paraphrased below, along with additional insight on the role of facilitators in the dialogue process. Dialogue characteristics include:

1. Listening: Being fully aware of others contributions and accepting new information for personal evaluation.
2. Respecting: Seeing others as having legitimacy and value in the group and conversation.
3. Suspending: Defer own thinking and feelings while remaining open to new information and perspectives.
4. Voicing: Quietly listening and learning before contributing precise observations or information that illuminate the issue.
5. Facilitating: Assisting in group participation, information exchange, resource support, and closure.
6. Establishing: Group expectations, topic scope, time allocation, and desired outcome.

Table 7.2: Learning-to-learn theory components summary.

Component	Description
Knowledge of domains of mental activity	Different people have different strengths, but all learners can strive to increase their attention and openness while experiencing a learning activity in each of three domains. • *Cognitive* (thinking/knowing) domain that involves the skills people use to know, understand, or comprehend information. • *Psychomotor* (physical) domain that involves neuromuscular coordination and the skills people use to control movements of their body. • *Affective or emotional* (behavioral/attitudinal) domain that involves skills in dealing with emotions and feelings, and focuses on valuing, organizing, and characterizing the human aspects of situations.
Knowledge of learning styles	Various learning-style inventories have been constructed to illustrate how individuals differ in perceiving and acting on information. Learning how to learn (Smith, 1982) is a resource of available instruments. It explains that individuals who become aware of their unique styles of learning have greater self-awareness, and potentially, are better able to communicate and learn from others and their experiences. Examples given are Kolb's Learning Style Inventory, the Myers-Briggs Type Indicator (MBTI), and the Herrmann Brain Dominance Inventory (HBDI).
Knowledge of formal learning strategies	Both trainers who design learning experiences and learners who participate in them perform more effectively when they are aware of the range of techniques available to enhance learning. General strategies include: • Rehearsal-activities to list, copy, or repeat items in order to commit them to memory. • Elaboration-mental imagery of connections and relationships among items. • Organizational-grouping items that share certain characteristics or that can be arranged in a graphic diagram.

Table 7.2: (*Continued*)

Component	Description
	• Comprehension — monitoring-ensuring individuals are aware of their learning process and are able to control their cognitive processes and change them as appropriate. • Affective and motivational — positive reinforcement and self-generated support to maintain one's focus and progress. When these strategies are understood and used in combination by the trainer and learner, the learner not only learns a subject better but *learns learning skills* transferable to other situations.
Knowledge of informal learning strategies	Occurring outside formally planned learning activities, they are valuable experiences if the learner is aware that they are occurring and takes advantage of them. The techniques for using experiences for learning requires one to assume a questioning or inquiry stance toward an issue that includes: • Identifying the assumptions that underlay individuals' perspectives and test them for validity before proceeding. • Generating and testing alternative interpretations of information in an effort to assess possible consequences of each choice. This approach improves a person's quality of learning by ensuring that misconstrued data or conclusions do not interfere with their reasoning.

7.3. Reasoning, Learning, and Action

The second situational learning foundational anchor focuses on promoting a cohesive learning environment that empowers reasoning, learning, and action. Several authors have attempted to develop frameworks that make fertile ground for learning for the individual, organization, and community. The ability to reason is an essential skill for situational learning. This chapter considers reasoning to be a cognitive process that identifies, assesses, and utilizes reasons for the learner's beliefs, feelings, conclusions, and actions. It includes both deductive (i.e., formal logic) and inductive (i.e., informal or critical thinking) reasoning.

7.3.1.   *Motives and Conditions for Learning*

In *Understanding and Facilitating Adult Learning*, Brookfield (1986) suggests that a society is able to realize its humanity through its ability to learn. It is through learning that we are able to both create and alter our beliefs, values, behaviors, and relationships which form our culture. He states: "The extent to which adults are engaged in a free exchange of ideas, beliefs, and practices is one gauge of whether society is open, democratic, and healthy. If adults of widely differing class and ethnic groups are actively exploring ideas, beliefs, and practices, then we are likely to have a society in which creativity, diversity, and the continuous recreation of social structures are the accepted norms." What is implied is that learning is a fundamental individual and collective function, and that the capability of a people to learn what they have in common and to forge agreements is essential for societal growth and development.

Brookfield (1986) emphasizes learning in adulthood as the basis for continued societal development and addresses the importance of adult motivation, styles of learning, and conditions that facilitate learning. He offers six principles of effective practice in establishing a learning environment. These are paraphrased for general use in this chapter as follows:

1. Learning should be voluntary. Better learning and commitment to what is learned is the result of voluntary participation wherein the learner's objectives create his or her own motivation.
2. Learning requires respect. Individuals whose self-worth is in doubt are limited in their ability to learn.
3. Learning is collaborative. The teacher (leader) and learner are engaged in a cooperative enterprise in which objectives, roles, and responsibilities are discussed and renegotiated as required.
4. Learning is reflection upon experience. It is through collaborative analysis of actions and consequences that strategies for obtaining improved results are established for future use.

5. Learning should include critical reflection. Learners can develop further if they are able to recognize the underlying values, beliefs, behaviors, and ideologies that are culturally transmitted during their experiences, and if they are thereby able to appreciate the situational nature of their experiences.
6. Learning should be self-directed. Learners who take responsibility for what and how they learn are empowered adults in control of themselves, and to some extent, their environment.

Brookfield (1986) expands on his views by adding insights provided by C. Suanmali in an unpublished doctoral dissertation entitled *The Core Concepts of Androgyny*. Suanmali suggests that adults have enhanced capability to function as self-directed learners when they are able to

1. decrease their dependence on educators (leaders),
2. identify and use learning resources,
3. define their learning needs and objectives,
4. organize what is to be learned in terms of their problems and level of understanding,
5. improve their decision-making and problem-solving capability, and
6. develop and apply criteria for judging experience.

7.3.2.   Orientations to Learning

Merriam and Caffarella (1991) in their book *Learning in Adulthood: A Comprehensive Guide* summarize major theories about the learning process into four orientations: behaviorist, cognitivist, humanist, and social learning. Each orientation poses a perspective on what happens during the learning process, and each offers insight into the multiple purposes and developmental outcomes from effective learning.

7.3.2.1.   The behaviorist orientation   Behaviorism focuses on the systematic design and delivery of instruction for the purpose of producing desired behavior change. Three underlying assumptions are held to be true. First, observable behavior rather than internal thought processes are the focus of study; in particular, learning is manifested by change in behavior. Second, the environment shapes one's behavior; what one learns is determined by the elements in the environment, not by the individual learner. And third, the principles of contiguity and reinforcement are central to explaining the learning process. "Stimulus-response" and "operant conditioning" theories hold sway in the behaviorist perspective as evidenced by the view attributed by the authors to B. F. Skinner (1971) that "... the ultimate goal of education is to bring about behavior that will ensure survival of the human species, societies, and individuals."

7.3.2.2. The cognitive orientation In contrast to the behaviorist viewpoint, cognitive orientation is based primarily on the Gestalt (German word for pattern or shape) or wholeness of a situation or event. The importance of individual perception, insight, and meaning are major contributions to cognitivism from Gestalt learning theorists. While behaviorists emphasize the environment as the locus of control over learning, the cognitivists (Gestaltists) place responsibility for learning with the individual or adult learning theory.

Cognitive psychologist Jean Piaget (1966) proposed a four-stage theory of cognitive development based on the view that one's internal cognitive structure changes partly because of maturational changes in the nervous system and partly because of the organism's experience with its external environment. Piaget explained that during childhood, individuals pass through four stages of cognitive development that represent different ways of making sense, understanding, and constructing knowledge of the world. He suggested that the individual was capable of mature adult thought by the age of 20. His four stages of cognitive development are

1. *Sensory-motor* in which thought is stimulated by innate reflex actions.
2. *Preoperational* wherein concrete objects may be represented in symbols and words.
3. *Concrete operational* in which there is understanding of concepts and relationships of ideas.
4. *Formal operational* wherein the ability to reason hypothetically, logically, and systematically is fully developed.

Others have built upon Piaget's foundational theory by adding their perspectives on various facets of cognitive learning and human development. Some of those directly applicable to this chapter include D. P. Ausubel's (1967) view that "meaningful learning" as opposed to "rote learning" occurs when it can be related to concepts that already exist in a person's cognitive structure and that "advance organizers" are necessary to prepare a person for new learning. Ausubel's work apparently stimulated research by others into schema theory wherein schemata — structures that organize the learner's worldview — in turn determine how new experiences are processed (Di Vesta, 1987; Greeno, 1980). The relationship of schema theory to learnership is discussed more fully later in this section under the subject of knowledge.

7.3.2.3. The humanist orientation Humanist theories consider learning from the perspective of the human potential for growth and include affective as well as cognitive dimensions of learning. Rather than accept that behavior is predetermined by environment (behaviorist) or subconscious (cognitivist), humanists see people in control of their own destiny, people that are inherently good and are striving for a better world, people that are free to act and whose behavior is a consequence of human choice, and people that possess an unlimited potential for growth and development (Rodgers, 1983; Maslow, 1970).

Maslow with his theory of motivation based on a hierarchy of human needs is considered to be the founder of humanistic psychology. Maslow stated that the need to learn is intrinsic and that it emanates from the learner. He believed that among growth motivations could be found the need for cognition — a desire to know and understand. In addition to the primary goal of self-actualization, Maslow identified other learning and understanding related goals that (selectively) include

- acquisition of a set of values,
- attainment of peak experiences,
- developing a sense of accomplishment,
- understanding of the critical existential issues of life,
- controlling of one's impulses, and
- learning to choose judiciously.

Carl Rodgers is another major figure who writes from a humanist orientation. In his view, "client-centered therapy" conducted by psychotherapists and "student-centered learning" led by educators are similar in outcome — both are concerned with significant learning in which the client and student, respectively, achieve personal growth and development. The characteristics of such learning are as follows:

- Personal involvement: the affective and cognitive aspects of a person should be involved in the learning event.
- Self-initiated: a sense of discovery must come from within.
- Pervasive: the learning makes a difference in the behavior.
- Evaluated by the learner: the learner can best determine whether the experience is meeting a need.
- Essence is meaning: when experiential learning takes place, its meaning to the learner becomes incorporated into the total experience.

7.3.2.4.   A social learning orientation   Social learning theory takes the position that people learn from observing other people in a variety of social settings. Bandura (1976) observes that "Virtually all learning phenomena resulting from direct experiences can occur on a vicarious basis through observation of other people's behavior and its consequences for the observer." He contends that what he calls "observational or social learning" may be characterized by the concept of self-regulation and that "persons can regulate their own behavior to some extent by visualizing self-generated consequences."

B. R. Hergenhahn (1988) adds the view that observational learning is influenced by the four processes of attention, retention or memory, behavioral research, and motivation. These processes are described as:

- Attention must first be given to someone who serves as a potentially worthy model for one's behavior modification.

- Information from observing the actions of the model and the consequences of those actions on the observer is set into the person's memory.
- Rehearsal in which the learner imitates what has been modeled and compares the results received to the modeled experience.
- Modeled behavior is accepted as being useful and is stored for future use.

Through this process, the interaction of the person with his or her social environment is described as a process of mutual influence, and learning is set completely within a social context.

7.3.3. Ten Philosophical Mistakes

Adler (1985) argues that modern reasoning and judgment are often poorly accomplished due to "little philosophical mistakes" that entered into the thinking of some noted philosophers of the seventeenth century — specifically Thomas Hobbes in England and René Descartes in France. These mistakes continue in modern thought and are witnessed as erroneous premises persistently leading to false conclusions, inappropriate decisions, and failed consequences. In most cases, when the little errors in the beginning are recognized, modern thinkers attempt to circumvent their impact further compounding the resulting difficulties. The 10 philosophical mistakes identified are as follows:

- Not recognizing that all of each person's ideas or viewpoints are subjective interpretations of his or her own knowledge and experience. Ideas, then, are not perfectly correct expressions of some objective reality.
- The failure to distinguish between perceptual thought about sensible objects and conceptual thought about those things that are constructed through the mind's power of intelligence. Only humans can deal with the unperceived and the unimaginable.
- Not recognizing that all ideas are meanings, and that they are the basis for all man-made words, signs, and symbols. Words, signs, and symbols cannot be said to be meaningless when they have referential ideas with which they are associated.
- The failure to distinguish between knowledge and opinion. Having knowledge connotes being in possession of true information, the certitude of which is beyond reasonable doubt. Opinions on the contrary may be asserted with little basis in evidence or reason. Decisions in this case have to do with whether something exists and requires descriptive judgment.
- The belief that there are no objectively valid and universally tenable moral standards or norms. The ability to distinguish and prefer human needs over human wants, and real goods over apparent goods, leads to a desire for knowledge and truth rather than opinion and the capacity to discern between "ought" and "ought not." Decisions in this case are said to be prescriptive judgment.
- The identification of happiness exclusively with the psychological state of contentment. This notion contributes to the inability to distinguish between

human needs and wants and between real and apparent goods — which undermines the development of a moral philosophy in which happiness also conveys attaining a life well lived and in balance.

- The misunderstanding of the relation between free choice and moral responsibility. Determinists argue that people do not have free will and choice and therefore should not be held fully accountable for their actions. The counterpoint is that moral virtue depends on the freedom of will and choice in one's learning and development that necessitates moral responsibility and accountability.
- The denial of common human nature among all people and cultures. Notwithstanding the deterministic characteristics common to species other than humans and the belief that humans have no essential similarity because they each receive a different genetic beginning (nature), humans do have in common potentialities — human being is a self-made creature who given a range of potentialities at birth may freely choose to develop him or herself within the guidelines of his or her culture (nurture).
- The belief that the "social contract" theory of Rousseau and others explains the origins of a civil society and the state. Rather than the view that human moved from an independent "state of nature" to political association for protection, a better informed perspective is that human beings by nature are both socially and politically oriented and have a natural inclination to participate in government. As such, true political community may only exist in democratic, constitutionally based civil government.
- Fallacy of reductionism — assigning a much greater reality to the parts of an organized whole than to the whole itself. Notwithstanding the trends within the scientific community to differentiate entities and human existence into their respective parts for analysis and identification of their attributes, and the consequential tendency to reduce the value and responsibilities of the larger whole through this process; the potentialities of those entities and human beings that become present when viewed from a whole perspective are, from a common sense viewpoint, the predominant concern. Individual human beings are whole units with identifiable identities and the ability to choose patterns of growth and development. As such, "There can be no question about the moral responsibility that each of us bears for his actions."

What may be derived from Adler's perspective is that while empirical science and mathematics have resulted in breathtaking technological advances and knowledge of physical system reality (primarily in the last two centuries), the greatest achievements in philosophy occurred in Greek antiquity and the Middle Ages and should be the basis for an equally important knowledge of human system reality.

7.4. Perspectives on Time, Change, and Complexity

The third situational learning foundational anchor illustrates the differing perspectives on the operational context (e.g., time, change, and complexity) of learning cycles and how this affects learning. Researchers have identified that the learner's sensitivity to stability and change can have dramatic impact on the effectiveness and urgency of learning. As the real world becomes more interdependent and involves more relationships (i.e., perceived complexity), the learner also experiences challenges with analysis paralysis, inability to be predictive, increased risk, and unclear causality.

7.4.1.   Attaining Temporal Balance

In *Marking Time*, Rappaport (1990) considers the impact of people's sense of time on their mental and emotional health, and their ability to attain a sense of balance within the social order. From childhood through adulthood, people's senses of time change from the infinite to the finite and they become aware that their time and their lives are passing by. They become more concerned with their identity and the directions in which they are tending as they reflect on their individual sense of past, present, and future. Rappaport (1990) refers to this aspect of human awareness as "temporal organization," and advises that human attention should be allocated to all three time dimensions of life for normal mental and emotional health. Apparently, fixation on the past or present with little thought for the future inhibits the development of a balanced sense of one's purpose and identity. The inability of individuals to develop this capacity often leads to a state of depression and social "maladaptation."

Normal human and social development progresses from the period of childhood dependency, in which stability and predictability are essential, through periods of adolescence and adulthood in which achievement of the senses of independence and interdependency denote maturity. Through this process, a greater understanding of one's purpose and history is obtained. The anticipation of the future and its potentialities creates the positive life force and necessary energy to pursue *a life well lived.*

The developmental challenge in modern society concerns our ability to sustain human and social system development amid the prevalent uncertainty, complexity, overload, contradiction, and values differences. Rappaport (1990) characterizes society today as being "... a culture struggling to find ways to cope with anxiety, depression, and addiction." He says that a major reason for the situation is the breakdown of our value system, the lack of social ideals, and the lack of meaningful future images. From what Rappaport suggests, "the solution seems to be for individuals and society to redefine their purpose, establish common values, dream of future possibilities, and commit to working for their interdependent development."

7.4.2.   Handling Discontinuous Change

The human race is experiencing several cultural ages marked by innovation and discontinuous change. The twenty-first century has arrived, thus ending the

Industrial Age and starting the Intelligence Age (Tyson, 1997). The new economy includes new sources of wealth generation and is increasingly reliant on the free flow of wisdom, knowledge, information, data, and measurement aligned with products and services (Allee, 1998). Innovation and creativity are the currency of this new knowledge economy and ongoing and continuous learning are the catalysts that ensure expertise and core competencies continue (Stewart, 2001; Bixler, 2000; Malhotra, 1998).

Today, enterprises are living in the world that Alvin Toffler (1970) predicted in his work *Future Shock*, where change is occurring at an ever-increasing rate as it enabled by the communications and information technologies. The accelerating pace of change is not just a function of increased technology but also a function of an increase in innovation. While technology has been a catalyst, the interconnectedness of people who share information and knowledge is the driver of this change (Bixler, 2000; van der Spek & Spijkervet, 1997).

Hock (1999), founder of Visa International, identified this as the "collapse of float." Before the world was so connected, concepts and things took time to travel. The knowledge about how to smelt iron took almost a century to cover the European continent, ushering in the Iron Age. Today, intelligence is available in minutes, if not seconds. Thus, information float has virtually disappeared. Technology floats are minimal, with new technology adoption happening in months or days. With cultural floats, popular trends sweep across the world almost instantaneously.

Increased speed in the new economy results in a compression of opportunity windows and less time to integrate competencies. It is now not good enough to just have the best mousetrap; it must also be the first to market (APQC, 1999a). In fact, Nadler and Tushman (1999) argue that timing is essential to gaining market advantage. This business environment demands innovation, adaptation, and vision, in contrast with the traditional emphasis on optimization (Malhotra, 1998).

Another result of this loss of change float is the loss of awareness that change is occurring and/or the loss of the predictability of the direction of change. The business environment is shifting from a world of long lead-time, controllable, predictable, stable, incremental, linear changes to the world of rapid discontinuous change reflected in Complexity Theory models of chaos and nonlinearity (Malhotra, 1998; Bixler, 2000). It also drives the need for adaptability and awareness of the environment.

In *The Age of Unreason*, Handy (1989) argues that change is no longer the same as it used to be. Change is now discontinuous and not part of a previously experienced or easily identified pattern. Instead, it is random, unpredictable, and is both confusing and disturbing. He notes that little changes may be seen making big differences, and that the way our work is organized is greatly impacting how we live our lives. His notion is that "Discontinuous change requires discontinuous upside-down thinking to deal with it." Regarding current organizations and systems, he opines that "For those in charge, continuity is comfort, and predictability ensures that they can continue in control. Revolutions may be required in order to unblock societies and shocks, to galvanize organizations."

Handy introduces the concept of *Triple I Organizations* of the future in which Intelligence, Information, and Ideas equal Added-Value (1 + 1 + 1 = 3.5 AV). He suggests that *quality is truth* in organizations, and that it takes "the right equipment, the right people, and the right environment to make quality happen." Top management in these organizations will be dedicated to continuous learning, will focus more on the conceptual and human vice technical skills of management, and will learn to listen more willingly to subordinates rather than just talking at them. The new focus, he predicts, will be that organizations will stop trying to manage employees' careers, and instead, will help them develop their capabilities to take advantage of opportunities as they appear. As a result, education will become an investment for future performance, and employees will be performing in teams and on projects in flatter organizations rather than the steeply hierarchical organizations of today.

In terms of a situational learning model (Figure 7.1), Handy's views are important in that they confirm the tension between the current infrastructure and forces for change, and illustrate that in order for organizations to cope, they will need to focus

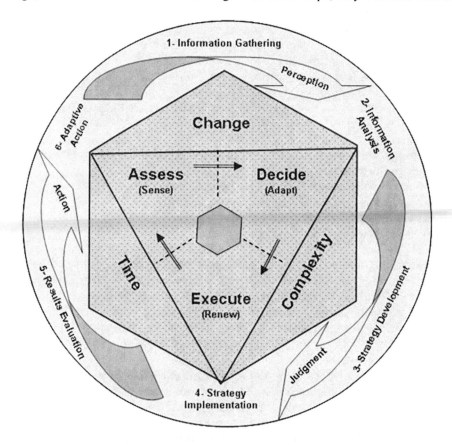

Figure 7.1: Situational learning model.

on quality and adding the value in their marketplaces. Continued quality learning, in terms of customer desires, need to become essential activities for managers and subordinates alike in an organization.

7.4.3. Wicked Problems and Social Complexity

Rittel and Webber(1973) first discussed the nature of ill-defined design and planning problems which he termed "wicked" (i.e., messy, circular, and aggressive) to contrast against the relatively "tame" mathematic problems of the past. In *Wicked Problems and Social Complexity* (2001), Jeff Conklin addresses these all too familiar concerns. These issues and problems that the modern society has to address are so dynamic and complex that they resist the thinking and efforts of even the most skillful of experts and leaders. Conklin states that wicked problems and social complexity are *forces of fragmentation* that challenge collective intelligence, doom projects, and make collaboration difficult or impossible. According to Conklin, fragmentation is "a condition in which the people involved see themselves as more separated than united, and in which information and knowledge are chaotic and scattered. The fragmented pieces are, in essence, the perspectives, understandings, and intentions of the collaborators ... and can be hidden as when stakeholders don't even realize that there are incompatible tacit assumptions about the problem, and each believes that his or her understandings are complete and shared by all."

Conklin attributes the definition of wicked problems to Rittel and Webber (1973), an early expert on the topic. Accordingly, problems are wicked when

- You do not understand the problem until you have developed a solution.
- Wicked problems have no stopping rule.
- Solutions to wicked problems are not right or wrong.
- Every wicked problem is essentially unique and novel.
- Every solution to a wicked problem is a "one-shot operation."
- Wicked problems have no solutions.

Conklin adds that when social complexity coconcurs with wicked problems, the combination fragmentation is virtually certain to be the result. "Social complexity is a property of the social network that is engaging with the problem." For example, when there are numerous organizations, experts, senior executives, and different skill sets actively involved, there is sure to be social complexity. And, if technical complexity is also a factor due to different levels of knowledge and experiences, the situation is really exacerbated.

Conklin advises that the only way to proceed effectively is by "creating shared understanding about the problem and shared commitment to the possible solution." He says that this occurs when an "opportunity-driven problem-solving" methodology is employed. He indicates that the *antidote for fragmentation is coherence* and that can only occur when both problems and solutions become subjects for iterative thinking, design, and dialogue that leads, incrementally, to clarification of what problems and solutions fit well together. Through iterative processing and learning, *coherence* begins to take shape and consensus is possible because the group involved comes to believe that something constructive has occurred. The caveat is that without leadership acceptance and support of the group's findings and suggestions, improvement may not be achieved.

7.5. Learning Systems: Cycles of Learning

In summary, it is useful to recapitulate the foundational themes of the *learnership* metasystem perspective: continuous learning in a dynamic environment. The construct proposes the idea that at the center of all human and social activity is the learning process. Through learning, individuals, organizations, and communities acquire the capacity for improved reasoning and action that supports the accomplishment of their respective goals. Learning occurs as new *information* is evaluated in terms of system *requirements* and *values* using current skills in *judgment* and *decision-making*. The learning process is interactive and integrative, and all subsystem development is inextricably linked in a network of mutual influences.

The context for learning and systems development is one of continuous change and turmoil. The availability of information from the various *fields of education* (physical science, social science, mathematics, etc.) is growing exponentially, and unfortunately, toward greater differentiation as specialties are added and experts establish their paradigms of thought and action within the boundaries of their respective fields of endeavor.

Forces for change are colliding with the *current infrastructure* that has been established to protect past traditions and accomplishments. An explosion of values, viewpoints, and technological capability is being experienced at an increasing pace, and in a discontinuous manner that negates social comprehension. The result appears to be greater alienation, social upheaval, and the suboptimization of the performance of most, if not all, societal systems.

7.6. Situational Learning Model

The proposed situational learning model (Figure 7.1) takes into consideration both the context that the learning takes place and the various types of learning cycles and their methodologies. This section addresses the major components of the model presented in Figure 7.1 as well as components of KM that are predicated upon such a learning model.

7.6.1. Learning Context

As presented in the early section, the context that directly impacts the ability to learn and to apply this learning can be summarized in three categories: time, change, and

Table 7.3: Learning context summary.

Context	Key points
Time	• Learning needs to address past, present, and future
Change	• Short floats in technology, culture, and learning introduce uncertainty
	• Tension exists between current infrastructure and forces of change
Complexity	• Nonlinearity of cause and effect
	• Iterative nature of the context and system relationships
	• Forces of fragmentation and agents of cohesion

complexity. The key considerations for the situational learning model are summarized in Table 7.3.

7.6.2. Learning Cycles

Variations of learning are illustrated in the learning cycle framework depicted in Figure 7.1. The figure has *two methodological features* that illustrate the basic learning cycle concept. The first methodology shown around the outer edge is the traditional, sequential approach used for decision-making and problem solving, which is composed of following stages:

1. Information gathering
2. Information analysis
3. Strategy development
4. Strategy implementation
5. Results evaluation
6. Adaptive action

The second methodology captured as transitions on the figure is the use of basic human cognitive and feelings shown as three stages of mental activity:

• Perception: use of sensing and intuition
• Judgment: use of thinking and feeling
• Action: representing (hard) cognitive results or (soft) social developmental accomplishment

The situational learning model has at its heart two development processes. The first process deals with the cognitive, objective (fact based, hard) learning cycle consisting of the assess, decide, and execute phases. Next is the affective, subjective (feeling consciousness, soft) learning cycle that follows the sense, adapt, and renew phases of internal learning. These are summarized in Table 7.4.

Table 7.4: Learning cycle overview.

Learning cycle	Description
Assess, decide, execute	This process is preferred when decisions and problems primarily require the acquisition and use of empirical facts and practical experience. The process requires the collection and *assessment* of explicit information in accordance with standard and best practices. Data and information collected is then reviewed using further inquiry and dialogue in a decision-making or problem-solving process in which analysis, synthesis, prioritization, decision criteria, and risk management are considered. *Decisions* are then codified into implementation plans and *executed* using good management practice. In practical experience, individuals, organization, and communities all need to use this approach on a daily basis.
Sense, adapt, renew	In this case, there are major tacit and/or feeling factors in play and the individual, using self-reflective intuition and/or emotional sensitivity, becomes aware or *senses* the need to attend to the situation. Using a sorting process similar to the cognitive decision process, the individual considers how to *adapt* to the new events or situation. Adaptation requires that new learning and knowledge be applied in the form of personal change or *renewal*, which in turn creates a new level of *"being"* or *"personal realization."* Again, practical experience indicates that everyone has the occasion to recognize their own personal dilemmas and treat them as learning opportunities.

7.6.3.   Situation-Handling

Karl Wiig, author of *People-Focused Knowledge Management* (2004), anchors his subject of KM in a four-stage process model with the following activities:

- Situation recognition
- Decision-making/problem-solving
- Execution method
- Process monitoring

While this approach works well for Wiig's purpose, it is in fact a restatement of the traditional learning cycle model advocated for decades by other researchers and authors explaining how *experiential learning* works. Of particular interest here is Wiig's emphasis on the fundamental need to understand the situation within which individuals and organizations find themselves — know the content and context of the situation — before attempting to determine a final solution or course of action.

According to Wiig, "People are required to act in all kinds of situations — large and small ... . The actions that are required depend upon the situation, its context and objectives, the person's understanding of the situation, and the person's capabilities. [And] Good situation-handling by people implies that the personal performance will be good. Personal situation-handling performance results from the quality of personal actions." His emphasis on this topic is similar to others who have written that unless we know the real problem and its context, it is certain that we cannot determine the best solution.

It should be noted that most decision-making models invoke similar process models that all value understanding the context and learning how to react appropriately. In the 1920s, Shewart proposed the initial decision cycle. Deming proposed the continuous plan, do, check, and act (PDCA) decision cycle (Deming, 1994, 1986). Simon (1977) proposed a four-phase decision cycle: intelligence, design, choice, and implementation. John Boyd (1987) proposed an organic model of the informed decision cycle. Known as the Boyd cycle or the observe, orient, decide, and act (OODA) loop, this decision cycle is used throughout the U.S. military. In the dynamic environment, the OODA loop requires shorter timelines and supports more interdependent action. With a continuous feedback loop, problems were identified and parts of the process be improved, thus all the proposed decision support models embody situational learning.

7.6.4.   Action Learning

David Garvin, in *Learning in Action* (2000), summarizes the three stages of the learning process (i.e., acquiring, interpreting, and applying information) and their potential disabilities. His recommended framework applies to organizational individuals and teams in the following manner:

7.6.4.1. Acquiring information   "The real challenge for managers is to distinguish relevant from irrelevant information, while remaining open to unexpected, and occasionally unwelcome, surprises. Effective organizational learning demands clear signals and minimal noise, as well as the ability to share critical insights so that they do not remain isolated or unacknowledged" (Garvin, 2000) (the *disability* = biased information). According to Garvin, data can be gathered in a variety of ways:

- Search. Identification and look-up data/information from known sources.
- Inquiry. Descriptive (closed-ended questions) or exploratory (open-ended questions) constructed and used to solicit data/information.
- Observation. Participate in and experience a situation, conduct interviews, and take notes.
- Reflection and review. Reflect on experiences and develop lessons for the future after situations have occurred.
- Experiential learning. Reflect on experience and conduct reviews for alternating periods during the experience.

7.6.4.2. Interpreting information   "Even if organizations were able to acquire all essential information, they would still have to interpret it …. Unadorned facts and opinions are therefore of limited value. They become useful only after they have been classified, grouped, or placed with a larger context." (The *disability* = illusion of information validity or causation.) Garvin notes that unfortunately people "routinely develop interpretations, causal connections, and probability estimates that are seriously biased." He identifies eight distinctive problems:

1. Illusory correlation. Assumes events are related because they have appeared together.
2. Illusory causation. Ascribes causality to earlier events in a sequence.
3. Illusion of validity. Increases confidence with more data, even though judgment accuracy has not changed.
4. Framing effects. Results in different responses given the same facts but different frame for evaluating.
5. Categorical bias. Classifies people and events with stereotypical categories, even when evidence indicates this is not effective or correct.
6. Availability bias. Assesses probability by the ease with which anecdotal examples come to mind, rather actual measured frequencies and likelihood.
7. Regression artifacts. Ascribes causality to actions when normal distribution of resulting events/value is the real factor in results.
8. Hindsight bias. Bias retrospective assessments with information only available after the fact about actual outcomes.

7.6.4.3. Applying information   "Managers must translate their interpretations into concrete behaviors and must then ensure that a critical mass of the organization adopts the new activities .... It is essential to eliminate unnecessary or outdated tasks as the same time that new ones are added. Otherwise, overload is inevitable." (The *disability* = inaction.) The shortcoming here pertains to passivity — an inability or unwillingness to act on new interpretations.

Garvin comments that "supportive learning environments" are essential to overcoming learning disabilities. He recommends four conditions for learning to flourish:

- Recognition and acceptance of differences
- Provision of timely, unvarnished feedback
- Pursuit of new ways of thinking and untapped sources of information
- Acceptance of errors, mistakes, and occasional failures as the price of improvement

7.6.5. Adaptive Learning

Stephen Haeckel, author of *Adaptive Enterprise: Creating Sense and Respond Organizations* (1999), contributes a contemporary view of how organizations should continuously learn so as to be competitive in their marketplace. He argues that today's organizations need to be continuously adaptive, and to do so, they have to increase the speed of their learning cycles — or if need be, shortchange the time allowed for learning cycles to reach a conclusion. Basically, he says that the need is to move rapidly from *sensing a situation* to *responding to the situation* by reducing the time spent on *interpretation* and *decision-making*. He proposes that organizational strategy is traditionally treated *as a strategy-plan* activity, but in many industries, it should now be understood as a *strategy-design* responsibility, that is, remake the organization by changing the operational structure and its locations through modularization of functions and the corresponding management policies and procedures. This way greater effort is spent in preparing client-stimulated action and providing the adaptive response that clients value.

7.7. Conclusion

Unless there is efficient, effective learning, KM will always operate with too much decision-making and implementation risk. The reason is that required knowledge will often be inaccurate, incomplete, or too late thereby causing decisions to be made under excessive uncertainty and risk. Without continual learning about the ever changing context, performance will be less than optimal and individuals and organizations will underperform their objectives.

Assertive learners cycling rapidly through numerous learning cycles are part of the remedy so too is an organization skilled in authentic dialogue and trusted collaboration wherein the parties involved know each other's needs, are committed to each other's success, and use critical thinking effectively without engaging in unnecessary game playing or politics. Skills in systems thinking and pattern recognition support situational learning, which, in turn, enables effective KM.

References

Adler. (1985). *Ten philosophical mistakes.* New York: Macmillan.

Allee, V. (1998). *The knowledge economy.* Available at http://www.vernaallee.com/library_articles/The_Knowledge_Economy.html

APQC. (1999). *Knowledge management. APQC benchmarking study best practice report.* American Productivity and Quality Center Consortium, Houston, TX, USA.

Ausbubel, D. P. (1967). A cognitive structure theory of school learning. In: L. Siegel (Ed.), *Instruction: Some contemporary viewpoints.* San Francisco: Chandler.

Bandura, A. (1976). Modeling theory. In: W. S. Sahakian (Ed.), *Learning: Systems, models, and theories* (2nd ed., Chicago, IL: Rand McNally.

Bixler, C. H. (2000). *Creating a dynamic knowledge management maturity continuum for increased enterprise performance and innovation.* Ph.D. dissertation, George Washington University, Washington, DC.

Boyd, J. R. (1987). *A discourse on winning and losing.* Unpublished data, August.

Brookfield, S. D. (1986). *Understanding and facilitating adult learning.* San Francisco, CA: Jossey-Bass.

Browne, M. N., & Keeley, S. (2001). *Asking the right questions: A guide to critical thinking.* Upper Saddle River, NJ: Prentice-Hall.

Carnevale, A. P., Gainer, L. J., & Meltzer, A. S. (1990). *Workplace basics: The essential skills employers want.* San Francisco, CA: Jossey-Bass.

Conklin, J. (2001). *Wicked problems and social complexity.* CogNexus Institute. Available at http://www.cognexus.org/wpf/wickedproblems.pdf

Deming, W. E. (1986). *Out of the crisis.* Cambridge, MA: MIT Center for Advanced Engineering Study.

Deming, W. E. (1994). *The new economics for industry government, education.* Cambridge, MA: MIT Center for Advanced Engineering Study.

DiVesta, F. J. (1987). The cognitive movement and education. In: J. Glover & R. Ronning (Eds), *Historical foundations of education.* New York: Plenum Press.

Garvin, D. A. (2000). *Learning in action: A guide to putting the learning organization to work.* Boston, MA: Harvard Business School Press.

Greeno, J. G. (1980). Psychology of learning, 1960–1980. *American Psychologist, 35*(8), 713–728.

Haeckel, S. H. (1999). *Adaptive enterprise: Creating sense and respond organizations.* Boston, MA: Harvard Business School Press.

Handy, C. (1989). *The age of unreason.* Boston, MA: Harvard Business School Press.

Hergenhahn, B. R. (1988). *An introduction to theories of learning* (3rd ed.). Englewood Cliffs, NJ: Prentice-Hall.

Hock, D. (1999). *Birth of the chaordic organization.* New York: Bantam Doubleday Dell Publishing Group.

Issacs, W. (1999). *Dialogue and the art of thinking together.* New York: Random House.

Malhotra, Y. (1998). Tools @ work: Deciphering the knowledge management hype. *Journal for Quality and Participation, 21*(July/August), 58–60.

Maslow, A. H. (1970). *Motivation and personality* (2nd ed.). New York: Harper and Row.

Merriam, S. B., & Caffarella, R. S. (1991). *Learning in adulthood: A comprehensive guide.* San Francisco, CA: Jossey-Bass.

Nadler, D. A., & Tushman, M. L. (1999). The organization of the future: Strategic imperatives and core competencies of the 21st century. *Organizational Dynamics, 28*(1), 45–60.

Piaget, J. (1966). *Psychology of intelligence.* Totowa, NJ: Little field, Adams.

Polanyi, M. (1962). *Personal knowledge. Towards a post critical philosophy.* London: Routledge.

Polanyi, M. (1967). *The tacit dimension.* New York: Anchor Books.

Rappaport, H. (1990). *Marking time: What our attitudes toward time reveal about our personalities and conflicts.* New York: Simon and Schuster.

Rittel, H., & Webber, M. (1973). Dilemmas in a general theory of planning. *Policy Sciences, 4,* 155–169 Amsterdam: Elsevier. [Reprinted in Cross, N. (Ed.). (1984). Developments in design methodology (pp. 135–144). Chichester: Wiley.].

Rodgers, C. R. (1983). *Freedom to learn in the 80's.* Columbus, OH: Charles E. Merrill.

Senge, P. (1990). *The fifth discipline: The art and practice of the learning organization.* New York: Doubleday Currency.

Simon, H. A. (1977). *The new science of management decision* (3rd ed.). Englewood Cliffs, NJ: Prentice-Hall.

Skinner, B. F. (1971). *Beyond freedom and dignity.* New York: Knopf.

Smith, R. M. (1982). *Learning how to learn: Applied theory for adults.* Buckingham, UK: Open University Press.

Stewart, T. A. (2001). *The wealth of knowledge: Intellectual capital and the twenty-first century organization.* New York: Doubleday.

Toffler, A. (1970). *Future shock.* New York: Bantam Books.

Tyson, K. W. (1997). *Competition in the 21st Century.* Delray Beach, FL: St. Lucie Press.

Van der Spek, R., & Spijkervet, A. (1997). *Knowledge management, dealing intelligently with knowledge.* Utrecht knowledge management network. Kennisecantrum CIBIT The Netherlands. Quoted by Bixler (2000).

Wiig, K. (2004). *People-centered knowledge management.* Burlington, MA: Elsevier.

Chapter 8

The Organizational Body Gets an Intelligent Brain

Annie Green

Abstract

Organizations have entered the knowledge era and do not have a reliable description of the path to intangible asset valuation in the context of business performance. Successful organizational performance measurement is in need of a methodology and system that enables managers to identify knowledge, document knowledge, and value knowledge. Today's knowledge era businesses are incorporating the development and use of knowledge in their improvement and corporate venture initiatives. However, in contradiction, development of their strategic plans to improve business performance and market valuation lack an understanding of how and where to start and the subsequent process to follow to obtain the expected outcome of performance measurement. The success of intangible asset valuation is contingent on an approach that increases certainty and minimizes the ambiguities and vagueness of valuing intangible assets. This chapter presents intangible asset valuation in the context of the business enterprise and attempts to identify its components, characteristics, and interrelationships. Intangible asset valuation is a system composed of interrelated components that embody the valuation of intellectual capital, assets, and properties. Core to this chapter is the identification of a theoretical model to follow when arriving at an intangible asset valuation for today's knowledge era business enterprise.

In Search of Knowledge Management: Pursuing Primary Principles
Copyright © 2010 by Emerald Group Publishing Limited
All rights of reproduction in any form reserved
ISBN: 978-1-84950-673-1

8.1. Introduction

> Around the world there has been carnage in performance management.
> Well-meaning balanced scorecard initiatives have resulted in seven
> figure consultancy bills and much cost in measuring performance —
> with no obvious benefit. Frustrated CEOs are throwing them out. This
> would be a grave mistake. The Balanced Scorecard concept will see the
> century out. We simply put garbage in and hence have garbage coming
> out. (Parmenter, 2008)

This is the message of an online business management seminar provided by
BetterManagement.com for an October 2008 Webinar. Why the frustration with
measuring performance? All indicators point to the "we are in the knowledge era"
category. In the knowledge era, value in the corporate enterprise is not where it
once was. Tangible assets of labor, physical capital, and raw materials are far less
indicative of a company's value. In the knowledge era, intangible assets like
innovation, relationships, and expertise are far more indicative of a company's value.
Approximately 80% of the respondents of a 1996 empirical study of knowledge
management (KM) said that the most significant part of a company's value chain is
knowledge and approximately 80% of the respondents also said they expect a
significant amount of knowledge to be used in future development of a business
enterprise value chain (VonKrough, 1998). Intangible assets are a major contributor
to company's value creation and need to be managed like traditional assets of labor,
physical capital, and raw materials within the business enterprise.

To define and manage intangible assets, leaders must know what to do with what
they know within the context of the business enterprise (Stewart, 1999). Business data
and information is the soil that grows business intelligence, which provides the
capability to reason, plan, solve problems, think abstractly, comprehend ideas
and language, learn and teach (Green, 2007a). Business intelligence is the utilization
of information aligned with business performance that is constructed on the
identification and modeling of focused operational data (Green, 2007a). Intelligence
as defined by Vandergriff (2008) in the intelligence pyramid (intelligence, wisdom,
knowledge, information, data, measurement [IWKIDM]) is the translation into the
user's frame of reference of the various levels wisdom, knowledge, information,
data, and measurement about the world. Vandergriff (2006) defines the following
WKIDM levels of abstraction:

- "Measurement" is defined as physical readings of phenomena from scientific
  instruments (e.g., photons) or event/object observations by individuals or groups.
- "Data" is the symbols, numbers, textual clauses, and other descriptive phrases or
  displays of measurements (e.g., evidence).
- "Information" is built from the organization of data sets through quantitative
  and/or qualitative analysis that relate those data sets, and can range from math
  equations, paragraphs, graphical illustrations, or images.

- "Knowledge" is created by applying experience to available measurements, data, and information.
- "Wisdom" results from the application of cognitive capability and judgment.
- "Intelligence" is defined as the result of the translation of wisdom, knowledge, information, data, or measurements into the user's frame of reference to support decision-making or decision implementation (Vandergriff, 2008).

Businesses need to define their knowledge, the value of their knowledge, and the approach to its valuation (Wiig, 1994). Today's business enterprise needs to become "intelligent" about the environment they seek to gain knowledge from before they can understand and define its valuation system. The following sections present the components and characteristics that represent a holistic approach to intangible asset valuation.

8.2. The System Component

We live in a world of systems. To understand systems people need to understand the underlying patterns. For example, people can only understand the system of a corporation by contemplating its whole, not its parts. Today's complex corporations are best viewed by looking for the patterns and understanding the whole. System thinking is a conceptual framework for making complete patterns clearer. Using and understanding systems thinking can help people see how to change the patterns effectively. (McNurlin & Sprague, 1998)

Peter Senge, in his book, *The Fifth Discipline* (1990), writes "We all know the metaphor of being able to 'step back' far enough from the details to 'see the forest for the trees.' But, unfortunately, for most of us when we step back we just see 'lots of trees.' We pick our favorite one or two and focus our attention and efforts for change on those. Businesses have not stepped far enough back to see the forest. In this knowledge era, businesses need to construct maps to include the details of the coherent picture to distinguish the high- from low-leverage changes." Businesses must view intangible asset valuation as a system within the context of the business enterprise and take a system approach that requires businesses to think about and define a language, for describing and understanding, the forces and interrelationships that shape the behavior of a valuation system (Senge, 1990). This discipline helps businesses to see how to change systems more effectively, and to act more in tune with the larger processes of the natural and economic world or business environment (Senge, 1990). The methodology to accomplish this is systems engineering/architecting and the overall goals and objectives are to: emulate business intelligence and knowledge in the structure of a performance-based valuation model and to provide a view of organizational performance with respect to changes attributable to knowledge functions.

8.3.　The Cognitive Component

Cognition is the science of reason, judgment, and learning. Cognitive science helps us to understand how individuals reason and make judgments. Being cognizant of thought patterns can help businesses create models that simulate business intelligence and knowledge and increase the business leader's certainty in the successful application of valuation in the context of performance measurement. The institution of a holistic approach to the construction of a performance-based valuation system places concentration on organizations understanding and constructing mental models of complex business systems.[1] Senge (1990) defines mental models as deeply ingrained assumptions, generalizations, or even pictures or images that influence how we understand the world and take action. Senge (1990) further states that working with mental models starts with turning the mirror inward; learning to unearth our internal pictures of the world, to bring them to the surface and hold them rigorously to scrutiny. Succinctly put, a business's "mental models" determine not only how they make sense of the business enterprise, but what guides their decisions and how they take action.

Allen Newell's *Unified Theories of Cognition* (1990) defines a single set of mechanisms for all of cognitive behavior as the following:

1. Problem-solving, decision-making, and routine action
2. Memory, learning, and skill
3. Perception and motor behavior
4. Language
5. Motivation and emotion
6. Imagining, dreaming, and daydreaming.

These mechanisms of behavior define how individuals deal with their external and internal environments. Our view of cognition as it relates to a business enterprise is to provide a unified model of these mechanisms that facilitate the appropriate behavior within the enterprise structure. It is critical that these mechanisms facilitate the appropriate behavior of the business enterprise, because a unified approach cannot be a pastiche, the parts must work together to achieve the expected goals (Newell, 1990). A cognitive theoretical model should express attributes of the mind, to include: (1) perception — the ability to influence, (2) awareness — the ability to

---

1. Complex systems as used here are defined as a class of open systems whose behavior are derived from the highly coupled elements/components/rules interrelationships and are other than just a sum of the parts or functions. The properties of such a system are modifiable as a result of environmental/contextual interactions as well as internal elements/components/rules. These interrelationships are usually highly nonlinear and organized on many spatial and temporal scales. (Derived from the Latin "plex" that means to weave; contrast with independent systems and may be composed of complicated and/or simple systems.) [Based on Jack Cowan and Marcus Feldman. Preview of Workshop on Complex Adaptive Systems, *Bulletin of the Santa Fe Institute*, Vol. 1, No 1] (Ross, 1924).

distinguish between events, (3) attention — the ability to be selective among percepts and thoughts, and (4) learning — the ability to store and recall experiences (Newell, 1990).

Foremost in the development of a cognitive model of enterprise business intelligence and knowledge is the identification of components of intelligence or business value drivers. A business has eight value drivers (Green, 2008) that compose its context, which are as follows:

1. *Customer*: The economic value that results from the associations (e.g., loyalty, satisfaction, longevity) an enterprise has built with consumers of its goods and services.
2. *Competitor*: The economic value that results from the position (e.g., reputation, market share, name recognition, image) an enterprise has built in the business marketplace.
3. *Employee*: The economic value that results from the collective capabilities (e.g., knowledge, skill, competence, know-how) of an enterprise's employees.
4. *Information*: The economic value that results from an enterprise's ability to collect and disseminate its information and knowledge in the right form and content to the right people at the right time.
5. *Partner*: The economic value that results from associations (e.g., financial, strategic, authority, power) an enterprise has established with external individuals and organizations (e.g., consultants, customers, suppliers, allies, competitors) in pursuit of advantageous outcomes.
6. *Process*: The economic value that results from an enterprise's ability (e.g., policies, procedures, methodologies, techniques) to leverage the ways in which the enterprise operates and creates value for its employees and customers.
7. *Product/service*: The economic value that results from an enterprise's ability to develop and deliver its offerings (i.e., products and services) in a timely manner that reflects an understanding of market and customer(s) requirements, expectations, and desires.
8. *Technology*: The economic value that results from the hardware and software an enterprise has invested in to support its operations, management and future renewal.

The challenge is to be able to identify within a business domain and in common language, what measurements and indicators the business needs to know from these value drivers (Green, 2007b)

8.4. The Intelligence Component

Organizations seek to have a view of negative and positive impacts on performance on the basis of intangible assets, which requires a body of knowledge that drives the goal of valuation. Organizations must establish a theoretical model of the body of knowledge to be called business intelligence that supports business reasoning, problem-solving, decision-making, and learning. Newell (1990) states in his definition of theory as it relates to his unified theories of cognition: "to state it positively and in general, let there be some body of explicit knowledge, from which answers can be obtained to questions by inquiries. Some answers can be obtained to questions by inquiries. Some answers might be predictions, some might be explanations, and some might be prescriptions for control. If this body of knowledge yields answers to those questions for you, you can call it a theory." "A theory is an explicit body of knowledge, from which answers can be obtained by anyone skilled in the art" (Senge, 1990).

Operational data provides a wealth of information that serves as a source of understanding and addresses the problems that face the enterprise in achieving its goals. The data and information are captured via the business functions of an enterprise and encoded for retention and recall for use in making decisions with respect to the business value chain. The right set of operational data grows intelligence, which is the ability to comprehend, understand and profit from experience (Wiig, 1994). The engineering of intelligence seeks to identify the major independent components of intellectual behavior and determine the importance of and interactions between functional components such that the degree of intelligence can be measured or evaluated. The structure and function are identified and defined as the conduit by which intelligence is achieved. To equate, business intellect is extracted from operational data and transformed into business intelligence, which must be aligned with business objectives and goals.

In the overall scheme of theory, business intelligence is just one component of a performance-based knowledge valuation system, just as intangible asset valuation is just one side of business performance, although it is the most valuable in the knowledge era. A performance-based valuation system must align with business needs and objectives and its body of knowledge or intelligence serves as the "core" of it functions. Intelligence engineering is the first step in the development lifecycle for a performance-based valuation system (Green, 2006).

8.5. The Knowledge Component

Knowledge is the psychological result of perception and learning and reasoning in accordance with a study conducted by the Princeton University. This may cause some debate among those who define knowledge as actionable. Most think that a positive action to knowing something indicates that it is knowledge; however, the lack of action based on perception, learning, and reasoning is also knowledge and the decision to not act can be measured and valued as much as the decision to act (Wiig, 1994). Knowledge engineering builds formal knowledge models based on rules or principles prescribing a particular course of action. Logical modeling is the tool of the problem solver in identifying a solution using knowledge in decision-making (Wiig, 1994).

Organizations are always at the mercy of expertise of the people it deals with — employees, vendors, customers, and other stakeholders who influence their business.

The quality of the work delivered depends on what they know and what they contribute. These associations are "agents" to the organization that provide expertise, know-how, competence, and other activities that drive the value system of the organization. Business knowledge in needed to deliver quality service and products to sustain competitively viable performance within the work place. "We postulate that the single most important factor in making the organization intelligent-acting is to make appropriate knowledge available and accessible — and to make sure it is used" (Wiig, 1994). Knowledge in the enterprise, to be effective, is well planned and implemented with deliberance, competence, and momentum (Wiig, 1994).

8.6. The Learning Component

"Learning may signify either a product (i.e., something learned) or the process that yields such a product. In the first sense, we might ask, "What have we learned?" referring to an accumulation of information in the form of knowledge or skill; in the second sense, "How do we learn?" referring to a learning activity that may be well or badly performed" (Argyris & Schön, 1996). An organization learns when it adds to its store of information or body of knowledge through organizational inquiry (Argyris & Schön, 1996). Thus, agents of an organization can only learn from what information and knowledge it captures, becomes aware of, discovers, and uses in its decision-making process.

In 1956, Benjamin Bloom developed a classification of levels of intellectual behavior important in learning. Bloom's (1984) taxonomy is a lexicon of labels that occur during learning. The levels of Bloom's taxonomy that represent intellectual activity are as follows: (1) knowledge-ability to recall previously learned material; (2) comprehension-ability to grasp meaning, explain, restate ideas; (3) application-ability to use learned material in new situations; (4) analysis-ability to separate material into component parts and show relationship between parts; (5) synthesis-ability to put together the separate ideas to form a new whole, establish new relationships; (6) evaluation-ability to judge the worth of material against stated criteria. A performance-based valuation model simulates the comprehension of information, organization of ideas, analysis and synthesis of data, application of knowledge, and the ability to choose among alternatives in problem-solving. A performance-based valuation model uses symbolic representation to simulate these components of learning.

8.7. The Change Component

Organizational inquiry can result in thinking and acting that yields a form of change in the design of organizational practices (Argyris & Schön, 1996). Senge et al. (1999) use the word "profound change" to describe organizational change.

Senge et al. (1999) view change as the combined inner shifts in people's values, aspirations, and behaviors with outer shifts in processes, strategies, practices, and systems. Senge et al. (1999) identify that learning is part of profound change as organizations not only do something new, but build a capacity for doing things in a new way. Doing something new, and new ways of doing work, impact the performance of individuals and groups involved in such work. Change measures the progress made toward achieving goals. However, the measurements of change are not just "hard" measures. It is imperative to measure not only the change itself, but the impact of the change. Petouhoff, Chandler, and Montag-Schultz (2006) describe a trend where improvement projects costs far outweigh their realized benefits. Reviewing 10 years of independent studies that evaluated the rate of return on projects, it was discovered that a McKinsey study showed the return on investment (ROI) was 143% when an excellent organizational change management program was part of the improvement initiative and 35% when there was a poor organizational change management program or no program. This demonstrates a major value difference from gaining 43 cents on every dollar to losing 65 cents on every dollar, which could significantly skew the valuation of intangible assets given the impact of change. "Soft" measures, such as motivation, commitment, ownership and resistance to change, are also included, as these are the critical variable for feedback that can help a team reflect, learn, and move forward (Senge et al., 1999)

8.8.   The Performance Measurement Component

> Performance measurement is a continuous and dynamic process in which measures are first constructed, based on strategically important success factors, then the measures are used to help implement planned strategies, and finally the analysis of measurement results provides feedback for new strategy formulations. (Okkonen, Pirttimaki, Lonnqvist, & Hannula, 2002)

Performance measurement deals with the implementation of an organization's strategy (Kaplan & Norton, 1996). When a balanced measurement system is used to measure performance, such performance is also used to identify and control critical factors that lead to success. It is usually carried out using a system that consists of several individual measures. The measures for the performance measurement system are chosen based on the organization's vision and strategy (Kaplan & Norton, 1996). The aim is to measure success factors from different perspectives, like customers, employees, business processes, and financial success, as well as from the perspective of past, current, and future performance, such that these different aspects of performance can be measured and managed (Okkonen et al., 2002). Differences in the use of performance measurement depend on the time frame monitored. Performance measurement at the short-term or operative level is used for guidance, control, and managing quality, whereas in long-term strategic issues it has a dual role in implementing and updating strategy (Okkonen et al., 2002). Performance measurement is translating a strategy into concrete objectives; communicating the objectives to knowledge workers; guiding and focusing knowledge workers' efforts toward achieving these objectives; controlling whether or not the strategic objectives are realized; using double-loop learning to challenge the validity of the strategy itself; and visualizing how individual employee's efforts contribute to the overall business objectives (Neely, 1998; Simons, 2000; Kaplan & Norton, 1996). In this chapter, a theoretical model that incorporates the integration of strategy, culture, and viability is discussed. The performance-based valuation system starts with the value drivers and their capacity, which evolves through intelligence, knowledge, learning, change, and translates into performance measures that identify and control critical factors aligned with success to meet the ultimate goal of identifying and controlling contribution of capital, assets, and property to organizational performance.

8.9. Characteristics of a Knowledge-Based Valuation System

The components of a performance-based valuation system share nine distinctive characteristics derived from their combination and interaction with each other. They are

1. Concept
2. Structure
3. Language
4. Data retrieval
5. Logic models
6. Pattern recognition
7. Knowledge Representation
8. Hypotheses
9. Evidence

8.9.1. Concept: Elements into a Basic Relationship

Concepts are the basic building blocks on which a system operates. Figure 8.1 depicts the diverse components of valuation within a business and brings these elements together into a basic relationship. This valuation concept is constructed on the research and understanding of valuing intangible assets within the business enterprise. This concept

- identifies sources of value that align with business performance,
- uses intelligence constructed from value chain elements of the business environment,

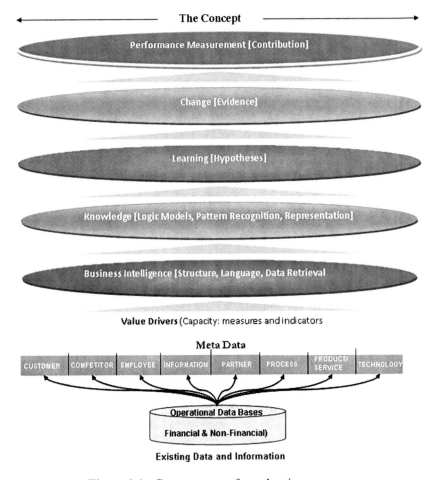

Figure 8.1: Components of a valuation system.

- formulates a model of potential improvements and corporate ventures that include levels of abstraction that apply to the business environment,
- develops hypotheses as the nature of improvements or corporate ventures being investigated, and
- verifies the findings or results rendered from the outcome.

8.9.2. Structure: Levels of Abstraction

Structure represents the relationships and orderings that should exist between and among business concepts and the language and symbols which represent them. The combined structure establishes a symbolic system or an ecological formation of inter- and intrarelationships as defined by Davenport (1997). The relationship between a company's organizational context and its information environment are of significant importance in its success as these relationships can enable or constrain the organization performance (Davenport, 1997). A performance-based valuation system provides structure that identifies and determines the relationships between business processes/functions, value drivers, data, information, and knowledge with the path from intangible asset capture to performance measurement. The valuation system exhibits the levels of abstraction from the business goals into their subsequent value drivers and primitive elements of capacity.

8.9.3. Language: Symbolic Communication

Language is the internal representation of data and external communications of value. A valuation system uses its terminology of the business enterprise to communicate. It is critical to state the semantics of a representation language, so it is known exactly what expressions mean and which inferences are valid (Cawsey, 1998). Proper understanding requires intelligence of both language and context. The semantics of language representation provides a way of mapping the valuation expressions in a formal language to the business components in the real business enterprise.

8.9.4. Data Retrieval: Interfaces

Interfaces to external and internal data of the business enterprise facilitate the extraction, transformation, and loading of data and information from business domain repositories. Business data is formed into information that is transformed into intelligence that evolves into knowledge and subsequently performance. The challenge is the retrieval of this data within a specific domain and in a useful form for its intended use. Businesses should think strategically about how to work with existing systems and data that represent key performance indicators (KPIs), both quantitative and qualitative.

8.9.5. Logic Models: Problem-Solving, Decision-Making, Learning

Logic models facilitate the transformation of business functions/conditions into a form that represents easily recognizable sets of objects in the real business world (Cawsey, 1998). Logic is a formal system that is described in terms of its syntax (i.e., allowable expressions), its semantics (i.e., meaning), and its proof theory (i.e., conclusions). Solving problems in the business domain requires knowledge of the business processes/functions and reasoning. Business logic models reflect the realities of the business enterprise and accommodate its explicit processes/functions. The problem solver performs analysis on the information to identify a course of action that best achieves the desired goal from amongst alternative course of actions. A valuation system contains inference processes to effectively make decisions and solve problems.

8.9.6. *Pattern Recognition: Variances and Trends*

Pattern recognition promotes the capture, analysis, and dissemination of better or best practices by identifying similarities among differences and differences among similarities. Newell (1990) states that problems are solved by searching a problem space, whose states include the initial situation (i.e., benchmarks) and potential desired situations (i.e., outcome) all as envisioned by the problem solver. Complex pattern computations rarely have a single right answer. Instead, they have a range of possible outcomes; the problem solver's job is to find one of the better ones. Developing good ways to search through the data for a good solution is vital to measuring change and its subsequent value.

8.9.7. *Knowledge Representation: Metadata*

Knowledge representation is the transformation of knowledge into a business fact. Business facts in a formal representation scheme are related to facts in the real business environment. General requirements when representing knowledge in a valuation model is: to adequately represent all the knowledge that is need for reasoning; adequately allow new knowledge to be inferred from a basic set of facts; efficient construction of inferences; and a well-defined syntax (i.e., language) and semantics (i.e., meaning) of allowable expressions (Cawsey, 1998).

8.9.8. *Hypotheses: Questions/Inquiries*

> We will have to learn, before understanding any task, to first ask the question, "What information do I need, and in what form, and when?" The next question people have to learn to ask is, "To whom do I owe which information and when and where." (Drucker, 1990)

A valuation system has the ability to formulate facts from relationships and orderings that are used for further investigation, using hypotheses or suggested explanations for observable phenomenon. Hypotheses can have varying scope and can provide potential for improvements and new corporate ventures in strategy development. Further investigation tests an explanation accounting for a set of facts. Hypothesis formulation is similar to induction, basic to knowledge, and essential to problem-solving. Hypothesis formulation is strategy development in the context of empirical games based on reasoning from detailed facts to general principles.

8.9.9. Evidence: Metrics

A valuation system supports the assertion of validity into the simulation of business knowledge. Metrics allow the recognition of change in both the enterprise and its context. Metrics for a valuation system are the collective set of measurements and indicators that define the eight value drivers aligned with enterprise objectives and goals. The key to the success of measuring value is the selection of meaningful measurements and indicators that provide insight into the enterprise and its context, which supports decision makers and implementers in learning and guiding the enterprise in its strategic direction. Unless there is evidence to validate the knowledge formulation process, the reasoning, collecting and utilization of data is useless.

8.10. The Theoretical Model: Enterprise Business Reasoning, Analytics and Intelligence Network (E-BRAIN©)

E-BRAIN© is a theoretical performance-based valuation system that integrates a technology implementation component, described below, with

- the seven valuation components described above: (1, system; 2, cognition; 3, intelligence; 4, knowledge; 5, learning; 6, change; and 7, performance measurement);
- the eight characteristics described above (1, concept; 2, structure; 3, language; 4, data retrieval; 5, logic models; 6, pattern recognition; 7, knowledge representation; 8, hypotheses); and
- the eight intangible asset value drivers described above (1, customer; 2, competitor; 3, employee; 4, information; 5, partner; 6, process; 7, product/service; 8, technology).

Through the integration of the valuation components, characteristics and value sources, E-BRAIN© (Figure 8.2) provides a holistic approach to the implementation of a performance-based valuation system. The theoretical model establishes a common language of valuation components in the context of the enterprise's decision-making processes. A holistic approach establishes intelligent components that promote cognitive learning from the data, information, and knowledge stored in enterprise operational repositories. Cognition in the context of valuation is designed in the structure, functions, and elements of the theoretical model. The model provides attributes that demonstrate recall and intellectual skills.

8.11. The Technology Implementation Component

Today's turbulent business environment increases the demand for effective intangible asset valuation. Information technology (IT) can contribute to meeting this objective.

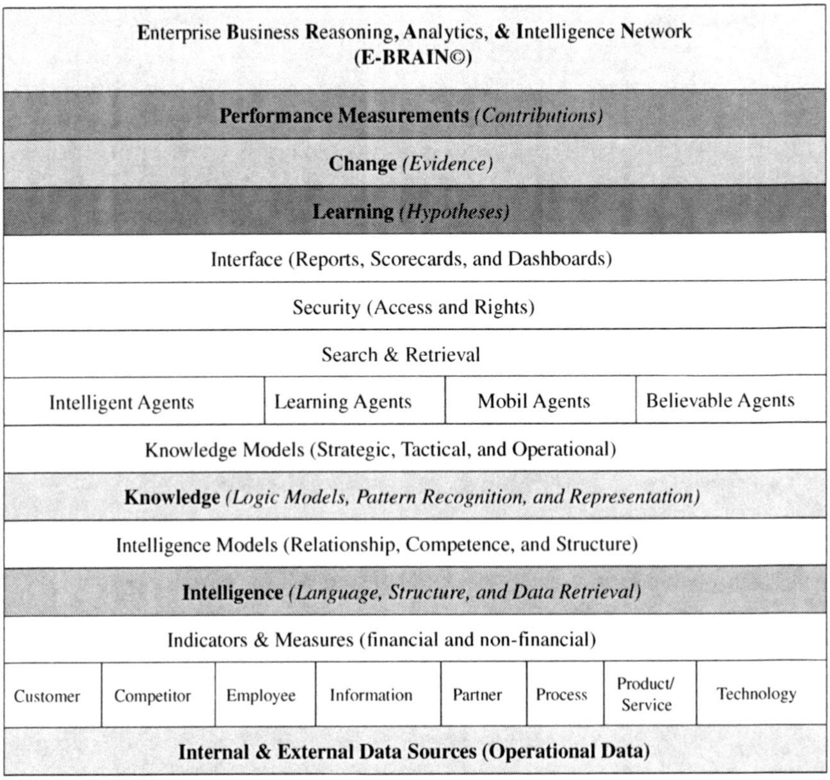

Enterprise Business Reasoning, Analytics, & Intelligence Network (E-BRAIN©)							
Performance Measurements *(Contributions)*							
Change *(Evidence)*							
Learning *(Hypotheses)*							
Interface (Reports, Scorecards, and Dashboards)							
Security (Access and Rights)							
Search & Retrieval							
Intelligent Agents		Learning Agents		Mobil Agents		Believable Agents	
Knowledge Models (Strategic, Tactical, and Operational)							
Knowledge *(Logic Models, Pattern Recognition, and Representation)*							
Intelligence Models (Relationship, Competence, and Structure)							
Intelligence *(Language, Structure, and Data Retrieval)*							
Indicators & Measures (financial and non-financial)							
Customer	Competitor	Employee	Information	Partner	Process	Product/ Service	Technology
Internal & External Data Sources (Operational Data)							

Figure 8.2: E-BRAIN© theoretical performance-based model.

In order to better understand the linkages between the use of IT, the business context, and performance measurement, in Figure 8.2, E-BRAIN© evolves the business concept of intangible asset valuation into a technology-based solution. The technological based elements depicted in E-BRAIN© above are as follows.

8.11.1.   Indicators and Measures (Financial and Nonfinancial)

> Capacity is the value-creating ability of an organization, an ability that takes in a wide variety of resources. (McNair & Vangermeersch, 1998)

The theoretical performance-based valuation model seeks to incorporate the basic economics of business within its structure by identifying a core set of value-adding activities (VAC), transformations, and transactions performed by the enterprise. This model seeks to provide attributes that have a direct or indirect relationship with the identification of profit, waste, and nonvalue-adding activities on resources. Decision-making is aided in effective management of intelligence and the ability to reduce or eliminate waste and nonvalue-adding activities, thus achieving an optimum level of organizational performance (McNair & Vangermeersch, 1998). Critical to the successful use of business intelligence is the capture of indicators and measure, to be known as capacity. Capacity is defined for every resource or value driver (Green, 2007a). Capacity is tied to the decision-making process of the organization (McNair & Vangermeersch, 1998). Capacity utilization is a primary goal of the operational, tactical, and strategic decision-making processes. Capacity should be represented in four categories of diagnostic information (Drucker, 1998): foundation, productivity, competence, and resource-allocation.[2] Drucker (1998) identifies these categories of information to provide results that inform and direct enterprise tactics and strategy development. The union of the proposed eight value drivers (i.e., customer, competitor, employee, information, partner, process, product/service, and technology) and capacity creates a body of knowledge for the construction of enterprise value and provides a basis for taking action to manage and improve performance. This body of knowledge is constructed in the form of an enterprise value database. The content of the enterprise value database is extracted, transformed, and loaded from operational data within organization data repositories that are aligned with the measurements and indicators of the value drivers.

8.11.2. Intelligence Models

Walter Fritz (1996) in his e-book, *Intelligent Systems and their Societies*, defines intelligence as the system's level of performance in reaching its objectives. In following this definition, it supports the creation of intelligence from the value drivers, which are aligned with the strategic decision-making capacity. Business Intelligence is not a single entity; it is composed from business data and information through cross-pollination of the eight value drivers defined at the beginning

---

2. Peter Drucker's (1998) chapter "The information executives truly need" of *Harvard Business Review on Measuring Corporate Performance* presents the following four categories of diagnostic information required by a business to manage wealth creation:

- *Foundation information*: Routine measures such as cash-flow and liquidity projections which when normal, basically do not tell much, however, when not normal, indicate a problem that needs to be identified.
- *Productivity information*: Measures that deal with performance of key resources. These measures must also include the total-factor productivity, which means that they should provide the value add of all costs, including the cost of capital. These measures incorporate such tools as economic-value-added analysis (EVA) and benchmarking to measure total-factor productivity and to manage it.
- *Competence information*: Measures associated with core competencies that link market or customer value with special skills and abilities of the producer or supplier of products and services.
- *Resource-allocation information*: Measures associated with the allocation of scarce resources, such as capital and performing people.

of this chapter (Green, 2007a, 2007b). Using the enterprise value database, the cross-pollination of business value drivers can construct the following three categories of intelligence: relationship, competence, and structure (Table 8.1). The modeling of business intelligence introduces a new level of abstraction that allows the conventional naming of these combinations and the elevation of them into strategic, tactical, and operational enterprise business models through a business intelligence database.

Table 8.1: Business intelligence: three major components (Green, 2007a, 2007b).

Relationship intelligence Understanding of how the interactions between knowledge workers influence organization performance	**Competence intelligence** Understanding of how the abilities/ proficiency of knowledge workers influences organizational performance
1. Employee-to-employee relationships 2. Employee-to-customer relationships 3. Employee-to-competitor relationships 4. Employee-to-partner relationships 5. Customer-to-customer relationships 6. Customer-to-competitor relationships 7. Customer-to-partner relationships 8. Competitor-to-competitor relationship 9. Competitor-to-partner relationship 10. Partner-to-partner relationships	1. Employee-to-information competencies 2. Employee-to-process competencies 3. Employee-to-product/service competencies 4. Employee-to-technology competencies 5. Partner-to-information competencies 6. Partner-to-process competencies 7. Partner-to-product/service competencies 8. Partner-to-technology competencies

Structure intelligence
Understanding of how the organization's infrastructure environment influences organizational performance

1. Customer-to-information structure 2. Customer-to-process structure 3. Customer-to-product/service structure 4. Customer-to-technology structure 5. Competitor-to-information structure 6. Competitor-to-process structure 7. Competitor-to-product/service structure 8. Competitor-to-technology structure 9. Information-to-information structure	10. Information-to-process structure 11. Information-to-product/service structure 12. Information-to-technology structure 13. Process-to-process structure 14. Process-to-product/service structure 15. Process-to-technology structure 16. Produce/service-to-product/service structure 17. Produce/service-to-technology structure 18. Technology-to-technology structure

8.11.3. Knowledge Models

Knowledge models are based on the identification of business events that can be symbolized and manipulated to achieve expected business results or enterprise business modeling. Enterprise business models utilize the routine and special statistical, financial, forecasting, management science, and other quantitative models that provide analysis capabilities (Turban & Aronson, 1998). A business logic model base is established on the knowledge needs for making business decisions and takes into consideration accounting, tax regulations, and compliance components and their affect on corporate transactions and profits. Some common measures of economic income include profit margin (gross or net), ROI (measured as total assets, net assets, or owners' equity), and net cash flow (before tax or after tax, before debt service or after debt service) (Reilly & Schweihs, 1999). Economic income measures can involve any increment in economic income or decrement in economic costs (Reilly & Schweihs, 1999). This is where the system engineers/architects and the expertise of economists come together. Using the enterprise intelligence database, the modeling of business knowledge introduces a new level of abstraction that allows the conventional naming of intangible assets and the elevation of them into strategic, tactical, and operational forms. This business knowledge can be learned from, decisions made based on change, and performance measures captured to evolve continuous strategy development aligned with organizational performance. The E-BRAIN© technology implementation component supports the levels of abstraction through the development of semantic networks and frames. Semantic networks and frames provide a simple and intuitive way of representing facts about objects (Stanfill & Waltz, 1986). Both schemes allow the representation of categories of objects and relationships between objects, and draw simple inferences based on this knowledge. Semantic networks are used in the definition of complex interrelationships in a knowledge base. Semantic networks provide the foundation of a sophisticated inference system. Frames emulate the mental recall of images of a particular object and its related attributes by human thought.

8.11.4. Search and Retrieval

The business enterprise is an ever-changing large and complex venture that has an overabundance of information requirements both internal and external. Search is the dominant paradigm for information retrieval, filtering, and management in computers, within corporations, and on the Internet as a whole. The use of classification technologies and the development of systems that enrich the user experience are paramount to the success of a performance-based valuation system.

Decisions in the knowledge economy require greater information content and analysis. The information required is not static; it is current and changes constantly.

The dynamic state and overabundance of information supports the use of agents[3] to do the search and retrieval of knowledge and perhaps even the negotiating in the decision-making process (Murch & Johnson, 1999). Agents search and retrieve a company's information as part of an evaluation of its business requirements using such attributes as adaptability, mobility, transparency, accountability, ruggedness, self-starter, and user-centered (Murch & Johnson, 1999). Agents facilitate reasoning in systems. Reasoning in a performance-based valuation system uses memory and/or case base reasoning. Memory-based reasoning (MBR) stores only the relationships between attributes of cases to measure similarity and recall based on a match (Talbot, 2003). Case-based reasoning (CBR) stores all of its outcomes as cases and knowledge or inference are derived from historical cases (Skyrme, 1999).

8.11.5. Security (Access and Rights)

> Every corporation culture is different, and there is no one right way to create and enforce security policies. But each company must find a way to make its security policy strategy effective, or risk losing immeasurable value in sensitive information and expensive resources. (Cisco, 2008)

Without adequate security in place, corporations are putting corporate and personal data at risk of intrusion. With too much or improperly implemented security in place, corporations are limiting corporate and personal opportunity and possibly diminishing the value to the corporation of information locked up with no access or untimely (slow) access. To store corporate knowledge under insecure conditions opens the corporation up to a phenomenal risk as corporate knowledge is the basis of its future renewal and succinctly put could be the life or death of the corporation. A performance-based valuation system's end product is intangible assets, which provide clients with accurate, relevant valuation information, which in turn presents defendable conclusions. This intelligence and knowledge should be protected as securely as tangible assets.

---

3. The use of agents has proven to be an effective approach to search and retrieval. These agents need a way to look at a company's information as part of a broader evaluation of its requirements. There is not a one size fits all agent. There are several categories of agents (Murch & Johnson, 1999), such as:

- Intelligent agents – uses reasoning and learned behavior to execute task or solve problems.
- Learning agents – learn from the user or owner, once tasks are learned, the agent can then instruct or suggest ways to improve: gradual and interactive (adaptive).
- Mobile agents – active, mobile, and can travel. They are frequently used to collect data, information, or changes.
- Believable agents – animation or perhaps personalities that make them believable.

8.11.6. Interface (Reports, Scorecards, and Dashboards)

Interfaces help organizations leverage information and perform analytics. They provide alignment, visibility, and collaboration across the organization by allowing business users to define, monitor, and analyze business performance. Visualization software should be easy to use, intuitive, and aid in finding information long after having forgotten where it was stored or what it was named. Interfaces for a performance-based knowledge valuation system include professional reports, scorecards, and dashboards. These interfaces contain strategic, operational, and tactical views as follows:

- Strategic reports, scorecards, and dashboards have a scorecard interface that support business leaders to tracking performance against strategic objectives.
- Operational reports, scorecards, and dashboards provide an interface that support senior and supervisory workers to monitor and optimize operational processes.
- Tactical reports, scorecards, and dashboards provide and interface that support business managers in improving their understanding of the processes and activities for which they accountable.

Visualization software for the purpose of measuring change should be designed by employees for learning, and not by the organization for control. A performance-based valuation system interface is constructed based on the value, intelligence, and knowledge repositories that feed its structure using its inherent models that are defined within its structure. This graphic tool is based upon user feedback to help monitor progress toward goals and the effect of actions taken and measurements that support interpretation and judgment in decision-making (Senge et al., 1999).

8.12. Conclusion

There is increasing recognition of the importance of intangible assets. In addition, there is a pressing need for a set of widely accepted metrics by which business leaders and the investment community can account for nonfinancial factors that affect value creation in the knowledge era business enterprise. E-BRAIN© is a comprehensive theoretical model that identifies the path from KPIs to performance measurement. The basis of its structure is intangible asset valuation using a systems engineering approach. The integration of key components establishes a path from the body of knowledge aligned with value through the measuring of performance. This path

- incorporates the eight enterprise value drivers of intangible assets;
- aligns measures and indicators from strategic, tactical, and operational data with the enterprise value drivers to establish a core "body of knowledge;"
- uses the comprehensive core "body of knowledge" to construct business intelligence;

- uses the three components of business intelligence to construct business knowledge;
- learns through hypothesis from knowledge gained to improve productivity of its enterprise value drivers;
- identifies by pattern recognition similarities and differences that support changes to business practices that are aligned with organizational performance; and
- measures the achievements of the business enterprise by using its capacity as its measurement of performance.

Value, capacity, and learning are key factors used in this path to measuring organizational performance and the major points to consider with respect to this approach are as follows:

1. The value chain of a business enterprise is the critical path to delivery of its products and services. This is a path that needs to be clearly defined. If it is not, how can a decision be made as to what, where, when, who, and why a change in necessary or desirable.
2. The capacity of an organization is the ultimate driver to its success. Profit has two views: the increase of revenue or the decrease of expenses. When viewing the bottom line, anything achievable, must be measurable and the final unit of measure within a business is the dollar. A business must be aware of the cost of its activities, in order to understand the location of its value and its waste.
3. Organizational learning is critical, as it is the ability to recognize what is or is not efficient and/or effective.
4. Change is inevitable: to ignore value-adding activities or to repeat nonvalue-adding activities over and over again without any consideration of change or improvement could be lethal.
5. Effective traceable planning and use of an IT-based solution is paramount to the success of a performance-based valuation system. IT solutions support greater pay-off in the dynamic knowledge-based environment given the overabundance of data and the complexity of the business enterprise.

References

Argyris, C., & Schön, D. A. (1996). *Organizational learning II: Theory, method, and practice.* Reading, MA: Addison-Wesley.

Bloom, B. S. (1984). *Taxonomy of educational objectives, book 1 cognitive domain.* White Plains, NY: Longman.

Cawsey, A. (1998). *The essense of artificial intelligence.* Europe, NJ: Prentice Hall.

Cisco. (2008). *Data leakage worldwide: The effectiveness of security policies.* San Jose, CA. Available at http://www.cisco.com/en/US/solutions/collateral/ns170/ns896/ns895/white_paperc11-499060.html. Retrieved on 30 January, 2008.

Davenport, T. H. (1997). *Information ecology.* New York: Oxford University Press.

Drucker, P. (1990). What executives need to learn. In: *Proceedings of Authur D. Little conference on implementing the information based organization*, March.

Drucker, P. (1998). The information executives truly need. In: Harvard Business Review (Ed.), *Harvard business review on measuring corporate performance* (pp. 1–24). Boston, MA: Harvard Business School.

Fritz, W. (1996). *Intelligence systems and their societies* (e-book). Fairhills, NJ: New Horizon Press. Available at http://www.intelligent-systems.com. Retrieved on 27 January, 1997.

Green, A. (2006). The starting block: Enterprise (business) intelligence-evolving towards knowledge valuation. *VINE: The Journal of Information and Knowledge Management Systems*, 36(3), 267–277.

Green, A. (2007a). Business information – A natural path to business intelligence: Knowing what to capture. *VINE: The Journal of Information and Knowledge Management Systems*, 37(1), 18–23.

Green, A. (2007b). Intangible assets in plain business language. *VINE: The Journal of Information and Knowledge Management Systems*, 37(3), 238–248.

Green, A. (2008). *A framework of intangible valuation areas: The sources of intangible assets within an organization*. Germany: VDM-Publishing.

Kaplan, R., & Norton, D. (1996). *The balance scorecard, translating strategy into action*. Boston, MA: Harvard Business School.

McNair, C., & Vangermeersch, R. (1998). *Total capacity management: Optimizing at the operational, tactical and strategic levels*. Boca Raton, FL: St. Lucie Press.

McNurlin, B. C., & Sprague, R. H., Jr. (1998). *Information systems management in practice* (4th ed.) Upper Saddle River, NJ: Prentice Hall.

Murch, R., & Johnson, T. (1999). *Intelligent software agents*. Upper Saddle River, NJ: Prentice Hall.

Neely, A. (1998). *Measuring business performance. Why, what and how?* London: Profile Books.

Newell, A. (1990). *Unified theories of cognition*. Cambridge, MA: Harvard University Press.

Okkonen, J., Pirttimaki, V., Lonnqvist, A., & Hannula, M. (2002). Triangle of performance measurement. *Business Intelligence and Knowledge Management*. Stockholm: Euram 2002.

Parmenter, D. (2008). *Revitalizing a floundering balanced scorecard with winning KPIs* (archived webcast). Available at http://www.bettermanagement.com. Retrieved on 29 October, 2008.

Petouhoff, N. L., Chandler, T., & Montag-Schultz, B. (2006). The business impact of change management, what is the common denominator for high project ROI's. Graziadio Business Report. *Journal of Relevant Business Information and Analysis*, 9(3). Pepperdine University. Available at http://gbr.pepperdine.edu/063/change.html#petouhoff

Reilly, R., & Schweihs, R. (1999). *Valuing intangible assets*. New York: McGraw-Hill.

Ross, W. D. (1924). *Aristotle's metaphysics* (Vol. 2). Oxford: Clarendon Press.

Senge, P. (1990). *The fifth discipline: The art & practice of the learning organization*. New York: Doubleday.

Senge, P., Kleiner, A., Roberts, C., Ross, R., Roth, G., & Smith, B. (1999). *The dance of change: The challenges to sustaining momentum in learning organizations*. New York: Doubleday.

Simons, R. (2000). *Performance measurement and control systems for implementing strategy*. Upper Saddle River, NJ: Prentice Hall.

Skyrme, D. J. (1999). *Knowledge networking, creating the* collaborative enterprise. Woburn, MA: Butterworth-Heinemann.

Stanfill, C., & Waltz, D. (1986). Toward memory-based reasoning. *Communication of the ACM*, 29(12), 1213–1228.

Stewart, T. A. (1999). *Intellectual capital: The new wealth of organizations.* New York, NY: Bantam Dell Publishing Group.

Talbot, P. J. (2003). Semantic networks: A unified framework for multistrategy reasoning. *Technology Review Journal* (Spring/Summer), 59–75.

Turban, E., & Aronson, J. E. (1998). *Decision support systems and intelligent systems* (5th ed.). Upper Saddle River, NJ: Prentice Hall.

Vandergriff, L. J. (2006). *Unified approach to decision support for agile knowledge-based enterprises.* D.Sc. dissertation, George Washington University, Washington, DC.

Vandergriff, L. J. (2008). Welcome to the intelligence age: An examination of intelligence as a complex venture emergent behavior. *VINE: The Journal of Information and Knowledge Management Systems, 38*(4), 2008.

VonKrough, G., Roos, J., & Kleine, D. (1998). *Knowing in firms: Understanding, managing and measuring knowledge.* London: Sage Publications.

Wiig, K. M. (1994). *Knowledge management, The central management focus for intelligent-acting organizations.* Arlington, TX: Schema Press.

Chapter 9

The University's Integrated Knowledge Space in Knowledge Management

Natalia Tikhomirova, Vladimir Tikhomirov,
Yury Telnov and Valentina Maksimova

Abstract

Globalization of higher education implies the integrated efforts and endeavors of universities, consortia, education institutions, and associations within international educational networks, and the integration of science, education, and business to build technological parks, joint competency centers, and other forms of effective intercommunication and interactions. This fosters the ever increasing importance of knowledge management (KM), which provides the intensive and dynamic accumulation and implementation of intellectual capital to improve and assure world-class education quality. These integrated efforts also seek to advance ongoing scientific and educational content and to arrange conditions for academic mobility of students, researchers, and the teaching staff.

This chapter examines the implementation of an integrated knowledge space (IKS) as an effective method for KM in a global university network. The IKS integrates all parties of the educational space — the faculty, scholars, and business people — in a framework of distributed departments on the basis of information center of disciplines (ICD). ICD enables higher education institutions to accumulate and support online renewal of knowledge for teaching and learning and to enhance the potential for innovation. Integrating and interconnecting education, research, and business communities allows ICD to facilitate the development of human and relational capital.

In Search of Knowledge Management: Pursuing Primary Principles
Copyright © 2010 by Emerald Group Publishing Limited
All rights of reproduction in any form reserved
ISBN: 978-1-84950-673-1

9.1. Introduction

In the knowledge economy, higher education institutions need to efficiently manage their intellectual capital (IC) for proper identification, acquisition, creation, sharing, development, transfer, protection, and evaluation of knowledge. The universities are considered to be institutions that provide society with qualified professionals and specialists that produce and disseminate knowledge of high quality. At present, universities must address the challenges of globalization and adapt to agile environments by applying their IC to maintain and increase competitive advantages and to develop their innovative capacity. IC, within the university environment, works effectively when all its elements (human, structural, and relational) are integrated, interconnected and directed to the creative activity of the university.

9.2. The Role of Universities and Their IC in the Knowledge Economy

Challenges facing the digital age have a direct impact on the education system. The knowledge economy is fueled by the rampant development of information technology, transformation of the education system, and ongoing innovation processes (Building Knowledge Economies, 2007). Today, the knowledge economy is much more knowledge intensive (Spender & Marr, 2005; Tissen et al., 2000; Andriessen, 2004). Its sustainability and economic growth depends on the innovation and professionalism of employees. Knowledge drives the way in which products and services are produced and sold, and the nature of competitive advantage in global, saturated markets in which differentiation and innovation are crucial (Williams, 2008).

Universities are the institutions that "prepare young people for life in a world where new technologies of information and communication place a premium on creative and innovating thinking" (OECD, 2008b, p. 62). They face the challenge to focus on education in a digital world as opposed an industrial world.

Knowledge is a driver of today's economy and it is the heart of IC. It is recognized that there is not a consensus on the definition of IC (Viedma, Arenas, & Grau, 2007). There are various definitions of IC (Brooking, 1996; Stewart, 1997; Edvinsson & Malone, 1997; Andriessen, 2004) or "Intellectual Assets." These multiple definitions are the result of a widespread tendency to interchangeably use the terms "intangibles," "intellectual capital," and "intangible assets" (OECD, 2006; Bounfour, 2002) and the classification of IC into three categories: human, structural, and relational capital (OECD, 2006).

Higher education systems, policies, and institutions are being transformed by globalization. The growing impact of the global environment is inescapable. The role of higher education institutions as mediums is growing for a wide range of cross-border relationships and continuous global flows of people, information, knowledge, technologies, products, and capital (OECD, 2008b). On the one hand, internationalization of educational institutions and systems entails cross-border cooperation, and on the other hand, it makes competition more acute. Intensive international cooperation in tertiary education is expected to enhance the global competitiveness as a whole, to engender a pattern of common changes and interconnectivity between national higher education systems (Tertiary Education for the Knowledge Society, 2008). The current trends in higher education are characterized by trends of convergence and diversification that sharp competitiveness in the knowledge economy. Commission of the European Communities (2005), for instance, advocates increased diversity as a condition for excellence and greater access.

Effective solutions to move the higher education system in the direction of accommodating diversity and convergence as well as the transformations associated with the knowledge economy have yet to be established, though major institutional changes have already been taken (OECD, 2008b). The challenges related to effectively combining strategies for cooperation and competition require the designing of adequate models of the higher education system. These models need to balance global competitiveness, national priorities, and interests within a wide international context.

The dramatic changes in the global higher education landscape are closely connected through innovation. Innovation is considered to be one of the main engines of sustainable economic growth and social development.

Since education systems provide the necessary knowledge, skills, and competences for a knowledge-based society, they must be innovative (OECD, 2008a). The scope for innovation is enormous. Let us start with ICT, which is considered to be a core instrument for adapting the education system to the knowledge economy (Commission of the European Communities, Brussels, 2008).

ICT has the advantage to redesign curricula and programs to offer e-learning, to bring improvements to teaching methods and materials, to adequately change the content of courses, and to foster the growing internationalization of higher education as a whole.

Innovative transformation embraces pedagogical, technological, and organizational innovation. Pedagogical innovation implies the implementation of novel ways of education and training together with traditional approaches. Interactive forms of e-learning lead to a more reflective, deeper, and participating learning, learning-by-doing, problem-solving, and creativity that can enrich the competencies of learners.

Technological innovation presupposes the need for new models of production, distribution, and access to digital resources. Contemporary technology has the potential to provide access to open educational resources (OER). The advantages of OER lie in their "adaptable functionality, lower overall costs, vendor independence, and adherence to open standards, interoperability, and security" (OECD, Background Report Technology, Paris, 2008b, p. 37). In addition, new technology can help to train students in innovative and creative thinking with the use of well-designed and sophisticated computer games for learning.

Computer games make it possible to learn by working on simulations of complex, real-world problems that do not have standardized answers. They are multiplayer, alternative-reality, role-playing games, in which the students develop valuable ways of thinking by simulating the process of participating in a professional practicum (OECD, 2008b). These kinds of games make it possible to learn by doing and emphasize the value of tacit and abstract ways of thinking that facilitate the knowing of intellectual and professional settings in a guided way, to simulate academic and professional practices. Computer games can prepare the learners for the intellectual life in the digital era. The authors of the research *The Future of Higher Education: How technology will Shape Learning* state: "On-line gaming and simulation software are cited by 54% of higher education respondents and 59% of corporate respondents as an innovation likely to be adopted among universities over the next five years" (The Economist Intelligent Unit, 2008, p. 6).Organizational innovation involves introducing a new organizational method of work between teachers, students, and other participants of the educational process.

In Russia, much attention is paid to the modernization of the national education system. The model "Russian education–2020" is being developed and discussed. The idea to create such a model was forwarded in 2007 and aimed at designing a model to transform the education system and tailoring the foundation for the development of the system within forthcoming years.

As compared with the previous approaches, the model differs in determining the directions of the education system development. First of all, the transformation of the education system is to be carried out with the respect of the consumer's interests in educational services. The education sphere is to be shaped for any person to have the chance of developing and enhancing his/her educational potential within their whole life. The system should be constructed in such a way that an individual may have the opportunity to renew his/her knowledge and to permanently raise their qualifications. Second, the public institutes, rating agencies are being involved into the process of assessing the curricula, programs, and employment of graduates. Some regional structural units are very active in selecting innovative schools and best teachers within the framework of the national project "Education." The feedback between the society and the educational system is being maintained.

The structure of the education model reflects the fundamental direction. The education system is to

- contribute to national and regional economic and social development,
- provide the adequate social relations and enhance an equal access of learners to education,
- facilitate greater responsiveness to learner and labor market needs,
- accommodate the growing diversity of occupational qualifications, and
- promote international competitiveness.

The other prominent development is closely associated with the objective of the education system to promote the innovative development of economy. Educational institutions of different levels are to shape various competences of the learners to solve complex problems, develop creative abilities, and take a proper orientation in an increasingly knowledge-driven global society.

The third direction of the education system is lifelong learning. The education system is a good opportunity to the people to continue learning throughout their lives.

The fourth direction is to facilitate the feedback between the social and educational institutes and external assessment of the education systems outcomes. Professional communities, social nongovernmental bodies, and agencies might have the opportunity to evaluate the results of education institutions activities and to conduct independent accreditation for certifying credibility of education institutions.

9.3. The Integrated Knowledge Space as the Foundation for Enhancing the Effectiveness of the University's Innovative Activity

The globalization of education implies the joint endeavors of universities within the framework of international educational networks, consortiums, and higher education associations and the integration of science, education, and business via the development of technology and knowledge parks, collaborative competence centers, and other forms of effective interaction. These diverse forms of collaboration foster the knowledge management (KM) that proposes to dynamically and intensively accrue and use IC to enhance education and research quality, to maintain the evolving content, and to provide the conditions for academic mobility of learners, scholars, and faculty. Universities play an important role in opening knowledge parks. In compliance with the knowledge parks conception, the parks are created on the basis of universities (Figure 9.1) and they facilitate the following processes:

- Collaborative research by universities and research institutions according to business orders
- Shaping of entrepreneurial environment for student's learning
- Searching and generating new knowledge with its reflection in a real-time format
- Technology transfer from universities to organizations
- Transfer of knowledge to small, medium, and corporative business

The organizational basis for knowledge parks is competence centers, research laboratories, and centers for technology transfer. The virtual environment for collaborative activities of participants in the scientific and educational process and the competence approach to learning necessitates the formation and wide use of the integrated knowledge space (IKS). The IKS incorporates the knowledge of scientific schools generated in grants, dissertations, and innovative projects within the competence centers and laboratories. As well, it embraces educational and methodological materials for educational courses. IKS provides the integration, accumulation, and support of the content of adjacent, contiguous disciplines within the framework of the KM system. It facilitates the access to research and educational materials. This enables

- the union of various sources of information on different disciplines, specialties, and educational process participants (teachers, scholars, representatives of business, postgraduate students, and students) within the integrated system;

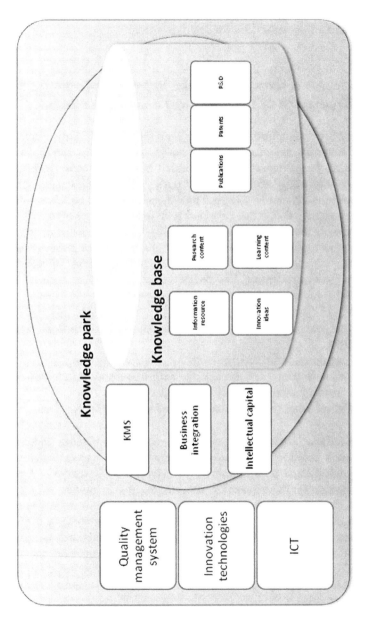

Figure 9.1: Components of a knowledge park.

- a continuous development of the system due to the renewal of academic theoretical knowledge and new experience obtained by the faculty and students in the course of the educational process;
- access of relevant information to each participant of the scientific educational process in harmony with his/her knowledge, needs, and preferences; and
- a distributed access of the participants to the content in a virtual environment.

The constituent unit of the IKS is the information center of disciplines (ICD). As a component of IKS, the purpose of this center is to be an information resource for making the interconnections of faculty, designers of learning and methodological content within a framework of separate disciplines. ICD facilitates a continuous process of collaborative, joint professional designing, developing, and usage of educational materials for all disciplines embedded in the curricula by interested participants. It includes and maintains a wide set of learning and methodological materials, integrated references to the research publications of scholars, teachers, postgraduate students and students, as well as to open educational recourses.

ICD goals are as follows:

- Creation and accumulation of research, learning and methodological materials for all disciplines
- Development of educational and methodological content at an adequate professional level
- Provision of ongoing work to update the materials and content
- Joint collaborative work of the distributed chairs of the university to develop the discipline and share knowledge

ICD can be considered as a center for integrating experience and IC of teachers, assistants, and professors within the framework of the IKS.

The objectives of ICD are summarized as follows:

- To create and update the materials in ICD by involving the teachers of the distributed chairs or the teachers from the educational consortium
- To use the R&D findings in developing the content
- To attract the organizations and business people as the developers of the content
- To use the findings of the postgraduate students' research in developing the content
- To organize educational and research work among the students
- To organize special service units

The ICD helps the teachers to store and accumulate the learning and methodological materials, to share ideas and information with colleagues, to cooperate with each other by using technological instruments (e.g., Web 2.0).

In comparison to traditional e-learning (Rosenberg, 2001), the ICD and the IKS can be referred to as a new generation of the systems of innovative learning (Figure 9.2).

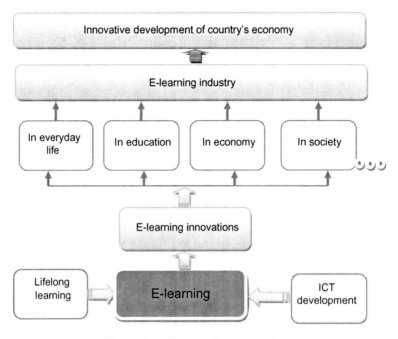

Figure 9.2: Innovative e-learning.

Innovative e-learning within the framework of the ICD has the following specific features:

- Learning process is being integrated into the organizational and social processes of knowledge transformation within the framework of the networking interconnection of educational, scientific, and business entities.
- New knowledge is being generated within the real-time regime that allows the participants to switch from periodically updating content to updating content when it is required.
- Several professional communities, communities of practice and partnerships are being created — "student–tutor," "student–student," "tutor–tutor," "department–enterprise," and "department–scientific organization."
- The quality of learning based on research and innovations becomes a leading factor in learning development.
- The scientific-methodological development of each discipline allows tutors to speed up their scientific research.
- Some new technological, pedagogical, and organizational innovations are being created during the scientific and educational process.

The integration of the ICD within the framework of the IKS changes the learning process in a way of self-learning. It allows the students to comprehend the theoretical materials, to perform practical and laboratory tasks, to properly describe common subject fields and particular situations in completing their terminal-, lab-, and term papers, projects, and diplomas. The internship program's role is also being transformed for the students to gather general information for the whole set of learning courses.

9.4. Technological Aspects in Shaping the IKS

The traditional and conventional process of creating the learning courses is implemented in accordance with the set of qualifying characteristics of specialties. The set of learning courses (disciplines), relevant to the qualifying characteristics of specialties, forms the general curriculum of a specialty. The consequent development of learning programs (syllabuses) by some departments leads to overlaps in some items; such overlaps are hard to be determined due to the specific terminology used in certain disciplines. At the level of the general curriculum, it is difficult to fully unify the whole volume of terminology used in particular disciplines. As a result, we are getting some rigid methodological and educational complexes that are hard to be adapted to a particular education institution or to individual's capabilities. To cope with such a problem and to enhance the quality of the educational process, it is viewed as necessary to integrate ICD at a department's level as well as at an interdepartmental level. This can be performed by coordinating the parallel-type work on the basis of a KM methodology, which rests on the object-oriented approach with ontological description of the conceptual model of knowledge used (Telnov, 2004).

In the object-oriented presentation of knowledge, every learning object is a complete semantic piece of knowledge of self-importance (Strijker, 2004). Separate objects could be configured into certain learning sequences in respect with regional and industrial needs of learning. As a result, there is a shift from small rigid courses to an array of reusable learning objects available for retrieval and involvement into certain learning sequence. Object-oriented methodology of learning courses has found its development in the activities of IMS Global Learning Consortium, which develops the system of basic standards in this field.

The development of objects could be done by different participants in various environments. All knowledge objects are placed into special banks — repositories, whereas at ICD only object references are being kept. Accordingly, results of scientific researches, innovative projects, and OER are presented through object type and getting linked with ICD via reference mechanism.

The integration of knowledge in the unified space, the decomposition of learning courses, and their components (learning objects) require a unified conceptual description of knowledge with the help of ontology (Gruber, 1993; Mizoguchi & Bourdeau, 2000). In order to organize the IKS, it is necessary to have

- subject ontology, reflecting subject field regardless of whom and how it's been taught;
- learning ontology that formalizes the structure of learning process with respect of competences of particular specialties and forms of study;
- learning objects' repository;

- objects of academic research and projects findings and outcomes; and
- objects of OER

The IKS is a KM system with a three-level architecture which at the outer level presents an array of the ICD, at the conceptual level — an ontology system, and at the storage level — an object-oriented repository of various knowledge sources (Figure 9.3).

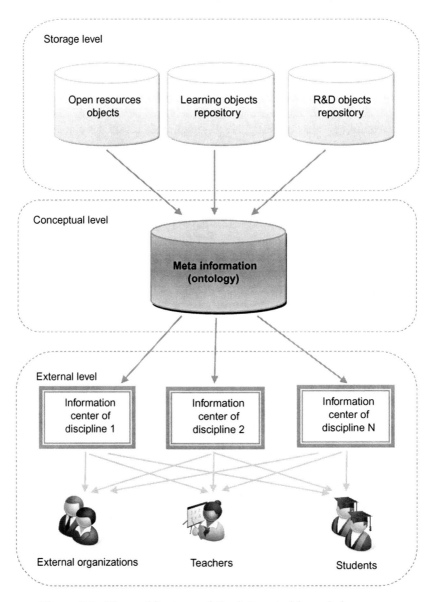

Figure 9.3: The architecture of the integrated knowledge space.

Therefore, the IKS seeks to increase the cooperation of tutors of the distributed departments and organizations interested in developing and presenting courses by organizing an exchange of educational, methodological and research materials, to be used in elaborating and designing adequate electronic courses. Also, the IKS can provide effective pedagogical scenarios for teaching in electronic environments.

The IKS enhances the quality of innovative activity of the university, thus enabling its capability to improve its IC (Figure 9.4).

The valuation of learning quality using the IKS is performed as a result of expertise of the IKS usage. This expertise takes into account the quality of learning resources used, the quality of organization of major learning processes, as well as the quality of organizational environment and participants' involvement in educational process. These metrics could be measured automatically by e-Metrics that include, for instance,

- amount of hits to the elements of the ICD,
- the quantity and level of updated elements in the ICD,
- busy time of information resources in learning process,
- knowledge search relevance, and
- occupancy of centers of disciplines' elements.

The quality of student's studying results associated with the IKS can be estimated by the demand on graduates in labor markets and by adequate usage of their received competences at the jobs. The values of these metrics are obtained through excellence methodology by polling all involved parties: employers, teachers, administration, and students.

The analysis of the effective usage of the IKS in the scientific and educational activity of a university shows the reduction of costs due to joint, collaborative endeavors of teachers of the distributed departments that diminishes overlapping

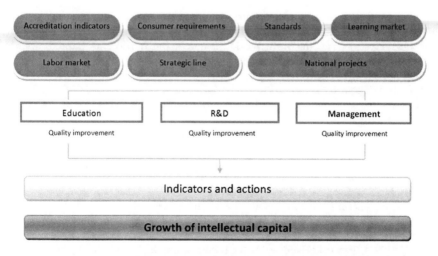

Figure 9.4: Quality of university's innovative activity.

materials, and leverages the relevance in matching educational objects to the specific features of individual learners. This approach seeks to increase the number of teachers, researchers and students in developing and updating the modern educational content.

9.5.   Conclusion

The improvement of the quality of educational content based on the IKS allows higher education institutions to achieve the following goals in the development of their IC:

- Alignment of Russian and international learning standards to facilitate academic mobility in online environment
- Improved professional competences on the basis of synergetic integration of educational, research and innovative process
- Updated learning and methodological content in a real-time regime to meet the requirements of today's development of science and practice
- A flexible educational process with the respect of concrete needs and problems to be solved
- The ability to enhance and leverage the effectiveness of scientific research and its innovation

The Moscow State University of Economics, Statistics, and Informatics is shaping the IKS and ICD within the framework described in this chapter.

References

Andriessen, D. (2004). *Making sense of intellectual capital.* Amsterdam: Elsevier.

Bounfour, A. (2002). *How to measure Intellectual Capital's dynamic value: The IC-dVAL approach.* Presented at the fifth World Congress on Intellectual Capital, McMaster University, Hamilton, Ontario, Canada.

Brooking, A. (1996). *Intellectual capital: Core asset for the third millennium.* London: International Thomson Business Press.

Building Knowledge Economies. (2007). *Advanced strategies for development.* Washington, DC: The World Bank.

Commission of the European Communities. (2005). *Integrated guidelines for growth and jobs (2005–2008),* COM (2005), Brussels, April.

Commission of the European Communities. (2008). *The use of ICT to support innovation and lifelong learning for all.* Brussels: Commission of the European Communities.

Edvinsson, L., & Malone, M. S. (1997). *Intellectual capital: Realizing your company's true value by finding it's hidden brainpower.* New York: HarperBusiness.

EIU. (2008). *The future of higher education: How technology will shape learning.* Paris: The Economist Intelligence Unit.

Gruber, T. (1993). Toward principles for the design of ontologies used for knowledge sharing. *International Journal of Human and Computer Studies, 43*(5 and 6), 907–928.

Mizoguchi, R., & Bourdeau, J. (2000). Using ontological engineering to overcome common AI-ED problems. *International Journal of Artificial Intelligence in Education* (11), 78–100.

OECD. (2006). Intellectual Assets and Value Creation. Paris.

OECD. (2008a). Innovation Strategy for Education and Training (2008). Paris: OECD, Centre for Educational Research and Innovation.

OECD/France International Conference. (2008b). *Higher education to 2030: What futures for quality access in the era of globalisation?* OECD, Paris.

Rosenberg, M. (2001). E-learning. Strategies for delivering knowledge in the digital age. In: *The Knowledge Management Magazine Series.* New York: McGraw-Hill.

Spender, J., & Marr, B. (2005). A knowledge-based perspective on intellectual capital. In: B. Marr (Ed.), *Perspectives on intellectual capital.* Oxford: Elsevier.

Stewart, T. A. (1997). *Intellectual capital: The new wealth of organizations.* New York: Doubleday.

Strijker, A. (2004). *Reuse of learning objects in context human and technical aspects.* Thesis, University of Twente, Enschede.

Telnov, Y. (2004). *The business process reengineering: Component methodology.* Moscow: Finance and Statistics.

Tertiary Education for the Knowledge Society (2008). OECD, Paris.

Tissen, R., Adriessen, D., & Lekanne Deprez, F. (2000). *The knowledge dividend: Creating high-performance companies through value-based knowledge management.* London, UK: Financial Times Prentice Hall.

Viedma, J. M., Arenas, T., & Grau, C. (2007). Diagnosing a region's intellectual capital to generate sustainable development strategies: A new approach. In: *Proceedings of the 8th European Conference on Knowledge Management*, Vol. 1, Barcelona, Spain, September 6–7.

Williams, R. (2008). The epistemology of knowledge and the knowledge process cycle: Beyond the "Objectivist" vs "Interpretivist". *Journal of Knowledge Management, 12*(4), 72–85.

SECTION IV

TECHNOLOGY APPLICATIONS

The competitive advantage is not the technology, but how the technology is applied. Dr. Charles Bixler (2000)

The KM technology pillar focuses on supporting business success through enabling decision support, data warehousing, process modeling, management tools, and overall communications (Baldanza & Stankosky, 1999). Calabrese (2000) validated this pillar and further defined subelements as the various types of KM-related technologies involved with data warehousing, database management, multimedia repositories, groupware, decision support systems, expert systems, corporate intranets, speech understanding, businesses modeling systems, intelligent agents, neural networks, etc. Today, efforts focus on archiving and retrieving structured data, information, and knowledge. Unfortunately, applications have often focused on what can be done and not what should be done. Archiving every piece of junk email is possible, but not of value. However, capturing and sharing knowledge has proved harder (Malhotra, 2000). The following chapters focus on technology-related applications.

References

Baldanza, C., & Stankosky, M. A. (1999). Knowledge management: An evolutionary architecture toward enterprise engineering. Paper read at International Council on Systems Engineering (INCOSE), Mid-Atlantic Regional Conference, 15 September.

Bixler, C. H. (2000). *Creating a dynamic knowledge management maturity continuum for increased enterprise performance and innovation.* D.Sc. dissertation, George Washington University, Washington, DC.

Calabrese, F. A. (2000). *A suggested framework of key elements defining effective enterprise knowledge management programs.* D.Sc. dissertation, George Washington University, Washington, DC.

Malhotra, Y. (2000). From information management to knowledge management: Beyond the "hi-tech hidebound" systems. In: K. Srikantaiah & M. E. D. Koenig (Eds), *Knowledge management for information professional* (pp. 37–61). Medford, NJ: Information Today Inc.

Chapter 10

Market Information Knowledge (MIK), a Systemic Model for Customer Knowledge Management, Which Changes the Enterprise Structure

Philippe van Berten

Abstract

In an environment which continues to grow in complexity, information systems are being increasingly relied on to provide organizations with appropriate knowledge management (KM) tools. Using the complexity paradigm as an epistemological framework, a systemic approach is undertaken to build a valorization model of the information flows circulating between the information system, the organization and their environment. Applied to the retail industry, this model seeks to transform information drawn from customer loyalty programs into customer knowledge.

10.1. Introduction

As business economics reaches an industrial level of development, the competitive market growth generates new management tools especially designed and adapted to its expansion. Marketing, a field introduced in the 1950s, was designed to facilitate mass diffusion to satisfy customer need. Since the end of the late twentieth century, major innovations such as communication and information technology (IT), globalization, and service economy introduce new patterns for the "old" marketing roots.

In Search of Knowledge Management: Pursuing Primary Principles
Copyright © 2010 by Emerald Group Publishing Limited
All rights of reproduction in any form reserved
ISBN: 978-1-84950-673-1

Recent tools create new knowledge management (KM) activities, for example, the mining of customers database allows managing the customer relationship (CRM), inducing competitive advantage out of the hosting of a data warehouse.

Kale (2004) observed that CRM project failure came from the mismanagement of many steps along the process:

- Taking the CRM only as a technology
- Having a no or partial customer-oriented sight (Humby & Hunt, 2003, p. 16)
- Neglecting customer lifetime value
- Poor involvement of executives and employees
- No change in the business process
- Badly converting data to customer knowledge

If the above listed pitfalls are true, it is possible to get a model which analyzes the success factors of the CRM (Reinartz, Thomas, & Kumar, 2005).

Customer knowledge appears to come from the interplay between the company stakeholders, the market, and the information system (IS). These many subsets that interact between each other must be integrated. It takes the form of an independent system, which needs to be understood and structured. The model hereafter answers this issue and can root the customer knowledge management (CKM) as a marketing innovation.

In order to better understand and refine the market information knowledge (MIK) model, it has been implemented in one of the marketing favorite sectors: the large retail sector.

This sector watches any shift of the society attentively. This makes the retail and particularly the large distributors an outstanding business for the second half of the past century. They anticipate the consumerist trends or adapt to the evolution of our societies. The constant growth of the retail part in the household expanse, a natural expansion of the demography, and an innovative know-how made possible its huge sales progression.

At the turn of the new century, the previously successful mass market model lost its efficiency. The market shares got sluggish or impaired, the margins went down as well as the stock global value of the sector.

The evolution of the perception and of the representation among individuals now impacts buying. Within this shifting environment, the retailer must permanently innovate in order to maintain image and market shares. Therefore, tremendous efforts occur, trying to limit the market share erosion.

Among the specific programs developed to this end, the loyalty card provides a new business relationship. Program managers face new opportunities and constraints. The IS compiles data on millions of customers who use their customized cards. Whether gathered on a voluntary basis, with a mandatory card application, or in a more passive manner at the checkout, such data can provide a deeper insight on individual's behavior and the relationship between the customer and her/his usual distributor. Tesco, in the UK, designed and now manage an IS based on data coming from the loyalty card processing and oriented toward a better knowledge of its customer.

The project case study has checked-out the properties of the theoretical model shown below and determined its applicative limits by answering the question: What can the IS bring to the CKM as part of a marketing process?

10.2. The Marketing Scheme Evolution

In an article dating back to the mid-1990s, Grönroos (1994) developed the idea that the marketing was about to change its own paradigm and possibly combine many different models. He asked if the development of the exchanges, parallel to the proliferation of relationship between the stakeholders would bring a new style of marketing, oriented toward the systems, the business actors, and their environment.

It appears in the research models that some variables stressing the interrelation between customer, seller, and public institutions are key to success. At the same time, the marketing mix tools are becoming less and less adapted to a fast changing environment. In various sectors (e.g., industry, services, distribution, marketing) techniques traditionally used for anonymous diffusion with an unknown consumer are progressively abandoned. To improve performance, marketing added to its existing tools the CRM. This results in a better identified customer.

Traditionally, the design of a marketing plan relies on a "marketing mix" based on the "4P"s (McCarthy, 1960) rule. The *product* is widely described and commercially positioned by its *price* (the pricing policy of the producer), its *place* (inclusive of the distribution channel and merchandising policy), and its *promotion*, dealing with sales strategy and advertising.

Still keeping the "4P" scheme as a universal mix, the construction and the management of the customer relationship becomes part of the marketing plan, making the center of gravity of the marketing shift from the product to the customer. The marketing of this relationship (which covers not only the final customer but the various stakeholders) fulfill new expectations beyond traditional marketing.

10.3. Information System and Customer Relationship Management

Every company gathers large amount of data out of the production activity. Such data (e.g., technical data, management data, marketing data, stock data) are continuously increasing by a twofold average every 20 months. These data are, like information assets, of great value for the business regarding the needs of the production department. However, it is estimated that only 10% is used afterward by other departments of the same company. Other needs of the company could be fulfilled by the data, but it is difficult to reuse data previously structured for separate primary goals than capitalizing and reusing. However, great endeavor is currently made in order to judiciously data mine this asset, created out of the production department computerized information. This is "computer-based decision making," so called because it is about to produce new data to help the decision-making after mining the existing data (Jambu, 1999). This concept covers new areas in the IS field, such as data mining, knowledge discovery from data (KDD), text mining, and data warehouse. Various tools are now widely used by the marketing department (Berry & Linoff, 2004; Tufféry, 2002).

The data warehouse is an IS, a tool set for identifying and targeting the prospects and the customers, allowing the optimization of basic marketing points:

- When is the customer willing to buy the products and the services?
- What triggers an interest for the product and helps to understand the customer's needs?
- How do the customer and the retailer interact?
- When and how does a customer switch to another brand?
- Who are the most profitable customers and how to identify them?
- Who are the most productive agents (or sale units) and their success criteria?

The data warehouse allows customer identification and targeting. This, combined with customer relationship, provides a real customer knowledge. In terms of marketing, bringing the right product to the right people on time can be dramatically improved thanks to the combination of CRM and data warehouse management. In a very competitive market, those tools can be of impressive corporate advantage. An instance of this tool combination has been given in 2000 by the Western and Southern Life Insurance Company. The shift from a mass marketing model (actually a nonindividualized direct marketing campaign) to a model of customer identification and targeting gave an easy to measure return, because marketing actions were managed by the same tool. The claimed return on investment of this project reached 600% (Kreyenhagen, Robbins, Crable, & Frolick, 2004).

A valuation of the retailer–customer relationship becomes more and more important. The primary goal is to make the customer loyal to the brand. It is widely admitted that such a set of loyal customers is part of the company assets. When millions of customers are involved, the value is real although figures are difficult to predict and track as a business asset.

CRM comes from a paradigm which no longer ignores the customer as an individual, compared to the indistinct mass market. This new model considers the customer as a real and differentiated entity, bearing wealth by him/herself. This is a significant evolution of the representation, which the retail sector has of the market and of itself. It is about to go from an activity adding to the products portfolio very little value (or no value at all), to the creation of a portfolio made of loyal customers with high value. This loyalty can be materialized by sharing an information media between the distributor and the customer. This information media can be a loyalty card (from a simple barcode label to a more sophisticated radio frequency identification [RFID]), a personal identification number (PIN), or a login combined to a password for online access.

Improving the customer knowledge, as well as increasing the number of customers and their profitability, requires also knowing their explicit and implicit needs. The assembled variables, coming from a household or from an individual, may pull the distributor out of the mass market paradigm and lead it to a new business model. This business model only works if the data gathered on the customer are real, accurate, and wisely used.

Customer relationship requires that the basic knowledge coming from the customer-guided choice of efficient variables. This manipulation will provide knowledge on each customer. It is fundamental to properly manage the data on this customer. Figure 10.1 (Tufféry, 2002) illustrates this concept.

The separation between operational and analytical CRM offers a multistage protocol but the actors of the process and the information media is not shown on this model. However, the place of the now well accessible IS becomes paramount and must be represented. Moreover, the stages of the model above set an order, which compartmentalizes this protocol and neglects the retroaction flows. The analysis of the information on the customers must influence the data collection. The campaigns management produces knowledge to be analyzed and used to improve the next cycle.

This type of model showing CRM techniques and data mining process combined to marketing is necessary but not sufficient. Many factors such as information flow, the origin of this information itself, and its conversion to knowledge (the customer knowledge is only a part of it), the location of the IS, all those elements must mingle within a systemic model further described in Figure 10.8.

10.4. From Customer Relationship to Customer Knowledge

The organizations knowing how to gain knowledge take from it a competitive advantage (Tzokas & Saren, 2004). These authors wonder how to retrieve new knowledge from the management of an existing customer relationship. Thus, they offer on Figure 10.2 a scheme of the process of the CRM keeping in mind that it must lead to innovation.

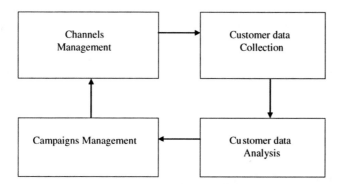

Figure 10.1: Customers relationship management. Based on Tufféry (2002).

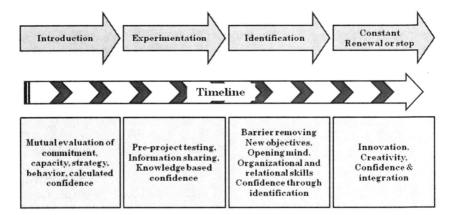

Figure 10.2: Customer relationship/customer knowledge life circle. Based on Tzokas and Saren (2004, p. 164).

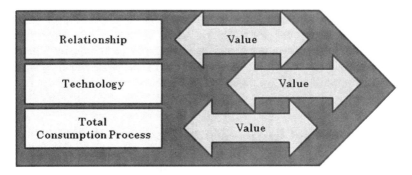

Figure 10.3: Customer value chain. Based on Tzokas and Saren (2004, p. 164).

Knowledge appears on this model, at the level of new projects *experimentation, as a confidence foundational element*. Confidence and knowledge are linked at this stage when the actors share common activities and exchange information.

However, knowledge clears of the model describing the process of the relational management, as if the thus existing exchange flows could not materialize, and therefore not feed the knowledge capital.

Trying afterwards to synthesis this previous model with the value chain in marketing practice (Porter, 1985), Tzokas and Saren (2004) suggest a model shown in Figure 10.3 which links the added value to:

- Information exchange flow (relationship)
- Operational tools (technology) of the CRM which, they say, allow an exchange of tacit knowledge between a company and its customers
- The entire consumption process (which presence there is not explained).

One step at a time, these models bring elements related to information flows, to the IS and to the knowledge. Intuition must be put at stake in order to understand the importance of those successive contributions in a systemic approach.

By the metaphor of the "knowledge house of the relational marketing" (Figure 10.4), Tzokas and Saren (2004) try to locate the knowledge off the customer relationship. By separating knowledge itself from the KM, this model put the organization and the stakeholders at the same level. The interactions and the flows on both sides of the knowledge are clearly represented.

This model of a system of knowledge in the relational marketing field is interesting in many ways.

First, at the level of the subsystem representation where the actors (firm, stakeholders) are next to the concepts (confidence, commitment, knowledge, and KM) and the flows (interaction, dialog, relationship). The tripod "actors, concepts, flows" insists on a fundamental element in systemic, which is the "flow," representing exchanges on various shapes and media bases.

Next is the analogy between this model and a house, which symbolizes protection and shelter, but remains a wall up against the environment by closing, dividing, isolating, and partitioning the space. It is not yet a perfect choice to represent the concept of opening, tautology of the systemic.

The complex systems do permanently exchange with their environment, making their milieu open. The representation and diagram with no openings do not suit the paradigm of complexity. Despite a good intuition at the beginning, this kind of Cartesian paradigm, which put walls and floors for clustering purpose, adds a strong segmentation to the knowledge by ignoring its environment.

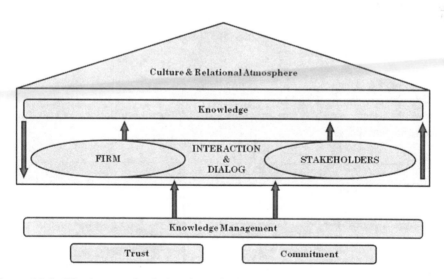

Figure 10.4: The house of relational marketing. Based on Christopher, Payne, and Ballantyne (1991).

10.5. Basic Principles of Systemic

10.5.1. The Missing Part

On the models above, shown in the academic literature, the "environment" component is generally missing in the representations as well as in the CRM (Figure 10.1) at relational level (Figure 10.2).

However, recent research insists on this component and on the transformation of the informational flows which accompany it. There are four flows or interactions (Emery & Trist, 1965; Wilkinson & Young, 2005), represented in Figure 10.5. The system is more designed by its relationships rather than by its content, especially when it is located in a hyper turbulent or restlessness environment.

The result of the company/environment interaction is unforeseeable and difficult to allot to a particular action. It is not any more the sole company which serves as a reference frame to measure the induced movements of market but the network of dependences and relationships to which it belongs.

These networks push the companies to continuously change and thus create value. A complex system's potential capacity of adaptation and response is much better suited for an agitated (i.e., chaotic or on the edge of chaos) environment. In this paradigm, a centralized management is not recommended to create value.

Exchanging, sharing, adaptation push the organizations toward a participative strategy, which creates dynamics and makes possible the network to self-organize and move forward.

10.5.2. The Essential of Systemic

In Figure 10.5, the letter "L" represents the "links" or interactions of various types. There are four types of links:

- Intrasystemic (L11)
- Inside the environment (L22)
- From the system toward the environment (L12 = interaction or adapted action plan and reactivity)

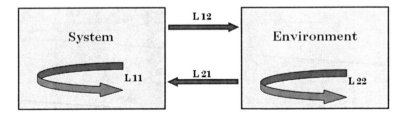

Figure 10.5: Interaction between a system and its surroundings. Based on Emery (1969).

- From the environment toward the system (L21 = selection or environmental changes process)

This representation (Emery, 1969) is a particularly interesting meta model, initialization of a true systemic representation where the system, the flows and the environment appear all together.

By adding to the model in Figure 10.5, a representation of knowledge and a representation of the base used by the information flow, a systemic modeling becomes applicable to many fields of management sciences.

The interaction (L21) is typically evolutionary in nature. It represents economical, social, and technical knowledge coming from the market. It includes marketing and customer relationship as well. Any KM system should consider these points by setting strong links between them and the heart of the company's essential knowledge.

These processes are:

- Inside the organization such as knowledge capitalizing and sharing, creativity, and learning.
- Outside the organization such as business intelligence, surveys, benchmarking, customers, and suppliers relationship.

10.6. Modeling with Systemic

The construction of the MIK model will be discussed in three steps: an initial "topological" version, a first version with the appearance of the concept of the "patron system," and finally the MIK model itself.

10.6.1. The Topology as a First Step

A first vision, presented in Figure 10.6 has an a priori intuitive and natural perspective. It is a topological representation where the customer is located within the market.

The organization's marketing has, thanks to surveys or to a proprietary IS, access to the data on the customer, the market, and other environmental parameters/metrics. This data helps the marketer to build up an adapted marketing plan.

This model, which combines classic and natural, introduces some issues. One of the paradoxes of the "open system" posed by complexity is "Should the group of the customers, being already Patrons, be represented inside the market?" It is difficult to exploit various resources from patrons' database as well as from contractor made market surveys or proprietary market surveys. The patrons, the customers, and the prospects are not clearly identified. Setting apart the patrons (i.e., segregated from the market) avoids the confusion between the groups. This shows a new path for

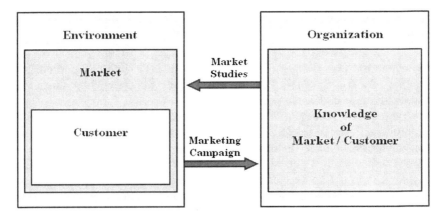

Figure 10.6: Topological modeling of the relationship between an organization and its market.

research. It becomes then possible to represent the knowledge exchange between the existing customers and the remainder of the market. In other words, the loyal customers (i.e., the patrons) in which meaningful variables have been gathered are no more, from a systemic point of view, within the market. They represent a subsystem on their own.

Pushing this reasoning to the limit, it could be said that:

> If all the customers of the market become loyal patrons, belonging to the proprietary data base, the market would be reduced to this group.

> Then, the company would get a market share of 100% of the customers. This monopoly could be reached when the loyalty rate hits 100% as well.

> The management capacity of the IS allows such loyalty programs to be done in order to primarily maintain the company's market share.

In order to get a representation of the exchange between the customers and the market, it is necessary to upgrade the first model (Figure 10.6) toward a more systemic design, where subsystems are not only exchanging through inclusion relationship. This design must have more shapes (loyalty program, prospects evaluation system, occasional customer identification, global market analysis, etc.) and more exchange flows. This can be managed as innovative marketing, which adds strong value to the company and to the customer in a win/win interaction.

10.7. Locating the Patrons Out of the Market

In the large retail, the concept of customer database is quite new. Its development was made possible thanks to powerful and inexpensive hardware material, animated (from the Latin *anima*, meaning the soul) by software managing input variables gathered from loyalty programs or proprietary credit card program.

The IS technology brings new practice and models. By doing an analogy with the four "Ps (i.e., price, promotion, product, and place) of the marketing mix described in (McCarthy, 1960; Borden, 1964), it is possible to describe here the three "Ps.

- The panelist is part of the survey sample of a market study. She/he can be shopping the brand or not, hold a loyalty card or not.
- The prospect is potential customer who never shops the brand.
- The patrons is shown in Figure 10.7, hold the loyalty card and uses it regularly

The loyalty card program is a logical follow-on from grocery "green stamps" loyalty merchants of the 1930s. This program rewards the steady customer and is now part of the usual offer of the retailer. These loyal customers could be treated by the marketing department as a special set of people, segregated from the remainder of the market.

The issue, from the marketer point of view, is not to bring a product to a mass market through the retail any more. It is about to know-how knowledge of patron's variables can be used to sell more, more often and to stimulate every single patron's demand in order to add value on the value chain. From that, it is possible to refine the topological model in Figure 10.6. Several systems there include customers. They segregate the patrons and the other two "Ps listed above as well as many different types of knowledge on the market. Some of them are refined knowledge on the patrons; some others are more "classical" as depicted in Figure 10.7.

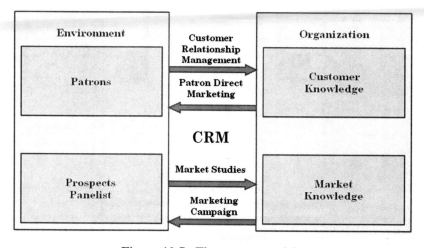

Figure 10.7: The patron model.

A stronger patron knowledge becomes a competitive advantage which no company can ignore any more. This customer-knowledge model brings a new perspective. The retailer can use powerful descriptive algorithms to improve this knowledge. Because the patron wishes to be treated well and get good bargains, they are ready to closely co-operate with the retailer in a win–win relationship. Therefore, the patron is willing to voluntarily communicate personal information to the IS on the condition they receive interesting offers in return. The IS becomes a confidence-based activated tool. The patrons express their personal information, for instance the detail of the contents of their market basket (e.g., purchase history). They use the information coming from the IS on various media such as emails, chat rooms, or personalized direct mailing. Information circulates directly between the patron system and the IS, but this direct flow does not exist with the other two "Ps.

Many other paths exist though for the brands to gather information on their customers. Such knowledge may come from customer relationship management (CRM) programs. The customer department officer, at the time of a call, can access in real time the customer history, which sorts all the exchanges already made (date and nature of all the purchases, previous requests, claims). This information is being processed afterwards, analyzed, and shared within the organization. This process makes new knowledge and therefore adds value to the company.

The IS operational importance is stressed by the management of the customer relationship. Being absent of the patrons model in Figure 10.7, the IS is thus inserted into a new model, thanks to a systemic modeling process (Figure 10.8).

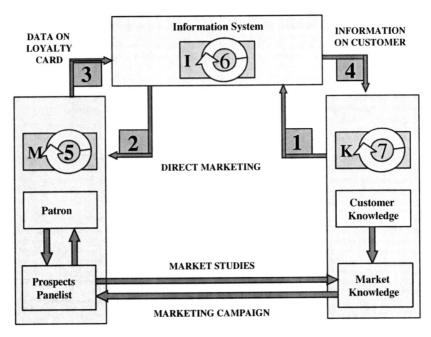

Figure 10.8: The market information knowledge (MIK) model.

10.8. Model and Environment

The MIK model, as any model using systemic, is a structuring tool of the management thinking, which should help decision-making and action. This obeys an epistemological approach made of multiple journeys between the two domains: empirical as well as conceptual.

The central position occupied by an intermediary who is mandatory in the process, e.g. the IS, stimulates reasoning and abstraction. The main difficulty for the searcher is about the choice and the design of the tools which make an interface between the two sides of the IS. This can be summarized with several questions:

- Which variables to choose?
- How to collect and combine them?
- How to display and organize them?
- How and to whom an access to the variables can be granted?

Another balance exists within the MIK model. The bottom of the model represents the marketing grassroots (i.e., the market studies and the mass marketing campaigns). The top of the model in Figure 10.8 shows the high speed reactivity capacity of direct marketing.

The IS makes possible to launch a targeted campaign by emails, which can be measured by the immediate online orders or store visits.

The difference between the top and the bottom of the model highlights the many actors of the marketing, the most reactive at the top and the middle and long-term planners at the bottom. They share and exchange information flows, represented by the vertical arrows on the right hand side the model.

The know-how demanded by this type of project described in MIK is new in the "brick and mortar" retail sector. A new professional position such as patron manager is likely to appear. This kind of job will be durable if it proves profitable result, which is easy to trace since the accurate measure of the patron's answer to direct and personalized campaign is computerized by the IS. Another task to be managed by the patron manager is to transfer his/her knowledge to others, through the IS.

Talking about systemic means that these systems are open and evolving over time. Some freedom is given by the organization to these departments let them self-organize and fix the place and importance of the IS. The now accurately measured result captured and shared by the IS will disrupt many of the company existing departments and processes.

The technology pillar, which is the origin of this evolution, is the swivel as well as the major reason of the failure of a lot of CRM projects. When it outlines mostly the technology (Kale, 2004), the belief in this computer-based panacea puts the entire marketing project at risk. It removes the focus away from the original purpose, which is to gain actionable knowledge on the customer (Reinartz, Kraft, & Hoyer, 2004).

Thinking that it is possible to master the technology first and then address the desired result and organizational profit causes many issues. It is important to focus on the company cornerstone and management needs realism as well as great knowledge on how the business domains behave. The IS must accommodate a methodology that matches the organization's needs. Thus, a proactive attitude is mandatory meaning that a list of specifications related to the project must be well designed. Also, the IS must facilitate the organization's intellectual capital support to perform the needed inductive knowledge development since the IS cannot have an automated nor independent algorithms producing inductive knowledge.

10.9. Model Structure

10.9.1. The Market

Systemics values the flows exchanged between the systems. An abstractive and intuitive hypothesis leads to represent the market separated from the organization (the retailer), making the graphical aspect of the flows easier. In math language setting a counterproposition, the company would locate inside the market. Although the common representation of the market in economy is a global entity, having the actors located inside it, this is topology, not systemics which objectives the relationship representation.

10.9.1.1. Patrons and nonpatrons All the retail brands have nowadays their own loyalty program. Putting the patron set off the market allows using math tools to build up a template, which brings new theoretical perspectives. An isomorphism exists between the patron/market and the customer knowledge/market both visible in Figure 10.8. The empirical application driven from that by the practitioners shall bring useful distinction, which will validate the MIK model.

For instance, for the patron set, it will be interesting to verify if these customers, participating in the loyalty program of the retailer, no longer belong to the market. To what extent the CKM is able to withdraw a patron from the market? Is it possible this patron does not act and react like the "average" customer? According to MIK, far beyond the behavioral posture influenced by the image of a brand, such as the preference when competition exists, it happens that a proper management by the patron manager of the customer knowledge should make the patron behave differently from the prospect or the panelist. Should it be right, the patron no longer belongs to the market, which is possibly unexpected from a common sense point of view.

10.9.2. The Information System

The exchanges between the IS of a retailer and its patron take many paths, such as the particular checkout of the after sale department, the regular checkout, or the online payment.

There are different data warehouses overseen by the IS of a large retailer. The amount of data grows with the number of variables and patrons. A hard to manage volume of data can be reached. This makes the investment in hardware expensive though the dollar per byte storage continues to drop. The real expense is more related to the management of data mining experts who must blend their analytical skills toward a customer-oriented approach.

The IS management has several questions that must be addressed:

- What power and place should be given to these experts?
- Who makes the decisions and who's accountable for it?
- Who should decide what the goals are?
- Who decides how should the then acquired knowledge be used for?
- Who should delineate the use of future knowledge?
- When to start a new project?
- What are the respective parts and responsibilities taken by the marketing department and by the IS department?

Depending on the given results, it is possible that these new tools call into question, with the help of statistics and probability, the relative weight of each department within the organization. This induces two questions in regard with the strategy elaborated by the managers. Should the IS department be externalized or should proprietary skills be developed? In the first case, how to preserve the competitive advantage which has been acquired, and how to prevent a third party transfer to the competitors sensitive skills?

10.9.2.1. Knowledge capital and customer knowledge Using the gathered and analyzed customer information the patron manger's experience creates an extensive customer knowledge capital for the organization. Modeling allows drawing dematerialized pattern such as knowledge. This theoretical construction is able to represent the customer knowledge ensemble, which is logically located within the organization using it, specially the customer knowledge capital.

Actual new scheme of the management domain, the central place now occupied by the customer have opened two research fields.

- One is oriented towards the customer relationship management (CRM).
- The other is focused on the customer knowledge capital (CKC).

Customer knowledge is a real intangible asset of the company, which must add strong value to the marketing activity. The MIK aids in both.

10.10. Math Approach of MIK: How it Works

Taking a variable within an ensemble and applying on it various changes equals to transform it with a function. The MIK model uses four of them described hereafter.

10.10.1.   The Traffic Functions between the Subsystems

10.10.1.1.   Information system and customer knowledge   The knowledge reception and organization by the IS, which is expressed by the knowledge actors, is a flow called *externalization* in the MIK model.

In Figure 10.8, these flows are depicted by the dark squares with numbers. It appears on the model like this:

The use of the data by the actors within the IS is called the *internalization* function and is represented on Figure 10.8 by:

These points are central for the use of the IS made by the organization. The empirical confirmation of this will come from the observation on how the practitioners send data from the data warehouse towards those who add value by using it.

The human–machine interaction transcends this issue. The way the databases are made available to the managers determines factor for smooth operation of the entire model. Poorly managed or unreachable data prevents internalization of the knowledge. Anyone knows that data exists and is stored inside the IS, but poor interface limits access, causes constant malfunctions and discourage use of the system. Failing software architecture does not allow the users to externalize their knowledge and seclude or isolate them, instead of sharing it.

10.10.1.2.   Information system and patron   There is a flow of data exchanged between the patron set and the IS. According to the MIK model, the customer access to the information and found them suitable, this is the *appropriation* function drawn like this:

What comes to mind after this is direct marketing, when customized commercials are sent to the customer through various media such as postal mail, telephone, or email, this is a stimulated appropriation. This can be information sought or simply observed by the customer on the Web site of the firm; this is a spontaneous appropriation.

The reverse direction of the appropriation is called the *expression* function and is shown by:

It is feeding the IS with direct data from the patrons. The patrons are voluntarily giving the exact value of selected individualized variables (e.g., income, household composition). This can be indirect data as well, with no active participation of the customer. Scanning only the loyalty card links transaction data (e.g., purchase receipts, mean of payment, time) to the data warehouse.

The patron can, now via internet, access limited areas of the company by appropriation, which is a change of the retail practice. In theory, nothing opposes a direct access to personal data or their alteration in order to obtain a better offer or service. In reality, patron concerns about privacy and data entry time/value perceptions can limit the amount and accuracy of the provided data.

Another MIK aspect is the indirect measure of the flow intensity between the IS and the patron set. The quantity of data exchanged is easily measurable and could be an index of the transaction level. This so measured value could be brought together with business exchange. The correlation between the volume of the data flow and the goods and services flow could help measuring other variables such as the image of the brand. Measuring the data flow is of common practice in media broadcasting, asking the audience to dial up a pay per call number. Before that, it was necessary to make a poll in the days after an event in order to scale the public interest. Today, the number of calls given from cell phones measures it instantaneously.

A majority of people being equipped with telecommunication terminals, by only knowing the value of few independent values, specific of the users, measuring the success of a novelty is made by counting the call or Internet page hits. The margin made on the call could be added to the then promoted product profit.

The near real-time analysis of this back flow, which is sent out by the patrons should allow adapting the marketing strategy. Some feedback action would therefore be produced by the patron manager who would be able to fine-tune the campaign. The IS makes now possible to adapt in real time the offer to the buyers' reaction. This put the retail close to the perfect market described by numerous theorists like Walras, Debreu, Arrow, or Pareto: to access with a network receiver (cellular device getting GSM, Bluetooth, Wi-Fi or other signals protocols) to the rate of the product or service, which before have been individually marked as the patron's preferences. As an adaptation in return, the electronic price tags on the shelves can be remotely monitored in order to match the demand and the available stock.

Such new IT techniques should have consequences on the environment as well, which is obvious in systemic and open systems. The relationship between the retailer and the producers/wholesalers/brands is about to change. The capacity to test new products and services with a tiny target of patrons brings to the retailer the skills formerly hold by the marketing companies. The buyers, negotiating with the brands, could share knowledge with the patron manager and then bring to the producer huge added value: no more consumer survey, no more market test, nor expensive market studies. Manage your knowledge with MIK and feel the patrons needs and behavioral trends on one side, adapt your purchase order and stock on the other side. Should the MIK model be managed properly, the waste of margin due to a poor stock management could be dramatically reduced as well.

10.11. Market Knowledge Capital of the Company

The MIK model, on its lower part, refers to the classical market studies and related campaign analysis. However, this area of MIK tends to dwindle as the patron subsystem grows. Having millions of patrons in a database gives more than a minimal sample for statistics. It explains that the flow between the customer knowledge and the market knowledge is going from top to bottom. The management of the prospect/panelist has more to gain from this knowledge flow direction.

This is not really a discovery. A retail manager knows more on his local market from his/her practice than from any market study, which is new though is the integration of the IS and all the functions going around and within the model. This is the basis for marketing management innovations to come.

10.11.1. *Internal Operators within the Subsystems*

Within the systems and subsystems, the exchanges have the same properties than the operators of

Sharing inside the market:

Combining inside the IS:

Socializing inside the Organization:

10.11.1.1. Correlation patrons-market Research in the future will improve the model and show how classical market studies will adapt to the arrival of the CKM in the "brick and mortar" retail sector. Future campaigns will preferably favor the growth of the patron set and mostly communicate in favor of the loyalty program instead of promoting products.

Operators help to exchange between the patron set and other customer categories. In other words, things which influence a loyalty card holder are going to exert on the nonholders. Since associations of consumers exist, an organized community of practice (COP) seems possible to be organized. Sometimes, information sharing or exchange happens between all the different customer categories of the market. Social relationship, links and bonds between people, families, and groups of individuals are the very basic of human relationship. By separating the patrons from the remainder of the market, the existing data flow exchanges between these categories have an effect which can be positive (e.g., recommendation, imitation, gregarious behavior) or negative (e.g., bad criticism, poor experience) shown in Figure 10.9.

On the other hand, the question is: up to what point is it possible to use the patron set as an extrapolation of the remainder of the market? Geography and size of this set are two obvious variables answering this question, but what other variables are going to moderate or increase this phenomenon?

What does influence the recommendation capacity of the patron? Which specificity has the patron subsystem in terms of purchase behavior and reactivity to the marketing campaigns?

Figure 10.10 represents the reverse operation that originates outside of the patrons. The loyalty card penetration rate could measure the external influences on the process, such as media campaigns, instant promotion at the till (checkout), store animations, etc. In addition, other questions that provide insight to the loyalty card program are:

- What is the specificity of the individuals who migrate to the patron category and of those who decline to do so?
- What is the key variable which is always found among the customers who sign a loyalty card application?
- Does this variable differ, depending on the type of retail?

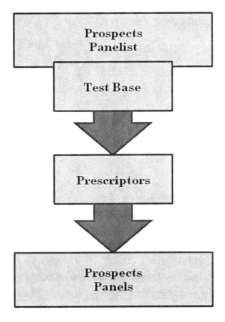

Figure 10.9: Correlation of patrons to market.

Becoming a patron does not always follow the same motivation. Some influences depend on whether patrons join at the beginning of the loyalty program or after millions have already subscribed. Depending upon what patron set size the aggregating operator working, the assumptions about representation of the total population are different.

A good question for the organization to evaluate is should the patron set be a representative sample of the entire market? If it does, this justifies the actions and validates the flow of data exchanged between the patrons and the IS. By comparing what happens inside the patron set in term of behavior with the remainder of the market (measured with a classical market survey), it proves that a captive database allows the retailer to gain knowledge on the entire market by "only" monitoring the patrons providing data in the IS.

On the other hand, people who participate in a loyalty program could be consider having an always positive attitude towards the brand, whatever pros and cons are in the environment of the brand.

10.11.1.2.   Correlation customer knowledge with market knowledge   Inside the organization is an exchange of knowledge which is represented by the operator of *socialization number 7*. To evaluate this operator several questions need to be addressed:

- How the various domains specialists do meet each other?
- What advantage, useful in their professional practice, are they going to withdraw?

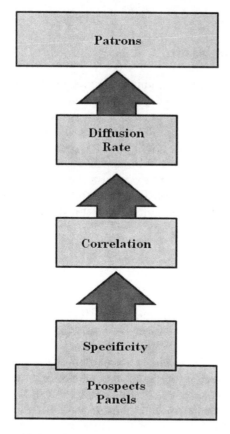

Figure 10.10: Correlation of market to patrons.

The MIK model could have a predictive capacity on the measure of the return on investment (ROI) of the marketing campaign by freeing the retailer from afterward market surveys. The model encourages an empirical checking on how the customer knowledge transforms to market knowledge; the opposite being in theory not possible. What are the variables bringing this knowledge and how can they convert to useful competences for the entire market?

10.11.1.3. Internal combinations in the information system The results to the queries sent to the database can concern one or more variables. The possible stepping and combinations are limited only by the statistical tools. Certain data mining tools claim they can automatically withdraw relevant correlations between the variables. This raises the question to know how the statisticians, who work for the large retail, combine the collected data, for what sake, and with which result.

10.12.   Conclusions

10.12.1.   *The patron set concept*

The immediate access to quasi unlimited amount of data makes it possible for the knowledge society to exist. Making various data available to the public requests through management by a combination of software tools and know-how is performed by the organization's IS. This concept can change the nature of the relationship existing between the retailer and the customer. It is made possible by the personal identification of the patron in real time and a trust relationship.

The patron set designates a group of customers having subscribed to a loyalty program either on premises or on line, monitored by an IS within a competitive frame in order to receive real or subjective incentives and add objective value to the brand.

10.12.2.   *The MIK model*

Depending on total or partial activation of the functions and operators of the model, managers are given many possibilities, from sending classical promotional material up to a live monitoring of the Patron reactions.

When all the model functions are activated, the purchase management, the marketing campaigns, the promotions and animations, the relationship with the advertising agencies, the auditing, the online sales, are all changing. It contributes to a new business model which can be applied to various business sectors.

The sales and the market share of the brand can noticeably increase due to the CKM, which changes the offer, the management practice, the image, and the profit. New skills appear like patron magazine editors, community of patrons managers, personalized financial services, and customer knowledge managers. The transformation of the traditional relationship between the customer and the firm raises the question about the representation the professionals have of their activity? It infers a disruption of the decisional and power balance within the organization.

10.12.3.   *Customer Knowledge and Shift in the Enterprise's Culture*

Applied advisedly, the MIK model can bring a demonstrated competitive advantage. This rupture in the practice of management changed the business model of the first British retailer, Tesco.

The communication agency, the market research institutes, the marketers and, to another extent, the market prospect and the financial analyst benefit from this model. To better understand how the exchanges between the three systems (the Patron, the IS and the Customer Knowledge) create value for the Organization. It enables all the stakeholders to act in their respective disciplines in regard.

The management of the customer knowledge has increased the market share of Tesco, the now largest retailer in the UK. It has contributed to the change of its management model, making the marketing department work in synergy with the IS managers.

As suggested by the MIK model, the functions of *knowledge sharing, socialization, internalization,* and *externalization* are essential with the activation of the operator of *combination.* In other words, this process involves a change in the culture of the teams. A new equilibrium of roles is reached when cooperation between data analyst and marketer becomes mandatory, as well as a rethinking of the communication strategy.

The diversification of the types of offers induces new business practices and allows a direct entry on other markets. The example of traditional retailer becoming a "click and mortar" firm demonstrates that the buildup of a brand can be spurred. The image of the brand as well as the confidence of the patrons must be carefully maintained. The credibility of the brand can be reinforced by every direct marketing campaign if creation of value for the patron is the goal.

The prospective buyers of the retailer's products and services, novelty part of the offer resulting from this diversification, are already in the patron database. They can be seen as people being already "in the store," even if it is a virtual facility.

Thorough knowledge compiled, a patron ensures the control of three essential rings of the value chain: production, storage, and distribution. This ability leads business to a diversification, not only of its offer but of its business model as well.

References

Berry, M. J. A., & Linoff, G. (2004). *Data mining techniques* (445 pp.). Indianapolis, IN: Wiley.

Borden, N. (1964). The concept of the marketing mix. *Journal of Advertising Research, 4*(June), 2–7.

Christopher, M., Payne, A., & Ballantyne, D. (1991). *Relationship Marketing* (264 pp.). Oxford: Butterworth-Heinemann.

Emery, F. E., & Trist, E. L. (1965). The causal texture of organisational environments. *Human Relations, 18,* 21–32.

Emery, J. (1969). *Organizational planning and control. Systems theory and technology* (166 pp.). New York: Macmillan.

Grönroos, C. (1994). From marketing mix to relationship marketing: Towards a paradigm shift in marketing. *Management decision, 32*(2), 4–20.

Humby, C., & Hunt, T. (2003). *Scoring points: How Tesco is winning customer loyalty* (276 pp.). London: Kogan Page.

Jambu, M. (1999). *Introduction au data mining: Analyse intelligente des données* (114 pp.). Paris: Eyrolles, France Telecom CNET.

Kale, S. H. (2004). CRM failure and the seven deadly sins. *Marketing Management, 13*(5), 42–46.

Kreyenhagen, M., Robbins, C. B., Crable, E., & Frolick, M. N. (2004). The western and southern life insurance company: A data warehousing success story. *Business Intelligence Journal, 9*(2), 57–63.

McCarthy, J. E. (1960). *Basic marketing: A managerial approach* (770 pp.). Homewood, IL: R. D. Irwin.

Porter, M. (1985). *Competitive advantage: Creating and sustaining superior performance* (557 pp.). New York: Free Press.

Reinartz, W., Kraft, M., & Hoyer, W. D. (2004). The customer relationship management process: Its measurement and impact on performance. *Journal of Marketing Research, 41*(3), 293–305.

Reinartz, W., Thomas, J. S., & Kumar, V. (2005). Balancing acquisition and retention resources to maximize customer profitability. *Journal of Marketing, 69*(1), 63.

Tufféry, S. (2002). *Data mining et scoring: Bases de données et gestion de la relation client* (311 pp.). Paris: Dunod.

Tzokas, N., & Saren, M. (2004). Competitive advantage, knowledge and relationship marketing: Where, what and how? *The Journal of Business & Industrial Marketing, 19*(2), 124(Business Module).

Wilkinson, I. F., & Young, L. C. (2005). Toward a normative theory of normative marketing theory. *Marketing Theory, 5*(4), 363–396.

Chapter 11

Targeting Information Technology on Organizational Needs

Linda Larson Kemp

Abstract

The right information technology (IT) systems can be essential enablers of the critical insights and predictive thinking necessary to keep enterprises viable and successful. These systems inform and remind decision makers of what the enterprise organization is, where it is in the world, and how prepared it is to cope with expected and unexpected challenges. This chapter outlines an approach for targeting IT investments on organizational needs viewed from this perspective by prioritizing information requirements, assessing technology options, and choosing and implementing the best holistic solutions. It discusses how to strategically align projects, determine criteria for selecting the best alternative approaches and products, factor in human elements, and ensure project success by planning well including planning for contingencies.

11.1. Introduction

How do you get the most value out of expensive technology? This is a chronic question that continues to frustrate executives — a quandary that requires at minimum three disciplined practices to resolve prudently: (i) a systems approach from the perspective of organizational survival and organizationwide performance; (ii) the alignment of investments with hierarchical business objectives; and (iii) a method of measurement to confirm that investments remain on track and to allow for timely corrections before failure occurs.

In Search of Knowledge Management: Pursuing Primary Principles
Copyright © 2010 by Emerald Group Publishing Limited
ISBN: 978-1-84950-673-1

[I]n the United States alone, a staggering 40 percent of [IT] investments fail to deliver their intended return each year. (Benko & McFarlan, 2003)

With regard to IT systems, getting the most value requires two additional disciplines: (iv) the identification and continual reassessment of the information needed most to make key decisions wisely and to conduct core operations effectively, efficiently, and sustainably; and (v) professional-level system design and implementation know-how that adequately accounts for user needs and for uncertainty.

Chapter organization:

- *Assessing needs and options* — Determining what information is most important (i.e., identifying and prioritizing key needs) and staying abreast of available technology (i.e., finding solution alternatives and considering overall appropriateness)
- *Selecting and applying solutions* — Choosing wisely among alternatives (i.e., determining selection criteria, weighing the alternatives, and providing for contingencies) and implementing the best alternatives given the implementation context (i.e., gaining buy-in and ensuring success)
- *Summary* — Addressing key questions for strategically aligning and pragmatically staging IT investments.

11.2. Assessing Needs and Options

11.2.1. Determining What Is Most Important

In the new economy, having vital information available to decision makers, including operations personnel, represents the foundation of an enterprise's core competency. Today's corporation is "designed around a skeleton: information" (Drucker, 1995). "[T]he internet and enterprise IT are now accelerating competition within traditional industries ... [n]ot because more products are becoming digital but because more processes are .... [And] the competitive shakeup brought on by IT is not nearly complete" (McAfee & Brynjolfsson, 2008). Knowledge not only represents a core business asset in the form of intellectual capital, it also serves as the chief generator of corporate and individual (and therefore national) wealth. What's more, having the right information available to the right people at the right time, in the right form, and at the right level of confidence is key to endurance as well as success.

Only some information is vital, though. Determining what is most important involves first identifying what is potentially key to enterprise success and failure (Kemp, 2000). Once identified, these needs should be prioritized. Allowing low-priority needs to dominate, spending limited assets to satisfy them, amounts to squandering the investments.

Conducting business is increasingly complex, dynamic, and interdependent, point out many pundits including Friedman (2005). Corporate competency must continuously evolve or the business becomes increasingly disjointed from reality. Therefore, intellectual capital must relentlessly be reappraised and ability to respond to change must continuously be planned for and adjusted (Dove, 2001).

11.2.2. Identifying Key Information Needs

The process of identifying the highest priority information needs involves evaluating the state of the business environment as well as the state of the organization. It also involves taking stock of enterprise risks, those often-ignored factors that can ultimately make or break any organization. Increasingly, the ability to assess and manage risks depends on the power of information and communications technology (Macgill & Siu, 2004, 2005).

11.2.2.1. Focusing knowledge competencies on business realities If the most important business information (Table 11.1) is to be supplied to decision makers, key knowledge management-related questions (Table 11.2) must be addressed:

- *What does the enterprise need to know most* — also when and to what degree of certainly does it need to know — to reach its primary goals and ensure its sustainability? Sorting this out helps to reveal which kinds of information are essential and should be highlighted versus which kinds are comparatively *un*important and, therefore, constitute "noise" that has no real bearing on success.
- *How does the enterprise go about knowing* and keeping its important knowledge current? Is its internal climate knowledge-centric? What cultural factors need to be understood and addressed? For example, are new facts, trends, and ideas constantly being sought? Or instead do convention and rigid expectations trample innovation? Is bad or controversial news welcomed objectively? Or instead does a "don't rock the boat" or "shoot the messenger" mentality inhibit attention and awareness by constricting the free sharing of insights and ideas? What expectations surround issues of control and privacy? Do shared organizational values include excellence, flexibility, learning, and customer focus? What must happen to improve the propensity for and process of absorbing, retaining, integrating, interpreting, predicting from, and refreshing critical knowledge to keep it a valuable asset that is actively employed to keep the organization strong? What must happen to instill confidence in important knowledge technology?

Table 11.1: Business context: key strategic questions requiring succinctly informed answers.

- What distinctive value do you provide to your stakeholders?
- What possibilities for great achievement are out there today? And tomorrow?
- What possibilities for disaster keep you awake at night? Or should?

Table 11.2: Knowledge focus: key KM questions for supplying succinct strategic information.

- What does an enterprise need to know most? What are the answers to the questions in Table 11.1?
- How does it go about knowing? How can that propensity and process be improved?
- How does it make the most out of what is known? How can that return on knowledge be improved?

- *How does the enterprise make the most out of what it knows?* Are lessons learned retained and reapplied, or do lessons often have to be relearned? Are distinctive intellectual assets leveraged in the marketplace, or are they squirreled away and lost? What needs to happen to improve the business return on knowledge assets?

11.2.2.2. Diagnosing business-context realities All of the above knowledge-oriented questions (summarized in Table 11.2) pertain to each of the following three categories of strategic questions (summarized in Table 11.1), which require succinctly informed answers:

- *What specific distinctive value do you provide to your stakeholders?* What distinguishes your contribution from that of your competitors or peer organizations? Are you monitoring demand trends or soliciting customer input? Are you watching what others are doing so that you can compare and contrast your own performance?
- *What possibilities for great achievement exist today? How about tomorrow's possibilities?* Are you constantly looking for new opportunities that distinguish you from others and for potential threats that can be turned into opportunities?
- *What possibilities for disaster keep you — or should keep you — awake at night?* What can make or break the success of your firm? Are you keeping an active eye or a blind eye on things in the periphery that could interfere with your ability to achieve?

11.2.2.3. Avoiding information overload

> Where is the wisdom we have lost in knowledge? Where is the knowledge we have lost in information?
>
> – T.S. Elliot

While having insufficient or erroneous information can mean having to make decisions blindly, having too much can overload and distract the process. Systems must support decision makers' ability to recognize signal amid noise (Benko & McFarlan, 2003). Therefore, gaining an understanding of what is truly important to know is crucial so that it can be distinguished from the unimportant. "People today are awash in information, but does that make them necessarily any more knowledgeable — never mind wiser?" (Bonabeau, 2002).

11.2.3. Determining Needed Information about the State of the World

Clear signals are needed about the state of the world as well as the state of the organization. Because success depends on managing factors in the environment (e.g., Rothberg & Erickson, 2005), the most fundamental step in identifying vital information is analyzing the organization from the perspective of its external context. That is, assessing outside forces such as changing legal, ecological, social, and political as well as economic and technological conditions (e.g., Stankosky & Baldanza, 2001). In addition to customer demand and competitor pressure, example forces can include threats associated with energy shortages, potential pandemics, terrorist acts, climate change, recession, and inflation/deflation, plus opportunities associated with scientific breakthroughs and demographic changes (Figure 11.1).

> [E]xecutives need to stay alert to peripheral threats and opportunities as well as concentrate on the job at hand. Failure to notice regulatory, political, or market-oriented changes in their environment will keep them from adapting their strategies so that their organizations can thrive. (Bazerman & Chugh, 2006)

To survive and thrive in a dynamic, often hostile world, an organization, like any living system, needs to continually and efficiently learn from experience, generate

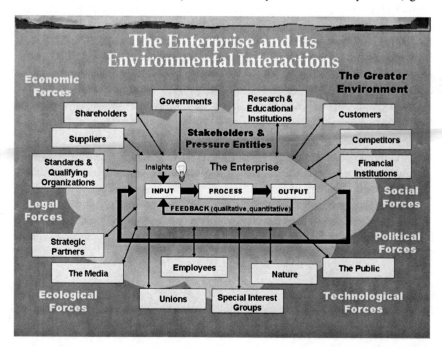

Figure 11.1: Enterprise stakeholders and environmental forces: Sources of shared and conflicting purposes and of ever-changing opportunities and threats.

new options, and adapt internally to match and overcome the pressures from its changing circumstances. Integration of the concepts and techniques of business intelligence[1] (BI) and knowledge management (KM) is central to managing an enterprise sustainably (Rothberg & Erickson, 2005). Decision makers need timely notification of potentially significant trends and events — also probabilities and insights into consequences as well as potential linkages between trends and events and potential secondary and tertiary consequences — in time to allow for appropriate adaptation and to enable wise response. Not obtaining and using such information proactively represents tremendous risk.

BI and KM offer powerful tools for continuously monitoring conditions, sensing change, detecting existing and emerging patterns, projecting probabilities, filtering noise, and sending signals to decision makers to help them stay alert to potentially significant change while helping them to stay focused on the job at hand.

11.2.3.1. Lessons from high-reliable organizations (HROs)

> The effectiveness of [HROs] stems from the ability to respond to fluctuating conditions.
> – Weick, Sutcliffe, & Obstfeld (2000)

Aircraft carriers are quintessential, often-described examples of HROs. They and other examples offer lessons for all organizations about how to perform successfully amid a context of chaos and danger (Carroll & Hatakenaka, 2001; Weick & Sutcliffe, 2005). Many of the properties of competence that allow HROs to avoid errors and recover quickly from failures can be leveraged by all organizations to deal more effectively with turbulence. As models of robustness, successful HROs stay focused on the job at hand while managing risks by staying alert to potential threats and by continuously monitoring performance and improving readiness.

> Effective HROs present a compelling picture of people working in fluid but orderly ways to focus energy and expertise where and when they are needed. The best HROs understand the dangers of complacency, inattention, and predictable routines .... They maintain a delicate and complex balance of processes that encourage continuous learning and improvement, while at the same time promoting order and reliable performance. (Weick, Sutcliffe, & Obstfeld, 2000)

---

1. BI is an "active, model-based, and prospective approach to discover and explain hidden, decision-relevant aspects in large amounts of business data to better inform business decision processes" (KMBI, 2005, in Liebowitz, 2006). BI is often assumed to focus primarily on internal information, however, while competitive intelligence (CI) is thought of as spanning external information as well. Thus BI is often considered to be subsumed within CI (Liebowitz, 2006). Nonetheless, for the purpose of this chapter, BI is viewed from the wider perspective, a view not inconsistent with KMBI's definition.

11.2.4. Determining Needed Information about the State of the Organization

The next fundamental step in assessing what information is vital is to analyze the organization's own internal competencies — measures of its strengths and weaknesses with regard to the depth and breadth of its assets, capabilities, and robustness. For example, how well does it truly perform when compared with leading competitive or peer organizations?

An integral part of maintaining vigorous operations is to constantly monitor those operations and make continual adjustments. Taking measures of input, process, output, outcome/impact, and context constitutes a primary form of feedback that is necessary for making these adjustments (Kemp, 2000). And since business operations are complex, many opportunities for measurement exist.

Figure 11.2 illustrates a basic way to categorize business operations and the information needed to perform them well. Classic authoritative models for deciphering the state of the organization include Porter's (1985) Value Chain, which analyzes business activities, and the McKinsey 7S Framework (Pascale & Athos, 1981), which analyzes strategy, structure, systems, skills, staff, management style, and shared values.

Determining what most needs to be measured begins with understanding what decision makers most need to know to make wise choices. Four basic categories of information are needed (Table 11.3): status of and projections about external conditions and internal capabilities. Status of external conditions can include benchmarks set by industry leaders and indicators of customer strength and supplier

Figure 11.2: Strategic alignment: The relationship between knowledge assets and performance competence (adapted from KPMG Consulting).

Table 11.3: Four basic categories of strategic information needs.

Status of external conditions	Projections about external conditions
Status of internal capabilities	Projections about internal capabilities

power. Status of internal capabilities can include performance against benchmarks, assessments of available skills, and indicators of culture (such as shared values). Projections of external conditions can include consumer trends, insights regarding emerging technologies, and indicators of capital market strength. Projections of internal capabilities can include measures of asset liquidity, indicators of structural flexibility, and assessments of intelligence systems.

11.2.4.1.   Lessons from Peter Drucker, the Father of Management   Drucker (1995), in describing the information executives need most to make sound operational judgments, emphasizes internal measures, although within a context of external measures:

- *Foundational information*: Traditional measures of cash flow and liquidity projections, which he compares to routine medical readings like pulse and blood pressure. If these are abnormal, further diagnosis is warranted.
- *Productivity information*: Beyond the classical measure of labor, he recommends measuring knowledge work, which is only now gaining a commonly accepted definition and wide interest (e.g., Green 2005, 2008). Drucker also advocates economic value-added analysis (EVA) and benchmarking:
  - EVA measures net return from operations after considering all factors of production. It can indicate how well things are going, what more needs to be known, and whether corrective action is needed.
  - Benchmarking compares the organization's performance to the best of its peers. The assumption is that, to compete successfully, an enterprise must perform at least as well as its industry's leaders.
- *Competence information*: Being an industry leader means generating special customer value by leveraging distinctive competencies. "Ever since C.K. Prahalad and Gary Hamel's (1990) pathbreaking article, we have known that leadership rests on being able to do something others cannot do at all or find difficult to do even poorly" (Drucker, 1995).
- *Resource-allocation information*: Drucker advises allocating human resources as rationally as financial resources, then considering the results just as carefully. Measures of these scarcest two resources are among the most important determinates of success because they show what can be converted into action.

11.2.5.   Determining Needed Information about Enterprise Risk

Hell is truth seen too late

– John Locke

Executives are responsible for the ongoing viability of their organizations. Yet a pervasive tendency persists: focusing primarily on internal conditions, machinations, and short-term results while ignoring or dismissing the importance of dynamic environmental forces that could have enormous impact if not addressed quickly and accurately.

11.2.5.1. Lessons from history The subprime mortgage debacle and ensuing worldwide credit crisis coming home to roost during the autumn of 2008 is a classic demonstration of problems arising from entrenched obliviousness to environmental conditions.

> The chief executive of the mortgage giant Freddie Mac rejected internal warnings that could have protected the company from some of the financial crises now engulfing it, according to more than two dozen current and former high-ranking executives and others. (Duhigg, 2008)

In hindsight, this fiasco echoes the same nature of failure that is at the heart of tragedies ranging from the Challenger accident, Enron, 9/11, Katrina, and a litany of other incidents occurring throughout history. Such catastrophes could have been avoided if decision makers had paid greater attention to a buildup of unfavorable circumstances; had heeded the warnings of more perceptive, more systems-thinking cohorts; and had made readiness a top priority. To illustrate:

> For six years, John O'Neill was the FBI's leading expert on Al Qaeda. He warned of its reach. He warned of its threat to the U.S. But to the people at FBI headquarters, O'Neill was too much of a maverick, and they stopped listening to him. He left the FBI in the summer of 2001 and took a new job as head of security at the World Trade Center [where he predicted the next major terrorist attack would take place and where he died on 9/11]. (Kirk & Gilmore, 2002)

> In highly uncertain circumstances, when [astronauts'] lives were immediately at risk, [NASA's] management failed to defer to its engineers and failed to recognize that different data standards ... and different processes ... were more appropriate. (CAIB & Gehman, 2003 in Weick & Sutcliffe, 2005)

> History has lessons to teach about the role of denial in the decline of companies. The stubborn refusal of the U.S. automobile industry to admit the changeability of consumer demand is one of the best examples. (Tedlow, 2008)

After a business failure, what often becomes apparent is that decision makers had at their disposal "abundant evidence in advance that the firm is in trouble. This evidence goes unheeded, however ... The organization ... cannot recognize impending threats, understand the implications of those threats, or come up with alternatives" (Senge, 1994). Examples abound of failures among businesses that once led their markets (Tiwana, 2002). Eastman Kodak dismissed digital cameras, for instance, and Sun Microsystems panned open-source software (Fuld, 2004). Denial ranges "from ignoring external forces such as technological innovation and

demographic change to overestimating a company's own capabilities and resources"
(Tedlow, 2008).

> [B]linding lack of situational awareness and disjointed decision making
> needlessly compounded and prolonged Katrina's horror. [A Failure of
> Initiative, draft congressional investigation report (in Hsu, 2006)]

11.2.5.2. Better lesson minding   "Fortunately," say Bazerman and Chugh (2006),
"people can learn to be more observant of changes in their environment, which will
help to remove their decision-making blinders." IT *should* be assisting in raising the
cognizance of change. Executive and management information systems (EIS and
MIS), competitive and business intelligence (CI and BI) systems, decision-support
systems (DSS), and KM systems all are intended to keep decision makers in the
know. But these technologies are typically focused only on internal conditions, even
though no real reason exists why smartly designed IT cannot help decision makers
learn to be more observant and appreciative of external conditions and enterprise
risk factors in addition to internal conditions and short-term economics.

> The extent to which ... managers are accurate in noticing aspects of
> their ... environment is ... likely ... a function of ... their ...
> information acquisition systems. (Sutcliffe, 1994)

The right IT is capable of presenting in an attention-getting manner the critical
information to which executives and others need to be attending in order to avert
calamities small and large. The targeting of IT to expand decision makers' useful field
of view and to advance enterprise risk management represents a large step toward
applying a holistic, systems-engineering approach to running the enterprise. Today's
fiercely competitive marketplace mandates that an enterprise be understood as a
complex system coevolving within a turbulent world and that total performance be
optimized over the long term as well as the short. Skilled managers use this holistic
mindset to optimize the entire organizational system — not just a few parts at the
expense of the whole (e.g., Senge, 1994).

11.2.6. Prioritizing Information Needs

Large IT investments should be clearly targeted toward and prioritized on the basis
of supplying that information which is needed most for keeping the organization
functioning optimally within its business context. Figure 11.3 illustrates the interplay
of many example factors to weigh during the process of targeting and prioritizing
investments. The critical information required for enterprise success should be
identified first; then the technical functionality required to supply that information;
and then the user and infrastructure requirements that define the appropriateness
of and the selectability criteria for judging candidate solutions to provide the
information.

Figure 11.3: Example factors influencing the identification of critical knowledge and the technology that enables it.

11.2.7. Understanding Key Decisions and Core Operations

How do you go about identifying information and IT needs associated with decisions and operations that are strategically imperative? A straightforward way is to list the highest-level organizational goals; identify the decisions and operations associated with these goals; identify and rate the information needs associated with these decisions and operations; and then identify the technology needed to supply this information in the most useful fashion. This normative, essentially goal-driven approach (exemplified in Table 11.4) represents a top-down view of needs. Its orientation and focus on organizational intent attend to mission-level questions like *what to accomplish* and *why*.

By contrast, the bottom-up, data-driven approach is oriented primarily on operations and focused on conditions. It attends to questions like *how, how well, how fast, what's changed,* and *what's possible.* From this perspective, information and IT needs are associated with circumstances and the feedback necessary to stay in synch with changing realities. Typically, IT is concentrated on gathering, manipulating, and presenting day-to-day information about internal composition and status and on supporting intraorganizational activities and collaboration (e.g., conventional information systems plus most planning and measurement systems, also portals and BI systems). However, providing information about nonroutine and external states of affairs (such as early warning systems) and supporting interorganizational collaboration (such as social networking) usually receives comparatively little attention. Nevertheless, the typical bottom-up approach can be a powerful catalyst for improving efficiency and innovation by revealing opportunity areas and encouraging idea sharing. But the key issue, still, is the relative importance of such improvements to enterprise viability and success.

Both the top-down and bottom-up approaches can identify crucial information and IT needs. The bottom-up approach is more likely to be reflected substantially already within an organization, though, while the top-down often receives short

Table 11.4: Example matrix for identifying critical knowledge and IT needs through alignment with mission-related goals.

Strategic Requirements				Critical Knowledge and IT Needs					
Support for Subgoal A	Support for Subgoal B	Associated Key Decisions	Associated Core Operations	Identified Knowledge Needs	Level of Criticality (H M L)	Sources of Information	Methods of Acquiring	Methods of Conveying	Enabling IT
Enterprise Goal 1. Continued Solvency: Safeguard assets through strong financial programs									
Subgoal A. Maintain successful collections: Continue to collect 99% of premiums due									
Subgoal B. Maintain sound investments: Continue to outperform index in down market									
1.A		D	O	Insuree bankruptcy predictions (8, 9)	H	External databases. Industry experts. Knowledgeable staff	Industry analysis. Competitive intelligence service. Risk analysis.		BI system
1.A		D	O	Premium collections (1,8)	H	Internal databases. Auditors	Accounting & financial systems.		BI system
	1.B	D		Portfolio performance (4, 8)	H	Internal & external databases. Investment analysts	Portfolio analysis.		BI system
	1.B	D		Cash flow projections (1,8)	H	Internal databases. Financial managers	Accounting & financial systems. Business rules.		BI system

Enterprise Goal 2. Premier Customer Service: Provide high-quality, responsive assistance and accurate, timely benefit payments

Subgoal A. In two years, receive "outstanding" from 85% of plan participants and benefit administrators

Subgoal B. In two years, send 95% of first benefit checks within two months of application

2.A	D		Customer ratings (3, 5)	H	Plan participants & benefit administrators (current & prospective).	Surveys & focus groups.	Performance reports.
2.A	D	O	Inquiry handling proficiency (3, 6)	H	HR, IT, & facilities staff & databases.	Evaluations (IT, workforce, infrastructure, etc.).	
2.B	D	O	Plan termination predictions ()	H	Internal analysts. External data services. Operations managers.	Econometric forecasts. Competitive intelligence services. Heuristics.	
2.B	D	O	Beneficiary application cycle times (2, 6)	H	Internal databases. Quality teams.	Application & payment systems. Statistics.	Performance reports.

- Operations management information that executives truly need (Drucker, 1995):
  - (1) Foundational measure (cash flow & liquidity projections).
  - (2) Productivity measure (knowledge work, economic value added, & benchmarks).
  - (3) Competence measure (comparative performance, success & nonsuccesses).
  - (4) Resource-allocation measure (use of capital & "performing people").
- Balanced Scorecard categories (Kaplan & Norton, 1996):
  - (5) Customer & other stakeholder measure.
  - (6) Internal business process measure.
  - (7) Learning, innovation, renewal, & maturity measure.
  - (8) Financial measure.
- Driving & constraining external forces:
  - (9) Business environment indicator (economic, technological, legal, ecological, social, & political)
  - (10) Stakeholder pressure indicator (customer, supplier, competitor, partner, shareholder, union, financial institution, government entity, interest group, media, etc.)
- Risks:
  - (11) Financial risk estimate
  - (12) Operational risk estimate
  - (13) Strategic (enterprise-level) risk estimate

shrift. Yet absent a clear goal-driven understanding of what is vital, tactics and day-to-day activities can be unfocused, wasteful, and even counterproductive, while at the same time myriad incoming data on environmental interactions and changing conditions can be missed, mishandled, and misleading. Both the top-down and bottom-up viewpoints are essential elements of a total-systems approach to enterprise management.

11.2.7.1. Taking a total-systems approach Note that strategically crucial information is not limited to executive audiences. Every organizational member is a decision maker and should be actively aware of those decisions and actions that have mission impact. Also note that strategically critical information is not limited to goal-driven norms. Collecting and providing information on certain activities or relationships or providing support for certain tactical decisions might be critical to viability. For example, to stay competitive or avoid a failure, operational personnel might need to have conveniently at hand up-to-the-minute customer history, inventory levels, or shipping alternatives or might need to be notified immediately if a quality problem occurs requiring immediate action.[2]

Table 11.4 illustrates a scheme for sorting through strategically crucial decisions and operations to identify associated information and IT needs. The sample data in the matrix, which is shown in an in-process state, is representative of some of the mission-related goals and related needs that might pertain to an employee benefits insurer. Parsing goals in this way helps to identify the most important, strategically aligned needs.

11.2.8. Understanding Strategic Aims and Tactical Options

How do you differentiate between strategy-driven needs and those that are tactics driven? Strategy specifies what mission-based outcomes are being sought and the basic principles guiding how they should be achieved. Tactics specify the means for achieving the outcomes.

> Business strategy has its origins in military thinking. In his classic *The Art of War* written over 2000 years ago, Sun Tzu states that "Strategy is the great Work of the organisation. In situations of life or death, it is the Tao of survival or extinction. Its study cannot be neglected." Definitions of strategy abound, but as a general rule, business strategy can be seen as long term, based on an understanding of the environment and an understanding of the business organisation or

---

2. Arguably, however, if having such information as customer history and quality-issue mitigations can be anticipated to be critical to enterprise viability, then these information needs ought to be linked already with specific strategic goals, thus they ought to be derivable from the normative, top-down orientation.

self-knowledge. Tactics on the other hand relate to short term actions to gain an advantage .... [In chess, for example,] strategy governs the way the entire game is played .... [whereas t]actical play involves the individual manoeuvres [sic] that help to achieve the strategy. (Marcus, 2007)

Strategic information illuminates progress toward these desired outcomes, the likelihood of further progress, and assorted risks affecting that likelihood. It answers questions like those posed in Table 11.2. Examples might include customer-base dependability and investment-portfolio performance. It also describes positive and negative impacts from organizational operations like patient health, technology advancements, industry consolidation, national security, and so on. Tactical information primarily illuminates output measures like units produced, customers contacted, and documents downloaded, also input measures like hours worked, funds allocated, and supplies consumed. Input and output measures may or may not be relevant indicators of mission-based outcomes.

Organizational alignment means synchronizing people, capital, and systems with overall objectives having to do with achieving success in the world. It requires appreciation of the interrelatedness of the environment and of the processes necessitated by it (Tiwana, 2002). Alignment is "about creating greater value and efficiency by managing the relationships among projects [as well as] building the organizational capability to respond effectively to whatever future presents itself" (Benko & McFarlan, 2003).

Before deciding on tactics, strategic aims should be thoroughly understood and embraced. IT investments are tactical decisions — they are means to desired ends, not ends in themselves. That means any significant IT decisions must be clearly grounded on the basis of which alternatives best further the organization's overall objectives.[3] Part of that grounding involves assessing which of the alternatives best

---

3. For example, by passing the Information Technology Management Reform Act of 1996 (ITMRA or Clinger-Cohen Act), the U.S. government mandated that, before receiving funding for any large IT investments, federal organizations must first justify the investments by explaining exactly how they would further the organization's strategic objectives.

readies the enterprise as a whole to deal with the often unexpected forces offered up by the world.

> [When managers think of KM as] investing in creating the conditions that are necessary for collaboration to ensue and [for] novel business insights, ideas, and capabilities to emerge [they] stimulate conversations that would otherwise never occur, create new lenses for old problems that might never have been used, and connect the views of experts and outsiders to generate fresh thinking. (Tiwana, 2002)

11.2.9. *Enabling Readiness to Deal with the Unexpected*

Ours is a high-speed world. Remaining a vital part of it requires rapidly and accurately taking in information about things happening in the periphery and making decisions based on that information. Constricting decision makers' fields of view impacts every aspect of operations. To ensure the organization can survive and thrive, executives must make a top priority the capacity to navigate in the long term and to weather unanticipated events. This means improving their ability to make rapid and accurate decisions and to adjust organizational structures and operations based on environmental interactions and changing circumstances.[4]

To do this means improving their ability to perform short-term prediction by developing their aptitude for understanding circumstances holistically and by increasing their speed of information processing to improve the trustworthiness of their understanding. It means broadening their window of attention and improving their useful field of view by increasing their capacity to see things in the periphery and their skill at distinguishing what's important from what's not. It means being cognizant of predisposed blind spots and proactive in avoiding change blindness. It means balancing two opposing demands on attention: the top-down and the bottom-up; that is, balancing the focus on goals with constant sensitivity to changing conditions.

This mode of thinking, which epitomizes the systems-science view, is startlingly consistent among divergent disciplines dealing with living systems. It reflects the latest findings in neuroscience, for example (Merzenich, Frackowiak, Gazzaley, Livingstone, & Moffett, 2008). It also reflects critical observations and conclusions—both new and classic—from business science giants like Beer (1959), Ackoff (1981), Gharajedaghi (1999), Haeckel (1999), Sheffi (2005), and Wheatley (2005) as well as Senge (1994). In neuroscience the ability to flourish amid difficulty is called plasticity;

---

4. This capacity is usually referred to in terms of "situational awareness" (SA), which means attentiveness to what is happening now and what might happen in the near term. SA has been most notably and heavily studied in military contexts since World War II, but its paradigm is fundamental and is being applied more and more in wide-ranging problem areas.

in business, agility; and in risk management, resilience. Everywhere such competence and readiness means the capacity to respond with vigor and adapt quickly. In business today, it requires also the ability to collaborate effectively, deemed by Benko and McFarlan (2003) as "not merely a 'nice to have' element, but a growing competitive necessity." Such capacity requires the aid of powerful IT.

11.2.10. Staying Abreast of Available Technology

Enterprise viability and competitive advantage can turn quickly as change accelerates (e.g., Friedman, 2005). Being alert to and comprehending of change and the possibilities it brings requires having convenient access to the right indicators and assessment tools, which in turn requires having the right suppliers of this information including the right IT.

But technology is also constantly advancing. Staying abreast of available IT requires not only scanning widely for existing and emerging options but also paying attention to the organization's capacity for exploiting such options. This does not mean that unnecessary assumptions are made and options are dismissed out of hand. It means that first a restrictionless view be taken to get a sense of the landscape of solution possibilities and then a broad view of feasibility be considered before a reasoned list of options are weighed against each other with sensitivity to human as well as both organizational and environmental factors.

In the investment-decision process, how do you include sufficiently broad, deep, and up-to-date knowledge about best-available technologies — whether they are mature, new, or emerging? And how do you include sufficient consideration of the organization's capacity to assimilate the technologies?

11.2.11. Finding Solution Alternatives

Discovering the best-available technologies most appropriate for the organization leverages, arguably, at least as much art and opportunism as science and reason. Scan the landscape for technological possibilities by being proactive in looking over the horizon for emerging options while at the same time being evenhanded in evaluating in-house or otherwise at-hand alternatives. Sometimes low tech is still the best solution. Expertise and experienced judgment are required along with creativity and out-of-box thinking to be able to recognize those possibilities that, alone or in unison, may become truly valuable options.

11.2.12. Scanning for Options

Researching solutions includes activities like surfing the Internet for news and product capability profiles, perusing industry publications for juried opinions and comparisons, joining in professional-association gatherings, attending conferences and seminars, participating in interoganizational communities of practice (CoPs), and engaging individual experts. Seek innovation.

In today's world, innovation is ever more important. "[A]s the art of the possible evolves at an ever-faster rate, the shelf life of innovations is shrinking" (Benko & McFarlan, 2003). Therefore, it is important to keep an open mind when idea seeking and not limit unnecessarily the range of options. At this stage, creativity is especially important; judging the options comes afterward. And flashes of insight can come serendipitously.

> I had thought that the magic of the information age was that it allowed us to know more, but then I realized … it allows us to know less. It provides us with external cognitive servants — silicon memory systems, collaborative online filters, … and networked knowledge. We can burden these servants and liberate ourselves. (Brooks, 2007)

11.2.13. Considering Feasibility

Researching solutions also includes considering the practical potential of the various ideas. While creativity and out-of-the-box thinking are imperatives for avoiding the trap of unnecessarily limiting possibilities, so is pragmatism with regard to feasibility after the possibilities have been identified.

11.2.13.1. Thinking pragmatically Being pragmatic means considering the possibilities in light of the organization's resources, infrastructure, regulatory constraints, culture, risk tolerance, and other imperatives and limitations.

Resources include budget, timeframes required, skills availability, and facilities compatibility and capacity. *Infrastructure* is the basic physical and organizational structures needed for the operation of an enterprise including its legacy systems; its main areas of concern include system compatibility, interoperability, scalability, and reliability. *Regulatory* constraints, especially in government, can include investment justifications as well as security mandates.

Culture can serve as a facilitator or an inhibitor of change and is often a combination of both. It consists of hard aspects (e.g., written policies, performance measures, and formal processes and models) and soft (e.g., informal traditions, expectations, and social rewards and tolerances for diverse expressions and behaviors). Culture includes "the degree of external focus as contrasted with internal focus" as well as "how action, change, and innovation are viewed," and it has been identified as a major factor in organizational malfunction (Bea, 2006). "Enterprise IT typically changes many jobs in major ways; this is never an easy sell to either employees or line managers" (McAfee & Brynjolfsson, 2008). Nevertheless, while parts of culture sometimes must be viewed as givens, often as a whole it needs to be viewed as a core element of the organization that can be cultivated to embrace change by showing people how the change will improve their work lives and professional futures.

> Plan for the worst case. Pleasant surprises are better than ugly ones.
> (Peters, 2007)

Risk tolerance addresses the proclivity to live with and exploit uncertainty. It involves the robustness of the organization's assets including finances, facilities, infrastructures, and people, also the kind and strength of forces and potential forces bearing upon the enterprise. All change represents a degree of uncertainty that must be considered along with opportunity costs. What other investments cannot be accomplished if this option is pursued? Compared with those other prospects, how is this change expected to increase resilience (the ability to be "robust under conditions of enormous stress and change" [Coutu, 2002])? What are the best- and worst-case scenarios that could ensue? To what extent does this change pose make-or-break possibilities? That is, to what extent might it leverage opportunities that can ensure long-term success? And to what extent, should failure occur or unanticipated events follow, might the change facilitate threats upon the enterprise's ability to survive?

Other imperatives and limitations affecting feasibility might include the technical capability to support staff remotely while working off-site. Other examples might include the capability to run on a certain computer platform, integrate a particular computer program, or meet specific security requirements.

11.2.13.2. Assessing feasibility A large part of the challenge of considering feasibility is determining which limitations, which feasibility factors, can or should be modified to enable implementation of the best overall solution and to ensure a successful outcome. For example, would major adjustments be required in facilities, infrastructures, systems, procedures, reporting, training, policies, commitments, or the like? If adjustments are needed, how large would be those secondary costs, how significant the disruptions, and how long the adjustments?

Another large part of the challenge is determining how best to go about accomplishing such adjustments. For example, is a familiarization (training) program or an information (marketing) campaign necessary? Sometimes a few management presentations, "brown bag" luncheons, and notifications are all that is needed. But other times traditions and expectations need to be altered, or policies modified, roles adapted, schedules changed, lines of communication tweaked, job performance criteria synchronized, or new social structures prompted and supported. Ultimately, if people are unable or unwilling to embrace a new technology, a multi-million-dollar investment can languish or be sabotaged through error, misuse, or duplicated effort.

11.2.14. Considering the General Appropriateness of Alternatives

Weighing the various solution options involves comparing and contrasting their relative plusses and minuses, including the ability to turn identified organizational weaknesses into strengths. Oftentimes, though, objective assessments are heavily swayed or even trumped by cultural factors. Organizational openness to and readiness for change should be a major consideration in assessing the appropriateness of any new system and in the acceptability of that assessment. Change, being a "significant environmental shift that challenge[s] the existing structure and functioning of work group communities and their ecosystems," compels people to adapt (Baba, 1995; Goldmacher, 2006). But established work groups that are averse to sharing knowledge will be resistant to change (Bock, Zmud, Kim, & Lee, 2005). Impediments to sharing can include fear, lack of time, rewards for hoarding, the not-invented-here syndrome, functional stovepiping, internal competition, and an autocratic tradition (Tiwana, 2002).

Discussion of such subjective assessments involving culture in any significant level of detail is outside the scope of this chapter. Please refer to experts like Argyris (1993), Baba, Falkenburg, and Hill (1996), Goldmacher (2006), or Román, Ribière, and Stankosky (2004) for more in-depth treatment.

11.2.15. *Understanding the Potential Value of Each Alternative*

While appreciating each alternative's potential added value requires sensitivity to the organization's current cultural climate, it also requires an open mind and the creativity necessary to envision new possibilities for furthering enterprise objectives over the long term.

What will be tomorrow's highest priority business needs? Will they be dependent on BI and a broader field of vision with special attention to changing externalities? Or dependent on a sophisticated process monitoring or decision-support system? Or on a community-based enterprise portal coupled with a new tradition of working collaboratively and sharing information, insights, and expertise toward a commonly agreed purpose and set of guiding principles? What technological options offer particular promise with regard to innovatively and flexibly providing for tomorrow's needs? What options hold the most promise for readying personnel, for enabling them to recognize and respond to the new business needs?

> The war taught us this lesson — that we had to collect intelligence in a manner that would make the information available where it was needed and when it was wanted, in an intelligent and understandable form. If it is not intelligent and understandable, it is useless. (Truman, 1956)

11.3. Selecting and Applying Solutions

11.3.1. *Choosing Wisely Among Alternatives*

> Develop KM into a buffer for uncertainty and internal, competitive, and industry-wide surprise. (Tiwana, 2002)

The best IT options are those possessing the most potential for making the greatest overall difference. Some options, while appearing to promise great value, may be out of synch with current objectives or be at cross-purposes with other initiatives. "[U]nintended disorder in a company's project portfolio consumes valuable time and energy, leaves good money on the table, and fails to provision the organization for the future" (Benko & McFarlan, 2003). For an IT developer, choosing objectively means appraising alternatives for the best fit given specific criteria within the context of a coherent organizational vision. The criteria must be well defined and prioritized on the basis of mission-aligned business needs and technological prerequisites. To what extent can each alternative be expected to contribute to the most needed business improvements? The selection criteria provide measures of this extent.

11.3.2. Defining Selection Criteria

11.3.2.1. Identifying the range of criteria Cost is one important aspect of the rationale that should drive selection, not only initial cost but also expected and potential long-term costs including future upgrade and switching costs. Additional criteria should be considered, selected, and prioritized as appropriate. Examples might include interoperability, robustness, scalability, maintainability, upgrade-ability, usability, expected life span, availability of qualified development and support staff, vendor strength, and expectations of managers and users. Also, for example, does workflow need to be supported? What degree of interface personalization will be expected by users? And are executives expecting a metrics dashboard?

11.3.2.2. Determining the relative importance of the criteria Which selection criteria are the most important decision factors? After identifying and defining appropriate criteria, determine their relative significance. Some will be have-to-haves, some nice-to-haves. The criteria and the alternatives can be laid out in a spreadsheet, for instance, with weights assigned to each criterion and ratings assigned to each alternative for each criterion. This technique quantifies the decision-making process, easing the selection and affording justifiability. Weighing solution alternatives against the criteria is but one approach, though. At times, a single criterion might drive a decision by eliminating all but one option. At other times, the best solution is one that merely satisfies all of the necessary capabilities.

11.3.2.3. Weighing the solution alternatives If the weighted approach is pursued, after each alternative is rated against each selection criteria, each rating is then multiplied by the relative weight assigned to each criteria. The results for each option are summed and the option with the highest overall score "wins." This elementary process can be done using a spreadsheet or one of a range of decision-support tools from Decide Right, to Expert Choice, to Cognos.

11.3.2.4. Considering quantitative and qualitative measures When considering the measures, it is important to weigh qualitative factors such as usability as well as quantitative such as cost. Financial factors can amount to potential revenues gained as well as costs reduced. Nonfinancial factors can include strategic advantage, social responsibility, and quality of work life. It is also important to give heavy consideration to long-term expected values such as reliability as well as short-term such as efficiency. Of course, the most useful measures of any IT solution are the ways in which it ensures organizational effectiveness.

11.3.2.5. Considering infrastructure, skill, and cultural requirements Think through the prerequisites of available personnel and infrastructure with regard to developing, implementing, and maintaining the various alternatives. Would major computer or communication system upgrades be necessary? Would technical or user personnel need extensive training? Who would prepare and conduct the training? Would significant alterations need to be made to formal or informal operating practices? Are there policy implications?

11.3.2.6. Considering trade-offs, dependencies, timing requirements, and project risks Also consider the strategic, tactical, cultural, and technological trade-offs, dependencies, and timing factors with regard to each alternative. What would be the lead time required to implement each alternative? What are the technical, social, and policy antecedents? What important functionality, if any, must be given up to pursue each alternative? What are other organizations' track records regarding successful implementation of each alternative? That is, how prone to failure is each option and what are the lessons learned about avoiding failure? To what extent is there risk of dependency on a particular product that is relatively untested, has a less-than-stellar reputation for dependability or interoperability, or could easily become unavailable, unaffordable, obsolete, or otherwise impractical? In other words, what are the staging implications, opportunity costs, and uncertainties? Answers to questions like these affect the fundamental feasibility of the potential solutions.

11.3.3. Providing for Contingencies

"Identify the critical success factors for the initiative" (Tiwana, 2002) and address them. For example, organizational circumstances or technological options can easily change after committing to a given alternative. Therefore, part of the selection process needs to include planning for contingencies. The unexpected *will* occur, so factor in the ability to sense and react in a timely, effective manner. Flexibility, adaptiveness, agility, and robustness, in addition to being imperatives for enterprise viability, are fundamental qualities to engineer into any technology change.

> What do armies, sports teams, and disaster-relief agencies have in common? In one way or another, they devise contingency plans for facing a reality that is different from what was expected. By being

prepared for different outcomes, they can quickly change course. (Benko & McFarlan, 2003)

11.3.4. Example: Selecting Business Intelligence Software

A BI system is a KM system that supports decision making by providing historical, current, and predictive views of business operations. The intelligence it yields can include, for example, customer product development efforts and customer evaluations of competitor products as well as economic indicators and news-service feeds (Tiwana, 2002). BI should stimulate innovation by presenting information in a way that facilitates insights for different kinds of users. A tailorable view is essential for successful BI because various types of users in different roles require different data, manipulations, timeliness, reliability, and so on.

> Data analytics drawn from enterprise IT applications, along with collective intelligence and other Web 2.0 technologies, can be important aids not just in propagating ideas but also in generating them. They ... can complement and speed the search for business process innovations [from where] the real value [of IT] comes. (McAfee & Brynjolfsson, 2008)

BI system capabilities include the following services:

- *Data extract, transform, and load (ETL)*: Access, parse, validate, standardize, organize, and consolidate data in various forms from internal and external sources, then store the data where it can be used conveniently to support analysis, decision making, and other business needs. Includes managing metadata (overall definitions of data structures).
- *Information delivery*: Convey information from multiple sources through multiple channels to the right people at the right time in the most useful form, such as Web pages, e-mail, cell-phone alerts, and documents.
- *Analysis support*: Enable users to easily extract, transform, and integrate information. Allow for time-based study and for easy customization and revision of business metrics.
- *Collaboration support*: Enable users to work together and share insights. Allow for real-time communication and use of groupware tools.
- *System integration and management*: Provide standardized features for external connectivity and applications integration as well as developer tools. Direct and administer the BI platform, infrastructure, and repository. Includes installing, supporting, and updating application servers; assuring system and data integrity; responding to disruptions and other problems; scheduling and following up on application-related activities; and extending BI to other computer system and organizational environments.

Establishing the criteria for selecting a BI system includes rating the importance of such services on the basis of business need and technical necessity. Ranking alternative products involves rating them according to their ability to deliver these services, then comparing and contrasting each product on the basis of the importance of the established criteria.

11.3.5. Implementing the Best Alternative

11.3.5.1. Gaining buy-in Gaining buy-in from decision-makers and staff before attempting to implement the change is crucial. "Lack of an active role of the top management has been identified as the primary reason that many projects fail; the second reason is failure of the users to buy in to the project" (Tiwana, 2002). Gaining buy-in requires justifying the choice in an understandable and culturally fitting way. But "changing people's behavior and attitudes toward technology is...challenging" (McAfee & Brynjolfsson, 2008).

11.3.5.2. Justifying the choice "Changing ingrained patterns of behavior is difficult without a rationale for why change is necessary" (Goldmacher, 2006). Rationale can be as varied as the organizations themselves. Reasons for IT updates often include costs that might be saved or revenues generated; human resources used more productively; or product quality improved. They might well also include risk or frequency of errors reduced given better situational awareness from an enriched field of view; customer base grown given increased ability to judge and respond to changing demand; or quality of work life improved given greater support for collaboration and a better user interface. But often such justifications pale when compared to the greatest potential added value, the strategic benefit.

> [I]f there had been something like co-ordination of information in the government it would have been more difficult, if not impossible, for the Japanese to succeed in the sneak attack at Pearl Harbor. (Truman, 1956)

Recognizing this importance, Kaplan and Norton (2008) are now recommending segregating strategic initiatives (which would include strategically aligned IT investments) to protect them from being reallocated by managers to meet short-term tactical financial targets —"a principal reason why most organizations have so much trouble sustaining their strategy execution process."

11.3.5.3. Achieving consensus and enthusiasm While gaining agreement from decision makers and thought leaders is important, it is even more important to gain the enthusiasm of all participants. Positive anticipation can be considered a prerequisite to success. If users view the change openly with positive anticipation instead of resistance, the likelihood that the technology will be made the most of, thus the investment pay off, goes up dramatically. Unless, of course, expectations are dashed by an overpromised capability, a faulty system, or a failed implementation.

11.3.6. Example: Implementing a Community-based Enterprise Portal

A portal is a KM system that connects people and encourages collaboration. It is a customizable Web environment that allows a group of people to aggregate and share knowledge and information, services, and applications among employees, partners, customers, suppliers, and other stakeholders (Kemp, Nidiffer, Rose, & Stankosky, 2001). As a depository and distribution center for collective content, it serves to generate and activate collective intelligence. It can be designed to support an entire enterprise or a small group such as a cross-organizational CoP.

An enterprise portal consists of a suite of shared workspaces and personalized views, which optimally are managed by work roles and individual knowledge use styles, where users can cooperate as well as access and contribute to various forms of content. Content consists of intellectual capital (human, social, and corporate) in addition to technical services, such as instant messaging and user profiling, and application tools, such as teleconferencing and online training.

Content can include assets such as BI services and findings like performance metrics, benchmarks, projections, and breaking news; internal and external references, templates, taxonomies, and search/query tools; other products and services such as software applications and an intranet; repositories of lessons learned and promising practices; expertise locators; discussions and meeting minutes; organizational and project plans; proposals and contracts; and the ever-ubiquitous documents and e-mail; plus a provision for responding to surveys and submitting suggestions.

Portals can range in sophistication from merely providing Web-enabled access to documents and raw data to supporting advanced decision analysis and data visualization capabilities with statistical and simulation tools. Portals contain multiple portlets that present content in the form of customized views, information access, services, and tools. Figures 11.4–11.6 illustrate example portal contents.

Figure 11.4: Example portlet for submitting ideas.

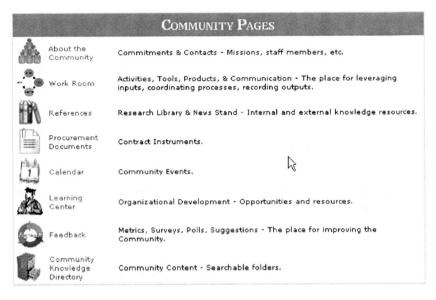

Figure 11.5: Example "table of contents" portlet explaining the portal community's pages and providing icon-identifiable, clickable access to the pages.

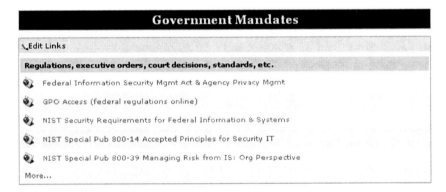

Figure 11.6: Example portlet containing links to regulations, standards, and so on that require operational compliance.

11.3.7.   Ensuring Implementation Success

Critical to the success of an IT system is ensuring professional development and management. This includes

- Staging the intervention intelligently and realistically by planning and preparing for implementation, including maintaining flexibility

- Designing practically by emphasizing information that is important and useful, organizing it logically, allowing for personalization, and insisting on high professional standards
- Preparing the organization for the change and engaging users by marketing the advantage of the change and leveraging its value

11.3.8. Staging the Intervention Realistically

11.3.8.1. Planning the implementation Staging development and roll-out appropriately and realistically is central to successful deployment. Implementation must be coordinated and prerequisites addressed. It is important to identify potential failure points such as end-user resistance and lack of management support and to implement preemptive measures (Tiwana, 2002). Prototyping and beta testing can help in detailing user requirements and working out problems. Issues might include required new or updated policies, procedures, roles, responsibilities, lines of communication, and technology upgrades as well as user preparation and training. Plan adequate time and resources to engage managers, prepare and train users, migrate data, and test the system (Kemp, Nidiffer, Rose, & Stankosky, 2001). Premature implementation can result in lost credibility as well as system failure.

11.3.8.2. Maintaining flexibility Care must be taken not to inadvertently or arbitrarily cut off backup means for accomplishing work. Staff should not be made anxious by the change; they need to be confident of their continued ability to perform their jobs productively. The ability to recover from failure also must be maintained; this may require keeping or putting alternative procedures or systems in place for a while to ensure a smooth transition.[5]

11.3.9. Designing Practically

People need convenient access to information used on day-to-day, periodic, and exception bases. Thus, the system needs to highlight the most useful information and the information needs to be organized logically. Implementation also needs to be compatible with organization-specific work requirements. Overnight content refreshment is of marginal value to staff who need hourly or instantaneous updates. The threat of serious impacts of invalid data being used could invoke significant

---

5. Unfortunately, however, maintaining alternative procedures or systems as assurance against failure can provide cover for, and thus can promote, an attitude of resistance to change. Some people may opt to depend on an old system for an extended period of time until they are at last persuaded of its value or are forced into the cutover by management mandate or eventual system failure. The advantages of maintaining the old as a safety net for the new must be weighed against the associated downsides.

vetting overhead. Finally, in a 24 × 7 world, what system down time will be tolerated when staff is dependent on the provided time-sensitive services? These are only a few example considerations; they constitute far from a comprehensive list.

Additional considerations pertain to portals. To illustrate, users who belong to multiple communities within the enterprise deserve some consistency among the pages so they do not lose their bearings going from one community to another. Standardized page and portlet layouts can be adopted. Example pages might include regular content and layout on, say, Work Room, Reference Library, and Feedback pages as well as Home and About pages. Example content portlets, shown in Figures 11.5 and 11.6, might include Contacts, Employee Search, News, Handy Links, Goals and Measures, Tool Kit (software, templates, procedures, checklists, benchmarks, and so on), Learning Resources, and Writing Aids in addition to Community Projects, Tasks, Calendar, Documents, and Discussions.

Sensible information organization and presentation are imperatives; in portals, so are content richness and navigability. Designers must put themselves in the shoes of the users they are attempting to assist. They must understand user responsibilities, activities, dependencies, frustrations, and needs for technical support. Ways of gaining this understanding can include research and observation, job analysis, structured interviews, workshops, use-case development, scenario building, and prototyping (an iterative process of involving users directly in the design process) along with large doses of experience and common sense. Take a holistic view of the strategic vision of the organization to create straw-model contents and structures to use as points of departure during requirements-gathering meetings.

Considerations also include numbers of clicks needed to find items; placement of the most-used contents in the most-obvious locations; labels that are descriptive yet succinct; and thresholds of information overload for each user group served (groups' thresholds will vary). Pay attention to the relative value of the content presented; for example, the utility of what is made available in a Toolbox, Professional Resources, or Learning Resources portlet.

11.3.9.1. Insisting on professional standards in design and execution What constitutes good design and execution and how do you achieve it? Usability is essential for gaining buy-in and enthusiasm (e.g., see Norman, 1988; Tufte, 1990), just like having the right information available in the right place at the right time in the right form. Users respond to aesthetics, so pay attention to detail. Be ruthless with regard to colors, fonts, sizes, spelling, grammar, graphics, and overall arrangement, balance, neatness, and consistency. Graphics and icons should be meaningful (in keeping with the gist of the content and not gratuitous or distracting), clear, and sized appropriately (usually the smaller the better but with sensitivity to legibility for all).

Also, it is important to be a knowledgeable professional. The IT designer is the one who bridges the gap between the users' needs and the technology solutions. Users deserve expert advice regarding design and execution. Shunting off this responsibility by acquiescing to a role of "order taker" forces users to have to become their own development experts in addition to doing their own jobs.

Analogies from other professions exist. Doctors do not depend on patients doing their own diagnoses; CPAs do not expect clients to show them how to keep books; and interior designers do not expect customers to tell them what styles and colors go together. Take seriously the role of professional and become truly an expert. Ask probing questions to help users think beyond the constraints of how they must work today. Provide rich examples from which they can pick and choose ideas. Provide learned advice, well thought-out models, and sound rationale for suggestions. Users may choose to override your suggestions, but at least they will have an informed choice, which cannot be the case if the design responsibility rests mainly on their shoulders.

11.3.10. Preparing the Organization and Engaging Users

11.3.10.1. Marketing the advantages and leveraging the potential The biggest incentive for users is the realization that the newly provided capability will make them successful with less effort. Thus, it is important for people to be excited about the opportunity to dig in and leverage their new tool. They also need to become comfortable with the change and adept at using the technology to perform their jobs better and easier. To help achieve the investment's potential, appropriate preparations might include e-mail announcements; informal briefings; formal training; one-on-one sessions with opportunities for individuals to "test drive" the technology; printed and electronic job aids; proactive support of CoPs; and even contests and recognition for participation and contribution. It should be noted, though, that a poor or mismatched design cannot be masked for long with ambitious marketing.

11.3.10.2. Overcoming bureaucratic barriers People also must be able and willing to act. Organizations often invest heavily in information systems but are stymied, for instance by approval-process blockages (Benko & McFarlan, 2003). Often the only way to ensure the investment will not be wasted is to engage the commitment of a high-ranking executive who can cut through the red tape by advocating key policy and procedure changes and broadcasting how important the tool is to the vision of organizational success.

11.4. Summary

You get the most value from technology by targeting it to satisfy the organization's highest priority business needs. Doing this requires a holistic systems-thinking perspective, which means the ultimate objectives are traceable to total enterprise performance and sustainability. It means investments must be aligned with strategic objectives and must be part of ongoing assessments of situational factors, including the availability of new technology. It means the technology must be, or must be made to be, compatible with internal factors including people's readiness to use it. It means

Table 11.5: Key question for targeting IT on organizational needs.

Information Needs Questions
1. How would you recognize emerging business threats or opportunities?
2. How fast would you need to act to avert a calamity or realize a gain?
3. How do you decide which action to take?
4. How do you know if you are prepared to act?
5. How will your stakeholders judge your actions?

Information Technology Questions
A. What do you need to know to answer the above business questions?
B. What is the prerequisite technology needed to gain this knowledge and make it easily available to those who need it most?
C. How can successful implementation be assured?
D. Which information and enabling technology are needed first?

---

rationally thinking through selection criteria rather than relying on assumptions, leaping to conclusions, succumbing to hype, or making impulse purchases. And it means preparing for contingencies as part of planning for roll-out.

In other words, it means following a shopping list prepared on the basis of highest priority needs, which requires first thinking through those needs systemically starting at the most basic level, enterprise survival. "Because [it] represents such a large percentage of capital spending...investment in technology is a de facto strategy [for the organization]" (Benko & McFarlan, 2003).

The approach to a successful IT program is holistically addressing the organizational questions posed in the upper portion of Table 11.5. The technology solution then must be designed within the context of these questions as illustrated in the lower section of Table 11.5. So for your next project, how would you answer these questions?

> Knowing what you're striving for with your knowledge management [system] makes it much easier to determine whether you're getting value for the money spent—even if the ROI never shows up on a balance sheet. (Cohen, 2006)

References

Ackoff, R. L. (1981). *Creating the corporate future*. New York: Wiley.

Argyris, C. (1993). *Knowledge for action: A guide to overcoming organizational barriers to organizational change*. San Fransisco, CA: Jossey-Bass.

Baba, M. L. (1995). The cultural ecology of the corporation: Explaining diversity in work group responses to organizational transformation. *Journal of Applied Behavioral Science, 31*(2), 202–233.

Baba, M. L., Falkenburg, D., & Hill, D. (1996). Technology management and American culture: Implications for business process redesign. *Research Technology Management*, *39*(6), 44–54.

Bazerman, M. H., & Chugh, D. (2006). Decisions without blinders. *Harvard Business Review*, *84*(January), 88–97 (Special Issue on Decision Making).

Bea, B. (2006). *Learning from failures: Lessons from the recent history of failures of engineered systems*. White Paper, Center for Catastrophic Risk Management, Department of Civil and Environmental Engineering, University of California, Berkeley, USA.

Beer, S. (1959). *Cybernetics and management*. London: English Universities Press.

Benko, C., & McFarlan, F. W. (2003). *Connecting the dots*. Boston, MA: Harvard Business School Press.

Bock, G.-W., Zmud, R. W., Kim, Y.-G., & Lee, J.-N. (2005). Behavioral intention formation in knowledge sharing: Examining the roles of extrinsic motivators, social-psychological forces, and organizational climate. *MIS Quarterly*, *29*(1), 87–111.

Bonabeau, E. (2002). Predicting the unpredictable. *Harvard Business Review*, *80*(March), 109–116.

Brooks, D. (2007). The outsourced brain. *New York Times*, October 26, A.25.

Carroll, J. S., & Hatakenaka, S. (2001). Driving organizational change in the midst of crisis. *MIT Sloan Management Review*, *42*, 70–79.

Cohen, D. (2006). What's your return on knowledge? *Harvard Business Review*, *84*(December), 28.

Columbia Accident Investigation Board (CAIB), & Gehman, H. W. (2003). *CAIB Report* (p. 201). Washington, DC: National Aeronautics & Space Administration (NASA). Available at http://www.nasa.gov/columbia/home/CAIB_Vol1.html. Accessed on February 2009).

Coutu, D. L. (2002). How resilience works. *Harvard Business Review*, *5*(May), 46–55.

Dove, R. (2001). *Response ability: The language, structure, and culture of the agile enterprise*. New York: Wiley.

Drucker, P. F. (1995). The information executives truly need. *Harvard Business Review*, *5*(January–February), 54–62.

Duhigg, C. (2008). At Freddie Mac, chief discarded warning signs. *New York Times*, August 5, A.1.

Friedman, T. L. (2005). *The world is flat: A brief history of the twenty-first century*. New York: Farrar, Straus & Giroux.

Fuld, L. (2004). How to anticipate wrenching change: CEOs can avoid being blindsided if they heed key signals. *Chief Executive*, *201*(August–September). http://www.fuld.com/News/08_04_How%20to%20Anticipate%20Wrenching%20Change.pdf. Accessed on October 2009.

Gharajedaghi, J. (1999). *Systems thinking: Managing chaos and complexity: A platform for designing business architecture*. Burlington, MA: Butterworth-Heinemann.

Goldmacher, A. (2006). The role of culture in managing change in a global automotive company. Avaialable at http://imeresearch.eng.wayne.edu/Proceedings2006/Amy.pdf. Accessed on December 2008.

Green, A. (2005). A framework of intangible valuation areas. In: M. Stankosky (Ed.), *Creating the discipline of knowledge management: The latest in university research* (pp. 189–208). Burlington, MA: Elsevier Butterworth-Heinemann.

Green, A. (2008). *A framework of intangible valuation areas: The sources of intangible assets within an organization*. Germany: VDM-Publishing.

Haeckel, S. H. (1999). *Adaptive enterprise: Creating and leading sense-and-respond organizations*. Boston, MA: Harvard Business School Press.

Hsu, S. (2006). Katrina report spreads blame. *Washington Post*, February 12, A.01. Available at http://www.washingtonpost.com/wp-dyn/content/article/2006/02/11/AR2006021101409_pf.html. Accessed on February 2006.

Kaplan, R. S., & Norton, D. P. (1996). *The balanced scorecard: Translating strategy into action*. Boston, MA: Harvard Business School Press.

Kaplan, R. S., & Norton, D. P. (2008). Protect strategic expenditures. *Harvard Business Review*, 86(December), 28.

Kemp, L. L. (2000). Measurement is fundamental to managing an enterprise knowledgeably. In: *Proceedings of the Government Electronics & Information Technology Association (GEIA) 2000 Vision Conference*, Washington, DC.

Kemp, L. L., Nidiffer, K., Rose, L., & Stankosky, M. (2001). Knowledge management: Insights from the trenches. *IEEE Software*, 18, 66–68.

Kirk, M., & Gilmore, J. (2002). *The man who knew*, PBS Frontline, Aired on 3 October. Transcript at http://www.pbs.org/wgbh/pages/frontline/shows/knew/. Accessed on July 2005.

KMBI. (2005). Knowledge Management and Business Intelligence (KMBI). Workshop organizer/chair: B. Rieger. In: K.-D. Althoff, A. Dengel, R. Bergmann, M. Nick & T. Roth-Berghofer (Eds), *Professional knowledge management, third Biennial Conference, WM 2005, Kaiserslautern, Germany, April 10–13, 2005, revised selected papers* (Vol. 3782, pp. 466–468). Berlin: Springer. Available at http://www.springerlink.com/content/pk3818tj507v4284/fulltext.pdf. Accessed on October 2009.

Liebowitz, J. (2006). *Strategic intelligence: Business intelligence, competitive intelligence, and knowledge management*. Boca Raton, FL: Auerbach.

Macgill, S., & Siu, Y.L. (2004). Risk management as risk knowledge management, *Journal of Risk Management*, Unpublished article.

Macgill, S., & Siu, Y. L. (2005). A new paradigm for risk analysis. *Futures*, 37(10), 1105–1131. December, copyright 2005 Elsevier. Available at http://www.sciencedirect.com/science?_ob = ArticleURL&_udi = B6V65-4GDKB0V-1&_user = 650615&_rdoc = 1&_fmt = &_orig = search&_sort = d&_docanchor = &view = c&_acct = C000035118&_version = 1&_urlVersion = 0&_userid = 650615&md5 = 2916c2ed783eef7238619d8b1941c7dd. Accessed on October 2009.

Marcus, B. (2007). *Business strategy versus tactics*. Helium, Inc. Available at http://www.helium.com/knowledge/104343-business-strategy-versus-tactics. Accessed on March 2009.

McAfee, A., & Brynjolfsson, E. (2008). Investing in the IT that makes a competitive difference. *Harvard Business Review*, 86(July–August), 98–107.

Merzenich, M., Frackowiak, R., Gazzaley, A., Livingstone, M., & Moffett, S. (2008). Brain Fitness 2: Sight and Sound, program aired on the Public Broadcasting System. Host Peter Coyote. Producer Tony Tiano, Santa Fe Productions.

Norman, D. A. (1988). *The psychology of everyday things*. New York: Basic Books.

Pascale, R. T., & Athos, A. G. (1981). *The art of Japanese management*. New york: Simon & Schuster.

Peters, R. (2007). Wanted: Occupation doctrine. *Armed Forces Journal*, 144(April), 39–47. Available at http://www.armedforcesjournal.com/2007/04/2591168. Accessed on April 2007.

Porter, M. E. (1985). *Competitive advantage*. New York: Free Press.

Prahalad, C. K., & Hamel, G. (1990). The core competence of the corporation. *Harvard Business Review*, 68(May–June), 79–91.

Román, J., Ribière, V. M., & Stankosky, M. A. (2004). Organizational culture types and their relationship with knowledge flow and knowledge management success: An empirical study in the U.S. government and nonprofit sectors. *Journal of Information and Knowledge Management, 3*(2), 167–178.

Rothberg, H. N., & Erickson, G. S. (2005). *From knowledge to intelligence: Creating competitive advantage in the next economy.* Burlington, MA: Elsevier Butterworth-Heinemann.

Senge, P. M. (1994). *The fifth discipline: The art and practice of the learning organization.* New York: Currency/Doubleday.

Sheffi, Y. (2005). *The resilient enterprise: Overcoming vulnerability for competitive advantage.* Cambridge, MA: MIT Press.

Stankosky, M. A., & Baldanza, C. (2001). A systems approach to engineering a knowledge management system. In: R. Barquin, A. Bennett & S. Remez (Eds), *Knowledge management: A catalyst for electronic government.* Vienna, VA: Management Concepts.

Sutcliffe, K. (1994). What executives notice: Accurate perceptions in top management teams. *Academy of Management Journal, 37*(5), 1360–1378.

Tedlow, R. S. (2008). Leaders in denial. *Harvard Business Review, 86*(July–August), 18–19.

Tiwana, A. (2002). *The knowledge management toolkit: Orchestrating it, strategy, and knowledge platforms* (2nd ed.). Upper Saddle River, NJ: Prentice Hall.

Truman, H. (1956). *Memoirs: Years of trial and hope* (vol. II). Garden City, NY: Doubleday.

Tufte, E. R. (1990). *Envisioning information.* Cheshire, CT: Graphics Press.

Weick, K. E., & Sutcliffe, K. M. (2005). *Managing the unexpected: High reliability organizing. course slides.* University of Michigan Ross School of Business (Unpublished data).

Weick, K. E., Sutcliffe, K. M., & Obstfeld, D. (2000). High reliability: The power of mindfulness. In: *Leader to leader.* San Francisco: Drucker Foundation/Jossey-Bass [Reprinted in Hesselbein, F. & Johnston, R. (Eds). (2002). *On high-performance organizations.* San Francisco: Jossey-Bass. Available at http://media.wiley.com/product_data/excerpt/91/07879606/0787960691.pdf. Accessed on October 2005.]. Unpublished course slide.

Wheatley, M. J. (2005). *Finding our way: Leadership for an uncertain time.* San Francisco, CA: Berrett-Koehler.

Chapter 12

Knowledge Management Technologies

Vincent M. Ribière and Aurilla Aurélie Bechina Arntzen

Abstract

This chapter presents the various technologies than can be used to support knowledge management initiatives. There is constant debate and confusion regarding the differences between IT solution and KM solutions. This chapter will help clarifying what is what and will present several frameworks to describe the various KM technologies available through different lenses. Over the past years, Web 2.0 technologies have gained a large visibility and adoption in the KM landscape and a portion of this chapter is dedicated to them.

12.1. Introduction: Knowledge or Information?

Can information technology be used to manage knowledge? Before we answer this question, let us look at the common definition of types of knowledge. Knowledge is often described as being explicit (which can be easily documented/codified and shared) or being tacit (acquired through experience). This oversimplified dichotomy is confusing and incomplete (Singh, 2007). As Mohamed (2008) pointed out, "Is it logical to use the current Information Technologies as Knowledge Management Technologies?" It is often mentioned in the knowledge management (KM) literature that tacit knowledge has to be converted into explicit knowledge. Since, by definition, tacit knowledge cannot be articulated, it cannot be converted into explicit knowledge. On the other hand, what can be articulated is implicit knowledge. Implicit knowledge is explicit knowledge that has not been yet articulated (Frappaolo, 2008; Nickhols, 2000). It has not been yet articulated because the owner does not know how to articulate it, or he/she did not think about articulating it or he/she did not want to do so. The help of a knowledge engineer, or of a person

In Search of Knowledge Management: Pursuing Primary Principles
Copyright © 2010 by Emerald Group Publishing Limited
All rights of reproduction in any form reserved
ISBN: 978-1-84950-673-1

that will observe the expert in performing a task, can help to capture and to articulate implicit knowledge.

> Knowledge is experience everything else is information
> — Albert Einstein

Without getting into philosophical debates, knowledge cannot exist without a knower (i.e., a person). A knowledge repository (e.g., computer, library) contains a lot of information but cannot be considered as "knowledgeable" (McDermott, 1999). The use and interpretation of this information repository might become source of knowledge for a person. Knowledge is part of the mind and body of a person and what comes in and out of it remains information (Al-Hawamdeh, 2003). Knowledge can eventually be recreated by a listener based on the information received (Bennet & Bennet, 2008). Knowledge is not an object, it is related to action and it is primary based on experience. That is one of the reasons why we often define knowledge as actionable information. For example, knowing how to drive a car requires some knowledge about rules on the road and safety that can be acquired by reading and understanding a driver's manual (i.e., information). It also requires some experience on how to operate a car and on how to handle different situations as well as emergency cases. An experienced driver will also develop over time some reflex actions that will become instinctive when there is no time to think (i.e., tacit). So if knowledge can only be embodied in people how can information technology (IT) help? IT can be used to manage the explicit representation of knowledge, often referred as knowledge artifacts (KAs) (McLerney, 2002; Newman & Conrad, 1999). In an IT context, KAs are explicit and implicit knowledge that have been articulated into documents, notes, procedures, policies, video, audio clips, and so forth (Kirsch, 2008). People should not say "Tacit knowledge needs to be converted into explicit knowledge" but "Implicit knowledge needs to be converted into explicit knowledge artifacts." Tacit knowledge can be transferred but cannot be articulated into explicit KAs.

Hence, IT cannot manage knowledge but it can manage information and KAs (i.e., passive objects) that will trigger and facilitate knowledge to be internally created by the user (i.e., dynamic action). Being able to provide the right information to the right person at the right time in the right format and in the right context can serve as catalyst for knowledge creation.

Once KM became a "hot topic," mid-1990s, a large number of software vendors saw an easy opportunity to sell their information management solutions under the new label of KM tools, without making fundamental changes to them. This situation created some confusion and disillusionment among the first adopters and gave a bad/false image to KM. KM was then considered as a new technology-based system without much consideration to the human side and to the change management aspects associated with it. Unfortunately, a lot of companies failed into their KM initiative because of this purely IT centered approach. As with any information system solution, if users do not adopt and do not use the system, benefits will be very limited. Fortunately the KM solution landscape has evolved and matured since then. In this chapter, we present three different frameworks that can be used to categorize them.

12.2. Frameworks of KM Technologies

In this section, we selected three frameworks that we believe complement each others in presenting how KM Technologies can contribute to the effective management of KAs.

12.3. Codification and Personalization Framework

This framework describes KM technologies at a very conceptual level. The framework is composed of two main and *complementary* categories of tools (and/or approaches): codification and personalization.

12.4. Codification Enabling Tools

Codification tools and practices intend to collect, codify, and disseminate information and knowledge artifacts. One of the benefits of the codification approach is the reuse of knowledge. "The aim of codification is to put organizational knowledge into a form that makes it accessible to those who need it. It literally turns knowledge into a code (though not necessarily a computer code) to make it as organized, explicit, portable, and easy to understand as possible" (Davenport & Prusak, 1998).

The codification approach has been named and described in different ways by various authors; the collecting dimension by Denning (1998), the transformation model by Natarajan and Shekhar (2000) and distributive applications by Zack and Michael (1996).

Hansen, Nohria, and Tierney (1999) published an article in the *Harvard Business Review* titled "What's your strategy for managing knowledge?" In this article, they described how different companies focus on different practices and tools to manage their knowledge. They described codification process as: "Knowledge is codified and stored in databases, where it can be accessed and used easily by anyone in the company. Knowledge is codified using a *people-to-documents approach*: it is extracted from the person who developed it, made independent of that person, and reused for various purposes" (Hansen, et al., 1999). They illustrated this strategy with the case of two consulting companies, Anderson Consulting and Ernst and Young, which adopted this strategy due to the fact that their activity mainly focused on implementation projects rather than on purely innovative projects.

Figure 12.1 illustrates the codification approach where a central knowledge repository is used to store the KAs captured and then provided to be reused by employees. The various tools that support the codification approach are represented on the right part of Figure 12.4.

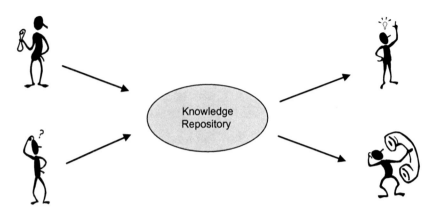

Figure 12.1: Representation of the codification approach.

12.5. Personalization Enabling Tools

Personalization tools and practices focus on developing networks for linking people so that tacit knowledge can be shared/transferred. Information and communication technologies (ICT) are moderately used in such type of approach. This approach corresponds to the Nonaka and Takeuchi personalization phase (Nonaka & Takeuchi, 1995; Nonaka & Toyama, 2003) of the socialization, externalization, combination, and internalization (SECI) model where knowledge flow and creation happened during an exchange of tacit knowledge. The authors who previously defined codification tools also provide their own definition of personalization tools; the connecting dimension by Denning (1998), the independent model by Natarajan and Shekhar (2000), and the collaborative approach by Zack and Michael (1996).

Figure 12.2 illustrates the personalization approach where technology is used to facilitate the social interactions between individuals. The various tools that support the personalization approach are represented on the left part of Figure 12.4.

12.6. Codification versus Personalization Tools

What is the best approach for managing knowledge? Hansen et al. (1999) noted that effective organizations excel by primarily emphasizing one of the approaches and using the other in a supporting role. They postulate that companies trying to excel at both approach risk failing at both. They refer to a 20–80 split between codification and personalization. This proposal raised much discussion in the literature (Koenig, 2004). Denning (1998) mentioned that organizations that focus entirely on a personalization approach, with little or no attempt at codification, can be very inefficient. After conducting a survey among 100 U.S. companies involved in KM, Ribière (2005) showed that the companies studied were more likely to use a balanced

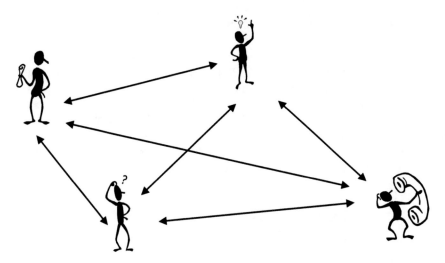

Figure 12.2: Representation of the personalization approach.

approach with a ratio closer from 45% to 55% than from 20% to 80%, as suggested by Hansen et al (1999).

In order to select an adoption approach, Tiwana (2002) designed a checklist based on the recommendations of Hansen et al (1999). They recommended examining the company's competitive strategy (e.g., What value do customers expect from the company? How does the knowledge that resides in the company add value to customers' goals?). Once the competitive strategy is clear three additional questions might be investigated:

- Does your company offer standardized or customized products?
- Does your company have a mature or innovative product?
- Do people rely on explicit or tacit knowledge to solve problems?

Companies having standardized products and/or mature products might want to focus on a codification approach. In contrast, companies having customized and/or innovative products might want to focus on personalization approach. People relying on explicit knowledge will also be more willing to adopt a codification approach. Furthermore, recent research highlights the critical role that organizational culture and organizational trust have in the selection of these two KM strategies (Ribière, 2001, 2009d; Ribière & Tuggle, 2005; Román-Velázquez, Ribière, & Stankosky, 2004). They demonstrated that the success of a KM strategy might be directly impacted by the type of organizational culture present in the organization.

The codification/personalization framework remains very general and another way to describe KM technologies is to organize them based on how they support the main KM processes/flows.

12.7.   A Process Oriented Framework: "L.A. R.O.S.A."

We selected the "LA ROSA" model developed by Ribière (2008) in order to describe the six main KM processes (Figure 12.3). The "LA ROSA" acronym stands for Locate, Acquire, Refine, Organize, Share, and Apply knowledge. *Rosa* is the Latin and botanic name of the flowering shrub rose. The six processes should *not* be seen as a cycle (i.e., a set of consecutive steps) but more as a set of interrelated processes. For instance, after applying knowledge you might want to directly refine it or maintain it (in the system), or you can locate knowledge (from someone) and acquire it directly without going through the "organize/storage" process.

Figure 12.3: Enabling IT tools supporting the "LA ROSA" knowledge flow model
(Ribière, 2009a, 2009b).

You will note that not all the tools presented are new; some of them have been available for quite some time for information management needs. However, they can also be used to support KM solutions in order to create a context to support KAs. An integration of various tools and solutions are required to efficiently manage KAs since currently there are no fully integrated KM solutions that cover all the various needs of different organization types. Note that the tools listed below are only technological tools, they will need to be associated with other KM practices in order to fully support each KM process. We will now describe the main ICT tools but other tools not discussed here might also help to support each subprocess of "LA ROSA."

12.8. Locate, Create, Discover, and Map Knowledge

Different tools can be used to support the KM processes. *Expertise locators* allow users to rapidly identify who has a particular set of skills or connections. These tools can use employees' profiles created by employees or which have been created dynamically by using semantic engines to learn from documents created by employees, from their emails, from their Web visits, and so forth. *Knowledge maps* are visual representations of KAs, their location, and their relationships. *Knowledge discovery tools* allow the mining of large data repositories in order to find pattern and relationships among data that will later on be integrated into knowledge bases or expert systems. *Data mining tools* fit in this category. *Text mining tools* (i.e., text analytics) allow extracting meaning from a document. They can be based on statistical analyses but those based on semantic engines typically provide better results. *E-learning* solutions allow you to train and transfer knowledge to employees by applying these learned procedures. These procedures instruct the employees on how to do things, why they should be done, when these actions are necessary, where to apply them, and what exactly needs to be considered. Through trial and error (i.e., experience), employees gain the tacit knowledge, allowing them to become proficient. *Intelligent and knowledge agents* can be programmed to perform knowledge searches in large data repository and on networks (e.g., Internet). *Social networking analysis* (SNA) is used to map informal relationships that exist between people within and outside a company. Such networks can be used to reveal employees who can be considered as experts, or knowledge brokers, or hubs between groups or communities. *Alert systems* allow you to be informed as soon as a new KA related to your interest has been made available in your corporate repository or on the Internet (indentified through a new Web search engine index). They belong to the category of push technologies and awareness systems. *Business intelligence* tools allow you to improve decision-making, and to ease access/manipulate enterprise information. They also allow you to stay updated on your competitors, market, and benchmarks. *Search engines* help not only to retrieve text based documents but also images, movies, people, bookmarks, etc. Meta search engines can be used to aggregate the results of queries performed by various search engines. *Visualization tools* are becoming more and more popular since they use interactive visual representations (e.g., maps, graphs) to display results of search and/or relationships between various knowledge artifacts. *Innovation and creativity supporting tools* help to foster innovation in organizations by providing a set of tools, like for instance mind maps, which can facilitate and support the process of thinking about the problem and solution in new more holistic ways. Group decision support systems (GDSS) help to take advantage of group brain power to develop new ideas (i.e., brainstorming), allow full collaboration, or to facilitate decision-making. Finally, online analytical processing (OLAP) tools use a cube representation to answer multidimensional analytical queries and to allow to slide and dice data in order to find the data or the response to a question or problem.

12.9. Acquire and Capture Knowledge

Knowledge acquisition usually requires the help of a knowledge engineer to articulate knowledge artifacts. Despite the involvement of a human being, some IT tools can help to capture knowledge artifacts. Audio and video recordings are an effective way to record interviews, debriefings, and after action reviews. People do not like to write reports and they are always careful regarding what they write. People share more freely and convey more meaning in their interviews than they will do in writing reports. Short video clips are then cut out from the full interview and can be meta tagged, indexed and made available through database of video clips or podcasts. *Recombination tools* are usually composed of aggregation, mashups, remixing, and embedding technologies. They allow to collect, like *content syndication tools*, information from various sources, to filter them and to deliver them, in a customized format, to all those interested. *Speech recognition tools* are used to capture and convert voice messages into text documents. They are very effective for people who are not comfortable with technology or who do not have time to type (e.g., doctors in hospitals or police detectives writing reports). *Semantic analysis technology* is often coupled with text mining tools in order, not only to extract meaning from text documents but, to abstract and summarize them. Translation tools can also become very useful to capture knowledge published in a different language or for international companies having to deal with different languages (e.g., multinational corporations). Finally, *forums* and discussion groups are wonderful tools to capture discussions and problem solving solutions shared between individuals (internal or external of the organization).

12.10. Refine, Validate, and Maintain Knowledge

Once the knowledge has been captured it needs to be validated and maintained over time. *Online expert communities* can be used to review and decide what should be considered as knowledge and what not. The validation can also be done directly by the members of the community or by people who used the knowledge artifacts. They will then use some assessment, *rating, ranking, and scoring mechanisms* in order to validate and eventually refine the knowledge artifact. *Contribution validation technologies* can also be used to pre-validate or automate some of the validation process. Finally, *workflow* systems can help to accelerate the validation and maintenance process flows and to improve workgroup productivity.

12.11. Organize, Store, and Protect Knowledge

The following technologies can be used to archive KAs. Most of these technologies are not new per se. *Document and content management systems* (DMS and CMS) are useful to manage the different phases of the document life cycle from drafting, to review, approval, and distribution. They also facilitate collaboration, storage, versioning, security, etc. DMS usually focus on structured information (e.g., word processing, spreadsheet, presentation, PDF, files) while CMS have the additional capability to manage and organize unstructured information (e.g., images, movies, multimedia). Database management systems (DBMS) are used to store operational and transactional data while *data warehouses* and *data marts* are used to store selected and cleaned historical data that may have been, to different extents, summarized. All three are used as data repositories for knowledge discovery tools (e.g., data mining) but also to structure and to easily retrieve records. Taxonomies are used to classify KAs into categories often following a hierarchical structure. *Ontologies*, at a higher level, help to define a domain, its components, and their relationships. Multiple taxonomies might be required to define a domain (i.e., ontology). *Taxonomies* are important since they facilitate the retrieval of a KA-assisting search engines and users who might take different paths to get to them. For instance, a lessons' learned document could be archived in a directory related to the project it emerged from, or in a directory associated with the type of practice (e.g., marketing, engineering, management) or in a directory related to a particular process or in other places. Taxonomies should allow users to easily retrieve the searched for KA following the logic (path) that makes sense to them without having to guess where the author may have stored it. *Folksonomies* and *tagging* techniques became popular with Web 2.0 technologies. These techniques allow authors, users, and anyone to describe and categorize content with their own keywords (i.e., tags) without using a rigid predefined structure (i.e., formal taxonomy). Tags are often visually represented on the Internet by tag clouds. Finally, information security techniques should be deployed to protect the intellectual digital asset of the organization. For instance, *authentication* techniques can be used to secure access to KA that might benefit, in specific cases, to be *encrypted* to decrease their likelihood to be stolen or viewed in case of security breaches. Disaster recovery systems, like *backup solutions* and policies, should also be present to protect the KA in case of emergency.

12.12. Share and Transfer Knowledge

Knowledge transfer and knowledge sharing are key KM processes. That is from the transfer and the application of knowledge that value is created. *Knowledge portals* provide a single point access to unified enterprise information and explicit KA. They integrate various technologies previously described and they provide a customized interface displaying only relevant information to the user. Online *communities of practice* (CoP) provide an environment where people, who share the same interest, can virtually meet to exchange tips, share best practices and documents, discuss issues, vote, collaborate, etc. Most portals provide a community-building feature but some tools are particularly designed to support the various needs of CoPs that can involve, not only employees of a company, but also partners, suppliers, customers, etc. *Groupware* is an umbrella term used to describe the technologies facilitating the collaboration of groups and teams. They are designed to support and increase the productivity and communication of the various team members. *Wiki technologies* allow anyone to contribute to a Web page by adding or changing content. It facilitates collaboration with various team members contributing online to the latest version of a shared Web document. *Blogs* are Web pages where authors share their experiences, passions, interests, etc. in a chronological manner. Originally used for personal use (i.e., online diary) they now have became a popular medium for employees to report on their daily activities, events, and to communicate. *Instant messaging* (IM) applications are synchronous communication tools that allow two or more people to communicate in real time through a text window. IM tools often offer voice over IP (VoIP) technologies that allow users to have a phone and/or video conversation using the Internet for free. Not all companies allow the use of IM, since some of them are worried about security issues or the distraction they can generate. IM are a good tool to get quick answers to questions when your colleagues are online. *Collaborative tools*, like groupware, is an umbrella term. They can support all kind of collaborations; synchronous, asynchronous (linked or separate), content development, project management, and group polling to name a few. *Publishing tools* allow users to directly share their KAs on the Internet or on an intranet or extranet in the form of documents, Web pages, blogs, and other communication devices. They can be part of DMS or CMS previously described. *Peer to peer* (P2P) *technologies* differ from client server technologies by the fact that a node (computer) can serve both as a client and as a server. They provide a easy decentralized way to share content (e.g., files, streaming media, telephony, discussion groups). *Email technology* might not require any explanation, but it is important to keep in mind that it is one of the most used collaboration and knowledge sharing tools even though its capabilities are very limited. It reinforces the fact that people like to use simple tools to do their routine work. *Online forums and discussion groups* are asynchronous linked type of technologies that work well for question-answers type of communications and collaborations. They can be easily searched and archived supporting codification mechanisms. Finally, video and audio conferencing allow real time communication between users. Through such kind of verbal and visual exchanges, richer content and explanations can be shared allowing implicit and tacit knowledge to be shared through conversations, discussions, etc.

12.13. Apply, Use, Adopt, and Adapt Knowledge

This last KM process is the one which is the least supported by technology but which provides the most benefits and value to individuals and to organizations. During the transfer process, knowledge sharing is supposed to take place. We used "supposed to" since a certain number of stickiness factors (i.e., knowledge characteristics, disseminative capacity, absorptive capacity, and organizational context) may interfere with the efficiency and effectiveness of the knowledge transfer process. If the transfer does take place, users can internalize and learn from the KAs passed to them. Then they can act on this newly internalized knowledge by solving problems, making decisions, performing activities, etc. This human learning process does not involve technology but the knowledge shared can also feed knowledge bases of *expert systems* (ES), *decision support systems* (DSS), *help desks*, or even *workflow collaborative tools*. These all help and support knowledge workers in diagnosing, planning, forecasting, supporting, designing, and decision-making processes.

12.14. A Knowledge Type Driven Framework of KM Technologies

This last framework illustrates the different KM technologies based on the type of information and KAs they manage (Figure 12.4). The bottom part (factory building) represents the corporate data, information and knowledge artifacts, The top part is linked to the Internet (cloud) and to the different stakeholders and environment factors.

The left part of Figure 12.4 represents tacit KAs and the right part explicit KAs that can be broken down into structured and unstructured information. The two parts overlap since most knowledge is neither fully tacit nor explicit.

Section 1 represents tools used to manage structured information (i.e., records). All these tools are supported by some sort of database management systems.

Section 2 represents tools that can be used to support both structured and unstructured information. These tools can be applied to search and manipulate information in database repositories but also in documents. For instance a semantic engine might be used to extract the key concepts out of a document and to display them on a map or on a tag cloud (e.g., visualization tool).

Section 3 represents tools that can be used to support unstructured information (e.g., documents, emails, presentation, Web content). A survey conducted in 2000 (Corporate Executive Board) showed that 85–95% of the information that an organization possesses is unstructured (5–15% is structured) and that only 10–20% of the IT spending was allocated to manage unstructured information (80–90% spent on structured information). We think that this imbalance is not as important these days but we are confident that a focus on structured information remains a priority for most organizations. A large amount of KAs are contained in reports, procedures,

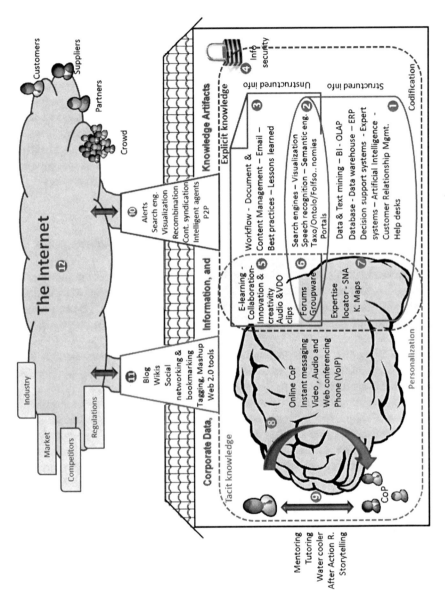

Figure 12.4: KM technologies framework (Ribière, 2009c).

and debriefings. This leads to the KAs are often hidden or that cannot be easily located or that are not searchable. Deploying some tools that can help to better take advantage of unstructured information can provide great benefits to an organization by better identifying and easily retrieving KAs.

As previously mentioned, since KAs represent a large proportion of the intellectual asset of an organization they need to be properly protected (section 4). Information security tools and practices need to be implemented to secure and to protect information (Ryan, 2004). Over-protecting information might impact the ability of employees to fully take advantage of the corporate knowledge asset, and leaving everyone access to everything might also result in knowledge leaks that might affect the company's competitiveness. So it is important to find the right balance between over protecting and under protecting your knowledge assets. Information security becomes also very important when companies share information with their partners and suppliers through extranets or other private networks.

Section 5 describes the tools that can support unstructured information (i.e., explicit KAs) and tacit KAs. If we refer to Nonaka's and Takeushi's SECI model (1995), these tools could support both the codification (i.e., conversion from tacit to explicit) and the internalization (i.e., conversion from explicit to tacit) phases. Creativity and innovation support tools as well as collaborative tools can facilitate the emergence of new ideas by supporting and stimulating interactions between groups. Audio and video recordings of expert interviews and any type of debriefing sessions can be valuable if they are, later on, properly converted into short video clips associated with meaningful keywords/tags that will make them easily retrievable. E-learning tools support the learning process and the creation of tacit knowledge through trial and errors.

Section 6 describes the tools that can support explicit KAs (based on both structured and unstructured information) as well as tacit KAs. Groupware application and online forums facilitate the capture and exchange of various types of information and documents. Database Management systems are used to link/connect these various types of information that makes them easier to manage and which also provide a context for their understanding.

Section 7 describes the tools that can support structured information (i.e., explicit KAs) and tacit KAs. Expertise locators (also called corporate yellow pages, or who is who) can be used to identify who in the organization has some particular expertise, skills, or knowledge about a specific topic. They help people to connect with each others. Usually a simple database managing employees' profiles can be used to meet this need. In the same way, knowledge maps can be used to identify where knowledge can be found and its flows. SNA allows you to identify the informal connection in between people inside and outside an organization. They can be used to identify who are the key holders of knowledge, who are knowledge brokers, hubs, etc.

Section 8 describes the tools that can support the transfer/flow or tacit knowledge between individuals, since tacit knowledge cannot be captured/articulated. Online CoPs often provide the capabilities for members to have interactions through instant messaging, video and audio Web conferencing, or through phone conversations (e.g., voice over IP).

Section 9 is not supported by technology but we represented it in order to reinforce the fact that tacit knowledge is best transferred by face to face interactions and socialization activities (e.g., mentoring, tutoring, water cooler discussions, after action reviews [AAR], and storytelling).

Section 10 described the tools that can be used to search, visualize, and automatically retrieve (i.e., push technologies) information located on the Internet. These tools are critical to increase awareness about any new available information regarding your stakeholders or your environment represented on the Internet cloud 12. Finally, section 11 represents the new generation of Web 2.0 tools which facilitate people to share and connect with each other inside and outside the organization. The next section describes these Web 2.0 tools in more detail.

12.15. Web 2.0 Tools

With the growing recognition that KM technologies have not fully delivered their promises (Rigby & Bilodeau, 2007), academic and KM practitioners have shifted their focus on solving "nontechnological issues" related to practices, cultures, and organizational changes (Allen, 2008). Knowledge sharing is seen as a challenging task, difficult to nurture within an organization. It requires prosocial behavior through social processes, for example, by cultivating a sense of community.

The persistent quest to achieve KM objectives and to foster collaboration has led strategist's people to adopt emerging technologies supporting new networked business structures. Web 2.0, Social software, could become one of the answers for improving the way people work together and to address some of the knowledge sharing challenges.

Close studies looking at the use of Web 2.0 communities show that knowledge sharing is the fundamental nature of such approaches. For example, strong user participations have created the recognized success of some Web sites such as Wikipedia, eBay, or Amazon.

With expanding capability to connect people and the need to enable corporate knowledge sharing, it is important to take a Swiss Army knife approach providing many tools and selecting the right tool or approach for each need at the point of use (O'Dell, 2008). Therefore, it is crucial to understand the Web 2.0 concept, how a new breed of open, networked organization — the Enterprise 2.0 (E2.0) is emerging and why nowadays it is gaining attention (Tapscott, 2006).

12.16. Introduction to Web 2.0

The Web 2.0 phenomenon has gained tremendous visibility and has attracted strong interests not only from the scientific community but as well from businesses and IT vendors (Smith, 2008). This has generated some conflicting definitions of Web 2.0

since IT vendors are trying to capitalize on this trend by associating their products with Web 2.0 attributes, like they did with KM technologies in the mid-1990s.

Web 2.0 should be seen as the convergence of two driving trends, one technology-oriented and one emphasizing social dimensions. This convergence leads to new business models with user-contributed content. The features leverage a diverse participatory intellectual capital to enhance the transparency of business processes and to distribute participatory services and products design.

The Web 2.0 definition by Tim O'Really, who first used this word, better reflects this new concept of gravitational core identified as the web as platform, user-controlled data, architectures of participation, cost-effective scalability, re-mixable data source and data transmissions, and harnessing collective intelligence (Tapscott, 2006).

In opposition to Web 1.0, users can easily generate and publish content. The collective intelligence of users encourages more democratic use and participation (Boulos & Wheeler, 2007). Initially, the primarily goal of the World Wide Web (WWW) was to foster a better collaboration among the scientific communities by sharing ideas and knowledge. However, it is only with the emergence of Web 2.0 technologies that we start to recognize its impacts on leveraging knowledge sharing and enhancing business processes in organizations.

Web 2.0 is a platform for interacting with content. Information is broken up into "microcontent" units that may be distributed across the Web. A new set of tools such as RSS (really simple syndication) provide mechanisms that creates a "feed" of updates from specified news sites, blogs and so forth. RSS contributes to publishing, aggregating, and combining microcontent in new and useful ways.

12.17. Social Software Tools

Literature reviews indicate that the main focus of Web 2.0 is oriented toward the social networking dimensions of Web 2.0 and it fosters the KM leitmotiv meaning from content collection to people connection. There is so far no common definition of the social software; however, there is a general consensus to recognize the strong interactive processes and networks as the backbone of such software. The interaction is mainly due the shift from push driven to pull driven information, in which user-generated content is prevailing (Hoogenboom, Kloos, Bouman, & Jansen, 2007).

Social software applications and services are perceived as the outcome of the popularity and the rapid development of Web 2.0 concepts. Web 2.0 services are: wiki's, like Wikipedia; blogging, such as Blogger; social networking such as Facebook; and social bookmarking, such as Del.Icio.Us.

The term *wiki* is derived from the Hawaiian word meaning fast. Wiki is a collaborative mechanism that allows people to contribute or modify content using a simplified markup language. Wiki is usually used to support the community-building Web site. Wikipedia, an open content encyclopedia, is considered as one of the most popular examples of a wikis. Wikis allow users to enter, aggregate, and annotate content. The underlying concept lies on the collective wisdom to produce an organized, thorough, and searchable database in various domains such as political, humanitarian, education, history, and so forth. Although security issues in organizational use of Wikis security have been tackled by putting in place some mechanisms to restrict viewing or editing content; there are still some concerns to limit the access as it against the concept of freely contribution. In addition, the quality of the content can be questionable if the self-organizing editing and vetting is not adequate.

Blogs are the most personal and controversial of the Web 2.0 applications and more especially in business contexts. Web sites can be created spontaneously and maintained by individuals, making it possible to maintain an online journal on which others can comment for private use or business purpose. Hence, activities discussions can emerge from dynamic use of the blogging feature. The biggest advantage resides in the possibility for participants to interact with others. For example, HP is encouraging its employee to use blog feature to discuss issues on printer compatibility with customers. Blogs have experienced exponential growth by enabling mass communication without requiring HTML knowledge. In fact, in 10 years, the blog sites number have increased to more than 200 million (Raskino, 2007). However, it is important to notice there is need to understand further the knowledge sharing process in this setting. May authors publish their own blog and if there are neither readers nor active participants, the interest of using a blog is quite limited.

Social networking is the practice of increasing the number of business or personal contact by making connections through individuals. This system allows members of a specific site to learn about other members' skills, talents, knowledge, or preferences regardless of geographic location. The concept of social networking is of course not new, however, the Internet has provided a strong potential to extend this phenomenon beyond the usual connections through a Web-based community. Popular Web sites dedicated to social networking include Myspace, Hi5, and Facebook. Professional Web sites dedicated to social networks include LinkedIn, XING, and Viadeo. These sites are said to create business opportunities by enhancing communication among employees, customers who can learn about each other's background such as undertaken contact information, education, employment history, employment opportunities, and so forth.

Social bookmarking allows users to manage, store, organize, and search bookmarks of web pages. The bookmarks can be public, private, or shared only with a specific people or a given community, or the public. Social bookmark services allow users to organize their bookmarks online with informal tags instead of the traditional browser-based system of folders. Therefore, authorized people can view these bookmarks chronologically, by category or tags, or via a search engine. An interesting additional feature relies on the possibility to comment online, annotate or rate on bookmarks. Some social book markings provide web feeds allowing subscribers to become aware of creation, tagging, and saving of new bookmarks by other users. Example includes Flickr and Delicious.

There are many tools that are available; however, it is important to understand the need of the Web 2.0 users and what type of limitation are encountered while using for instance social software.

12.18. Who Are the Users of Web 2.0?

There is strong recognition that people responsible of implementing KM initiative also called KM practitioners are early adopters of knowledge related technologies. Hence, the novel Web 2.0 tools having social computing features were used easily by the KM practitioners. Usually, they are always looking for better tools and practices for the KM initiatives implemented in their workplaces. Examples include the large use of Wiki or blogging (Redmiles & Wilensky, 2008).

However, with the expansion of Web 2.0 technologies, the concepts of *digital natives* and *digital immigrants* have emerged (Figure 12.5). Digital natives are individuals who were born and grew up during the era of the Web, in which instant online access, instant communication with multiple peer groups are part of their thinking mode. Computers, mobile phones, and video gaming are part of their lives. Digital immigrants were born and grew up before this era; thus, these technologies and concepts are not native to them. Individuals belong either to digital native or to digital immigrant groups. Digital natives have a more intuitive potential than digital immigrant to adopt quickly what can Web 2.0 offer (Phifer, 2008). However, the motivation for using Web 2.0 technologies is the decisive element.

For a successful deployment and use of Web 2.0 technologies, it is crucial to categorize the Web 2.0 users in order for enterprises to understand how to deal with employees and customers. Psychographics are essential, because they relate to the user's lifestyle, interests, aspirations, and attitudes toward the use of tool such blogs, wiki, and social networks. It is not the age of the person that determines the categories but rather the people inclination to use Web 2.0 technologies.

One manifestation and application of Web 2.0 in the business domain refers to the concept of E2.0.

12.19. Enterprise 2.0: A New Way To Do Business

During the last decade, enterprise strategists started to recognize that business success and performance improvement was more and more related to the degree to

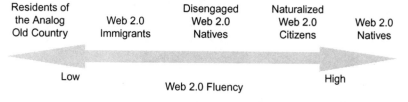

Figure 12.5: Spectrum of Web 2.0 fluency (Phifer, 2008).

which it is a knowledge based organization. There is no doubt that sharing knowledge culture, building a strong sense of community, collaborating, and networking people can drastically contribute to the business process improvement and give to the organization a competitive advantage. Based on collaboration and cooperation, the renaissance of KM and its underlying concepts is leading to a new concept of E2.0 (Gotta, 2007).

The term "Enterprise 2.0" (E2.0) describes a collection of organizational and IT practices that help organizations establish flexible work models, visible knowledge-sharing practices, and higher levels of community participation. An additional interesting feature of E2.0 is the "mashup," a Web site or Web application that uses content from more than one source to create a completely new service.

E2.0 refers to the use of social software in order to improve knowledge sharing and foster collaboration between companies, employees, theirs customers, and partners. To illustrate this approach, Tapscott (2006) introduced "the term of wikinomics to describe an economy in which companies are gaining competitive advantage by successfully managing a trust-based relationships with external collaborators and customers" (Johnston, 2007; Tapscott, 2006). The last decade has seen a clear evolution toward a networked enterprises concept as a means for companies to be more competitive. Figure 12.6 illustrates the evolution from Web 1.0 to E2.0.

The growing adoption of E2.0 is dictated by the need to capitalize knowledge and to retain the corporate knowledge assets through a well thought human resource strategies and competence based management. In addition, the pressure on firms to

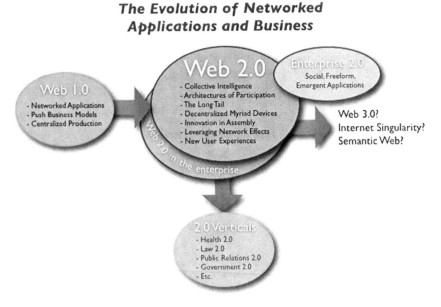

Figure 12.6: Evolution of networked enterprises (Hinchcliffe, 2007).

innovate has forced firms to look for ways to improve their business performances. E2.0 represents a new paradigm for strategic collaboration and KM.

There is no doubt that KM initiatives coupled with collaboration efforts are the best strategy to address the needs to retain people and reach performance goals. Although E2.0 seems to bring the right answer, it is necessary to examine what constitutes its framework.

McAfee (2006) introduced the terms and concepts behind E2.0. He has coined a mnemonic SLATES to describe the key aspects of these social platforms with a description of the essential elements. SLATES stands for Search, Links, Authorship, Tags, Extensions, and Signals.

Search technologies should allow the discovery of the E2.0 content. So that it can be reused or leveraged. This is an important feature that will enhance the collaboration aspects by incorporating this function into business processes.

Links denotes the possibility to integrate content such as Mashup (i.e., remixing the contents in other to create a new one) by facilitating the interconnections between content. It facilitates as well the navigation through the content.

Authorship refers to the usability of the system by allowing access to every worker without having to enter into an extensive training program.

Tags allow the use of meta-tags in order to identify the relevancy of tagged content. Tags create a taxonomy, or several taxonomies, and can be combined to create a folksonomy. Tags can be used to capture individual and collective opinions on the value of content, a form of knowledge in itself, which can also be used as a navigational path through content in a manner similar to links.

Extensions introduce technology to expose patterns of user activity in order to get an insight from the knowledge base. Mechanisms for searching user activity and its behavior are as well provided such for instance Users who have searched on this topic, have also looked at this.

Signal refers to the use of specific technology to push content to potential interested users. It gives a proactively collaborative feature to E2.0. For example, users can subscribe to a Web site and get immediately informed if any changes occurred in meantime.

Dion Hinchcliffe (2007) expanded the SLATES framework by adding four others dimensions: freeform, network-oriented, social, and emergence.

This extended framework called FLATNESS stands for Freeform, Links, Authorship, Tagging, Network-oriented, Extensions, Search, Social, Emergence, and Signals as illustrated in Figure 12.7.

Freeform, stresses that authorship should not be hampered by barriers; such as restriction or learning curves. It stresses as well the need for freeform interfaces to functionality.

Network-oriented stresses that all content must be Web-addressable by giving special rules on authorship. It suggests encouraging the use of blog within the enterprise.

Social highlights the need for transparency, diversity, and openness. Content and community should have easy access by providing the right structure. The cultural facet is a very important ingredient to E2.0 environment.

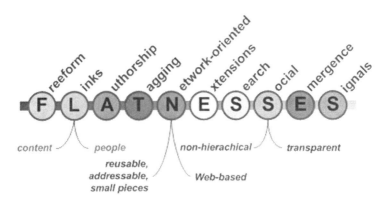

Figure 12.7: The FLATNESS framework (Hinchcliffe, 2007).

Emergence refers to the use of methods and approaches that leverage the interaction of the collective wisdom of the community to produce more than the mere sum of the whole.

Therefore, the two frameworks presented above should be better understood and further investigated as an organization adopts them. The organizational challenges presented by such an adoption are best meet by understanding the critical success factors that drive an E2.0 strategy. The next section discusses the encountered organizational challenges while adopting of E2.0 and identifies the main success drivers.

12.20. Limitations and Barriers

It is recognized among the KM practitioners that focusing only on technologies will not insure the success of Web 2.0 deployment. E2.0 could have happen even without technologies due to the fact that it is a socially driven evolution that did not originate from a technology push nor from a demand pull (Frappaolo & Keldsen, 2008). Hence, adopting E2.0 is not about using others software tools but rather means that people have to reconsider their business routine by incorporating the collaborative paradigm in their daily work. Organizational dimension should be considered by fostering change management strategy while trying to implement new technology. Understanding organizational challenges means understanding the E2.0 adoption barriers, which identify the critical success factors.

The penetration of new technologies in the workplace has generated new type of issues and challenges. For example, selection and adoption of technology is a complex process that is based on a number of alternatives including technological choices, perceived benefits, cost-based models, and organizational strategies. However, technology itself needs adaptation to organizational goals and strategies (Laulmann, Nadler, & O'Farrell, 1991).

Motivations for technology use are both intrinsic and extrinsic. Adaptability of technology to user needs, user confidence, and motivation to its adoption are key factors to undertand. Kanter's (1990) has identified five characteristics of successful technology adoption, the five Fs: focused, fast, flexible, friendly, and fun.

Dias (2002) identified three motivation factors for using technology, namely, perceived usefulness, perceived ease of use, and perceived enjoyment. He argues that "information technology implementation is an intervention we make in order to improve the effectiveness and efficiency of a socio-technical system".

The deployment of novel Web 2.0 tools requires understanding the factors that will facilitate or inhibit the full adoption of their use in the workplace. It is important to examine some of the organizational issues that E2.0 must face such as governance, culture, leadership, incentive schemes, and value capture.

One factor related to the organizational culture arises from the fact that some organizations do not promote extensive collaboration and knowledge sharing outside their project teams. Thus, the Web 2.0 deployment is a challenging task.

Another factor common in many industries (e.g., manufacturing's, aerospace, automation) is the generation gap. Workforces in these sectors are aging and belong mainly to the digital immigrant group. Hence, it is challenging for some of them to use or see a need for social software in their daily work.

12.21. Web 2.0 and E2.0: Conclusion

During the past few years, there has been a growing interest in social software under the name of Web 2.0 for both the business world and the academic communities. Web 2.0 represents the revolution that is happening since more and more users are transforming from passive consumers status to active participants.

However, technological innovations are not magic bullets, and will not provoke organizational change by just being deployed. E2.0 technologies must be introduced into a dynamic environment that participants can see value in. This can be done by taking into accounts human and social contexts and providing appropriate management visioning of the future.

Just as organizations are beginning to grapple with the potential of Web 2.0 and E2.0, there are more opportunities being developed. At this point, there is a concept that looks to be the most promising and that is gaining a large amount of interest (Burkhardt, 2009). The concept refers to the Semantic Web that should be understood as a means for machines to be able to understand, relate, and compile information without human intervention. This could be the starting point for the Web 3.0.

12.22. Conclusion

The purpose of this chapter is to present the most commonly used technologies to support KM through different lenses (i.e., frameworks). We did not address the adoptions factors that will make users use such systems but numerous researches have addressed this issue based on various popular information system adoption models (2008). We also decided not to present any knowledge management systems (KMS) architecture but we recommend looking at the work of Tiwana (2002) as well as white papers from different KMS vendors.

We purposely did not mention any brand or any particular software to illustrate each technology since listing all vendors will be impossible and the IT market is constantly changing. One reference that could be used is the *KM World Buyers Guide* (www.kmworld.com). Various open source applications should also be considered while looking for KM tools and platforms.

Even though KM technologies have matured and take more and more in consideration the human side and relationships between people, we would like to end this chapter by a quote to always keep in mind once implementing KM:

KM is something you do, not something you buy! (Mann, 2007)

References

Al-Hawamdeh, S. (2003). *Knowledge management.* Oxford: Chandos Publishing.

Allen, P. J. (2008). How Web 2.0 communities solve the knowledge sharing problem. Paper presented at the Technology and Society, IEEE International Symposium, ISTAS Fredericton, New Brunswick, Canada, June 26–28.

Bennet, D., & Bennet, A. (2008). The depth of knowledge: Surface, shallow or deep? *VINE: The Journal of Information and Knowledge Management Systems, 38*(7), 405–420.

Boulos, K. M. N., & Wheeler, S. (2007). The emerging Web 2.0 social software: An enabling suite of sociable technologies in health and health care education. *Health Information and Libraries Journal, 24*(24), 2–23.

Burkhardt, P. (2009). Social software trends in business. Retrieved from http://www. igi-global.com/downloads/excerpts/8352.pdf. Retrieved on February 11, 2009.

Davenport, T., & Prusak, L. (1998). *Working knowledge. How organizations manage what they know.* Boston, MA.

Denning, S. (1998). *What is knowledge management?* Available at http://www.stevedenning. com/Find_what_is_km.html. Retrieved on February 11, 2009.

Dias, D. D. S. (2002). Motivation for using information technology. In: E. Szewczak & C. Snodgrass (Eds), *Human factors in information systems* (pp. 55–60). Hershey, PA: IGI Press.

Frappaolo, C. (2008). Implicit knowledge. *Knowledge Management Research and Practice, 6,* 23–25.

Frappaolo, C., & Keldsen, D (2008). *Enterprise 2.0: Agile, emergent & integrated.* Silver Spring, MD: AAIM.

Gotta, M. (2007). *Enterprise 2.0: Collaboration and knowledge management renaissance.* Collaboration and content strategies – In Depth Research Report. Midvale, Utah, Burton Group. Doc number. 77421. http://files.meetup.com/314479/enterprise2%200.pdf

Hansen, M. T., Nohria, N., & Tierney, T. (1999). What's your strategy for managing knowledge? *Harvard Business Review, 77*(2), 106–116.

Hinchcliffe, D. (2007). The state of Enterprise 2.0. *ZDNET*. Retrieved from http://blogs.zdnet.com/Hinchcliffe/?p = 143. Retrieved on February 11, 2009.

Hoogenboom, T., Kloos, M., Bouman, W., & Jansen, R. (2007). Sociality and learning in social software. *International Journal of Knowledge and Learning, 3*(4–5), 501–514.

Johnston, K. (2007). Folksonomies, collaborative filtering and e-business: Is Enterprise 2.0 one step forward and two steps back? *Electronic Journal of Knowledge Management, 5*(4), 411–418. Retrieved from http://www.ejkm.com/volume-5/v5-i4/Johnston.pdf

Kanter, R. M. (1990). *When giants learn to dance*. New York: Free Press.

Kirsch, D. (2008). Knowledge artifacts. Available at http://it.toolbox.com/wiki/index.php/Knowledge_Artifacts. Retrieved on February 11, 2009.

Koenig, M. E. D. (2004). Knowledge management strategy codification versus personalization (a false dichotomy). In: M. E. D. Koenig & K. T. Srikantaiah (Eds), *Knowledge management lessons learned. What works and what doesn't*. Medford, NJ: Information Today.

Laulmann, E., Nadler, G., & O'Farrell, B. (1991). Designing for technological change: People in the process. In: N. R. C. National Academy of Engineering & Commission on Behavioral and Social Sciences and Education (Eds.), *People and technology in the workplace* (pp. 1–14). Washington, DC: The National Academic Press.

Mann, J. (2007). *Why knowledge management is no longer on the Gartner hype cycles*. No. G00151237. Gartner Research, Stamford, CT, USA.

McAfee, A. (2006). Enterprise 2.0: The dawn of emergent collaboration. *MIT Sloan Management Review, 47*(3), 21–28.

McDermott, R. (1999). Why information technology inspired but cannot deliver knowledge management. *California Management Review, 41*(4), 103–117.

McLerney, C. (2002). Knowledge management and the dynamic nature of knowledge. *Journal of the American Society for Information Science and Technology, 53*(12), 1009–1018.

Mohamed, M. A., & Mohamed, M. S. (2008). Knowledge management technologies: Compendious reflections on VINE's technology inquiries. *VINE: The Journal of Information and Knowledge Management Systems, 38*(4), 388–397.

Natarajan, G., & Shekhar, S. (2000). *Knowledge management: Enabling business growth*. New Delhi: Tata McGraw-Hill.

Newman, B., & Conrad, K. K. (1999, February). A framework for charactering knowledge management methods, practices, and technologies. Paper presented at the Choosing Knowledge Management Technology Panel, Santa Clara, CA, USA.

Nickhols, F. (2000). The knowledge in Knowledge Management (KM). Retrieved on March 1, 2009, from http://home.att.net/~nickols/Knowledge_in_KM.htm

Nonaka, I., & Takeuchi, H. (1995). *The knowledge creating company*. Oxford.

Nonaka, I., & Toyama, R. (2003). The knowledge-creation theory revisited: Knowledge creation a synthesizing process. *Knowledge Management Research and Practice, 1*(1), 2–10.

O'Dell, C. (2008). Web 2.0 and knowledge management. *The role of evolving technologies: Accelerating collaboration and knowledge transfer*. Houston, TX: APQC. http://wiki.sla.org/download/attachments/11371006/APQC+2008+Web+2+and+KM.pdf?version = 1

Phifer, G. (2008). *Web 2.0 user categories: Beyond digital natives and digital immigrants*. Gartner Research, Doc no G00164326.

Raskino, M. (2007). *In 2008, Enterprise Web 2.0 goes mainstream*. Gartner, No. G00153218. Gartner Research, Houston, TX, USA.

Redmiles, D., & Wilensky, H. (2008). Adoption of Web 2.0 in the enterprise: Technological frames of KM practitioners and users. Paper presented at the workshop for CSCW 2008. http://swiki.cs.colorado.edu/CSCW2008_Web20/33. Retrieved on February 11, 2009.

Ribière, V. (2001). *Assessing knowledge management initiative successes as a* function *of organizational culture*. Unpublished D.Sc. dissertation, The George Washington University, Washington, DC.

Ribière, V. (2005). *The critical role of trust in knowledge management* [*Le rôle primordial de la confiance dans les démarches de gestion du savoir*]. Unpublished Ph.D. dissertation (Management Sciences), Université Paul Cézanne, Aix en Provence (France). Available at http://proquest.umi.com/pqdweb?did = 1127190691&sid = 3&Fmt = 2&clientId = 31812& RQT = 309&VName = PQD&cfc = 1

Ribière, V. (2008). Knowledge management processes. *CIO World & Business Magazine*, November–December, pp. 52–54.

Ribière, V. (2009a), KM technologies (Part 1). *CIO World & Business Magazine*, January–February, pp. 56–58.

Ribière, V. (2009b). KM technologies (Part 2). *CIO World & Business Magazine*, May, pp. 58–60.

Ribière, V. (2009c). KM technologies (Part 3). *CIO World & Business Magazine*, June, pp. 53–55.

Ribière, V. (2009d). A model for understanding the relationships between organizational trust, KM initiatives and successes. Paper presented at the Hawaii International Conference on System Sciences-HICSS-42, Hawaii.

Ribière, V., & Tuggle, F. D. (2005). The role of organizational trust in knowledge management tools and technology use and success. *International Journal of Knowledge Management*, *1*(1), 60–78.

Rigby, D., & Bilodeau, B. (2007). *Management tools and trends 2007*. Bain & Company. http://www.bain.com/management_tools/Management_Tools_and_Trends_2007.pdf

Román-Velázquez, J. A., Ribière, V., & Stankosky, M. A. (2004). Organizational culture types and their relationship with knowledge flow and knowledge management success: An empirical study in the US Government and Nonprofit Sectors. *Journal of Information & Knowledge Management*, *3*(2).

Ryan, J. J. C. H. (2004). Information security tools and practices: What works? *IEEE Transactions on Computers*, *53*(8), 1060–1063.

Singh, S. P. (2007). *VINE: The Journal of Information and Knowledge Management Systems*, *37*(2), 169–179.

Smith, D. M. (2008). *Web 2.0 and beyond: Evolving the discussion*. Gartner, No. G00154767. Retrieved from http://mslibrary/research/MktResearch/Gartner2/research/154700/154767/154767.html

Tapscott, D. (2006). Winning with the Enterprise 2.0. Retrieved from http://www.cob.sjsu.edu/jerrell_l/Tapscott%20on%20Collab%20Advantage.pdf. Retrieved on February 11, 2009.

Tiwana, A. (2002). *The knowledge management toolkit, orchestrating IT, strategy, and knowledge platforms* (2nd ed.). Upper Saddle River, NJ: Prentice Hall.

Zack, M. H., & Michael, S. (1996). *Knowledge management and collaboration technologies*. White Paper. The Lotus Institute, Lotus Development Corporation. July, 1996.

SECTION V

RESEARCH IN KNOWLEDGE MANAGEMENT

As society transforms from one age to the next, to be successful, the operating paradigms used by individuals and organizations must change. This was true as the world changed from the Agricultural Age to the Industrial Age, and it is also true as we move from the Industrial Age to the Intelligence Age. Luddites cling to the past where they were successful. Practitioners tinker with new approaches randomly finding success, and researchers examine the new world looking for the underlying truths that can support continual success.

The George Washington University's (GWU) School of Engineering and Applied Science (SEAS) Department of Engineering Management and Systems Engineering with its integrated approach to research, teaching, and public service is one of the largest academic departments of its kind. It includes nine academic concentrations built on the premise that engineers eventually become managers and need the necessary management competencies to function in the modern world. It is from the knowledge management (KM) concentration that researchers have approached with academic rigor the understanding of the KM and its organizational framework. As in our first book, it is clear that knowledge was the prime currency for the coming Intelligence Age, and its proper or improper application directly impacted the bottom line and success. As Dr. Stankosky emphasizes in our work:

> Our economic well-being and competitive advantage are dependent on knowledge resources—our knowledge, experiences, education, training, professional networks, collaborative, and innovative skills.

In fact, KM as popularized by practioners in the mid-1990s has seen many successes and failures. This section represents the research of an interdisciplinary group examining the complex world of the Intelligence Age with a knowledge and information management emphasis. We have built upon such KM giants as Peter Drucker, Karl Wiig, Ikujiro Nonaka, Larry Prusack, Tom Davenport, Tom Stewart, Hubert St. Onge, and Karl-Eric Sveiby, to name just a few. Our work has been guided by the KM framework with the four pillars of leadership, organization, learning, and technology, all supported by a communication infrastructure developed by Dr. Mike Stankosky and Dr. Francesco Calabrese.

The following chapters address work done in several related KM areas: decision support, innovation, implementation practices, and communities of practice.

Chapter 13

Application of Knowledge Management in a Unified Approach to Decision Support for Agile Knowledge-Based Enterprises

Linda J. Vandergriff

Abstract

This exploratory study is focused on defining an agile knowledge-based enterprise comprehensive menu of decision support capabilities that includes dynamic knowledge management (KM). The research identifies current (e.g., quantitative analysis), inadequate (e.g., real-time risk management), and new (e.g., reliable knowledge) decision support capabilities. The resulting list of 30 validated and 14 proposed decision support capabilities define an informed decision cycle operational needs, guides decision support theory and application development, and provides a meaningful framework to guide infrastructure investment.

The study finds that an informed decision cycle requires integration of decision-making, decision implementation, and knowledge management activities (Deming, 1986, 1994; Boyd, 1987; Simon, 1977). These solutions support the move from the complicated efficiency-driven Industrial Age to the complex effectiveness-driven Intelligence Age enterprises.

13.1. Introduction

Agile knowledge-based enterprises drive a need for a more aware, inclusive, and responsive decision support system. Goldman, Nagel, and Preiss (1995) observe that organizations are responding to these needs in a piecemeal fashion. Although

In Search of Knowledge Management: Pursuing Primary Principles
Copyright © 2010 by Emerald Group Publishing Limited
All rights of reproduction in any form reserved
ISBN: 978-1-84950-673-1

significant research exists on agile manufacturing, decision-making tools, knowledge management (KM), decision analysis, and other decision support applications, Vahidov and Kersten (2004) assert that researchers and developers lack a unified decision support approach with a decision support theory, framework, or architectures. Without an overarching decision support framework for identification and evaluation of needed capabilities, investment choices can provide incompatible or wrong with substantial chance of missing needed capabilities for a decision support system (DSS) as defined by Power (1997, 2003). All of these situations lessen the organization's return on investment expected from a unified approach.

This exploratory study focused on defining an agile knowledge-based enterprise comprehensive menu of decision support capabilities. The research identifies current (e.g., quantitative analysis), inadequate (e.g., real-time risk management), and new (e.g., reliable knowledge) decision support capabilities. The resulting list of validated decision support capabilities defines informed decision cycle operational needs, guides decision support theory and application development, and provides a meaningful framework to guide organization infrastructure investment.

The study finds that an informed decision cycle requires integration of decision-making, decision implementation, and KM activities (Deming, 1986, 1994; Boyd, 1987; Simon, 1977). These solutions support the move from the complicated efficiency-driven Industrial Age to the complex effectiveness-driven Intelligence Age[1] enterprises.

Using exploratory research, this study established a comprehensive menu of decision support capabilities to support enterprises in building the "right" decision support solutions. Stebbins (2001) defines such exploratory research as a "broad-ranging purposive, systematic, prearranged undertaking to maximize the discovery of generalizations leading to description and understanding of an area...." First, the study conducted a systematic review of existing decision support and related complexity theory scholarly research for previous work in this area. Second, the study reviewed interdisciplinary theoretical and application-based decision support literature to identify current (e.g., quantitative analysis), inadequate (e.g., real-time risk management), and new (e.g., reliable knowledge) decision support capabilities. Third, the study identified needed decision support (e.g., decision-making, decision implementation, and KM) capabilities using qualitative architecting techniques. Fourth, the study surveyed a stratified convenience sample of system engineers, decision support developers, and knowledge workers to evaluate the desirability of the proposed decision support capabilities and missing capabilities.

The literature suggests that the "perfect" decision support would provide for an informed decision cycle. An informed decision cycle provides the ability to adaptively sense and respond. It allows an organization to take advantage of the dynamics of

---

1. First coined by Kirk Tyson (1997) is a more accurate representation of the current era than the term "Information Age" hyped by the AT&T Marketing department to sell Information related technologies. (Kushnick, 1998)

the fitness landscape and the empowered enterprise competencies. In this construct, the primary decision support activities are

- Decision-making aided by appropriate KM and computerized assistance with problem definition, alternative generation, decision analysis, and decision communication
- Decision implementation informed by effective decision coordination, execution planning, and change feedback in an co-evolving environment and enterprise

13.2. Decision-Making Capabilities

For this study, the term capability means the ability to execute a specified course of action or activity. For most enterprises, capabilities result from a tailored blend of people, processes, and technology. This study, however, only identifies and prioritizes capabilities needed by the Enterprise. The implementation strategies and designs are outside the scope of this study.

Good decision definition contributes to successful outcomes. To frame the decision one must consider the decision context that drives the need for the decision. Setting up the decision context includes identifying the decision scope, the objectives for the decision, related decisions, and interested parties. For all but the simplest of decisions, it is important to understand the ground rules, evaluation criteria, and assumptions that will govern the choices.

Tyson (1997) identifies the need to inform the decision cycle with business intelligence (BI). This intelligence is the translation of wisdom, knowledge, information, data, or measurement (IWKIDM[2]) into the decision-maker and implementer frames of reference (Vandergriff, 2006, 2008).

Decision support needs the capability to let a decision-maker or analyst identify and gather all the supporting IWKIDM for decision definition, alternative development, and solution selection. Decision support assists in this process by automating IWKIDM gathering and providing a framework for the decision context (Nutt, 1993, 2004).

---

2. Describes the intelligence pyramid, where intelligence is the translation in to the user's frame of reference of the various levels wisdom, knowledge, information, data, and measurement about the world. Based on my dissertation work (Vandergriff, 2006), the following WKIDM levels of abstraction are defined. "Measurement" is defined as physical readings of phenomena from scientific instruments (e.g., photons) or event/object observations by individuals or groups. "Data" is the symbols, numbers, textual clauses, and other descriptive phrases or displays of measurements (e.g., evidence). "Information" is built from the organization of data sets through quantitative and/or qualitative analysis that relate data sets, and can range from math equations, paragraphs, graphical illustrations, or images. "Knowledge" is created by applying experience to available measurements, data, and information. "Wisdom" results from the application of cognitive capability and judgment.

Decision-making implies a choice between two or more alternatives. Simon (1977) described the design related activities as inventing, developing, and analyzing possible courses of action. Kepner and Tregoe (1981) advocate a stand-alone decision-making approach that includes defining the problem, formulating decision objectives, generating selection criteria, inventing or identifying alternatives, and analyzing alternatives. Nutt (1993) cites that strategic decisions fail due to improper attention to problem definition and alternative generation.

Nutt (1993) identifies that 28% of decisions are driven by a single alternative. These single choice decisions are failure-prone. Thus, knowledge workers need to identify and characterize multiple alternatives to allow proper evaluation. The use of multiple perspectives helps identify the widest range of these potential solutions.

Nutt (2004) identifies several traps for alternative generation:

- Relying on initial impressions alone to define decision scope and objectives
- Allocating too few resources to develop alternatives
- Devoting too little time to identifying viable alternatives and characterizing them appropriately
- Requiring fully defined alternatives before committing
- Using current or available alternatives with limited or no search
- Promoting of self-serving alternatives
- Narrowing of alternatives too early based on belief or intuition

Alternatives result from either a search for readymade solutions or a development of new solutions (Mihtzberg, Théorêt, & Raisingham, 1976). Innovation literature discusses approaches to identify readymade or new solutions. These approaches include knowledge base searching, soliciting suggestions, brainstorming, repurposing, serendipity, experimentation, and research (Robinson & Schroeder, 2004; Kemp, Moerman, & Prieto, 2001; Matheson & Matheson, 2001; Kinni & Ries, 2000; Malhotra, 1998; Vicari, von Krogh, Roos, & Mahnke ,1996; Nutt, 1993; Osborn, 1993; Nunamaker, Dennis, Valacich, & Vogel, 1991; 3M, 1977; Hayek, 1945). Creation of alternatives improves with group participation. The ideation (e.g., creation of ideas) process is more productive and varied (Briggs, Nunamaker, & Sprague, 1998).

In searching for readymade solutions, the technical infrastructure must enable idea capture, as well as, domain-specific and organization-specific knowledge searches. These tools range from Intranets, email, and yellow pages to more sophisticated data repositories, data mining, and groupware (Skyrme, 2003; Hargadon & Sutton, 2001; Baek, 1998). To support analysis and evaluation of the alternatives, the capability to characterize and capture the expected outcomes, projected benefits, and negative consequence is needed. In addition, any implementation barriers should be noted (Nutt, 1993).

To fit the enterprise and its decision making to an ever changing context, Boyd (1987) proposed the observe, orient, decide, and act (OODA) loop with constant feedback and re-evaluation. This iterative decision-making and assessing loop creates a process with self-awareness (observe), analysis based on culture and knowledge (orient), decision-making (decision), and decision implementation (act). The process repeats observing the results of the decision implementation and reacting to the changing context.

Thus, decision support analysis seeks to increase problem understanding. It assesses the relative value or risk of alternatives. Calculating the relative costs and time to realize each alternative provides a basis for initial planning. In addition, this analysis provides the tacit understanding of operations and the interactions derived from modeling and simulations.

Usually, analysis of the alternatives revolves around the three-value axis of cost, benefit, and risk. The decision-making tool kit consists mainly of quantitative analysis tools. Analysts are often uncomfortable with qualitative approaches that rely upon experience (Courtney, Kirtland, & Viguerie, 1997). For a variety of decisions faced by knowledge workers, the analysis portfolio needs to contain both qualitative and quantitative analysis tools (Alessandri, 2002).

Decision-making needs to occur at the lowest level possible (i.e., closest to the point of contact), but at a high enough level to ensure that all activities and objectives are considered. Decision-making must address the consequences deriving from multiple decisions made by diverse entities and the emergent behaviors that result (e.g., the law of unexpected consequences).

With expansion of the number of people involved in the decision cycle, decision support assumptions about familiarity and ability must be re-examined. Decision guidance aids users to effectively and efficiently structure and execute the decision cycle (Parikh, Fazlollahi, & Verma, 2001). Silver (1991) categorizes decision guidance by target (i.e., decision-making or decision implementation), form (i.e., informational or suggestive), mode (i.e., predefined, dynamic, or participatory), and scope (i.e., short or long term). For the enterprise, all of these decision guidance types provide improved capability. This capability, though necessary, will cost resources (Sambamurthy, Bharadwaj, & Grover, 2003).

The agile nature of the enterprise drives the need for dynamic decision guidance. The decision support updates not only provides decision guidance, but also, the IWKIDM necessary to inform decisions (Robbins & de Cenzo, 2000; Ashmos, Duchon, & McDaniel, 1998). As organizations become more knowledge intensive and addressing unpredictable situations, rules alone become overly restrictive. Decision support for these unstructured decisions requires more guidance and decision aids (White, 2004; Ashmos et al., 1998; Perrow, 1986). This growth of dynamic unstructured decisions drives enterprises to further empower their knowledge workers. These workers participate in updating and collaborating on decision guidance. Indeed, the learning organization captures and updates guidance as the context changes (Silver, 1991).

As earlier discussions have pointed out, in the Industrial Age, decision-making was considered an isolated process done by senior managers with off-line tools and no traceability to the organization's vision or mission. This paradigm of decision-making assumes an ability to predict the future and that the best decisions arrive from long term planning. In fact, with complex enterprises in turbulent environments none of these basic assumptions applies. One of the more successful strategies for decision-making in uncertain environments is to make a series of small decisions with option decision points based on future situational awareness. Thus, for an agile enterprise each decision depends on and influences other decisions. Situational awareness of the decision-making and implementation status of other projects and divisions is a critical input to the decision-making, as well as, implementation status of other projects and divisions is a critical input to the decision support processes, which drives a need for the ability to track and notify the decision-maker of decision points based on various implementation and environmental parameters.

This could become a paralyzing realization, unless timely communications provides the right IWKIDM. In fact, decision support, to be useful, must be accessible, convenient, responsive, and interactive (Costanza, 1983). Once an alternative is selected or resource committed, the implementers coordinate an implementation plan that has monitoring metrics and that reports on decision success to ensure better informed decision-making in the future and better implementation course-correction in the present (Hammond, 2001).

The decision-making activities fall into four main areas. For three of these the corresponding capabilities are at too high a level for desirability evaluation. Thus, for active decision-making management, multilevel IWKIDM access, and facilitated decision-making these activities were further decomposed into discrete implementable capabilities as seen in Figure 13.1.

13.3. Decision Implementation Capabilities

Communication is at the heart of all good decision-making and implementation. In a distributed enterprise, localized dynamic decision-making drives the need for automating notification. Thus, decision support must track and inform those impacted by these decisions and those who will be responsible for the implementation (Markulla, 1999; O'Leary, 1998; Russo & Schoemaker, 1989; Sridhar, 1998).

Communication and planning are an iterative process, with a need for consensus building and a need for sharing and internalizing knowledge (Beers & Kirschner, 2002; Bryson & Bromiley, 1993) Often a decision transmitted to implementers through memos or email is not sufficient for action. In fact, a significant amount of tacit knowledge used in implementing a decision is never really captured (Valle, Prinz, & Borges, 2002). The follow-up communication between decision-makers and decision implementers is usually informal and ad-hoc. Many researchers have found that this leads to loss of decision total context and can lead to something other than implementation of the agreed-to decision (Borges, Pino, & Valle, 2002).

The informed decision cycle requires tracking of business processes, detection of deviations in business process performance, and identification of changes in the external business fitness landscape (e.g., unfolding interaction with environment). The Gartner Group calls this process business activity monitoring (BAM). It emphasizes identifying significant business events and providing actionable intelligence to the knowledge worker (Medicke, Chen, & Mago, 2003).

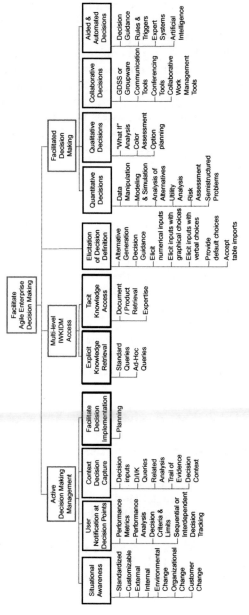

Figure 13.1: Decision-making capability tree.

Monitoring allows characterization, evaluation, prediction, and diagnosis of implementation. This situational awareness allows timely mid-course corrections, triggers future decision points and enables organizational learning (APQC, 2004).

The enterprise benefits from the ability to continuously learn (Hickson, Miller, & Wilson, 2003; Zack, 2003; March & Levitt, 1999; Argyris, 1996; Senge, 1990; Lee & Courtney, 1989). Thus, learning organizations develop a perpetual cycle of observing, knowing/orienting, deciding, and implementing that is constantly learning within one decision cycle in preparation for the next (Barry, 2004; Hall, Paradice, & Courtney, 2001; Matheson & Matheson, 2001). To realize learning benefits, the agile enterprise needs some decision support infrastructure. The knowledge, innovation, and lessons learned flow into a retention process that properly captures, catalogs, and validates it (DAU, 2003; Park, 2002; Newman & Conrad, 1999; Turban & Aronson, 1998). Due to the volume and time constraints, these retention processes are more effective when utilizing technology support rather than relying upon knowledge workers after action reporting (APQC, 1999).

Decision-making informs decision implementation. Those already involved in enterprise operations implement the decisions. For significant decisions, the action-able implementation plan (AIP) contains schedules, resources, lists of projected products/services, and anticipated risks and opportunities. The AIP is commu-nicated, and, preferably, coordinated with all those affected by the decision. Implementation is monitored using AIP measures. The organization learns and captures lessons learned during the implementation (Turban & Aronson, 1998).

The summation of the decision implementation literature identifies three main activities: manage implementation, monitor implementation, and facilitate learning. These capabilities are still at too high a level for evaluation of desirability. Thus, these activities were further decomposed into discrete implementable capabilities. These capability leaf nodes were then selected, defined, and summarized in Figure 13.2.

13.4. Knowledge Management Capabilities

A key point made throughout the literature is that, to be effective, decision support must have a reliable body of knowledge that dynamically updates. It must do so in a user-friendly manner that provides all levels of decision-makers and implementers with the proper levels of security and access.

With the need for informed decisions comes the problem of information overload. The University of California Berkeley's School of Information estimated that in 2002 the world's production of data and information amounts to 250 megabytes for every person on earth and it is growing exponentially (Lyman & Varian, 2002). It is important for the user to understand that too much data disguises the goal, confuses the vision, produces overload, and shuts down processing. In this environment, users desire decision support that provides only relevant reliable knowledge in an actionable way (DAU, 2003; Marchand, Kettinger, & Rollins, 2001; Kauffman, 1995).

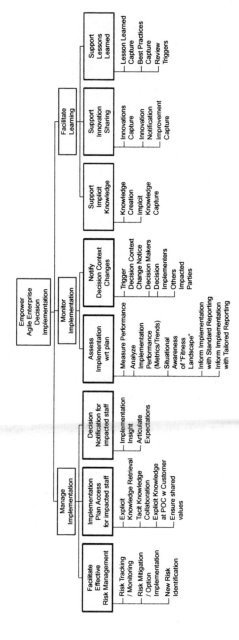

Figure 13.2: Decision implementation capability tree.

For some, the goal of KM is to capture only the essential data, information, and experience an employee needs and filter out the rest (Bair, 1997). This is a response to the data glut seen throughout the business environment. Unfortunately, this approach is based upon the paradigm that somehow one can predict what will be necessary. In an agile enterprise, it is difficult to automatically push the right information to the right people. It is also challenging to identify what will be of importance to the ever-changing organizational priorities and projects. Thus, KM becomes more critical in an agile enterprise. Active decision support needs smarter access with features such as expert systems, specialized agents, search, and verification (Vahidov & Kersten, 2004; Malhotra, 2000; Sviokla, 1990).

In this mode, a significant problem for the enterprise is not in the making of a wrong or poor decision, but in the absence of a decision made in a timely manner (Hammond, 2001). With the increasing amount of BI and workload, it becomes difficult for the knowledge worker to identify and respond to conditions calling for decision. Active decision support advocates call for decision support that provides user notification of decision needs (Vahidov & Kersten, 2004).

Thus, the informed decision cycle requires support by feedback and learning loops. In addition, the organizational IWKIDM must be able to present in an ad-hoc or standardized manner (Holsapple & Whinston, 1996). In fact, current research has shown that in for-profit organizations the primary focus of KM is to improve decision-making and implementation (Anantatmula, 2004).

Agile enterprises cannot stop at their boundaries for their DSS and KM needs. It is very often the case that the needed IWKIDM are found in the extended enterprise: in extranets, Internet, and subscription centers (Intelliseek, 2002; Park, 2002; Zack, 1999, 2003). In addition, KM must accommodate transparency to outside interest groups and regulators (Allee, 2004). Unfortunately, applications have often been focused on what can be done instead of what should be done. Permanently archiving every piece of junk email is possible, but may not be of value to the overall business processes. Indeed it is the harder to capture IWKIDM that contributes more to the bottom-line of the enterprise and thus is more desirable (Malhotra, 2000).

Vahidov and Kersten (2004) propose the use of intelligent agents to identify decision opportunities. This approach uses observations from the informed decision cycle to provide timely notification of change in the environment, enterprise, or performance. With these notifications, knowledge workers evaluate the new situation and translate "global" business objectives into actionable "localized" decisions.

The agile enterprises need KM that provides both distributive (integrative) and collaborative (interactive) capabilities (Park, 2002). KM allows informed decision-making and implementation. Some of these KM activities support other enterprise activities. Other KM activities that did not directly contribute to decision support are not included. These decompositions are from the operator point of view; infrastructure implicit activities (e.g., communications, maintenance) were not included.

The KM activities found that the functions of use, transfer, codification, generation, and assurance were performed differently for the different entities of the IWKIDM pyramid. So, this research developed six main activities based on the types of IWKIDM. These are to ensure reliable knowledge sources, provide user-friendly support, ensure access and security, manage tacit knowledge, manage explicit knowledge, and facilitate workforce learning. The first three activities were considered defined enough to be categorized as capabilities for desirability evaluation. The second three are still at too high a level for desirability evaluation. Thus, these activities were further decomposed into discrete implementable capabilities. Thus, these activities were decomposed into discreet implementable leaf node capabilities as shown in Figure 13.3.

13.5. Summary of Findings

The art of eliciting and refining needs from stakeholders involves defining what is needed, when it is needed, and where it is needed. This research developed and validated a comprehensive set of decision support capabilities. Building on the capability definition work, the research used a survey to evaluate decision support capabilities for desirability. This assessment was based on the respondents understanding of their organizations current and projected needs.

The respondent population consists of knowledge workers, their managers, and decision support developers. With a response rate of 3.1%, the respondent population consists of 81 individuals. Respondents mainly represent for-profit organizations (i.e., 76%) from the defense, intelligence, and aerospace business area (i.e., 47%).

The respondents represent a very experienced group (i.e., 67% with 20 + years of experience) composed mainly of the nonexclusive groupings of knowledge workers (i.e., 62%) and managers (i.e., 44%). Most of the respondents (i.e., 97%) identified their awareness of key study concepts. Thus, the respondent population is considered qualified to evaluate decision support capability desirability.

The instrument uses desirability scales ranging from 1 to 5 (Table 13.1) to evaluate each proposed decision support capability (Gay & Diehl, 1992; Likert, 1932).

The survey tool provided the ability to randomize the order of the capabilities to reduce question order bias. At the end of each category of capabilities, the respondent had to prioritize the capabilities (i.e., rank capabilities from highest to lowest) and provide any missing essential capabilities.

Since this evaluation used a 5-point desirability scale, nonparametric statistics characterize the ordinal data central tendency, variance, and correlation. This study has successfully achieved its stated goal of generating, vetting, and ranking a comprehensive set of decision support capabilities.

For this study, the confidence level has been set at 95% ($\alpha = 0.05$). With the sample size ($n = 81$), the confidence interval for the 75% and 25% population is $\pm 9.43\%$. To be considered valid for the purposes of this study, the proposed capability met the following two conditions:

- More than three-fourths of the respondents rank the capability as desired or higher
- More than one-fourth of the respondents rank the capability as highly desired or essential

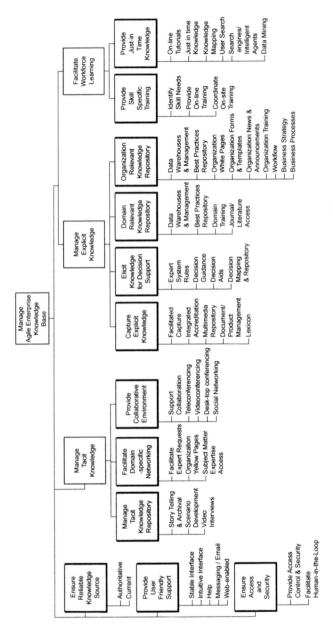

Figure 13.3: Knowledge management capability tree.

Table 13.1: Decision Support Capability Desirability Scale.

Desirability Scale	Description
1	Not needed
2	No opinion (neutral point)
3	Desirable
4	Highly desirable
5	Essential

All of the proposed capabilities met these criteria. When comparing rankings, the researcher evaluates the statistical significance of the differences seen in comparison with the uncertainty of the data sampling. A nondirectional Wilcoxon signed rank test ($z > 1.960$) evaluates the statistical significance of differences between capabilities. For the ranked capabilities, significant statistical differences occur over the range of the desirability ranking. This ranking difference is also of practical significance. The capabilities ranked highest are the most likely to have funds invested for development. In addition, these highest ranked capabilities should contribute most to user satisfaction when provided.

Table 13.2 provides the integrated ranked list of all the study proposed DSS capabilities.

Six decision-making capabilities rank as essential by over one-fourth of the respondents. These were the explicit knowledge, quantitative decision-making, decision definition, situation awareness, decision points, and decision context. The lowest ranked decision-making capability is expert system. This ranking agrees with the observed trends in the literature valuing decision support integration into the enterprise infrastructure. The survey data ranks explicit knowledge highest of all the decision support capabilities. To provide this capability decision support must leverage the information technology (IT) infrastructure to retrieve the appropriate IWKIDM. The respondents rank the traditional focus of decision support; quantitative decision-making capability very high. Both the survey respondents and researchers in the field view the use of computer applications to help define the decision as valuable. As observed by Nutt (1993), a key contributor to decision success is correctly scoping the decision, identifying the objectives, and the evaluation criteria. Situation awareness enables an enterprise to react quicker to the changing environment. The decision points capability aids future decision management by notifying appropriate users of upcoming decisions. The ability to monitor and identify opportunities to make decisions extends the cognitive reach of those involved in enterprise operations. The other essential capability was providing the decision context to both those who have to implement a decision or who are affected by it. This capability was ranked higher than providing an implementation plan. It is surmised that the implementation plan was considered more an implementation activity and should be developed by the implementers based on the provided decision context.

Table 13.2: Decision support capabilities: overall ranking.

DS type[a]	Capability name	Capability description	Essential frequency
DM	Explicit knowledge	Provide retrieval of knowledge that is codified and articulate. Explicit knowledge appears in the form of documents, procedures and in databases. In contrast with "tacit knowledge"	39
DI	Risk management	A well defined process to identify risks, analyze the probability of their occurrence and potential impacts, develop mitigation or containment strategies, monitor and report risk status, and identify when strategies are to be implemented with minimal impact to the project or organization	35
KM	Reliable knowledge	Provide an assured knowledge source that is current, vetted and configuration managed	35
DM	Quantitative analysis	Support quantitative decision analysis and trades	33
DI	Decision notification	Provide timely communication of a decision and its associated implementation plans that affects the operations of the individual or team involved to impacted staff	33
DI	Capture lessons learned	Leverage organizational learning throughout the organization with capture of lessons learned and best practices during decision implementation	32
KM	User-friendly access	Ensure user-friendly access to knowledge	30
DM	Decision definition	Elicit decision definition (e.g., frame decision, identify decision objectives, develop evaluation framework)	27
DI	Notify context changes	Notify decision makers and implementers of decision context changes	27
DM	Situational awareness	Provide knowledge of the state, condition, or progress of the organization's operations environment, performance, cost, and schedule	26
KM	Control and security	Provide assured access control and security to Enterprise Information Portals	26
DM	Decision points	Notify user of the critical moment before which a decision must be made (e.g., triggers)	25
DM	Decision context	Provide decision related assumptions, reasoning, and analysis that support a decision with decision notification (e.g., decision diary)	25
KM	Organization-specific repository	Provide organization-specific knowledge repository (e.g., Processes, Forms)	24

Table 13.2: (*Continued*)

DS type[a]	Capability name	Capability description	Essential frequency
KM	Collaborative knowledge environment	Support collaborative knowledge environment	22
KM	Explicit knowledge capture	Enables explicit knowledge capture	21
KM	Knowledge elicitation	Elicit knowledge to support decisions (e.g., explicit knowledge bases, expert system rules)	20
KM	Just-in-time knowledge	Allow knowledge pull at time of need to minimize information overload from broadcast	19
DM	Qualitative analysis	Support qualitative analysis, decision priority assignments, and judgments	18
KM	Domain-specific repository	Provide domain specific knowledge repository (e.g. Journals, White Papers)	18
DM	Tacit knowledge	Enable tacit knowledge retrieval (e.g., collaboration /networking, yellow pages)	17
DI	Monitor progress	Monitor implementation progress and notify with respect to plan	17
KM	Domain-specific networking	Enable domain-specific knowledge workers networking to access tacit knowledge	16
DM	Group decision-making	Enable collaborative or group decision-making	15
DI	Access plans	Provide access to decision implementation plans	14
DM	Implementation planning	Enable decision implementation planning	12
DI	Implicit knowledge	Captures and provides implicit knowledge to support implementation	12
DI	Capture innovation	Enable organizational learning through capture of serendipity innovations (e.g., support knowledge cycle capture, evaluation, and distribution of innovations) realized during decision implementation	12
KM	Skill-specific training	Provides for needed training needed for implementation of specific decisions when needed	9
DM	Expert system	Support expert system-aided decision-making	7

[a]Decision support types include decision-making (DM), decision implementation (DI), and knowledge management (KM).

The different ranking approaches used in the analysis identified expert system capability as the lowest priority. This lack of desirability may stem from the over promise, under delivery history of this capability or the stealth nature of successful expert system/artificial intelligence applications that are already incorporated into operational systems.

When evaluating the decision implementation capabilities, respondents identified risk management as the highest priority. It can be speculated that this ranking results from a need for increased risk-taking in the dynamic and ambiguous environment. With more risk taking in decision-making, decision support needs an implementation capability that effectively identifies, monitors, mitigates, and reports on risks (i.e., unrealized issues).

With the glut of information bombarding the decision-makers and implementers, the respondents identify the need for timely decision notification. In the environment of expanded decision-makers and complex interactions, traditional chains of command are insufficient to provide decision notification. Decision support need to provide an expanded web of notification to all those involved and impacted by the decision.

In knowledge-based enterprises, the literature indicates that intellectual capital is a major contributor to competitive advantage (Green, 2004). In such an environment, it is necessary that all functionality of the organization support learning (Senge, 1990). Thus, during decision implementation, capturing lessons learned and improving the best practices become challenging and more important. Thus, it was expected the capability to capture lessons learned was ranked as high as it was by the respondents.

With knowledge workers focused on implementation, this fourth decision implementation capability helps extend their cognitive capability to identify opportunities. This capability requires monitoring the changing landscape for opportunities, definition of bounding conditions, and identification of key events. Authors such as Vahidov and Kersten (2004) have identified the need for situated decision support to deploy intelligent agents to do this functionality.

The two lowest ranked decision implementation capabilities potentially reflect the respondent's evaluation of KM's ability to capture and manage tacit knowledge. The innovation literature talks about the need for an organization to capture and repurpose ideas (Robinson & Schroeder, 2004; Kemp et al., 2001; Matheson & Matheson, 2001; Kinni & Ries, 2000; Vicari, von Krogh, Roos, & Mahnke, 1996; Nutt, 1993; Osborn, 1993; Nunamaker, Dennis, Valacich, & Vogel, 1991; 3M, 1977; Hayek, 1945). However, attempts to create IT capability to create, capture, organize, and transfer tacit knowledge fail due to IT's static off-line database nature (Malhotra, 1998). The potential to infer knowledge from the explicit knowledge (i.e., implicit knowledge) is not a strong point for IT. Most success seen in these areas comes through connecting the right people with the applicable tacit knowledge to those who need the knowledge.

Decision support has significantly more KM capabilities ranked as essential for over a one-fourth of the respondents as either decision-making and decision implementation. These capabilities are reliable knowledge, user-friendly access, control and security, organization-specific repository, collaborative knowledge environment, explicit knowledge capture, and knowledge elicitation. The lowest ranked KM capability is skill-specific training. This underscores the need to create a viable KM strategy.

Several authors have proposed that KM literature continues to struggle with what KM is and how it should be measured because of its infrastructure nature (Stankosky, 2005; Anantatmula, 2004; KPMG, 2000; Goldman et al., 1995). This study identifies that the KM strategy for decision support needs to provide the enterprise secure access to the right knowledge in a timely manner. Decision support research traditionally does not address developing such strategies.

The literature review observed that KM systems focus on acquisition, creation, retention, and distribution (DAU, 2003; Park, 2002; Newman & Conrad, 1999; Turban & Aronson, 1998). The questionnaire reflects the desire for KM systems to ensure content currency and reliability. This has large implications on structures that are not easy to keep current and vetted.

In a collaborative environment, both organization and domain-specific knowledge needs to be stored and shared. This knowledge must have appropriate configuration control throughout the organization. Concepts such as those proposed by Delic and Douillet (2004) represent an initial step to KM content management.

The informed decision cycle needs empowered knowledge workers for success (Hickson, Miller, & Wilson, 2003). The role of organizational-specific knowledge repository (e.g., processes and best practices) is important to this goal on several levels. For the relatively new team member, this repository can represent a starting point that has captured the tacit knowledge of what has worked in the past for this organization. For the seasoned veteran, they can serve as a check for missed steps or coordination. For the organization, they reflect the coherent values and allow efficient development of "standard" processes across the organization. Hope and Fraser (1997) describe the processes and best practices used by an organization as the "DNA" of an organization's core competencies. In traditional enterprises, processes reflected the stovepipe functional and organizational boundaries. However, now processes tend to extend across multiple organizations and have many levels of participation. No one "controls" the whole process. The process is an adaptable collection of simple rules and actions producing the desired complex emergent behaviors.

The respondents recognize the need, not only for group decision-making, but also, for collaboration in the enterprise's decision support. This collaboration can occur at the same time and location, at the same time in different locations, different times at the same location, or different times at different locations. In these collaboration settings, the DSS must accommodate decision-makers, decision implementers, customers, and regulators. This requires sharing of IWKIDM and forming collaborative relationships. Current DSS tools fall short, focusing only on communication technology (Ullman, 2004).

The decision implementation capabilities show that the enterprise needs to be a learning organization. This recognition of the value of learning is reflected in the essential ranking of both the explicit knowledge capture and the knowledge elicitation capabilities. Current IT structures develop explicit knowledge repositories. Support of the informed decision cycle must be considered in developing these repositories. Knowledge elicitation supports the collection of knowledge needed for development of the rule sets and boundary conditions for decision points and other monitoring related capabilities.

The difficulty with all questionnaires using closed-ended questions is that the researchers cannot encompass all the possible choices. Thus, when the value of the respondents' views is worth the additional processing involved, it is normal for an open-ended question to be added. Since the goal of this study is to identify all the capabilities needed by agile enterprises for decision support, the corresponding question below was asked at the end of each section: For your organization, what other capabilities do you consider essential?

The survey participants proposed 14 new decision support capabilities. Table 13.3 provides a summary of all these new decision support capabilities. Although these were not evaluated for desirability, they do provide valuable insight into additional capabilities that a Decision Support provider should consider.

For decision-making capabilities, several additional types of quantitative analysis were identified that addressed the financial and time aspects, as well as business modeling. In addition, the need to have graphical interface to the elicit decision definition capability was identified. The respondents added two capabilities that help manage the decisions: decision tracking and decision reporting/archival.

The decision tracking capability allowed the use of decision trees and linkages to facilitate decision points and option mapping. This capability also included the ability to define decision authority and accountability of future decisions. To allow better notification and feedback on a decision, the tracking capability also added the ability to map decision related impacts and feedback. The second new decision-making capability facilitated archiving decision-making material for record management with standard reporting/analysis products (e.g., capability maturity model integration [CMMI]) that were aligned to appropriate KM capabilities.

The respondents identified the need for the risk management capability to include the ability to perform risk assessment. The other two new capabilities address the need to ensure implementations do no damage to operations. The first capability is the ability to model decision impacts and implementation problems at the source of the concern. This capability to model from small value calculations through end-to-end simulations exists in an ad-hoc fashion in today's enterprises. The second decision implementation capability would be the change control management. Decisions to change processes and procedures, implementation plans, reporting structures, etc. must be coordinated and managed to avoid confusion during implementation and uneven application across the enterprise.

Several of the responses address an expanded collaborative environment. This environment includes not only diverse groups and locations of a given organization, but also, serves the wider multicontractor implementation team and customers. Interoperability and visibility (e.g., transparency) are essential to the enterprise.

Table 13.3: Decision support: new capabilities.

DS type	Short descriptor	Activity description
DM	Decision tracking	Tracks decision trees and linkages, maps potential decision impacts, provides feedback on decision success or failure, and provides clearly stated decision authority and accountability trails
DM	Decision reporting and archiving	Reports and archives decision-making material with standard reporting/analysis products using aligned KM practices and procedures
DI	Implementation quantitative modeling	Modeling to evaluate implementation issues or to identify emerging trends and patterns
DI	Change control management	Change control management of processes, products, and services
DI	Implementation collaboration	Implementation team support for collaboration
DI	Interoperable implementation tool suite	For diverse groups and locations, especially in multi-company teams provide ability to integrate any separate tools used to implement decisions
DI	Customer-friendly visualization	Process visible to customer
DI	Asset visualization and tracking	Visualization of current and projected manpower/ tasking intensity and critical failure points
KM	Assurance and security	Ensure IWKIDM availability, integrity, authentication, confidentiality, and nonrepudiation. This includes the ability to restore IWKIDM by incorporating protection, detection, and reaction
KM	Project collaboration map	Identify objectives of related developments to minimize duplication and enhance collaboration
KM	Enable tacit knowledge capture	Create and maintain tacit knowledge repositories to support informed decision-making and decision implementation based on organizational experience base
KM	Knowledge map	Build and maintain maps for knowledge repositories that provide information literacy and maximize knowledge worker efficiency
KM	Knowledge map for captured explicit and tacit knowledge sources	Recognition of knowledge production sources
KM	Knowledge base management	Knowledge reuse metrics to validate importance to core competencies and mission requirements, alignment with organizational goals and reporting/tracking of these metrics

In realization of the increasing importance of human capital, a new decision implementation capability was recommended to manage the unique manpower assets in real time.

The new KM capability recommendations focused on providing a knowledge map capability and expanding assurance and security. The first comment identified the capability to manage security for proprietary data. For this study, the control and security capability should include access as appropriate across the enterprise information portal to the individual's roles and responsibilities. Other comments recommended the need for maintenance and validation of the organization's knowledge bases. Configuration control capability may include more than just the structure or content of the knowledge sources and thus it was maintained as a separate capability.

The ability to perform an analysis and identify emerging trends is very important to adapting to the fitness landscape. This capability is reflected in the respondent's comments. The role of modeling and simulation differs in decision-making and decision implementation. The quantitative analysis capabilities proposed for these two activities was considered sufficient for the list of proposed capabilities.

The capability to support organizational learning and collaboration was cited as an essential capability (Senge, 1990). The concept would include helping coordinate development efforts that have similar or identical development objects, in order to minimize duplication of effort and to leverage reuse. This is a manifestation of the need for "loose" interaction to aid in innovation and learning. The capability has been added as project collaboration map KM capability.

Explicit knowledge is usually found in repositories while most tacit knowledge is stored in the human capital of an organization. Thus, the approach to capturing and sharing these two types of knowledge is different. The initial capabilities reflected this with the capabilities focused on explicit knowledge capture and enable tacit domain-specific networking. However, some work is currently being done to capture tacit knowledge in the form of storytelling, videotaping interviews, and online interactive learning for specific implementation efforts. To properly reflect this capability, a new facilitate tacit knowledge capture capability was added.

The new KM capability recommendations focused on providing a knowledge map capability and expanding assurance and security. This first capability addresses the need to aid those making and implementing decisions to locate the most current knowledge for the application at hand. This theme was present in several of the KM comments. This requires the capability to ensure that the sources of knowledge are known and used to support both decision-making and implementation. The second capability expands the concerns of security to include concepts such as information and knowledge assurance. This capability ensures availability, integrity, authentication, confidentiality, and nonrepudiation of the decision support–related IWKIDM (NSA, 2003).

The resulting list of 30 validated and 14 additional decision support capabilities defines informed decision cycle operational needs, guides decision support theory and application development, and provides a meaningful framework to guide organization infrastructure investment.

This ranking and the list of additional capabilities provide insight into the expanded role of decision support. These 44 capabilities go far beyond the traditional focus of quantitative analysis techniques (ranked fourth overall by respondents). The respondent's evaluation and comments highlight the vital role integrated KM capabilities play in the enterprise decision support. KM capabilities not only inform decision choices with explicit knowledge, but also, aid in managing risks and uncertainties, ensuring organizational coherence, empowering knowledge workers, enabling a learning organization, and facilitating the decision cycle.

The capability-related findings are as follows:

- Decision support consists of decision-making, decision implementation, and KM capabilities
- All proposed capabilities are as highly desirable or essential based on median desirability scores and all are considered needed capabilities
- Automation of the decision-making activities related to intelligence, design, and choice are important for knowledge workers
- Difficult to achieve capabilities were identified by the respondents
- Reliable knowledge requires content management that provides timely updates and configuration control
- Decision support should provide decision notification
- Decision support aids capture and use of lessons learned as part of the learning organization
- Some proposed capabilities rank higher by those identified coming from high empowerment organizations

13.6. Study Observations and Generalizations

Because of the array of decision necessary, decision support must be flexible to address a wide "scope" (e.g., range) of decision support applications with common services and IWKIDM sharing. In addition, decision support must address "scale" issues arise from both the increased number and variety of users and the significant amount of intelligence used. Due to the exploratory rather than confirmatory nature of this study, a main goal was to discover generalizations about enterprise decision support (Stebbins, 2001). These generalizations derive from the literature review, architecture development, and questionnaire analysis. Table 13.4 groups these generalizations into four distinct categories.

The above generalizations and observations inform the Intelligence Age enterprise. Success demands the enterprise maintain awareness of a coevolving context and enterprise and provide an active decision support. In addition, the enterprise must leverage its intellectual capital through empowerment, automation, and collaboration. The knowledge workers represent a significant part of this intellectual capital. They operate as individuals and in teams at single or diverse locations. To be effective, the decision support needs to become a resource for all of

Table 13.4: Study generalizations.

Type	Generalization
Enterprise	• Operates in a dynamic, unpredictable environment/context • Maneuvers in a complex operating context with many competing demands for service • Requires empowerment to make and implement decisions at the point of need • Increases risk-taking and opportunity recognition to achieve competitive advantage • Values organizational learning from successes and failures • Uses technology to automate communication, knowledge capture and sharing, performance monitoring, and decision notification and tracking • Benefits from collaboration for distributed decision-making and virtual team implementation
Knowledge workers	• Operate in multiple of settings and environments and need mobile support structures • Work as individuals and as teams driving need for compatible individual and collaborative tools • Desire a user friendly more graphical interface and appropriate level of training and help to ensure effective use • Extend cognitive abilities with increased decision definition, situational awareness, context change notification, and decision opportunity identification • Benefit from access to organization-specific knowledge that provides a valuable source of intellectual capital especially in dynamic environments
Decision support	• Consists of decision-making and decision implementation with extensive support by KM capabilities • Requires integration into the enterprise infrastructure to support timely analysis and response • Improves modeling and simulation for both alternative evaluation and implementation planning • Requires configuration control of decisions, business process, and knowledge to ensure consistency and reduce confusion across the enterprise
Decision support success	• Depends upon reliable timely knowledge about the context and the enterprise • Relies upon early identification, management, and mitigation of risks • Needs realistic and adaptable quantitative analysis techniques • Requires effective communication of decision with those who implement or are affected by it

the knowledge workers providing more value than it cost in effort to use. This decision support must become seamless with components of decision-making, decision implementation, and knowledge management facilitating the knowledge workers in performing their jobs.

13.7. Conclusion

For the agile knowledge-based enterprises of the 21st century to be successful, they must provide the demanded services and products with improved productivity and customer-focused delivery. This requires the effective use of all assets, especially intellectual capital. One of the main contributors to this effective use is an informed decision cycle.

This study finds that an informed decision cycle requires integration of decision-making, decision implementation, and KM capabilities. An enterprise return on investment can be improved by using a unified approach to solutions in DSS related capabilities. The research has developed a *comprehensive menu of decision support capabilities that include dynamic knowledge management (KM). The research identifies current (e.g., quantitative analysis), inadequate (e.g., real-time risk management), and new (e.g., reliable knowledge) decision support capabilities. The resulting list of 30 validated and 14 proposed decision support capabilities define an informed decision cycle operational needs, guides decision support theory and application development, and provides a meaningful framework to guide infrastructure investment.* Thus, an enterprise-specific tailored set of decision support capabilities will support the move from the complicated efficiency-driven industrial age to the complex effectiveness-driven Intelligence Age Enterprises.

References

3M. (1977). *Our story so far: Notes from the first seventy-five years of 3M company.* St Paul, MN: Minnesota Mining and Manufacturing Company.

Alessandri, T. M. (2002). *A portfolio of decision processes: Rationality in capital investments under perceptions of risk and uncertainty.* Ph.D. dissertation, The University of North Carolina at Chapel Hill.

Allee, V. (2004). 360-Degree transparency and the sustainable economy. *Transformation, 18*(2), World Business Academy. Verna Allee Value Net Works™. Available at http://www.vernaallee.com/library%20articles/Transformation%20020404.pdf. Accessed on September 9, 2005.

Anantatmula, V. (2004). *Criteria for measuring knowledge management efforts in organizations.* DSc. dissertation, George Washington University, Washington, DC.

APQC. (1999). *Knowledge Management. APQC benchmarking study best practice report.* Houston, TX: American Productivity and Quality Center Consortium.

APQC. (2004). *Measurement in the 21st century.* White Paper. American Productivity and Quality Center, Houston, TX.

Argyris, C. (1996). *On organizational learning*. Oxford: Blackwell.

Ashmos, P., Duchon, D. D., & McDaniel, R. R., Jr. (1998). Participation in strategic decision making: The role of organizational predisposition and issue interpretation. *Decision Sciences, 29*(1), 25–51.

Baek, S. Ik. (1998). *Knowledge management for multimedia systems design- toward intelligent web-based collaboration*. DSc dissertation, George Washington University, Washington, DC.

Bair, J. (1997). Knowledge management: The era of shared ideas. *Forbes, 1*(1) (The Future of IT Supplement, September 22). Quoted by Malhotra (2000).

Barry, M. (Ed.). (2004). The agile organization. *EINFORM, 4*(1). Available at http://monkey. biz/Content/Default/Support/Resources/IDC_TheAgileOrganization_1710.pdf. Accessed on September 9, 2005.

Beers, P., & Kirschner, P. A. (2002). Decision-support and complexity in decision making. Academic track educational technology expertise center, Open University of the Netherlands. Available at http://www.alba.edu.gr/OKLC2002/Proceedings/pdf_files/ID106.pdf. Accessed on September 9, 2005.

Borges, M. R. S., Pino, J. A., & Valle, C. (2002). On the implementation and follow-up of decisions. In: *Proceedings of the DSIAge – International conference on decision making and decision support in the Internet age*, Cork, Ireland, July (pp. 366–375).

Boyd, J. R. (1987). *A discourse on winning and losing*. Unpublished briefing, August.

Briggs, R. O., Nunamaker, J. F., Jr., & Sprague, R. (1998). 1001 unanswered research questions in GSS. *Journal of Management Information Systems, 14*(3), 3–22.

Bryson, J. M., & Bromiley, P. (1993). Critical factors affecting the planning and implementation of major projects. *Strategic Management Journal, 14*, 319–337.

Costanza, C. (1983). *Microcomputers and decision support systems*. DSc dissertation, George Washington University, Washington, DC.

Courtney, H., Kirtland, J., & Viguerie, P. (1997). Strategy under uncertainty. *Harvard Business Review, 75*(6), 66–79.

DAU. (2003). *What is knowledge management?* Fort Belvoir, VA: Defense Acquisition University.

Delic, K. A., & Douillet, L. (2004). Corporate IT knowledge work bench: Case study. In: *Database and expert systems application proceedings of 15 international workshop*, 30 August to 3 September (pp. 494–497).

Deming, W. E. (1986). *Out of the crisis*. Cambridge, MA: MIT Center for Advanced Engineering Study.

Deming, W. E. (1994). *The new economics: For industry, government, education*. Cambridge, MA: MIT Center for Advanced Engineering Study.

Gay, L. R., & Diehl, P. L. (1992). *Research methods for business and management*. New York: Macmillan.

Goldman, S. L., Nagel, R. N., & Preiss, K. (1995). *Agile competitors and virtual organizations: Strategies for enriching the customer*. New York: Van Nostrand Rinhold.

Green, A. (2004). *Prioritization of value drivers of intangible assets for use in enterprise balance scorecard valuation models of information technology (IT) firms*. D.Sc. dissertation, George Washington University, Washington, DC.

Hall, D. J., Paradice, D. B., & Courtney, J. F. (2001). Creating feedback loops to support organizational learning and knowledge management in inquiring organizations. In: *Proceedings of the 34th Hawaii international conference on system sciences*, 3–6 January (pp. 1–10).

Hammond, G. T. (2001). *The mind of war: John Boyd and American Security*. Washington, DC: Smithsonian Institution Press.

Hargadon, A., & Sutton, R. I. (2001). *Harvard business review on innovation*. Boston, MA: Harvard Business School Press.

Hayek, F. (1945). The use of knowledge in society. *American Economic Review, 35*(4), 519–530.

Hickson, D. J., Miller, S. J., & Wilson, D. C. (2003). Planned or prioritzed? Two options in managing the implementation of strategic decisions. *Journal of Management Studies, 40*(7), 1803–1836.

Holsapple, C. W., & Whinston, A. B. (1996). *Decision support systems: A knowledge based approach*. Minneapolis, MN: West Publishing.

Hope, J., & Fraser, R. (1997). Beyond budgeting, breaking through the barrier to the Third Wave. *Management Accounting, 75*(11), 20–23.

Intelliseek. (2002). *True enterprise search: Leveraging knowledge from the extended enterprise*. Intelliseek™ White Paper. Cincinnati, OH. Available at http://www.intelliseek.com. Accessed on April 4, 2004.

Kauffman, S. A. (1995). *At home in the universe: The search for the laws of self-organization and complexity*. Oxford: Oxford University Press.

Kemp, J. L. C., Moerman, P. A., & Prieto, J. (2001). On the Nature of knowledge-intensive organizations: Strategy and organization in the new economy. In: T. Klaus-Dieter, F. Weber, & K. S. Pawar (Eds), *Proceedings of the 7th international conference on concurrent enterprising*, June (pp. 27–29). Bremen, Germany: ICE.

Kepner, C. H., & Tregoe, B. B. (1981). *The new rational manager: An updated edition for a New World*. Princeton, NJ: Kepner-Tregoe.

Kinni, T. B., & Ries, A. (2000). *Future focus: How 21 companies are capturing 21st century success*. Milford, CT: Capstone Publishing.

KPMG. (2000). *Knowledge Management Research Report*. Knowledge Processing Management Group (KMPG) Consulting, London.

Kushnick, B. (1998). *The unauthorized biography of the Baby Bells and Info-Scandal*. New York: New Networks Institute.

Lee, S., & Courtney, J. F., Jr. (1998). Organizational learning systems. System Sciences Vol. 3. In: *Proceedings of the 22nd Hawaii international conference on system sciences: Decision support and knowledge based systems track*, 3–6 January (pp. 492–502).

Likert, R. (1932). A technique for the measurement of attitudes. *Archives of Psychology* (140), 55–64.

Lyman, P., & Varian, H. R. (2002). How much information? UC Berkley School of Information Management. http://www.sims.berkeley.edu/research/projects/how-much-info/. (Accessed 7 September 2005).

Malhotra, Y. (1998). Tools @ work: Deciphering the knowledge management hype. *Journal for Quality and Participation, 21*(4), 58–60.

Malhotra, Y. (2000). From information management to knowledge management: Beyond the 'Hi-Tech Hidebound' systems. In: K. Srikantaiah & M. E. D. Koenig (Eds), *Knowledge Management for Information Professional* (pp. 37–61). Medford, NJ: Information Today Inc.

March, J. G., & Levitt, B. (1999). Organizational learning. In: J. G. March (Ed.), *The pursuit of organizational intelligence* (pp. 75–99). Oxford: Blackwell.

Marchand, D., Kettinger, W., & Rollins, J. (2001). *Making the invisible visible: How companies win with the right information, people and IT*. New York: Wiley.

Markulla, M. (1999). Knowledge management in software engineering projects. In: *Proceedings of the 11th software engineering and knowledge engineering conference*, Kaiserslautern, Germany (pp. 20–27).

Matheson, D., & Matheson, J. E. (2001). Smart organizations perform better. *Research Technology Management, 44*(4), 49–54.

Medicke, J., Mago, M., & Chen, F.-W. (2003). Creating an intelligent and flexible solution with bpm, business rules, and business intelligence part I. IBM website, 9 October. Available at http://www-128.ibm.com/developerworks/db2/library/techarticle/dm-0312medicke/index.html. Accessed on September 7, 2005.

Mihtzberg, H., Théorêt, A., & Raisingham, D. (1976). The structure of the unstructured decision-making process. *Administrative Science Quarterly, 21*(2), 246–275.

Newman, B., & Conrad, K. K. (1999). A framework for characterizing knowledge management methods, practices, and technologies. Paper read at Choosing Knowledge Management Technology Panel, February. Santa Clara, CA.

NSA. (2003). National Information Assurance (IA) glossary. NSA CNSS Instruction #4009. Committee on National Security Systems. Revised May 2003.

Nunamaker, J. F., Jr., Dennis, A. R., Valacich, J. S., & Vogel, D. R. (1991). Information technology for negotiating groups: Generation options for mutual gain. *Management Science, 37*(10), 1325–1346.

Nutt, P. C. (1993). The identification of solution ideas during organizational decision making. *Management Science, 39*(9), 1071–1085.

Nutt, P. C. (2004). Expanding the search for alternatives during strategic decision-making. *Academy of Management Executive, 18*(4), 13–28.

O'Leary, D. E. (1998). Enterprise knowledge management (March). *IEEE Computer, 31*(3), 54–61.

Osborn, A. F. (1993). *Applied imagination: Principles and procedures of creative problem-solving* (3rd ed.). Hadley, MA: Creative Education Foundation.

Parikh, M., Fazlollahi, B., & Verma, S. (2001). The effectiveness of decisional guidance: An empirical evaluation. *Decision Sciences, 32*(2), 303–324.

Park, H. (2002). *Assessing the success of knowledge management technology implementation as a function of organizational culture*. DSc dissertation, George Washington University, Washington, DC.

Perrow, C. (1986). *Complex organizations*. New York: Random House.

Power, D. J. (1997). What is a DSS? DS*. *The On-Line Executive Journal for Data-Intensive Decision Support, 1*(3)http://www.dssresources.com/papers/whatisadss/index.html. Accessed on September 7, 2005.

Power, D. J. (2003). What are the characteristics of a decision support system? *DSSNews e-newsletter, 4*(7).

Robbins, S. P., & de Cenzo, D. A. (2000). *Fundamentals of management: Essential concepts and applications* (3rd ed.). Englewood Cliffs, NJ: Prentice Hall.

Robinson, A. G., & Schroeder, D. M. (2004). *Ideas are free: How the idea revolution is liberating people and transforming organizations*. San Francisco, CA: Berrett-Koehler Publishers.

Russo, J. E., & Schoemaker, P. J. H. (1989). *Decision traps: Ten barriers to brilliant decision-making and how to overcome them*. New York: Simon and Schuster.

Sambamurthy, V., Bharadwaj, A., & Grover, V. (2003). Shaping agility through digital options: Reconceptualizing the role of information technology in competitive firms. *MIS Quarterly, 27*(2), 237–263.

Senge, P. M. (1990). *The fifth discipline: The art and practice of the learning organization.* New York: Doubleday.

Silver, M. (1991). Decisional guidance for computer-based decision support. *MIS Quarterly, 15*(1), 105–122.

Simon, H. A. (1977). *The new science of management decision* (3rd ed.). Englewood Cliffs, NJ: Prentice-Hall.

Skyrme, D. J. (2003). KM basics. Resources David Skyrme Associates. Available at http://www.skyrme.com/resource/kmbasics.htm. Accessed on September 7, 2005.

Sridhar, S. (1998). Decision support using the Intranet. *Decision Support Systems, 23*(1), 19–28.

Stankosky, M. A. (Ed.) (2005). *Creating the discipline of knowledge management: The latest university research.* Burlington, MA: Elsevier Butterworth-Heinemann.

Stebbins, R. A. (2001). *Exploratory research in the social sciences. Qualitative Research Methods Series 48.* Thousand Oaks, CA: Sage Publications.

Sviokla, J. J. (1990). An examination of the impact of expert systems on the firm. *MIS Quarterly, 14*(2), 127–140.

Turban, E., & Aronson, J. E. (1998). *Decision support systems and intelligent systems. Instructor manual.* Upper Saddle River, NJ: Prentice Hall.

Tyson, K. W. (1997). *Competition in the 21st century.* Delray Beach, FL: St. Lucie Press.

Ullman, D. G. (2004). Decision management: Punctuating the process. *Incose Insight, 6*(2).

Vahidov, R., & Kersten, G. E. (2004). Decision station: Situating decision support system. *Decision Support Systems, 38*(2), 283–303.

Valle, C., Prinz, W., & Borges, M. R. S. (2002). Generation of group storytelling in post-decision implementation process. In: *Proceedings of the 7th international conference on computer supported cooperative work in design CSCWD'2002*, Rio de Janeiro, Brazil, September (pp. 361–367).

Vandergriff, L. J. (2006). *Unified approach to decision support for agile knowledge-based enterprises.* DSc. dissertation, George Washington University, Washington, DC.

Vandergriff, L. J. (2008). Welcome to the Intelligence Age: An examination of intelligence as a complex venture emergent behavior. *VINE: The Journal of Information and Knowledge Management Systems, 38*(4).

Vicari, S., von Krogh, G., Roos, J., & Mahnke, V. (1996). Knowledge creation through cooperative experimentation. In: G. von Krogh & J. Roos (Eds), *Managing knowledge: Perspectives on cooperation and competition* (pp. 184–202). Thousand Oaks, CA: Sage Publications.

White, C. (2004). *Building the smart business: Connecting people, processes, and information.* BI Research White Paper. Version 1. BI Research, Ashland, OR.

Zack, M. H. (1999). Managing codified knowledge. *Sloan Management Review, 40*(4), 45–58.

Zack, M. H. (2003). Rethinking the knowledge-based organization. *MIT Sloan Management Review, 44*(4), 67–71.

Chapter 14

Knowledge Management and Innovation: What Must Governments Do to Increase Innovation?

Alfredo Federico Revilak De La Vega

Abstract

This research assesses the relevance of knowledge management (KM) initiatives to a government's role in promoting innovation. Today, governments at all levels (federal, state, and municipal) have started projects with the goal of fostering innovation to promote economic growth. Nevertheless, most of those efforts are incomplete, not standardized, diverse, and not in compliance with needs. The research locates and evaluates the KM components that were successful in fostering innovation and were implemented by the correspondent governments. In addition, this study will use empirical methods to identify the existing elements that prompt innovation in countries with low research and development investment, since it is predictable that financial capabilities will be a significant factor in promoting innovation.

14.1. Introduction

Knowledge, and the ability to create, access, and use it effectively, has long been a tool of innovation, competition, and economic success and a key driver of economic and social development. Traditional economist (Schumpeter, 1949), contemporary authors (Porter, 1989), and multilateral organizations (OECD, 1995) agree that innovation represents the engine that brings motion to the economy and growth to nations. However, the theoretical attempt to incorporate innovation as a formal systematic method into a national or supranational economy is only a recent preoccupation (Fagerberg, 2004).

In Search of Knowledge Management: Pursuing Primary Principles
Copyright © 2010 by Emerald Group Publishing Limited
All rights of reproduction in any form reserved
ISBN: 978-1-84950-673-1

Knowledge is being developed and applied in new ways. The information revolution, supported by the technical advances in information and communication technologies (ICT), has expanded academic, scientific, and community networks and provided new opportunities for accessing data, information, and knowledge in a timely manner (Economist, 2004). It has also created new opportunities for generating and transferring all kinds of knowledge artifacts such as manuals, interviews, processes, and business procedures. Knowledge management (KM) and sharing of information have demonstrated increase in innovation output (OECD, 2004a, 2004b).

Today, a typical government is engaged in many innovation activities with the challenges of understanding the nature, mechanics, and expected results from these. Examples of these activities include multi agency budgeted research and development (R&D), grant funds for education sector, fiscal breaks, new innovation institutions, innovation clusters, deployment of new technology, and so on.

However, these programs are not yet standardized or validated, and many of them lack a formal framework to apply and assure an adequate level of success. Governments will keep ignoring the needs of these activities if they are not methodically studied, identified, and assessed. These activities all have knowledge needs and products that must be incorporated in an existing KM framework to be of use in future innovation policy setting situations.

There are a set of existing knowledge related best practices used by some government agencies with success in some countries that helped to leverage the innovation output, and those knowledge management practices are not identified nor accounted for. This research aims to identify such practices and provide policy makers a blueprint for developing, monitoring, and measuring national efforts to enhance innovation.

14.2. Innovation

According to Webster's dictionary, innovation means "bringing into effect new and more effective products, services, or approaches" (Webster, 1987). Studies from contemporary economic authors agree that innovation "is the process through which economic or social value is extracted from knowledge" (Freeman, 1982).

14.3. Types of Innovation

Innovation may be classified by type in two different ways. While Schumpeter (1949) refers to innovation as an entity taking different forms as later on explained. Others authors like Mensch (1978) introduce a critical distinction regarding the impact of innovation: *basic innovation* and *incremental innovation*. According to Mensch, basic innovation creates a new type of human activity, whereas the improvement innovation furthers develop an established human activity.

For other researchers, innovation may take the form of a new device, a better delivery method, or a new means of providing a service. In a seminal work, remarkably relevant to present times, Schumpeter (1949) distinguished between five different types of innovation:

- New products or services
- Methods of production
- Sources of production
- New markets
- Business organization

Since innovation may take any of these forms as well as new knowledge, governments should establish mechanism and support infrastructure to foster any type of flourishing innovation.

14.4. Models of Innovation

To facilitate the representation of the innovation process, two models have been widely used with different characteristics. The first one, "linear innovation" identified by earlier versions of the OECD Oslo manual (OECD, 1997), sees innovation as a process of discovery, which proceeds via fixed and linear sequence of phases. In this view, linear innovation begins with new scientific research, progresses sequentially through stages of product development, production and marketing, and terminates with the successful sale of new products, processes, and services.

However, as other authors explain, innovation can assume many forms, including incremental improvements to existing products, applications of technology to new markets, and uses of new technology to serve an existing market. This process is not completely linear. Innovation requires considerable communication among different actors — firms, laboratories, academic institutions, and consumers — as well as feedback between science, engineering, product development, manufacturing, and marketing.

Kline and Rosenberg (1986) presented an integrated model of the innovation process, called the "chain-linked model." The biggest difference between this new model and the linear one was that there is not just one major path of activity in the innovation process. Innovation can take many different routes.

The chain-linked innovation model achieved wide popularity among innovation and R&D researchers, since it facilitated the understanding of managing the process of innovation as a system in which several orderly elements interact to reach a specific goal.

Abrunhosa (2003) asserts that the ability of the chain-linked model to recognize the interactions and interdependencies between the different components of the innovation process and the complexity and uncertainty of the process. This model makes it easier to understand the concept of National Innovation Systems to the decision-maker.

However, there are still separate policies for research, education, innovation, industry, commerce, competition, etc. These must be taking into account, as well as, the interdependency of a multiplicity of elements involved in the innovation process. In addition, it is important that the production, diffusion, and adoption of innovation/knowledge are considered with respect to growth and development for a coordinated and integrated set of policies.

14.5. Innovation Measurement

Understanding the nature and causes of innovation requires analysis of its activity; it means that despite the difficulties to measure innovation, it is necessary to quantify the results and characteristics with hard, objective data.

Measurement indicators must be capable of reflecting innovation of all types of tangible and intangible activity. Under these complicated circumstances, the reality is that the performance of an innovation environment is hard to measure. A complete innovation measurement method able to translate and display the rate in which knowledge is created, shared, used, and transformed has been a topic of research and discussion.

Rogers (1998) established that innovation measurement indicators may be classified as either inputs or outputs. Inputs could consist of number of researchers, amount of expenditure, outputs could be new products, publications, and so on; this idea is expanded by Varga (1999) stating that there are three measurements have been applied in innovation studies.

- Research & development expenditures
- Literature-based innovation output indicators
- Patent-based measures

14.6. Measurement by Patents

Patents are probably the most widely used Industrial Age indicator of innovation (Griliches, Pakes, & Hall, 1987). Patent citation data is used in a growing body of economics and business research on innovation (Coombs & Richards, 1996). Many countries and organizations have adopted the ratios of patents per inhabitants and patents by time.

Although this indicator provides the best existing documentation of innovation activity, it has some shortcomings. Duguet and MacGarvie (2003) show that patent citations are indeed related to companies' statements about their acquisition and dispersion of new technology. However, the strength and statistical significance of this relationship varies across geographical regions and across channels of knowledge diffusion.

An issue that generates different positions is the quality of patents and techno-logical exhaustion. A clever solution to that problem is proposed by Lanjouw & Mark (2004) with the index of patent "quality" using detailed patent information and showing that using multiple indicators substantially reduces the measured variance in quality.

14.7. Knowledge Management

Organizations have always managed knowledge, even without noticing it. But in today's competitive environment, organizations realize that it is necessary to engage in a systematic approach to capture, store, and share organization knowledge in order to become more competitive.

Stankosky and Baldanza (2001) defines KM as "the systematic leverage of intellectual capital to improve organizational performance."

As KM became an important area of study, the richness of concepts encompassing KM such as knowledge itself, process, codification, human resources, learning, leadership, and technology management has unfortunately made the discipline hard to manipulate. In order to alleviate this problem, Stankosky and Baldanza (2001) proposed the KM framework in a holistic view associating all the components in four spheres or dimensions (i.e., leadership, learning, organization, and technology). These dimensions contain several factors affecting the KM "system."

This framework proposed by Stankosky was revisited and validated by Calabrese (2000). His work found through empirical demonstration that the model was valid and added to the framework the four model pillar depicted in Figure 14.1.

In a recent study (OECD, 2004a, 2004b), KM was identified as a positive variable to increase innovation inside organizations. The research consisted of a pilot evaluating the KM influence on patent production inside organizations in France, which included more than 5500 companies.

The present study will extend the scope of this line of investigation by trying to establish the same relation between KM and innovation — not just limited to considering the corporation level, but expanding to the national level.

14.8. Research Methodology

In this study, the research objective is to reveal if there exists a correlation between the establishment of KM initiatives by local governments and innovation per-formance in companies. It is worth mentioning that a great effort to start addressing this problem is found in the so called "Innovation Policy Terrain" developed by the Organization for Economic Cooperation and Development (OECD, 1997) in which a framework is presented with the variables associated to be taken into consideration to develop policies regarding innovation. Nevertheless, the study keeps a general tone

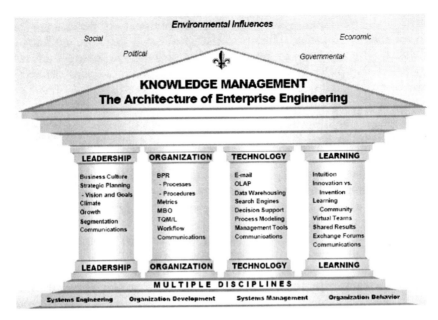

Figure 14.1: KM framework (Stankosky and Baldanza, 2001).

and leaves the reader (e.g., local governments) to establish rules to connect innovation systems and foster knowledge sharing.

To reach our goal, we proposed to answer the following research question: Do government's KM initiatives affect an innovation environment?

In order to answer the research question we established the research preamble with the following elements:

1. A validated KM Framework that allows the incorporation in a systematic manner of the aforementioned knowledge elements, in this case The George Washington University Four Pillar Framework (GWUFPF).
2. A selection of 13 of the government's KM factors that represent the closely represent the GWUFPF from the countless number of economic, environmental, health, financial, variables found in the international arena.
3. The sample of this research is composed of 50 successful national innovation systems (countries with more than 100 patents filled at the United States Trademark and Patent Office). The countries are shown in Table 14.1.
4. Correlation analysis was performed to corroborate and measure the impact of the 13 selected KM factors controlled by the Government. This research also executed Factor analysis to test the validity of the GWUFPF in the level of National Innovation System.

Table 14.1: Selected countries.

Country	Patents per 1,000,000 inhabitants	Country	Patents per 1,000,000 inhabitants
USA	7565.158	South Africa	84.436
Switzerland	6711.300	Slovenia	74.587
Japan	4646.737	Bulgaria	66.171
Sweden	4016.069	Greece	42.275
Germany	3349.655	Argentina	28.277
Canada	2187.993	Venezuela	25.615
Finland	2095.306	Croatia	22.242
Taiwan	2052.059	Portugal	21.578
Netherlands	2037.664	Mexico	21.456
Israel	1999.030	Poland	19.645
United Kingdom	1935.219	Czech Republic	19.236
France	1730.134	Malaysia	18.202
Denmark	1618.763	Romania	17.644
Austria	1592.218	Chile	14.392
Belgium	1385.738	Russian Federation	12.028
Norway	1060.867	Brazil	9.161
Australia	787.369	Saudi Arabia	8.441
Italy	704.631	Colombia	5.075
South Korea	696.837	Peru	4.297
Singapore	584.994	Ukraine	3.732
New Zealand	530.570	Thailand	3.407
Ireland	466.803	Philippines	3.028
China, Hongkong S.A.R.	374.173	Turkey	2.139
Hungary	265.441	India	1.909
Spain	124.526	People's Republic of China	1.628

14.9. Results

The results of this study point out that in at least 10 of the 13 governments, KM factors selected had an influence on the number of patents produced in Countries. Such KM factors ordered by weight of impact are in Table 14.2.

Four principal KM factors showed significant positive relation to production of patents per 1000 residents in a country: Size of the ICT sector, e-government maturity, intellectual property protection, and the ratio of researchers to employees in a country. The government's effectiveness is also significant and positive to predict patents in a country.

What it was unexpected is the negative and statistically significant relation of the government's funds to support R&D to the number of patents. This translates to a

Table 14.2: KM factors.

KM Factor	r	p
Size of information and communications sector	0.66	<0.0005
e-Government maturity	0.62	<0.0005
Intellectual property rights enforcement	0.61	<0.0005
Researchers per 1000 total employment	0.59	<0.0005
Government effectiveness	0.48	<0.0005
Government's support in R&D	0.46	0.001
Collaboration between companies	0.42	0.002
Impact of government regulations on business competitiveness	0.37	0.007
Quality of public education	0.37	0.008
ICT expenditure as percentage of gross domestic product (GDP)	0.29	0.037
Government prioritization of ICT	0.27	0.058
Population enrolled in tertiary education	0.2	0.153
Subject matter expert (SME) activity by country	0.13	0.354

r, Pearson product–moment correlation coefficient; p, test of significance, a value < 0.05 is statistically significant.

illogical but real fact: when countries assign more funds to public R&D, the resulting number of patents decreases. A suggested explanation would be that when government invests more in R&D, the private sector stays latent, waiting for the government to produce new knowledge. In some countries such as the United States, patents are not always rewarded for government-funded research. Other explanation could be that the least developed countries (without many patents filed) are the ones engaged in supporting large pieces of their gross domestic product (GDP) to R&D from the government, thus in the long run, the situation may switch to observe a logical result.

The second part of the study carried out a factor analysis with the intention to test the GWUFPF in a national level. The GWUFPF has been validated by Calabrese in an organizational level. The test consisted in locate the underlying components from the 13 KM factors selected. The expectation of the study is that the components found would bear a resemblance to the four pillars mentioned (i.e., leadership, organization, technology, and learning organization).

A principal component analysis with varimax rotation was performed on the 13 KM indicators in an attempt to validate the four-pillar model, Varimax rotation seeks that each individual can be well described by a linear combination of only a few basis functions (KM factors). The results of this analysis (varimax-rotated principal component loadings) are shown in Table 14.3.

A partial validation of the GWUPFP is observed with this particular set of 13 KM factors. Here is a possible interpretation to the results obtained:

Component number one may be related to the *leadership* pillar since it is strongly supported by intellectual property protection and collaboration between companies.

Table 14.3: Principal component analysis results.

	Component number			
	1	2	3	4
e-Government maturity index	0.59	0.57	0.39	0.26
Intellectual property protection	0.85	0.27	0.28	0.14
Research and development	−0.20	−0.30	−0.26	−0.69
Government effectiveness	0.62	0.34	0.58	0.00
SME funding	0.28	0.49	0.02	−0.64
Collaboration between companies	0.85	−0.07	0.07	0.26
Impact of government regulations	0.60	0.26	0.54	−0.12
Size of information, communication, and technology sector	0.71	0.56	0.31	0.09
ICT expenditure	0.27	0.12	0.02	0.70
Government prioritization of ICT	0.15	0.02	0.88	0.21
Quality of public education	0.37	0.51	0.51	0.06
Proportion with tertiary education	0.00	0.86	0.02	0.06
Proportion of employees who are researchers	0.45	0.68	0.31	0.16
Sum of squared loadings	3.61	2.69	2.16	1.63
Percentage of variance explained	27.75	20.70	16.61	12.51

Component number two may be linked to the *learning organization* pillar since it is sustained by the people in the tertiary level and the number of researchers in a country.

The *technology* pillar is supported by component number three but it is also sustained by component number one, this has a possible high correlation between variables.

The *organization* pillar is not sustained by this specific rotation and set of KM factors, although the presence of the IPR and collaboration has a cross sector influence in the leadership pillar.

Nevertheless, the results are open to interpretation since factor analysis is used here to study the patterns of relationship among many dependent variables. Thus, the answers are more hypothetical and tentative than when independent variables are observed directly.

The present research was restricted by the availability of data. The number of countries and KM factors were limited by the availability. Unfortunately, there is a trade-off between these two elements. With fewer countries (let us say 20), the study could have used more representative and complete KM variables (such produced by the European Innovation Scoreboard, or OECD), but the study would reflect the reality of only a small group of developed countries. In the other hand, if less KM variables were to be used (lets say 4 or 5), a very subjective result would have been presented with gaps for interpretations and with no real application. On the other side, with many countries, the constraint becomes the availability of data.

This research also has been restricted by the measurement of innovation. Patents are not the best yet but the most used measurement stick for innovation. It is generally accepted that innovation exists in many other forms other than patents, and patents sometimes are not equal to innovation (some patents never get to the market). But until we could articulate a better measurement indicator, patents are to be used in the scientific world as a synonym of innovation.

14.10. Conclusion

The impact of government's KM investments on innovation was mixed do limitations on population and innovation indicators (e.g., patents). The desire at all levels of government to promote innovation and thus economic growth has resulted in many various approaches.

For governments, a logical step, after reading this research is to engage KM initiatives to enhance innovation.

The supporting KM leadership-related activities are among others to design policies to create a foundation for innovation such as patent protection, government regulation, and evident government support to business creation and development (Ireland is a good example of this actions).

Investment in KM organization related activities such as SME funding, enhancement of the collaboration among companies via forums, conferences, or expos via fiscal incentives or direct support. Reduce the impact of government regulations to support business creation and collaboration (Singapore is a good example of this behavior).

KM learning-related activities to be shaped and enhanced are the promotion of tertiary education and all kind of education for adults, continuous education and certifications, support to research and development with hybrid formulas (private–public), and support education for employees at all levels (Sweden has been consistent with this policies for many years).

In technology KM related activities, the government needs to update the infrastructure and services with more ICT expenditure and prioritize ICT in their budgets. Examples of this are Wi-Fi connected cities, digital libraries, digital government procurement, etc. Following these policies, the e-government index and the size of the ICT sector will find a growing path to support new solutions and create a better environment for innovation (Japan is a good example of these policies).

References

Abrunhosa, A. (2003). The national innovation systems approach and the innovation matrix. In: *Creating, sharing and transferring knowledge.* Denmark: Copenhagen.

Calabrese, F. A. (2000). *A suggested framework of key elements defining effective enterprise KM programs, in SEAS.* Doctoral dissertation. The George Washington University, Washington, DC.

Coombs, R. N. P., & Richards, A. (1996). A literature based innovation output indicator. *Research Policy, 25,* 403–413.

Duguet, E., & MacGarvie, M. (2003). How well do patent citations measure flows of technology? Evidence from French Innovation Surveys (September). Available at SSRN: http://ssrn.com/abstract = 452000 or DOI: 10.2139/ssrn.452000. Retrieved on May 26, 2006.

Economist, T. (2004). *Reaping the benefits of ICT, Europe's productivity challenge.* London: T.E.i. unit.

Fagerberg, J. (2004). Innovation: A guide to the literature. In: J. Fagerberg, D. Mowery & R. Nelson (Eds), *The Oxford handbook of innovation.* Oxford University Press: Oxford.

Freeman, C. (Ed.) (1982). *The economics of industrial innovation.* England: Pinter

Griliches, Z., Pakes, A., & Hall, B. H. (1987). The value of patents as indicators of inventive activity. In: P. Dasgupta, P. Stoneman (Eds), *Economic policy and technological performance,* Cambridge, UK: Cambridge University Press.

Kline, S., & Rosenberg, N. (1986). An overview of innovation. In: R. Landau & N. Rosenberg (Eds), *The positive sum strategy* (pp. 275–305). Washington, DC: National Academy Press.

Lanjouw, J. O. a. S., & Mark, A. (2004). Patent quality and research productivity: Measuring innovation with multiple indicators. *Economic Journal, 114,* 441–465.

Mensch, G. (1978). *Stalemate in technology: Innovations overcome the depression.* MA: Ballingar Pub Co. ISBN 088410611X.

OECD. (1995). *The knowledge economy* Paris, France: OECD.

OECD. (1997). *Oslo manual: Proposed guidelines for collecting and interpreting technological innovation data measurement of scientific and technological activities.* Paris: OECD.

OECD. (2004a). The significance of knowledge management in the business sector. In: OECD (Ed.), *OECD observer.*Paris: OECD.

OECD. (2004b). Knowledge management: Innovation in the knowledge economy: Implications for learning and education. In: CERI (Ed.), *Knowledge management.* Paris, France: OECD.

Porter, M. E. (1989). *The competitive advantage of nations.* New York, USA: The Free Press.

Rogers, M. (1998). *The definition and measurement of innovation.* Working Paper. Institute of Applied Economic and Social Research, Melbourne: The University of Melbourne.

Schumpeter, J. (1949). Economic theory and entrepreneurial history. *Change and the entrepreneur* (pp. 63–84). Reprinted in Schumpeter, J. (1989). In: R. V. Clemence (Ed.), *Essays on entrepreneurs, innovations, business cycles and the evolution of capitalism* (pp. 253–271). New Brunswick, NJ: Transaction Publishers.

Stankosky, M. A., & Baldanza, C. (2001). *A systems approach to engineering a KM system.* Working Paper. The George Washington University, Washington, DC.

Varga, A. (1999). Time–space patterns of US innovation: Stability or change? In: A. Taudes (Ed.), *Innovation, networks and nocalities.* Berlin: Springer.

Webster's New World Dictionary, 11th edition (1987).

Chapter 15

From the Periphery to the Core: Understanding the Process Whereby Members of a Distributed Community of Practice Become Leaders of the Community (and What the Experience Means to Them)

Anthony P. Burgess

Abstract

The core-group phenomenon in a distributed community of practice is the development of a small, socially connected and committed group of members that takes responsibility for the majority of activity in the system. The success of the larger community is contingent upon the vitality of the core group. Previous research has been limited largely to naming the phenomenon and establishing a relationship between the core group and the effectiveness of the community of practice. The purpose of this study was to provide a greater understanding of the core-group phenomenon by studying the lived experience of actual core-group members in one particular community of practice: a distributed community of company commanders in the U.S. Army. This research took an inductive, phenomenological approach and created insights based on multiple in-depth interviews of 10 core-group members. The study explored the process whereby members of the core group traveled from the periphery of the community to the core and what their experiences mean to them. The process was found to be an iterative, mutually reinforcing process of participation and connection. A key finding was that core-group-members' experiences are meaningful in particular ways, and the meaningful nature of the experience reinforces their participation. Analysis yielded a definition for

In Search of Knowledge Management: Pursuing Primary Principles
Copyright © 2010 by Emerald Group Publishing Limited
All rights of reproduction in any form reserved
ISBN: 978-1-84950-673-1

meaningful action in a community of practice, which builds on the work of Podolny et al. (2005): An action, situated in the purposeful context of the community of practice, is meaningful to me when I make a tangible contribution to a valued other and/or the community (*to contribute*); I become more socially connected and achieve greater solidarity with other members (*to connect*); and I become more personally effective (*to develop personally*). Finally, this research found that a definition for leadership in communities of practice should position leadership as a process whereby members foster the creation of meaning for each other. This study contributes to the growing field of communities of practice by providing an empirically grounded understanding of the core-group phenomenon.

15.1.   Introduction

Members of informal social systems exhibit varying degrees of participation in the system. A snapshot at one point in time, looking specifically at member participation, typically reveals a large number of people who are nominally active (or peripheral), and progressively smaller numbers of people who are more active and especially active. The smaller, especially active group within the system has been called the core group.

This pattern of a small, core-group taking responsibility for the majority of activity within the system has been observed in many types of informal social systems to include geographic communities, online networks, and distributed communities of practice. For example, Keller (2003, p. 211), in a 30-year longitudinal study of a New Jersey urban community, found that a "fraction of the residents" — a "nucleus of concerned leaders" — was responsible for the majority of activity and played a "crucial role" in the community. Wasko and Teigland (2002) found that a small, "critical mass" of individuals — 4% of the community — sustained knowledge exchange within one particular online network. Two separate studies of open-source-software-development communities report that a small core team creates the vast majority of new knowledge. For example, a core team of 15 Apache developers contributed more than 88% of added lines and 91% of deleted lines of code (Mockus, Fielding, & Herbsleb, 2002); and 50% of responses on an Apache Usenet were provided by "the 100 most prolific [knowledge] providers (2% of all providers)" (Lakhani & Hippel, 2003). Finally, community leaders at Buckman Laboratories estimated that 10–20% of community members respond to questions and sustain knowledge sharing in the community (Dixon, 2000). See also Bruckman (2004) and Kling and Courtright (2004).

Wenger, McDermott, and Snyder (2002, p. 56) provide a visual representation of this participation pattern (Figure 15.1) and describe the core group as one of three main levels of participation in a community of practice (emphasis added):

> The first [of three levels of participation] is a small core group of people who actively participate in discussions, even debates, in the public

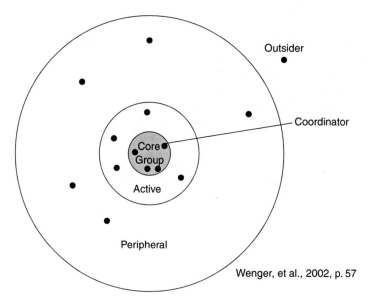

Figure 15.1: Participation in a community of practice. Reproduced with permission.

community forum. They often take on community projects, identify topics for the community to address, and move the community along its learning agenda. *This group is the heart of the community.* As the community matures, this core group takes on much of the community's leadership, its members becoming auxiliaries to the community coordinator. But this group is usually rather small, only 10 to 15 percent of the whole community.

Research has established that the core group is critical to the success of communities of practice. For example, Snyder and de Souza Briggs(2003, p. 9) state that "Leadership by an effective community coordinator and core group is essential", and McDermott (2000) found "building a core group" to be a critical success factor in successful communities of practice.

15.1.1. *Discussion of Key Terms and Army-Specific Context*

First, drawing upon the work of Katz and Kahn (1966, p. 17), I conceive of a *social system* as "the patterned activities of a number of individuals. Moreover, these patterned activities are complementary or interdependent with respect to some common output or outcome; they are repeated [and] relatively enduring ... . Social systems are open systems, which is to emphasize their interdependence with the environment in which they are situated. I use the word *informal* as Weick (1979, p. 17) defines it: "The interaction patterns that develop in addition to those that are prescribed by lines of authority". Informal social systems are characterized by voluntary human interactions and relationships and are emergent rather than hierarchically driven. *Communities of practice* are one type of informal social system. They are "groups of people who share a concern, a set of problems, or a passion about a topic, and who deepen their knowledge and expertise in this area by interacting on an ongoing basis" (Wenger et al., 2002). The term "distributed" is added to community of practice in this study to specify a geographically distributed community of practice whose members connect in various ways. See Wenger et al. (2002, p. 249):

> 'Distributed' is the preferred term over 'virtual' or 'online' because, as is the case for 'distance education' initiatives, these communities generally connect in many ways — including face-to-face — although they may rely primarily on 'virtual' communications.

15.1.1.1.   What is a company commander?   A company (also battery, troop, detachment) is an organizational unit in the U.S. Army comprised of approximately 100 soldiers. A captain with anywhere from five to eight years of service in the Army leads this organization for an average of eighteen months as the company commander. This is the first level of leadership granted full command authority, to include the authority to administer the Uniform Code of Military Justice (UCMJ). Due to the nature of the current operating environment — complex and rapidly evolving — power and responsibility are being increasingly delegated to the company level. The decentralized nature of modern warfare, combined with a significant increase in technological capabilities, has resulted in company commanders having more responsibility and power than ever before.

15.1.1.2.   What is the company command professional forum (the CC forum)?   This is a distributed community of practice in the U.S. Army focused on the practice of company command. Membership and domain are continually negotiated, but have tended to make the current company commander and the practical requirements of leading a company the central focus. The stated purpose of the CC forum is: To improve the effectiveness of company commanders, and to advance the practice of company command. The term professional forum is introduced by Dixon, Allen, Burgess, Kilner, and Schweitzer (2005) to clarify the "profession" as a defining aspect of this type of community of practice. The term *professional forum* is used interchangeably with *community of practice* throughout this chapter.

15.1.1.3.   Who are topic leads?   These are Army officers who volunteer to undertake informal leadership roles in the CC forum. In other communities of practice, topic leads are typically called informal community leaders, editors, facilitators, or topic coordinators. The term *topic lead* has been defined this way:

> These are CC members who take responsibility for particular topic areas within CompanyCommand.army.mil. They manage and

facilitate the main topics of the forum — leadership, warfighting, training, fitness, force protection, maintenance, supply, and Soldiers & families. Other topic leads provide leadership to "Rally Points," which are forums within CC that serve specific types of company commanders — for example, ADA [air defense artillery], EOD [explosive ordnance detachment], and HQ [headquarters]. Still other topic leads coordinate special topic areas such as professional reading. (Dixon et al., 2005, p. 4)

15.2. Research Methodology

In order to understand a group, it can be helpful to study the experience of the people who are the group — the people who carry out the practices, processes, and policies of the group. The purpose of this study was to come to a greater understanding of the core-group phenomenon by studying the lived experience of core-group members in one particular community of practice: a distributed community of company commanders in the U.S. Army. This research took an inductive, phenomenological approach and created insights based on in-depth interviews of the core-group members. The study was shaped by two guiding questions:

1. What is the process whereby members journey from the periphery to the core?
2. What does it mean to the members to be part of the core group?

This research placed the lived experience of core-group members front and center, and insights were induced from that lived experience. Research was conducted using a qualitative, in-depth interview method based largely on the work of Seidman (1998) that calls for three 90-minute interviews with each participant: an initial interview focused on establishing rapport and exploring the participants' life history and values; a second interview focused specifically on the participants' experience as core-group members; and a third interview that encouraged the participants to reflect upon the meaning they make of their experience as core-group members. Interviewing core-group members gave me access to the context of their behavior and allowed me to gain understanding into the meaning of their active participation.

15.2.1. Participant Selection and the Role of the Researcher

Participants were selected "purposefully," meaning I intentionally selected members of the CC core group (Creswell, 2003, p. 185). I identified approximately 50 potential core-group members based on their demonstrated participation and then, using the principle of "sufficiency," I sought to maximize variance and ensure I interviewed members that reflected the range of participants in the core-group population (Seidman, 1998; Weiss, 1994). I paid close attention to these factors: amount of time in the core group (I wanted to include core-group members representing a range of time spent as members of the core group); basic branches or specialty fields (I wanted to include participants that represented a range of different branches in the Army); current status as a company commander (I wanted to include participants who were still in company command jobs, as well as participants who were no longer in command); and experience commanding in combat (to reflect the overwhelming number of company commanders currently in combat or preparing for combat).

The principle of theoretical saturation further helped me judge how many participants to interview. Glaser and Strauss (1967) use this idea to describe when additional interviews (or data gathering) no longer add new ideas. Weiss (1994, p. 21) writes: "You stop when you encounter diminishing returns, when the information you obtain is redundant or peripheral, when what you do learn that is new adds little to what you already know to justify the time and cost of the interviewing". This is supported by Seidman, who puts it succinctly: "If you stop learning, you've reached the point of saturation" (conversation with the author; June 5, 2004). I sensed that I was at or close to saturation after closing out the three interviews with the eighth participant. I continued with two more participants to ensure the principle of saturation was met.

In the end, I selected 10 participants and interviewed each of them three times. All 10 participants are active-duty U.S. Army officers who are either currently serving in the job of company commander or previously were company commanders. The prototypical participant is a thirty-something, well-educated, married male Army captain with seven to ten years of military service, which includes significant experience commanding a company in combat. He used the CC forum in preparation for and during company command and either became part of the core group while in command or soon after coming out of command. I created a first-name pseudonym for the members of the core group named in this chapter, to include the 10 participants. I italicize the name as a reminder to the reader that the name is a pseudonym and that the person is part of the core group.

Research participants	Alan, Chris, Dale, John, Martin, Matt, Randy, Roy, Terry, Shawn
Additional core group members referred to	Michael, Mitch, Nick, Paul, Roy, Tommy

One key underlying assumption in this research is that the researcher influences the nature of the knowledge that is created. Rubin and Rubin write, "Interviewers are not neutral actors, but participants in an interviewing relationship. Their emotions and cultural understanding have an impact on the interview" (Rubin & Rubin, 1995, p. 19). This is certainly the case with me because although I am a researcher, I also helped found the CC forum and consider myself to be, like the participants, a member of the CC core group. Moreover, Kvale (1996, p. 2) writes, "The qualitative research interview is a construction site of knowledge. An interview is literally an inter view, an inter change of views between two persons conversing about a theme of mutual interest". Eden and Spender (1998, p. 21) write, "Narrative ... involves activity, not only from the storyteller, but also from the listener who must actively reconstruct its meaning". The active reconstruction of or negotiation of meaning, as Wenger (1998) describes it, occurs during the interview as well as during the subsequent analysis and writing.

Interviews were primarily conducted via telephone due to the geographic distribution of the core group. Interviews were recorded using a digital recorder, and the recordings were transcribed verbatim by a professional transcriptionist. After checking transcripts for accuracy by listening to the recording while reading the transcript, I uploaded all three transcripts for a participant into Atlas.ti, which is the software package I used to help manage the material.[1] I reviewed any handwritten notes taken during the actual interviews and then began coding the transcripts. The initial process used could be called line-by-line, open coding, which is to say that I created and assigned labels to the text as I read through the transcripts (Charmaz, 2001; Coffey & Atkinson, 1996). I then worked with the data, looking for and writing about overall patterns and themes. Additionally, I provided the participants the opportunity to "check" my interpretations, which is something that Lincoln and Guba (1985, p. 314) call "the most crucial technique for establishing credibility". This research was an iterative process of analyzing, writing, and reflecting.

15.3. Discussion

15.3.1. Research Question 1: What is the Process Whereby Members of a Community of Practice Journey from the Periphery to the Core?

The first research question focused on understanding the process whereby members of a community of practice become more actively involved — how they move from being members on the periphery to being leaders that are essential to the success of the community. During the second interview in the three-interview series, I asked participants to describe their experiences with CC chronologically, beginning with first finding out about it and continuing all the way through to the present. This story was interwoven with the story of being in the Army, so it is helpful to begin with establishing the basic pattern for the participants' careers (Figure 15.2):

The prototypical participant is commissioned as an officer in the Army and attends basic officer training. After an initial assignment as a platoon leader (PLT LDR) and company executive officer (XO), the newly promoted captain attends the five-month captain's career course (CCC), and then transitions to a new location where he undergoes some period of time working on staff and preparing for company command. At some point, he or she takes command of a company, commands, and

---

1. Atlas.ti is a qualitative data analysis software that facilitates qualitative coding of interview transcripts. Find out more at www.atlasti.com.

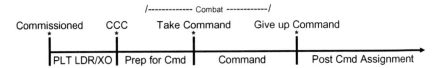

Figure 15.2: Typical officer career pattern.

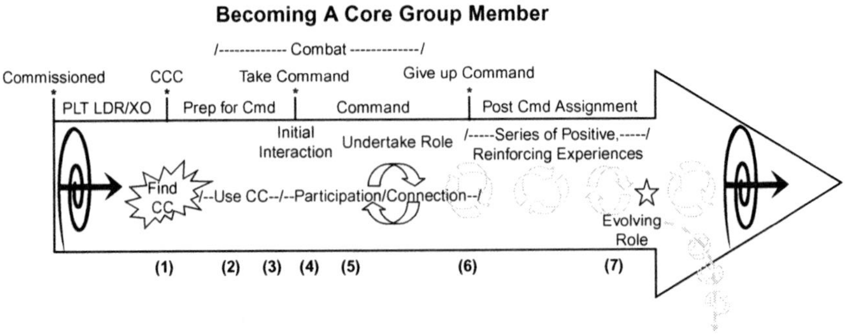

Becoming A Core Group Member

Figure 15.3: Core group becoming structure.

then gives up command. The period of command time is typically eighteen months to two years; some officers — like five of the ten participants in this study — are selected to command a second company and therefore go through two iterations of prepare, command, give up command. In the current world situation, almost every officer experiences a combat deployment, and often more than one. After command, officers — like seven of the participants at the time of these interviews — transition into postcommand assignments such as graduate school, instructing at the captain's career course, serving on higher-level staff assignments, or teaching at West Point.

In the process of studying the interview transcripts, I began to refer to these stories (the stories of the participants' relationship with and activity in the community of practice) as becoming-core-group-member stories, or simply, *becoming* stories. After studying the participants' *becoming* stories, an underlying structure began to emerge — a structure that describes the *becoming* process. Combining this structure with the career pattern previously described (Figure 15.3) provides an indication of the general pattern of moving from the periphery to the center:

The basic storyline is that the participant (1) finds CC either while attending or close to the time he or she is attending the captain's career course. The participant (2) uses CC to help him or her prepare for command and continues to use it while in command. At some point, there occurs (3) an initial interaction between the participant and member(s) of the core group. Over time, there is (4) a pattern of increasing participation in the forum and increasing interaction (or connection) with core-group members, leading to (5) an invitation to take on a leadership role with CC. Undertaking a role is followed by an iterative process of increasing participation and connection, which can be described as (6) a series of meaningful experiences that

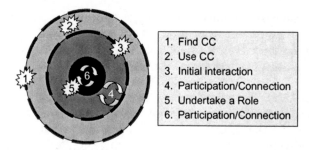

Figure 15.4: Cross-section view of core-group becoming structure.

have a cumulative, positive effect. At some point, often in conjunction with increasing time and distance from his or her command experience, the person's role begins (7) to evolve — either toward greater leadership and support roles, or towards a gradual disengagement from the core group. Of note, becoming a core-group member is not something that you ever fully arrive at; you are always becoming, never arriving.

Figure 15.4 is a second image of the prototypical becoming story, which takes a cross-section view of Figure 15.3 and follows the key events in a prototypical core-group-member's becoming story over time.

Moreover, this *becoming* story fits into the larger story of becoming a member of the Army profession, a career-long process. One way to think about both of these stories is in terms of identity and commitment. Over time, identity evolves and officers become more committed members of the profession. Disengagement from the CC core group may not change the person's trajectory toward becoming a member of the profession and, in fact, it may be a positive step in that longer-term story as the person becomes more active in the professional forum at the next level of leadership.

For the purposes of this chapter, I will limit discussion to the most important theme when it comes to understanding the core-group phenomenon: the iterative and mutually reinforcing process of participation and connection, which can be further broken down into four subthemes: (1) use of and gaining value from CC, (2) undertaking a leadership role, (3) series of positive (and reinforcing) experiences, and (4) evolving role.

15.3.2. Participation and Connection

Alan provides an exceptional introduction to this theme:

> I was getting ready to come home for a couple of months before going back in for a second tour in Iraq. I had command under control, I knew what I was doing, we had kicked ass and we are now in for the long haul. The first sergeant and I were clicking, the FRG

[family readiness group] was clicking, I had all my guys below me clicking — everything was good. [And] now I actually had things to say that were relevant. I went out of take, take, take, take, take to take/give, take/give, take/give, take/give.

And there was also something else that happened right around then, and it just sort of happened. People started contacting me on email outside of the site. For the most part up to that point all the action associated with the site I had seen in postings, in files that were being put up, in products that people could use, and in the comments that people were putting up there. But somewhere around that time, I started doing business offline with people and that made it more personal. You start thinking about, okay, these aren't just random people out there. You now see the pattern where all these guys are showing up and ... they go from being just names on a screen to people that you associate things with.

At some point, typically during or shortly after company command — and less often, before taking command — the participants transitioned from strictly reading and using content to contributing in some way. Although I could argue that simply reading content and even the act of joining and entering the online space is a form of participation, I am using the term here to specifically refer to observable acts of participation; for example, posting a question, or engaging in an online discussion, or completing the Web-based combat-leader interview. Participation, thus, makes a member visible to the community, and it is that visibility that creates the awareness in the minds of the core group to communicate or to connect with the member. This initial connection typically includes a warm welcoming, acknowledgment, and appreciation of participation, and — sometimes — a gift or token of appreciation such as a CC coin, book, or hat. *Alan*, for example, spoke endearingly about the broken-handled CC coffee mug he received while in Germany, which he referred to as an "unsolicited attaboy."

I use the word connection in the sense of an invisible thread between two people. Sometimes the very act of participation creates a connection between two people, such as when a person responds to another's question in a discussion, or when a person emails or otherwise communicates with another person. When multiple iterations of connection-making activity occur between two people, the thread grows thicker and a human relationship develops. Of note, not all connection-making activities are equal in impact. For example, a face-to-face, personal, one-on-one conversation is more powerful than two members becoming aware of each other in a casual threaded discussion.

What is evident in the participants' *becoming* stories is that participation and connection are co-creative. Participation creates connection, which creates participation. It is often a mutually reinforcing process that can propel the person to a more central position in the community of practice. For example, *Martin* — a current company commander in Iraq at the time — became involved in a threaded discussion about air-to-ground coordination, which led to him being emailed by core-group members:

> One of the guys wrote me and said, "Hey, saw your post — it's good stuff; we're glad to have you; welcome aboard; we think you're gonna enjoy the website, etc., etc." And then I wrote him back and said, "Well, thanks for such a warm welcome," you know, and we started a little conversation about who I was and what the website was about, and then they just came right out and said … "Hey, we're looking for somebody to run the Aviation site. Are you interested?" And I allowed as how I wasn't sure how much time I could dedicate to it being as how we were deployed, but, yes, I was definitely interested in doing it, and it kind of grew from there.

Similar conversations began after *Roy*, *John*, and *Chris* each began participating in online discussions and contributing content. *Roy* had used CC as a resource during his two-year company command; however, it wasn't until he shared some of his knowledge and core-group members corresponded with him that we would say that human connections had formed.

Interestingly, participation does not always initiate this cycle. In some cases, a connection is a catalyst for the initial act of participation. *Randy* had matter-of-factly used CC content to help him prepare for command, but he had never participated in the sense we are using the term here. While in Iraq he met *Paul*, a CC core-group member. *Paul* interviewed *Randy* — putting a face to the CC name — and he explained to *Randy* how he could share his valuable knowledge with leaders preparing for Iraq. This face-to-face connection was a catalyst for *Randy's* first overt act of participation:

> I'll be honest with you, I didn't really pay much attention to [CC] after I took command until *Paul* — I ran into *Paul* in Mosul — and he was doing his interviews … He was talking to me about it and I [agreed to be interviewed] and then he told me, "Maybe you ought to go on [CC] and share some of these things that you've told me." … [Then] I remember answering those [combat-leader interview] questions. I think I remember going back in CC like two or three times and editing, you know, changing up my answers as things were becoming clearer. And after that I thought, you know what, this is probably a good way because there's a lot of guys coming over and then you start reading some of the questions and guys are [asking questions I can answer] … At that point I was like, you know what, maybe I ought to start throwing some of this stuff up there because really how else are they gonna get some of the information because the Army does a good job at pre-producing stuff, it's just very slow in lessons learned and things like that. So // and that's // at that point I thought, well, you

know, there's a lot of utility here and that's when I started getting very
involved, I guess you could say.

And in some cases, a previous relationship (thick connection) exists between a person
and a core-group member first. For example, *Matt* was good friends with *Mitch* and
had a preexisting relationship with *Nick*. Based on those connections, *Tommy* invited
him to help facilitate a leader-development seminar for captains who were preparing
for command. Over the course of six months, *Matt* and *Tommy* were involved in
multiple connection-making activities, to include three iterations of the leader-
development seminar, ultimately leading to *Matt* becoming an active leader in
the online forum. And, in *Dale*'s case, his act of joining CC gave core-group member
James — who he had previously served with — the opportunity to warmly welcome
him. In that case, there was a preexisting connection and *Dale*'s entering the online
forum created the chance for that connection to be updated.

One interesting activity in CC that serves as a mechanism to foster this participation and connection cycle is the featuring of members on the main page of the forum.
The core group collaboratively identifies an experienced company commander
who has begun to emerge as an active participant, and then invites that person
to be the CC featured member. A conversation ensues during which the member
to-be-featured provides a photograph, talks about his or her experiences and current
situation, and participates in a short email interview (which becomes part of the
featured-member package). Interestingly, six of the ten participants in this study were
featured members. *Chris* talks about that experience:

> I really like the website and I like contributing and I think it was an
> exchange of emails between *Tommy* and I [that prompted my becoming
> a "Featured Member."] We had emailed a couple of more times, and
> I had posted some more [discussion posts in the forum] and — I don't
> know if it was [the things I had contributed] or maybe my blossoming
> personality, [but] from there it was just, "Hey *Chris* would you mind,"
> you know, "If you can send us a picture and then if you can answer
> these questions for us." I was hesitant at first but heck, I'd gotten a lot
> from the website so why not, you know, and that's the way it came
> about. It was a long process ...

In this process, a thicker connection is established between *Chris* and the core group.
Moreover, this activity intensifies *Chris*' visibility in the community and serves, in
some way, as a public announcement of his commitment to CC and the profession.
Chris goes on to say,

> [A friend] made fun of me at first when ... my mug [picture] went up on
> the web page but, you know, after that he started using the web page
> and whatnot. Oh [he] definitely [gave me a hard time about being the
> featured member], yeah, because the picture was so cheesy ... I didn't
> know how big of a deal it was gonna be until I had some of my old

roommates from Fort Bragg being like, "cheese dick," [laughs] — just hassling me. I didn't care because you know what happened? People started writing me for information, and I felt as though I was giving back to the Army community that has given me so much. So it was good; it was awesome, the good month that I was up there, however long, a month and a half I guess it was. [laughs] And, you know, I got emails two or three times a week — guys I went to [ROTC] Advanced Camp with nine years ago would be like "Hey, man, I saw you up on CompanyCommand.com." And I was like, wow, okay, what's up man, and started writing back and forth. And guys I went to the captain's career course with that I lost touch ... There were just so many people that came out of the woodwork, like, "*Chris*, I saw you." ... People keeping in touch — great ... And that's cool ...

Thus, the activity of being the featured member sparks a whole new cycle of participation and connection for *Chris*. It is an important part of his *becoming* story.

15.3.2.1. Using and benefiting from participating in the CC forum Most of the participants used CC during their time in command, such that they had a clear sense of the value they gained by being involved. For example, solving problems, getting ideas and tools, and generally integrating CC into their work as company commanders — to include as a tool to develop their subordinate leaders. Becoming a core-group member is, most importantly, a result of members engaging deeply in the forum, and — as *Randy* described — when you are given a leadership role in the forum, "you keep contributing in the way you've always contributed." In the process of gaining value from participating, the participants began to perceive the forum as integral to their effectiveness. "I valued the forum because I personally experienced what being involved can do for you" was a sentiment that echoed across many of the interviews. Core-group members do not have to make a case for the value of CC to active members because the members have personally experienced that value. In addition to the sense of value for the forum that develops when members personally benefit from participating, they often feel a responsibility to reciprocate — to give back. *Terry* makes the point well:

> A basic underlying assumption I operate on is that you don't just take ... That's a basic value that I have: always try and give back to the folks who give to you ... If anybody contributes to your development or anybody helps you out in some way you help them back.

And *John* says, "When I have a question or need some information, this is one of the resources I look to. So, I feel that it's my obligation to post any information I have ..." Thus, gaining personal benefit invokes a level of reciprocity that would not exist if the member had not personally benefited from being a member. This sense of value for the forum, as well as the desire to reciprocate, sets the conditions for the member to respond positively when core-group members connect with the member.

15.3.2.2. Undertaking a leadership role   At some point in the iterative cycle of participation and connection, the participants in this study were invited to take greater responsibility in an area that matched up with their already existing passion and talent. In order to know what a person's talents are and what they are passionate about, you must know that person. In the previous excerpt from *Martin*, he describes a back-and-forth process with core-group members, which — among other things — allows the core-group members to get to know him. *Martin* became involved in a threaded discussion and then a core-group member warmly welcomed him and let him know his participation was noticed and valuable. "And then I wrote him back and said, 'Well, thanks for such a warm welcome,' you know, and we started kind of a little conversation about who I was and what the website was about." The core group discovered that *Martin* has significant experience with and passion for aviation and especially air-to-ground coordination. It was a natural fit to invite *Martin* to take lead in this subject matter. His increased responsibility in CC became a natural extension of who he already is.

The underlying assumption driving this CC core-group behavior is that company commanders who become active members have experience with and passion for an aspect (or aspects) of company command. It is therefore the CC goal to discover the person's talent/passion first, and then to give them a platform to more fully be themselves — and to more fully bring themselves to the community. *Roy* provides an especially valuable insight into how this can occur:

> And it was at that point that *Tommy* contacted me and sent me an email saying, "Hey, I saw your post, I looked at your dog tags [member profile]. I really think you are somebody that we would benefit from having on our team. Are you in a position to contribute to the profession?" ... And so *Tommy* and I had a phone conversation; we talked about different places to contribute, different ways to contribute ... [We] finally settled that I would jump into the *Soldiers and Families* [topic] ... I felt strongly about the topic because in my experience it was something that really mattered to soldiers and it was one of those intangibles that really made a difference in how prepared your soldiers were and how prepared they felt ... *Soldiers and Families* was a place where I felt that I could advance the level of knowledge and the level of discussion that was present and it was an area where I felt that I could really make a difference ...

During the course of this research, I found that core-group members do not limit their participation to one topic; however, it seems that giving them a leadership role in a topic that they especially like and have experience with serves as an invitation for them to take additional responsibility, and it grants them permission to take more initiative and to become stewards of the community. This was the case, for example, with *Shawn* and *professional reading* and *John* and his passion and expertise in the area of *physical fitness*.

This leads us to a key point, which is that having a role is a key step in the *becoming* stories. With that role come additional editing privileges as well as access to a "team only" part of the forum, which is essentially an online community within the community, for core-group members. Most importantly, members' identity within the forum evolves with the taking on of a role: participation in the forum takes on new meaning. *John* provides us with an absolutely fascinating case study of this because he was invited to be the co-topic lead of the *Fitness* topic after my first interview with him, but before the last interview. Here, before he has undertaken a role in the CC forum, he talks about his commitment to have an exceptional web page for the company he commands:

> When you're given a responsibility, it carries over ... // Right now I have a company web page. It's not like CompanyCommand website — where ok, I really don't have to do anything. I can just go on there and get stuff, but [pause] on the company website I have a responsibility to update it not because I have to // ... If I've taken on this thing I'm gonna do it and it's gonna be right. You know? ...

And with regards to his role with CC, he says: "I'm just one of many who have possibly something good that they can contribute ... I don't run that fitness page or really control anything on there ... I don't have an unrealistic vision of what my role is there." By the final interview, after having accepted *Michael's* invitation to help him lead the *Fitness* topic, we see that *John's* perspective has evolved:

> [As far as the experiences with CC that stand out to me?] Well, just finding the page was a pretty neat experience for one. [And] all this recently has been pretty interesting, with you coming in [the research interviews], and the whole Fitness thing — this is definitely a turning point or a // maybe not a turning point but one of the milestones if you will that I'll remember or look back on through time ... This has definitely given me a different perspective and almost // well a responsibility and more ownership now in what's going on. So it's more personal now.

Finally, *Roy* reflects on how the invitation to a leadership role influenced the nature of his participation:

> [Without having a role], I think I would have been active but I would not have taken any type of leadership or organizational role because I simply would not have felt the confidence to do that. I would have felt like it was not my role. All of us want to take initiative and all of us want to be out front leading, but if you don't feel like you have the authority to do that // authority and responsibility are a pair and you can't have one without the other. And so I certainly felt like I had a responsibility to do it, but without that conversation, without that

outreach from another team member and that empowering of, "We want you to take this part of it," I would not have felt that I had the authority to do the kinds of things like reaching out to team members and saying, "Hey, we want you on board, we think you're a great person" — and doing all of those things. So, yeah, I don't think I would have been anywhere near as involved ... I would not have been anywhere near as engaged in CompanyCommand as I have been over the last two years.

Thus, we see that having a leadership role — and especially one that is aligned with the member's talents and expertise — plays an important role in the *becoming* process.

15.3.2.3. Iterative process of increasing participation and connection

In the *becoming* stories, what occurs next is an iterative process of increasing participation and connection. Of critical importance, the *becoming* story does not end with taking on a leadership role; it is more appropriate to think of that event as an initial commitment that develops depth and meaning as the core-group member experiences being a core-group member, and as he continues to participate and connect with the people who are the CC forum. It is also important to observe that the participants experienced a series of meaningful experiences — one after the other — that had a cumulative, positive effect. I draw attention to this by including "series of positive (and reinforcing) experiences" in the *becoming* structure diagram. If the initial interaction and participation/connection cycle is the key to growing a core group, it is the series of positive (and reinforcing) experiences that is key to sustaining the core group.

Each of the participants experienced this series of positive (and reinforcing) experiences, though each is at a different location along their journey. For example, between September 2003 and May 2004, *Roy* took on responsibility for leading the *Soldiers and Families* topic, connected with *Matt* who was attending the same graduate school, received tangible evidence of his having an impact on a member seeking input on casualty operations, attended an On Fire Rendezvous (meeting of the core group) in Washington D.C., reorganized the *Soldiers and Families* topic, began developing relationships with members, and represented the forum/presented his experience with the forum at the Navy knowledge management conference in San Diego. These are the concrete experiences *Roy* talks about when asked to describe his experience as a core-group member. When we look at his reflections about these experiences, we begin to get a sense for their impact on his overall experience as a core-group member:

- *Volunteering to be a leader in the forum*: "And I think there was a real conscious shift in my mind of, yeah, this is something different."
- *Contributing to a member in need (in Iraq)*: "It was really a great thing for her, and it was a great thing for me to have that validation of my actions. And, again, going back to this idea of I'm looking for ways to reconnect with the profession and

contribute to an Army at war, well this was it. You know, this was me giving some kind of tangible assistance, to people directly involved in the fight. And so it was a tremendous boost for my dealings with that."

- *Face-to-face meeting with the core group*: "That was huge because that brought together such a group of like-minded professionals, and staying with that group of people for three or four days, talking with them, generating ideas, was a huge energy boost. It really just kind of got me reenergized and back into the thick of it. It gave me some huge ideas on reorganizing the taxonomy of how *Soldiers and Families* was organized and trying to make it more content friendly and trying to make it more user-friendly. And it really just kind of reaffirmed what I thought I was doing with CompanyCommand and why it was valuable to me and why it was valuable to the profession. So that was a huge boost ... "

- *Presentation at Navy conference*: "The advantage of going down and talking about something and briefing something is that it forces you to kind of reorganize in your own head — just like teaching makes you better about a subject [pause] because when you have to teach something or you have to talk about it you really have to get it straight in your head. By the same token, doing this briefing really got it straight in my head about what it is that I think I'm doing here; so doing that briefing was not only a great outreach to another group of military professionals — which is always worthwhile — but for me personally it really helped me sort it out in my head what am I doing here, what the purpose of this is."

- *Developing relationships with members*: "I would see a note about something on the website that was a request for assistance and I'd post something to try and help out or I'd send a note to somebody to say thanks. That would generate follow-on request for content or follow-on request for this or that [and] helped draw people in, helped them contribute more and also helped kind of reinforce my sense of belonging and my sense of value in working with this site."

What stands out in *Roy's* story is that each of the experiences is important to him, and they build on each other. When he reflects on the January 2004 face-to-face meeting in D.C., he says, "It really just kind of got me reenergized and back into the thick of it." He implies that he was in need of being reenergized; i.e., his energy was waning. And the things *Roy* learned at the meeting motivated and equipped him to reorganize his topic in the online space. Moreover, the San Diego conference in May caused him to really think through the purpose of the whole thing and what he was doing with it. In the interview, he explained that the experience of personally making a difference for the member in Iraq gave him the confidence to speak at the conference; whereas without that personal sense that he was a true contributor, he may not have felt like he was the right person to present at the conference. Thus, he underwent a series of positive experiences that built on each other and made an important impact on his *becoming*.

These types of memorable experiences occurred for all the participants. Other examples include *Randy* traveling to Germany to help facilitate a leader-development seminar, *Dale* and *Shawn* taking advantage of the professional reading challenge — which included CC sending them copies of a book of their choosing to read with their lieutenants, and *Matt* developing and launching a completely new topic to honor members who are killed in combat. Perhaps the rendezvous — which *Roy* described above — is the experience that made the most impact on the participants. Because the impact comes across so strong in the interviews, I will share a few more comments from the participants about it here:

> *Dale*: "The On Fire Rendezvous [in Colorado] absolutely without a doubt was critical [to my becoming more involved] ... That was another one of those experiences that was just incredible ... And it's hard to put into words how that On Fire thing really kind of kept me hooked because had I not gone to that I'm not sure I would be // I would have continued to post, but I'm not sure I would have been as involved as I am. I probably would have looked at *James* and told him he's nuts if he wants me to come on as a co-topic lead for Headquarters Commander Rally Point ... And there's a cool factor involved with this ... It's just a cool thing to be a part of."

> *Terry*: "[The On-Fire Rendezvous] for me personally it gave me some new ways to look at how to build conversations ... It changed my perspective ... The other great thing that came out of it was meeting people like *Roy*, meeting *James* and *Gary*, and a lot of the others that were just a name and an occasional conversation on the site — *Matt* and all the other folks ... and being able to network with them because being able to put a face with the name ... I was less intimidated to ask a question ... Surrounded by so many awesome people, for me personally, I was just like, wow ... what a great bunch as far as having a support system, bouncing ideas off: "Hey, what do you think about this? What do you think about that," and broadening out // whatever I was weak in or didn't know about or didn't have an experience in, I knew I had a great group of friends that I could rely on to make up for that shortfall and who I could also learn a lot from."

> *Matt*: "The turning point for me is when we went to DC [for the first rendezvous]"

> *Randy*: "Being invited out to the [rendezvous] meant a lot to me ... I was blown away by it. It was so awesome."

> *Alan*: "It was fantastic to get the rest of the story about what was going on with the site, and to be able to talk about where it's going ... I actually got to see a lot of people and see mirrors of myself because the folks that were there all had that same stupid smirk on their face of, you know, what we're doing is the absolute coolest thing

on the entire planet. It's so cool that, really, if you expose anybody to it they're gonna agree that, damn, this is pretty cool ... So it was good because that built upon the whole idea that it's not just the site, it's the people; it's just not what's posted on there, it's the means by which you can get things done ... I got to know that there are a lot of other people out there who are bit by the bug — who have the same crazy devotion to the movement of CompanyCommand."

In summary, the participants experienced a series of positive (and reinforcing) experiences that happened in succession over time. Moreover, the experiences have a cumulative impact.

15.3.2.4. Evolving role As time passes and core-group members become more experienced and more senior as far as their time away from their company commander experience, their role within the forum often evolves. While still in command and during the time immediately following command, core-group members are in an ideal situation to contribute. They are at the cutting-edge of knowledge in the company command domain. On the other hand, they often have limited time available and may not yet be equipped with the skills that go with the other roles (e.g., facilitator and steward). After they come out of command, they might have more time available and they continue to gain experience that allows them to be more effective core-group members. However, at the same time that they are gaining skill and experience as core-group members, they are also getting farther away from personal experience as company commanders. Given the rapidly changing environment, it doesn't take long for past company commanders to perceive themselves to be less relevant to the community, and this perception increases the longer they are out of command. One experienced participant said, "With each passing day, my opinion of myself is I'm less relevant." A second participant, not yet even out of command, said:

> Since I've now been back from Iraq for a year and my major's board has already convened, I probably ought to start looking to see if I can find another young commander who would like to get in there and post a lot of the new TTPs [tactics, techniques, & procedures] and kind of take over the stuff because I'll be leaving command here. I'm not really sure I'll be relevant more than about maybe two years after command ...

A third participant reinforces this perception of losing relevance with each passing day away from the company command job:

> You go outside your relevance window. And I'm quickly getting there in terms of HHC [headquarters and headquarters company] specific stuff simply because I look now at the way an HHC commander // it's

been a little over eighteen months since I've been back from Iraq. I don't know what tank company commanders are doing there so much anymore and I'm not exactly sure how HHC guys are being utilized there.

And a fourth participant said:

That's where I see my role has changed ... It's interesting that some of us who have been around [CC] for a couple of years now and // ... I don't wanna say we've moved on because we haven't; I think we still have something to contribute, but it's not in the same way we did when we were commanders ... I'm not sure how to articulate it.

Thus core-group members often perceive that they are becoming less relevant to the specific knowledge domain of the community over time.

Being promoted to major is another factor that, for some participants, has reinforced this shift in identity. Within CC, there is a strong — and intentional — focus on the current company commander as far as the identity of the forum. The forum is called CompanyCommand and the symbol greeting members is a pair of captain bars (rank insignia). Everything in the forum clarifies that this is a place for company commanders, who are captains in the U.S. Army. So, as one participant who had been a major for a couple years by the time of the interviews put it, "If you pull up the website, one of the first things you bump into on the homepage is the captain's bars, which is the way it should be, but I don't have captain's bars [pause] Where does a major's oak leaf fit into that captain bar picture?" Given the clear message that the forum sends members, this core-group member is asking, "How do I fit into this picture?"

One option for core-group members is to transition from being especially active contributors of their personal knowledge about commanding a company to being exceptional connectors, facilitators, social catalysts, and stewards for the community. *Alan, Matt*, and *Roy* are good examples of experienced core-group members whose roles have evolved over time to include activities like coaching newer core-group members and taking the lead on coordinating activities involving core-group members. In *Alan's becoming* story, he talks about how at some point people started contacting him on email outside of the site. He says, "People go from being just names on a screen to people ... It becomes personal." During his experience at the rendezvous in Colorado, the importance of relationships outside the online space crystallized for him. When he returned to Germany, he worked with two other core-group members to develop and send out personal welcome emails to members that were either stationed in Germany or who were military intelligence officers like himself. He also continued, now with more clarity of purpose, hosting barbeque (BBQs) at his house for current and potential core-group members. This type of leadership indicates a core-group member whose role is evolving.

Both *Matt* and *Roy* — the only two participants who attended two rendezvous — describe how their role evolved from strictly learning during the first rendezvous to coaching and mentoring newer members at the second rendezvous:

> *Matt*: A year later, when we were in Colorado at the ... second Rendezvous, I felt like my role switched a little bit from consumer to more of seeing how I could contribute to the learning process for the new people ... Having been in the CompanyCommand system for two years by this point, I kind of understood how to do stuff. I started trying to help teach others how to do stuff and how to look at the website in terms of the philosophy and that sort of thing because I felt kind of like a disciple at this point now that I knew and understood what was going on a little bit better than those guys fresh off the block ... I personally saw the lights go on for guys. They're just like, huh, you know, I can do that. And then next thing you know everyone's got their laptops open and they're fiddling around with the website ... I definitely felt that [my role was changing] — in a good way. And I think it kind of felt good ...

> *Roy*: Somehow at this next rendezvous I was the guy that some people were turning to and saying, "What do you think about this? Is this feasible?" And that kind of caught me off guard; I was like what the hell are you asking me for? ... And understand, I'm not saying that I became like a leader of the group or anything because I don't think that's the case // but somehow I became something resembling an old hand when in reality I was only a guy who had been doing this for about a year or so. And I'm not sure where that transition happened, but it happened. And so I found myself at the Colorado meeting being a little more active and taking a little more of a mentoring and shaping approach with other members, as well as with the site content, which was a very odd transition for me. And I'm still kind of sorting through, still kind of sorting through that transition in my mind.

Their experience as core-group members allows them to have a significant impact on newer core-group members — and their distance from command does not lessen that impact. This realization can be liberating for leaders like *Matt* and *Roy*. Thus, core-group members often take on additional responsibility commensurate with their experience as core-group members. As they evolve, so do their roles, becoming coaches and mentors for the emerging leaders in the forum.

It is important to note that not all core-group members make this transition. One of the participants provides an interesting example of a core-group member who did not enjoy the evolving role. He had been a prolific contributor and took great satisfaction from that role in the community. In this excerpt, he describes the sense of loss that he felt when he realized that his role was evolving.

My "what have I done to help you out" role has changed to, "what can I do to find the other people who have had this experience, and get them involved with those guys who are over there now." [As I've acted in the facilitator and steward roles], I've realized that this is kind of what it's gonna be like now from here on out and I was, you know, it kind of, it kind of [pause] not bothered // I guess it bothered me a little bit because I had really enjoyed being the active member as opposed to being the guy who now is a facilitator, so to speak, because I don't know if I fall into that role really well; I don't, I don't know.

There is an element of tension for this participant as he negotiates his own identity in the forum. This excerpt introduces the idea that some core-group members may not naturally transition into other roles in support of the community.

Another option for core-group members, which is perhaps an option that arrives for everyone at some point, is to gradually disengage from the CC forum while simultaneously engaging in the community of practice associated with their next job: for example, jobs like operations officer and battalion executive officer, which are jobs that majors hold. In this way, the *becoming* story is much larger than just the CC forum. These leaders are becoming members of the profession — a career-long process — and their time engaged in the CC forum propels them forward in that developmental journey. One way to think about both of these stories is in terms of identity and commitment. Over time, identity evolves and officers become more committed members of the profession. Disengagement from the CC core group is likely a seamless part of a professional's centripetal movement, where full participation is couched in terms of the never-ending process of becoming a professional Army officer.

And, interestingly, the nature of the core-group-member roles — especially the connector and social catalyst roles — are such that a core-group member can continue to live those roles out, even when they are no longer active in the online forum proper. Past core-group members stay loosely connected and remain available to the core group as a source of knowledge should they be needed; moreover, they often encourage the junior leaders they work with to participate in the forum. The sentiment of the participants is "once a member, always a member." *Martin* captures this: "The truth is, I'll be coming back to CompanyCommand for the rest of my career now." The sense one gets is that although the participants may transition out of an active core-group-member role, they will always be committed to the purpose of the forum and will continue to be advocates and remain part of the wider CC network.

15.3.3. *The Core Group Phenomenon is a* Social *Phenomenon*

One finding of this research is that the core-group phenomenon is a social phenomenon. This is a critical point, one which I did not fully appreciate before the research began. Initially, I defined *core group* as the small group of active members that is responsible for the majority of activity in the community of practice. Notwithstanding the use of the word group in the definition, the social nature of the phenomenon is missing. One interpretation of this definition could be that the core group is simply a grouping of the most active, but not necessarily interdependent, members. The literature which I relied on most in the shaping of my early understanding likewise does not clarify the interdependencies of the core-group members:

> The first [of three levels of participation] is a small core group of people who actively participate in discussions, even debates, in the public community forum. They often take on community projects, identify topics for the community to address, and move the community along its learning agenda. This group is the heart of the community. As the community matures, this core group takes on much of the community's leadership, its members becoming auxiliaries to the community coordinator. But this group is usually rather small, only 10 to 15 percent of the whole community. (Wenger et al., 2002, p. 56)

Although these interdependencies are implicit, I initially put my emphasis on understanding the individual core-group members. What became quite clear in the research is that social interdependencies in the core group are of critical import, and I therefore introduce an updated definition: *The core-group phenomenon in a distributed community of practice is the development of a small, socially connected and committed group of members that takes responsibility for the majority of activity in the system.*

15.3.4. Research Question 2: What Does It Mean to the Members to be Part of the Core Group?

The three-interview method is structured such that the final interview creates the opportunity for the participants to reflect upon what they have shared in the first two interviews, to create new connections, and to articulate the meaning that their experience holds for them. Schutz (1967, p. 69), in *The Phenomenology of the Social World*, writes:

> It is misleading to say that experiences have meaning. Meaning does not lie in the experience. Rather, those experiences are meaningful which are grasped reflectively. The meaning is the way in which the Ego regards its experience. The meaning lies in the attitude of the Ego toward that part of its stream of consciousness which has already flowed by ...

In line with Schutz' concept that experiences become meaningful reflectively, I began the third interviews with this question: "As you've reflected on the first two interviews, has anything emerged for you? Have you made any connections that weren't there before?" What I found in every case was that the first two interviews had stimulated the participants' thinking and new ideas and connections had in fact emerged. By starting with this question, I was able to reestablish rapport and to get us back into the flow of conversation. When I felt the timing was appropriate, I asked a question directly about meaning. For example, "As you reflect back on your time being part of this team, what has it meant to you to be involved like this?" And I asked a third question focused on meaning that underpinned their ongoing commitment to the work — in other words, meaning-making that has influenced their continued participation: "You invest a lot of time and thought into your role with the team. I'm wondering what drives you to do this. What causes you to continue investing so much into this?" Talking about meaning is not something people do very often, and these were not easy questions for me to ask. However, the participants — at this point in the three-interview process — were willing and able to respond. I also noticed that when I looked at the transcripts of the earlier interviews through a "meaning" lens, there were connections to meaning in most of the stories that the participants told.

Wenger (1991, p. 114) writes, "Meaning arises out of active participation in practice." Moreover, he makes the point that the "process by which we experience the world and our engagement in it as meaningful" is negotiated:

> Meaning is not pre-existing, but neither is it simply made up. Negotiated meaning is at once both historical and dynamic, contextual and unique ... The meaningfulness of our engagement in the world is not a state of affairs, but a continual process of renewed negotiation ... Meaning exists neither in us, nor in the world, but in the dynamic relation of living in the world. (Wenger, 1998, p. 54)

For the participants in this study, their experiences as core-group members are iterative and ongoing, and the meaningfulness of their engagement in the community of practice is, as Wenger wrote, "a continual process of renewed negotiation."

When I studied the participants' stories, looking specifically at the idea of meaning, topics that are common across the participants emerged. The topics crystallized into three major themes that influence the creation of meaning for people when it comes to their work with the CC forum (Figure 15.5):

1. *To contribute* (give back): "It is meaningful for me to give back, to make a contribution to something I value." This occurs both in terms of contributing to another person as well as to the corporate body.
2. *To connect* (relationships and solidarity): "It is meaningful for me that I am becoming more connected to this band of brothers — this community of like-hearted leaders who are committed to a common cause." This includes a sense of camaraderie and being part of something bigger than self.
3. *To develop personally* (improved effectiveness): "It is meaningful that I am becoming more personally effective as a result of being involved."

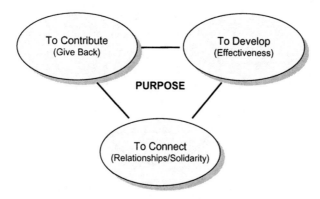

Figure 15.5: Meaning-making components (situated in purpose).

All three themes are meaningful as they relate to the context and purpose of the CC forum, which is to improve the effectiveness of company commanders and to advance the practice of company command. To clarify this important point, *contribution, connection,* and *personal development* are purposeful in that they all relate directly back to the work to which these leaders have committed themselves: being Army professionals. The members' *contribution* is situated in the context of helping Army company commanders become more effective as well as advancing the profession more generally. The members' *connection* occurs in the context of relationships with people who share their professional aspirations; and the members' *personal development* is situated in the context of becoming more effective Army leaders. In this way, meaning is situated in purpose.

When they engage in the work of being core-group members, they have experiences that are personally meaningful. In other words, meaning cannot be separated from behavior. The participants, like most human beings, desire their work to be meaningful; however, it is less likely that the desire for meaning creates the initial behavior (what they do as core-group leaders), and more likely that the experiences they have, as a result of what they do, are meaningful to them in the context of who they are and what they value. As a result of their having meaningful experiences in the process of being core-group members, the participants' behavior is reinforced. Thus, over time, behavior and meaning are self-reinforcing, and we could therefore say that the meaning core-group members make of their experiences helps sustain their participation and their participation provides them meaning. Lave and Wenger (1991, pp. 51–52), writing in the book in which they coined the term community of practice, describe it this way:

> Participation [in a community of practice] is always based on situated negotiation and renegotiation of meaning in the world. This implies that understanding and experience are in constant interaction — indeed, are mutually constitutive".

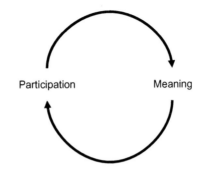

Figure 15.6: Participation and meaning.

Participation and meaning are mutually constitutive (Figure 15.6): participation provides meaning to members and the meaning members make of their experiences sustains their participation.[2]

In *Revisiting the Meaning of Leadership*, Podolny, Khurana, and Hill-Popper (2005, pp. 13–14) derive a definition of meaningful action within organizations, drawing from French and German social theory (e.g., Rousseau, Weber, and Durkheim):

> An action is meaningful when its undertaking: (1) supports some ultimate end that the individual personally values; and (2) affirms the individual's connection to the community of which he or she is a part ... One component ... emphasizes that meaning is created when action is directed toward a broader ideal; the other component ... emphasizes the importance of [social] relationships to meaning.

The first two meaning themes that emerged in my research — contribution and connection — strongly support this definition. I will discuss those themes now, and I will add one more component to this definition for meaningful action in a community of practice: action is meaningful when it *develops the individual*.

15.3.4.1.   To contribute (give back)   "It is meaningful for me to give back, to make a contribution to something I value."

This occurs in terms of contributing to someone or something I value. The intrinsic desire core-group members have to give back and to make a difference for other members and for the Army profession — both of which they hold in high

---

2. We might also say that human activity produces a world and the world (and the meaning we make of it) produces human activity. See Wenger's work on "participation and reification" (1998); Karl Weick's "enactment" (1979); Weber's "iron cage" (2002); Giddens' dual nature of structure known as "structuration" (1986); and Berger and Luckmann's description of "the relationship between man, the producer, and the social world, his product as a *dialectical relationship*" (1966).

regard — feeds this. This was, perhaps, the most obvious of the three meaning themes.

Matt introduces the theme nicely:

> It's neat to be reeled back into something bigger and better than an Army of one ... I think [leaders are all] ... looking for job satisfaction. They want to know that they are doing something that matters, something meaningful and they're making an impact. When you leave command, you leave the band of brothers. [While in command], we all thought that we were making an impact ... and that's what really fueled us ... We would be willing to work 24/7. And then once you leave command you are just kind of like, "Oh, what do I do now?" [And so you appreciate it when] someone bumps into you and asks you to do something that's meaningful, that has a purpose — it gives you a reason to wake up on Saturdays.[3]

Several participants talk about the meaning of their contribution in terms of their legacy. *Martin* says, "We gotta look out for each other; we gotta try and make a difference for each other. I guess it really comes down to that. When I retire I want to be able to look back on my career and say I made a difference; I made it better in some way, shape or form." *Dale* puts it this way:

> Every commander wants to leave a legacy ... and the best thing that I can think of as a legacy is how well your people work ... after you've gone; the missions they executed and how you have affected the junior leaders' development ... That's kind of what CompanyCommand gives you an ability to do if you're a guy who has already commanded — it gives you a way to reach back and maybe help one other guy. If you leave one piece of your knowledge, it may help another guy. And that becomes part of your command legacy.

Terry adds:

> The concept of CompanyCommand is so cool: there is no personal gain to be had; [rather], it is a matter of making our profession better. I was just so profoundly impacted by that and inspired myself to look above how this is gonna benefit me ... I always looked at trying to give back, but this was a way where I could go above and beyond just providing leadership to a unit by contributing to my fellow commanders and in so doing, reach so many more people in the profession and help them be more proficient ...

---

3. Here *Matt* was reflecting on being asked to help facilitate leader-development seminars for future company commanders, which took place on Saturdays.

I only have a little bit of time left on earth to contribute ... Aside from my religious affiliation ... how can I contribute to those that are around me? How can I make this career or profession I chose be meaningful? ... Being a member of CompanyCommand.com, I'm now a part of a team that is reaching across the world, very quickly sharing and growing the expertise of the profession. You could be helping somebody [within minutes] of them posting the comment. And not only are you helping them and answering their question, you may be generating thinking or developing others who just like to read and were like, "Wow, I never thought of that." And so it's contributing to our profession in a powerful way at the company level, and the same people that we're affecting now are gonna be the future generals and sergeants major. And so, you know, being able to have that kind of impact on somebody now and into the future is just cool — what else can you say? [chuckle] There's probably a lot better words than that but, you know, it's huge. [pause] And it covers a lifetime, and it's just a meaningful way to // one, it provides meaning to what I do being a member of this Army profession — it gives back — it contributes to others. I think it's important to leave a unit or organization a little better than when you found it. What better way to leave an organization than developing the leaders that lead those organizations?

And *Roy* provides another example of how contributing to others is meaningful:

It is enormously personally satisfying to me to see stories like [Name], where I can say I had a tangible impact. All of us love to be able to look back at our career and be able to see tangible impacts and effects of our leadership ... And all of us have had those times in our careers where we just didn't feel like we were contributing anything, and so being able to look back and put your finger on those tangible moments I think is really gratifying for all of us. And CompanyCommand gives me another opportunity to do that ...

It is interesting that many of the participants couched the meaning of their participation in the CC forum in terms of their legacy, both to people and to the profession.

Roy identifies an important point: Contribution takes on greater meaning when the person contributing has tangible evidence of the impact he is making — something that does not always occur when the contribution occurs via the Internet. The experience of contributing to the captain who needs advice dealing with her first casualty situation takes on meaning for *Roy* when he becomes aware of her receiving his email and finding his input beneficial. Without her reply, he is not sure she even got the email. It is the tangible evidence of contribution that infuses the experience with meaning for *Roy*.

John found meaning in the personal feedback from other members who responded to his contribution. He says, "It's nice, and it feels good when you contribute and it's appreciated. You know, when you get a comment or something. That feels good because I like to get an azimuth check on what I'm thinking." This is another example of how feedback from another person can infuse one's contribution experience with meaning.

And, in some cases, this feedback can be designed into the technology system. *Shawn* describes how he was frustrated early on when he thought that no one was seeing his topic; and, he describes how a little feedback — designed into the online system — gave him a better sense for the impact that his contribution was having.

> [Lately] I have been clicking on that upper right-hand corner [link that shows you the names of members who have visited the page] ... [Before], I was getting cheesed off because I'm like, "Why is it that nobody's adding stuff to *Pro Reading*?" And I finally clicked up on that upper right-hand corner and I'm like, "Damn," you know — 197 hits last week — *that's* cool. It kind of shows you the // ... It's just cool to see that there are guys out there that actually give a crap, and that's the kind of thing that fires me up.

And *Terry* reinforces this point when he says,

> In the beginning I'm going, "Is anybody using this *Supply* topic?" Then [Technology Leader] figured out how to show how many hits one particular Web page is getting within the site ... And so now it's meaningful to me 'cause I'm like, "Wow, there are a lot of people using this!"

Shawn and *Terry's* contribution took on new meaning when they gained awareness of who was visiting their online topics. A sense for the social presence in their topic changed the meaning of their experience.

Part of the sense of meaning that the participants draw from their involvement is related to the combat experience theme. They understand the life-and-death stakes involved and their contribution therefore becomes more meaningful. Take *Martin*, for example:

> Maybe they're deeply disturbed about the fact that they're gonna be deploying, they're scared to death that one of their guys is gonna get killed, and he's out there looking for that information that's gonna try and keep his guy alive. Well, when we get on there and we start talking about this stuff maybe some guy just off-handedly gives him that one piece of information that's gonna tie it all together, that's gonna allay this leader's fears and let him bring everybody back, you know?

And *Shawn* reinforces this:

> [Our] soldiers deserve the best and most competent leaders, and I do it
> [actively participate in CC] because of that, and I do it because I've
> looked a spouse in the face and said, "I'm gonna bring your husband
> home safe," and I do it because I love being a soldier, and I do it
> because I love those soldiers — and that's why. Does it cause me
> to ... lose a bit of sleep? Sure. But the rewards ... it's the word priceless.
> I know that when I leave CompanyCommand.com as a topic lead ...
> I will have improved the Army profession and I will have, hopefully,
> saved soldiers' lives.

Chris adds to this:

> I'm giving back to my profession ... I'm helping as much as I
> can ... It's something personal ... I like the memorial for our fallen
> comrades ... The bottom line [purpose of what we are doing] is
> to shorten that list of fallen comrades ... I've lost two friends in
> combat so far, and it hit me kind of hard [when I found out about
> one of them dying when my wife] and I sat up next to the screen
> together and read about it. [Name] was a good guy; he was a good
> man, and people need to realize that the work is ... being done so that
> you can ... make your organization better, [and] so we can shorten
> that list.

Thus, the context in which core-group members contribute influences the potential
for their participation to be meaningful. The fact that the CC community is so
focused on leadership in combat likely magnifies the potential for contribution to be
meaningful.

Another aspect of contribution that creates meaning for the participants is when
they have a sense of ownership for contributing to something new, something that
would not exist without their having been a part of the team. In a separate study of
four company command core-group members, Dixon et al. (2005, p. 71) referred to
this as license to be creative:

> They feel the pride that comes from knowing that their own ideas and
> energy are making a difference. This ability to take responsibility for a
> certain product is also self-reinforcing; people always have the most
> energy and enthusiasm for something they have built themselves, for
> something they create.

Matt provides an exceptional example of this. He created a new topic in the online
forum specifically to honor company commanders who die in combat. In this story,
you see the power of relationships and personal development themes; however,

I share the story here to highlight how meaningful it can be for a person to create something new:

> For me the real turning point in terms of me being inspired to participate was [during an on-fire rendezvous] when I was sitting in Starbucks with *Nick*, and he was teaching me how to do stuff on the website ... It was a one-on-one training session. And that was important to me for a couple of reasons. One, you know, *Nick's* one I always looked up to a lot and to me it was just like, wow, I get an hour with *Nick* — that's cool. But second though was I had an idea in my mind and it was called the *Hall of Honor* ... and I told *Nick* as we were sitting there in Starbucks. He and I built that part of the site like in twenty minutes, and we put up the first guy on ... the *Hall of Honor*. So he and I put a guy named [name] ... *Nick* showed me how to put the picture in there, how to hyperlink the article about [Name], and we had our first honoree in our *Hall of Honor* and I thought, wow, this is cool — not only did I get to hang out with *Nick* for an hour, but he took an idea that I had and basically ran with me to bring it to fruition — it was no longer an idea. And so that inspired me to start, when I got home, I was, "Well, let's see who else deserves to be in here." ... It started to snowball and I was like, "Wow, this is kind of cool, this is something I was able to contribute that wasn't there before." ... And so that's kind of what really inspired me to get deeper, to deepen my involvement in the website.

Matt contributed by creating a new topic to honor fallen commanders, and that experience inspired him to become more involved. When people create new things that contribute to something that they value, it is meaningful.

Additionally, core-group members find it meaningful when people they know, and perhaps recruited, contribute. *Randy*, talking about a member who worked for him at one time says, "In a sense, his contribution to the website — when he posts something — I feel that I had a hand in that ... Just maybe, I had something to do with getting him to share. When I see guys that I've worked with get out there and contribute like that, that makes me feel good." In a similar way, people find it meaningful to be part of a group that is making a valued contribution. In other words, by being part of the core-group, members can feel good about the contributions of the CC forum in general. This aspect will be covered further in the *connect* theme.

In summary, members find it meaningful to give back and to make a contribution to someone or something they value. They often think about this in terms of what their legacy will be. Moreover, for a contribution to be meaningful, the person must be able to see the connection between action and impact. Contributions are more meaningful when the person contributing has tangible evidence of the difference their contribution made. Some contribution experiences, simply by the nature of the situation, have more potential for meaning. For example, helping someone in a life-or-death situation will likely be more meaningful than helping someone cross the street. Moreover, the more involved in the creation process members are — especially bringing their own ideas to fruition — the more meaningful their participation will likely be. Finally, core-group members find it meaningful when people they have recruited, or otherwise are connected to, contribute, and they also find meaning as a result of the collective contribution the forum is making.

15.3.4.2. To connect (relationships and solidarity)   "It is meaningful for me that I am becoming more connected to this band of brothers — this community of like-hearted leaders who are committed to a common cause."

The members' *connection* occurs in the context of relationships with people that share their professional aspirations, which is why the word solidarity is important. Providing a basic definition, the American Heritage Dictionary (American-Heritage, 2000) defines solidarity as "a union of interests, purposes, or sympathies among members of a group; fellowship of responsibilities and interests." Drawing upon the work of Rousseau, Podolny et al. (2005, p. 14) add complexity to the concept when they write: "the quest for meaning is attained through social communion, a process in which an individual realizes herself through achieving solidarity in transparent relationships with others". They go on to write, "As was the case for Rousseau, Durkheim proposes that for action to be meaningful, the enactment of values or purpose needs to occur in the context of community" — which Durkheim calls the "conscience collective" (2005, p. 14).

It is quite obvious from the beginning of this chapter that the core-group phenomenon is truly a human phenomenon. The *becoming* stories and especially the discussion of the on-fire rendezvous (team meetings), communicate how meaningful the relationship and social cohesion component of the participants' experience is.

One aspect of *connection* that is meaningful to the participants is when their participation in the CC forum transcends the online forum. *John* talks about his experience becoming "personal" when he began meeting people as a result of his involvement. And *Alan* says,

But somewhere around that time, I started doing business offline with people and that made it more personal. You start thinking about, okay, these aren't just random people out there; You now see the pattern where all these guys are showing up and ... they go from being just names on a screen to people that you associate things with.

Participation in the forum becomes personal, or, as some participants described it, "real," when they begin interacting with people and developing relationships. This kind of experience changes the way that the participants look at the CC forum. And when that "off-line" interaction occurs face-to-face, it is especially powerful. Several months after *Alan* noticed that his participation had transcended the online forum, he attended the annual team meeting: "I got to know that there are a lot of other people out there who are bit by the bug — who have the same crazy devotion to the movement of CompanyCommand." The meeting crystallized for *Alan* the sense of solidarity — that fellowship of responsibilities and aspirations that the core-group members share.

Another way that the importance of relationships is evident in this study is in the number of times that names were mentioned in the interviews. And, perhaps not surprisingly, the names the participants mentioned are often the names of the other core-group members. If there truly were threads of connection running between the core-group members, the core group would be woven together in a tapestry of relationships. *Tommy* and *Nick* are life-long friends; *Martin's* unit took over from *Roy's* unit in Iraq; *Roy* and *Matt* attended graduate school together; *Chris* previously served in the same battalion with *Rick* and went to the officer basic course with *Luke*; *Dale* served with *James*; *Matt* was close friends with *Mitch* and knew *Nick*; *Paul* met *Randy* in Iraq; a relationship between *Alan* and *Roy* formed online; *Alan* invited *Martin* over for a BBQ; *Shawn* met *Nick* years prior in Korea, etc. And the interconnections radically increased when these leaders became core-group members and started interacting in that capacity online, meeting at face-to-face events like the annual rendezvous meeting, and sharing developmental experiences like presenting at a leader development seminar.

The stories of the participants reveal the value that they place on the relationships that they have as a result of being actively involved. *Terry* says:

> I have enjoyed being a part of the experience, the ride and even more so getting to meet all of [the core group] because just what a great bunch of people … The people of CompanyCommand.com make it all worthwhile, let alone the mission and just seeing all the good that comes out of it — units that much more prepared for combat or being that much more successful than maybe they would have been because they had somebody they could go and ask a question of or they could go and find something out. So, yeah, it's been awesome.

This excerpt highlights the value *Terry* places on the relationships and it also underscores the sense of solidarity he feels because of the common cause to which the core-group members are committed: "the mission." *Dale* values the contacts he has developed as a result of being involved, and again draws attention to the solidarity aspect of this theme:

> And, really, you know, the personal contacts that you form between people, you know, it's contagious, man. I just think it feeds on itself when you got a group of people that are all willing or all have a desire to make something grow. I think that's just part of being a leader in the Army — you wanna be a part of something bigger and better than yourself.

He finds it meaningful to be connected to other people who, like himself, are committed to something "bigger and better" than self. And here *Shawn* reflects about some of the people he has valued relationships with because of his involvement with the CC forum:

> It's amazing to me how diverse the site is. There are so many things out there that I never would have known, I never would have thought about // I never would have talked to *Tommy*; I never would have talked to *Nick* after he left Korea; I never would have talked to *Roy*; I never would have talked to *Randy*; I never would have talked to, you know, anybody who is not in my immediate circle of peers inside of 1st Brigade, 10th Mountain or the guys down here. And, you know, like I said, I'm a people person; I like to talk to people ...

The participants value the connections because they genuinely appreciate the people — the relationships are meaningful in-and-of themselves; and, there is a sense that, together, they are forming something bigger and better than what they are alone. This is, to borrow from *Matt*'s description, the "band-of-brothers" effect. The relationships, camaraderie, and common commitment to advancing the profession are all very meaningful to them.

15.3.4.3.   To develop personally (improved effectiveness)   "It is meaningful that I am becoming more personally effective as a result of being involved."

The participants recognize that their participation is having a personally developmental impact — and they value this. This theme is less obvious to the participants than were the other two *meaning themes*; it was less obvious to me as well. In the end, however, *personal development* experiences may prove to be the most powerful meaning-inducing type of experiences that the participants have.

Recall the impact that *using and benefiting from participating in the CC forum* had on the participants' *becoming* stories. Many of the participants consider the CC forum to be integral to their work effectiveness. *Dale*'s development as a company commander was integrated with his participation in the CC forum. When he had a training dilemma, for example, he posed it as a question in the forum and was able to pull together a significant training event based in part on what he learned:

> Based on the discussions and all the training strategies and ideas that were brought to me through the forum, I pulled everything together ... And it was just an awesome training event that I might not have stumbled across if I didn't have all these great guys in CompanyCommand.mil kind of feeding me: "Hey, look, think about ways to do these types of things." And so because of the professional discussions we were having, I was able to make that leap and grow not

only as an HHC commander, but grow some really good training for
my troopers ...

I was able to pull other things [off CC] that were just awesome —
like the training SOPs [standard operating procedures] that
[Name] wrote. I mean that was just kick ass ... I tweaked it for
an Armor HHC and I went and I put it into play and it had huge
benefits for me.

There appears to be a correlation between *Dale*'s participation in the forum and his
effectiveness commanding his unit; *Dale* certainly takes that for granted, and as
a result, his participation is more meaningful to him.

Moreover, the participants recognize that in the process of sharing their
own experiences in the online forum, they are learning. *Dale* is very aware
of this and describes learning and giving back (contributing) as two sides of the
same coin:

It's a way to give back and I can continue to learn from giving back.
And that's the real beauty of it — by giving back to that site and giving
back to company commanders in general, I continue to learn more
about myself and what I did in command ... It gives me a chance to put
what I know out there, continue to learn from others, and then it gives
me a frame of reference or a snapshot into a segment of the Army at a
given point in time, and that's invaluable ...

Dale loves to learn. To him, participation is "almost like a drug, it's addictive in
nature," and it's powerful:

And it's a powerful thing when a whole segment of the Army comes
together and says, okay, let's look critically at ourselves, let's look
critically at what we're doing and let's figure out on our own how to go
ahead ... To be involved as I am has been an opportunity (a) to affect
future generations of commanders, and (b) to help maybe commanders
like myself who are just out of command to understand a little bit more
what the heck it was we actually did or those on the back side now that
it's all done and we got a chance to catch our breath // What does it
all mean — when you boil it down — what does it really mean to have
commanded soldiers.

He recognizes that sharing what he has learned and getting feedback from others will
help him more fully understand and learn from his command experience. This is an
interesting insight. What *Dale* recognizes is that an experienced commander has an
opportunity to learn after his command experience is over through the social process
of active reflection in community.

Another way that participants integrated the CC forum into their work, and became more effective as a result, was by participating in the CC professional reading program. *Dale, Shawn, Roy,* and *Alan* all selected books to read and discuss with the leaders that they were developing.[4] In the participants' stories about the reading program, it is evident that the experience was developmental for them as well as for their subordinate leaders — which further reinforced the value that they placed on their participation in the forum.

There also seems to be an intentional effort by the CC forum coordinators to introduce core-group members to leadership development books. The participants are becoming more personally effective as a result of reading and discussing the books with each other. Although all the participants experienced this, perhaps *Terry* gained the most personally as a result. During the interviews, he rattled off the titles of a dozen books he has read as a direct result of being part of the core group, one of which was Malcolm Gladwell's, *The Tipping Point* (2000). Here *Terry* describes the impact the book had on his work as a tactical officer developing cadets at the United States Military Academy:

> *The Tipping Point* was very influential in changing how I did business as a TAC [tactical officer] ... It greatly influenced [me], and I shared it with my company commander and my platoon leaders as a way they could be better at what they do. We saw a lot of great changes and improved performance ... And Malcolm Gladwell [the author] was just here [at West Point]. I got to hear the man directly ... But, like I said, none of that would have been possible without CompanyCommand.-com.

Terry, in the process of reflecting on this aspect of his involvement with CC, commented that not only has he and the leaders he leads been positively influenced, but so has his family.

The *personal development* theme is interconnected with the participants' desire to learn, and professionally develop. Here, you see how professional-development-type experiences — and even the possibility for them — are meaningful for *Dale*:

> Think about it, though — by getting involved in the site I had an opportunity to go to the Land Combat Expo [in Germany]. Didn't do it because of family reasons, but the opportunity was extended to me to do it. The opportunity was extended to me to do the On Fire Rendezvous [in Colorado]. I have no doubt in the future that there may be other opportunities for me to do things that I didn't think I'd

---

4. When a company commander selects a book to read and discuss with his or her team, the CC forum sends him or her copies of the book and creates an online discussion forum for the team to discuss the reading. For a description of this, see Chapter 3: "Talking About Books," in *CompanyCommand: Unleashing the Power of the Army Profession* (Dixon et al., 2005).

get to do otherwise. So I mean it's professional development for me at the same time as it is giving back to company commanders, as it is helping out the team. There are so many different ways in which it's professional development — it's cool. There's no other word to really say it — it's a great group of people. Everybody understands we're all volunteers so, you know, it's not this additional duty that you have to do.

Randy, who traveled to Germany with the team, found that experience professionally and personally rewarding:

> I had never been to Germany, so I was like, "Yeah, I wanna go." ... It was a great deal. I tell you what — I really enjoyed that. I listened to the Sergeant Major of the Army speak and General Bell speak and General Wallace. General Wallace was interesting because he obviously was our corps commander [in Iraq] ... There was a lot of talk about transformation which was doubly interesting for me working at TRADOC and that focused me when I got back to Fort Monroe ... That was a great thing about going to Heidelberg — you are exposed to some of that stuff and you get to talk to a bunch of people ...

The participants value these types of experiences that introduce them to new ideas, people, and places.

Building on this idea, several participants were given opportunities to participate in leadership and knowledge management conferences, to include presenting their own stories. Presenting in public about the CC forum seems to be an especially meaningful experience. *Roy* talked about the impact that such an experience had on him. *Matt* also was a part of several conferences and seminars, and served as a facilitator in a few. Reflecting on his first face-to-face facilitation experience at a leader-development seminar, *Matt* describes how much of a learning experience it was for him. In his description, you see that this invitation required him to move a little out of his comfort zone:

> I remember not really being sure of what I was getting into. I remember going across the river [driving to the seminar location on a Saturday morning] and getting lost. I got lost on the way there and I was so worried about being late. I think *Tommy* was the only dude I knew there that first time ... He put me on a table [as a facilitator] with some very junior captains and I remember that he went through the rock and the sand analogy from the books ... I remember some discussion at round tables, but it was just as new for me as it was for the captains. I might as well have been one of the captains, because I thought I was less of a contributor and more of a consumer ... And

then [there I was], a facilitator [chuckle] The second one was definitely
a lot easier.

Matt talks about how meaningful it was to be around those young captains, and to
feel like he was making a contribution; however, another reason he valued the
experience, though he did not state it explicitly at first, is that he was learning and
gaining new skills as a facilitator. Later, *Matt* describes his experience presenting at
three iterations of a civilian leadership/knowledge management forum and describes
it as a two-way learning experience, to include becoming a more effective public
speaker:

> As a topic lead I think [the KLF conference] definitely helped me out,
> and I think the reason why is because it forced me to take the idea and
> intent of the website — the website's purpose — and to be able to //
> You can't talk about it unless you understand it, and so it forced me to
> understand what is the purpose of CompanyCommand.com, why does
> it exist, and how do we as the team try to achieve the vision ... When
> we prepared to talk about this stuff with a civilian group, you have to
> convert the whole military thing to "civilian speak," you know, and it's
> almost like a translation if you will ... [Each time I've done one of these
> presentations], I've gone back to the *CompanyCommand* book [Dixon,
> et al., 2005] to review ... what we are before I can communicate it to
> others. And so you almost have to become a subject matter expert.
> And I remember at my first KLF function I was not there at all [in
> terms of my own knowledge], and then what compounded it was I only
> had like a ten minute window to talk. It was like boom, boom — you
> know, ten minutes is nothing. And so, you know, what was my sound
> bite out of that? What was the take away for the people? I don't
> know — I don't even remember it was so fast. And so now I've kind of
> figured it out a little bit better since then, but you really gotta be able to
> know what you're talking about especially when you're dealing with
> this completely different group who is not military.

And, finally, *Matt* describes his sense for the development that he underwent from
the first seminar he helped facilitate to the present:

> The professional growth that I feel like I've made since my first Rally
> Point to my most recent KLF function ... is huge. My whole way of
> looking at things, my whole way of expressing things, and my way of
> looking at leadership totally changed.

The process of reflecting on these experiences during the interviews triggered this "ah
ha" moment for *Matt* and allowed him to more fully appreciate his own development
as a leader.

In summary, the participants find it especially meaningful to be learning and developing as a result of their participation in the forum. Increasing participation leads to increasing access to people, ideas, and opportunities for *personal development* — all of which they appreciate.

The second research question led me to look at the experience of core-group members through the lens of meaning. A finding of this research is that the participants' experience as core-group members is meaningful to them in particular ways. When the participants engage in the work of being a core-group member, they have meaningful experiences. Building on the research of Podolny et al., the types of experiences that are meaningful to the participants can be organized in three main categories, something I call the three *meaning-making components: contribution, connection,* and *personal development*.

Moreover, drawing from previous research by Lave and Wenger, I found that participation and meaning are mutually constitutive: participation provides meaning to the participant and the meaning participants make of their experiences influences the nature of their continued participation.

It is possible now to update the *becoming-a-core-group-member* structure to include the iterative process of participation and meaning (Figures 15.7 and 15.8). At some point in the iterative process of participation and connection — often in conjunction with the member undertaking a leadership role — participation evolves, the connection component is integrated into the member's participation, and the experience begins to take on greater meaning.

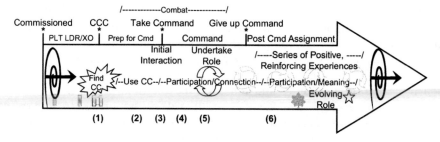

Figure 15.7: Updated core-group becoming structure.

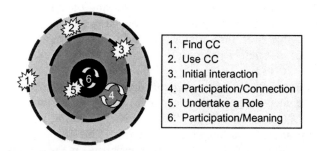

Figure 15.8: Updated cross-section view of core-group becoming structure.

15.4. Conclusion

The core-group phenomenon is the development of a small, socially connected and committed group of members that takes responsibility for the majority of activity in an informal social system. It is remarkable, for example, that as few as fifty interconnected, informal leaders generate the majority of activity within the CC forum, which has over 10,000 members. I conducted in-depth interviews with 10 individual members of the CC core group to gain understanding into this phenomenon with a focus on two main research questions: (1) What is the process whereby members travel from the periphery of the community to become part of the core group and (2) What does it mean to the members to be part of the core group. The first part of the research focused on identifying the concrete experiences that stand out as important in the lived experience of the participants. The *becoming*-a-core-group-member structure was depicted as a process, over time. A second, cross-section view of the process drew attention to the centripetal spiral of a member over time.

The most significant parts of this structure, as far as gaining understanding into the core-group phenomenon, were identified. The essential nature of the *becoming* story is most evident in the process of participation and connection (where initial participation is an observable "act" and connection is a thread of affiliation connecting two members). This process begins with the initial interaction and it is continuous thereafter, with a positive, cumulative effect over time. "Acts" of participation increase and connections between people thicken into relationships. At some point in the iterative process of participation and connection, often in conjunction with the member undertaking a leadership role, participation evolves to include additional roles; the connection component is integrated into the member's participation, and the experience begins to take on greater meaning.

The second part of the research described the participants' lived experience through the lens of meaning — and addressed the question, "What does it mean to be a core-group member?" Schutz (1967, p. 70) explains that people are immersed in a stream of lived experience, and their experiences become meaningful only when they step out of the stream and reflect, or shine a "cone of light," retrospectively upon the concrete experiences:

> Each Act of attention to one's own stream of duration may be compared to a cone of light. This cone illuminates already elapsed individual phases of that stream, rendering them bright and sharply defined and, as such, meaningful.

The three-interview method was the impetus for participants to take details from the "stream," and to reconstruct and reflect upon them, to include the meaning they make of them. Wenger (1991, p. 114) writes, "Meaning arises out of active participation in practice". Building on this, I argued that meaning arises out of core-group-members' active participation in their practice, in the context of who they are and what they value. Finally, participation and meaning are "in constant interaction — indeed, are mutually constitutive" (Lave & Wenger, 1991, pp. 51–52). In this way, the meaning core-group members make of their experiences helps sustain their participation and their participation provides them meaning.

Finally, analysis of the core-group-members' participation experiences yielded a definition of meaningful action in a community of practice, which builds upon the work of Podolny et al. (2005). An action is meaningful to me when, in the process or as a result, I

(1) make a tangible contribution to another valued member(s) and/or to the community (*to contribute*);
(2) become more socially connected with and achieve greater solidarity with other members (*to connect*); and
(3) become more personally effective (*to develop personally*).

15.4.1. Implications for Leadership

"Maybe there's a lot more people out there that would want to be, that would find it really meaningful and personally satisfying to be involved in this way."[5]

Because participation is so important to the success of communities of practice, it is natural for researchers and practitioners to ask, "What can be done to increase member participation?" This research, however, indicates that a subtle shift in thinking could yield more positive results. A question that might be more aligned with the reality of the informal social system is this: "What can be done to increase the frequency and quality of member experiences, in terms of the meaningfulness of those experiences, as perceived by the members?" One way of framing this shift is in terms of leadership: a shift away from leadership as influence, toward leadership as meaning-creation. We could define leadership in a community of practice as a process whereby members foster the creation of meaning for each other. Given the findings of this research, it is possible to be more specific: leadership in a community of practice is a process whereby members engage in experiences that (1) make a tangible contribution to each other (*to contribute*); (2) cultivate a more connected social network of members (*to connect*); and (3) develop each other (*personal development*).

This view is reinforced by Drath and Palus (1994, p. 18), who provide a conception of leadership in a community of practice. They write that members of a community of practice are:

> already motivated by a desire for increased centrality in the community — increased participation in the more skilled, more

---

5. When I listened to the interview recordings, I heard the participants *and* I heard myself. This was me thinking out loud, in a give-and-take conversation with a participant — a mutual inquiry about the core-group phenomenon.

knowledgeable aspects of whatever activity the community is organized around. The purpose of the process of leadership in this view is therefore not to create motivation; rather it is to offer legitimate channels for members to act in ways that will increase their feelings of significance and their actual importance to the community.

And:

The criteria of effectiveness will ... look more to the involvement of community members in increasingly central ways — the movement of people from relatively less important, marginal roles toward more important, more central roles; in other words, the criteria will tend to be the rate of increase of significance. (Drath & Palus, 1994, p. 14)

If we use these insights to build upon the implications of this research, the criteria by which we measure the rate of increase of significance (or meaningfulness) may be the vitality of the core group. In other words, we know that leadership is occurring in a community of practice when there are increasing numbers of members who are active and engaged in doing the work of the core group.

As members take action (participate), they have meaningful experiences. Their sense of meaning reinforces their participation. The three *meaning components — contribution, connection, development* — can be envisioned as a pathway to meaning, with stepping stones along that pathway representing the concrete experiences of members' journeys toward meaning in their work (Figure 15.9).

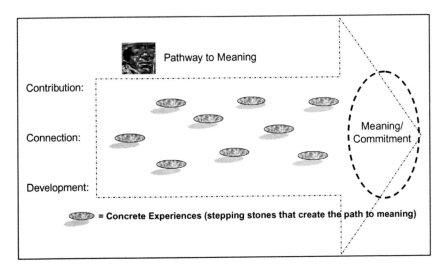

Figure 15.9: Pathway to meaning.

The process of leadership, from this perspective, helps provide stepping stones or creates the conditions for those stepping stones to emerge. Concrete experiences, for example, might include:

- I answer a member's question and receive feedback/tangible evidence that my specific contribution made a difference for him or her.
- I attend a rendezvous meeting with other core-group members.
- I undertake responsibility for an idea or topic.
- I travel to Germany and facilitate a leader-development seminar with younger members of the profession, etc.

And, finally, we can conceive of any person acting in a way that fosters participation and the creation of meaning to be providing leadership in a community of practice.

I complete this research with a greater understanding of the core-group phenomenon: the idea that a small, socially connected and committed group of people can make a positive difference — for themselves and for the greater community. This research suggests that the experience of being a core-group member is anchored in a mutually reinforcing cycle of participation and meaning, and that core-group-members' participation experiences are meaningful in particular ways. Further analysis yielded a definition for meaningful action in a community of practice. Finally, the research found that a definition for leadership in communities of practice should position leadership as a process whereby members foster the creation of meaning for each other.

15.5. Postscript

"So among those who cooperate the things that are seen are moved by the things unseen. Out of the void comes the spirit that shapes the end of men."

— Chester Barnard (1968)

"[Adults seeking to live life to the fullest] want to count for something; they want their experiences to be vivid and meaningful; they want their talents to be utilized; they want to know beauty and joy; and they want all of these realizations of their total personalities to be shared in communities of fellowship. Briefly, they want to improve themselves; this is their realistic and primary aim. But they want also to change the social order so that vital personalities will be creating a new environment in which their aspirations may be properly expressed."

— Eduard Lindeman (1961)

References

American-Heritage. (2000). *American-Heritage Dictionary of the English Language*. Houghton Mifflin Company.

Barnard, C. (1968). *The functions of the executive*. Boston, MA: Harvard University Press.

Berger, P. L., & Luckmann, T. (1966). *The social construction of reality: A treatise in the sociology of knowledge*. New York: Anchor Books.

Bruckman, A. (2004). Co-evolution of technological design and pedagogy in an online learning community. In: S. A. Barab, R. Kling & J. H. Gray (Eds), *Designing for virtual communities in the service of learning*. Cambridge: Cambridge University Press.

Charmaz, K. (2001). Grounded theory. In: R. M. Emberson (Ed.), *Contemporary field research*. Prospect Heights, IL: Waveland Press.

Coffey, A., & Atkinson, P. (1996). *Making sense of qualitative data*. Thousand Oaks, CA: Sage.

Creswell, J. W. (2003). *Research design: Qualitative, quantitative, and mixed methods approaches*. University of Nebraska, Lincoln: Sage.

Dixon, N. (2000). *Common knowledge: How companies thrive by sharing what they know*. Boston, MA: Harvard Business School Press.

Dixon, N. M., Allen, N., Burgess, T., Kilner, V., & Schweitzer, S. (2005). *Company command: Unleashing the power of the army profession*. West Point, NY: The Center for the Advancement of Leader Development and Organizational Learning.

Drath, W. H., & Palus, C. J. (1994). *Making common sense: Leadership as meaning-making in a community of practice*. Greensboro, NC: Center for Creative Leadership.

Eden, C., & Spender, J. C. (1998). *Managerial and organizational cognition*. London: Sage.

Giddens, A. (1986). *The constitution of society: Outline of the theory of structuration*. Berkely, CA: University of California Press.

Gladwell, M. (2000). *The tipping point: How little things can make a big difference*. Boston, MA: Little, Brown and Co.

Glaser, B. G., & Strauss, A. L. (1967). *The discovery of grounded theory: Strategies for qualitative research*. Chicago, IL: Aldine Publishing Company.

Katz, D., & Kahn, R. L. (1966). *The social psychology of organizations*. New York: Wiley.

Keller, S. (2003). *Community: Pursuing the dream, living the reality*. Princeton, NJ: Princeton University Press.

Kling, R., & Courtright, C. (2004). Group behavior and learning in electronic forums: A socio-technical approach. In: S. A. Barab, R. Kling & J. H. Gray (Eds), *Designing for virtual communities in the service of learning*. Cambridge: Cambridge University Press.

Kvale, S. (1996). *Interviews: An introduction to qualitative research interviewing*. London: Sage.

Lakhani, K. R., & von Hippel, E. (2003). How open source software works: "Free" user to user assistance. *Research Policy, 32*(6), 923–943.

Lave, J., & Wenger, E. (1991). *Situated learning: Legitimate peripheral participation*. Cambridge, UK: Cambridge University Press.

Lincoln, Y. S., & Guba, E. G. (1985). *Naturalistic inquiry*. Beverly Hills, CA: Sage.

Lindeman, E. C. (1961). *The meaning of adult education*. Canada: Harvest House, Ltd.

McDermott, R. (2000). Knowing in community: 10 Critical success factors in building communities of practice. *IHRIM Journal* (March), 19–26.

Mockus, A., Fielding, R. T., & Herbsleb, J. (2002). Two case studies of open source software development: Apache and mozilla. *ACM Transactions on Software Engineering and Methodology, 11*(3), 309–346.

Podolny, J., Khurana, R., & Hill-Popper, M. L. (2005). Revisiting the meaning of leadership. *Research in Organizational Behavior, 26*, 1–36.

Rubin, H. J., & Rubin, I. S. (1995). *Qualitative interviewing: The art of hearing data*. London: Sage.

Schutz, A. (1967). *The phenomenology of the social world*. G. Walsh & F. Lenhert (Trans.). Chicago, IL: Northwestern University Press.

Seidman, I. (1998). *Interviewing as qualitative research: A guide for researchers in education and the social sciences*. New York: Teachers College Press.

Snyder, W. M., & de Souza Briggs, X. (2003). *Communities of practice: A new tool for government managers*. Washington, DC: IBM Center for The Business of Government.

Wasko, M. M., & Teigland, R. (2002). The provision of online public goods: Examining social structure in a network of practice. In: *International conference on information systems (ICIS)*. Organization, Culture, Decision-Making and Knowledge, Barcelona.

Weber, M. (2002). In: P. Baehr (Trans., Ed.) & G. C. Wells (Trans.) *The protestant ethic and the spirit of capitalism: and other writings*. New York, NY: Penguin Classics.

Weick, K. E. (1979). *The social psychology of organizing*. New York: McGraw Hill.

Weiss, R. S. (1994). *Learning from strangers: The art and method of qualitative interview studies*. New York: The Free Press.

Wenger, E. (1991). *Toward a theory of cultural transparency: Elements of a social discourse of the visible and the invisible*. Dissertation, Palo Alto.

Wenger, E. (1998). *Communities of practice: Learning, meaning, and identity*. Cambridge, UK: Cambridge University Press.

Wenger, E., McDermott, R., & Snyder, W. M. (2002). *Cultivating communities of practice: A guide to managing knowledge*. Boston, MA: Harvard Business School Press.

Chapter 16

Evaluation of Knowledge Management Practices in U.S. Federal Agencies

Elsa Rhoads and Vincent M. Ribière

Abstract

The opening perspective for this research was to use two searing events – "9/11" and "Katrina" – to bring to bear a rationale for continuing to press for the open exchange of knowledge and collaboration (1) between individual departments within the same agency (intra-agency); (2) between different agencies working together to serve the same general public (inter-agency or cross-agency); and (3) between agencies that must collaborate across vertical boundaries (federal, state, and agencies in local communities).

It is essential that agencies join together to collaborate across boundaries to best serve their country in national emergencies. This is the successful "whole of government" approach to knowledge management promulgated by the 30 member countries of the Organization of Economic Cooperation and Development (OECD) headquartered in Paris.

This chapter is based on dissertation research conducted on the subject of knowledge management practices in U.S. federal agencies. A survey was designed and conducted to evaluate the status and results of knowledge management (KM) programs implemented within U.S. federal agencies by asking questions of the KM practitioners themselves who were then and are now continuing to bring these practices into the daily work of federal employees. Why? To establish trust, encourage transparency, and expect a positive transformation of the accomplishments of the agencies of the U.S. federal government.

In Search of Knowledge Management: Pursuing Primary Principles
Copyright © 2010 by Emerald Group Publishing Limited
All rights of reproduction in any form reserved
ISBN: 978-1-84950-673-1

16.1. Introduction

The specific KM practices chosen for evaluation in this research are drawn from both the statistics Canada KM Practices Survey and the KM practices survey conducted by the OECD. The questions from the Canadian survey conducted in 2001 form the basis of this research instrument (OECD, 2003). Three additional KM Practice surveys, all based on the Canadian survey, were carried out in France, Germany, and Denmark. An appreciation of the results of these surveys can be gained from a book published by the OECD (2003) about this experience, entitled "Measuring Knowledge Management in the Business Sector: First Steps." This book was written primarily by Dominique Foray of the Center for Educational Research and Innovation, OECD, and by Fred Gault of Statistics Canada. In a discussion about measuring KM practices, the survey results, tables, and figures are described for each country. Their recommendations for conducting surveys to measure KM practices have been taken into consideration for our current research survey.

Louise Earl, a lead statistician with Statistics Canada in the Science, Innovation, and Electronic Information Division, developed the original Canadian survey. The core of these survey questions were also used by the OECD to conduct their own survey in 2002 entitled "Survey on Knowledge Management Practices for Ministries/Departments/Agencies of Central Government" in OECD member countries (OECD, 2002).

In response to feedback from some the countries that had agreed to participate, the OECD added many additional questions to the base survey. The survey was developed to compare specific KM practices across each country relative to seven specific functional areas of public management. The stated goal of this research was to compare the experiences of federal agencies in terms of KM practices. The objective was to conduct cross-national (across member countries) and cross-sector (across functional areas) analyses on the implementation of KM strategies in public organizations.

In many of the OECD member countries, KM is implemented by the central government and applied countrywide, resulting in an effectual mandate. KM programs and practices in the United States are not mandated by a U.S. central government. Both the Office of Management and Budget (OMB) and the Government Accountability Office (GAO) share these responsibilities, reporting to the president, and to Congress, respectively. It is difficult to pinpoint how the lack of a U.S. mandate for the establishment of KM practices might negatively affect the progress of U.S. federal agencies towards an e-government transformation, as contrasted to the progress of OECD countries.

The United States participated in the OECD survey "The Survey of Knowledge Management Practices for Ministries/Departments/Agencies of Central Government in OECD Member Countries under the auspices of the Knowledge Management Working Group (KM WG) of the Federal Chief Information Office (CIO) Council, which distributed and collected the survey for analysis by the OECD in 2002. As co-chair of the KM WG at that time, the author of this research tested the survey to provide feedback to the OECD, and distributed the survey in the United States by contacting the CIOs of six major agencies respond to the survey, and attended a "Learning Symposium" hosted by the OECD in Paris in April 2003 to hear reports of the survey results from each participating country.

Belgium, Canada, Denmark, Finland, France, Germany, Greece, Hungary, Iceland, Ireland, Korea, Norway, Poland, Portugal, Slovak Republic, Sweden, United Kingdom, and the United States participated in the OECD KM Practices Survey.

16.2. Research Goals

The two primary goals of this research are:

Goal 1: Identify the status of the implementation of KM practices in U.S. federal agencies

Goal 2: Examine the types of KM practices implemented by agencies, as well as the agency's perception of results from the use of KM practices

16.2.1. Goal 1: Identify the Status of the Implementation of KM Practices in U.S. Federal Agencies

The KM WG of the Federal CIO Council is comprised of 400 plus members who are KM practitioners, working to establish knowledge-sharing and KM practices in federal agencies. From its inception in January 2000, this working group was unable to satisfactorily quantify the information from its membership base to locate which agencies have established KM activities. This survey research provides the first empirical evidence to fill this knowledge gap.

16.2.2. Goal 2: Examine the Types of KM Practices Implemented by Agencies and the Perception of Agency Results

There was no definitive research into which types of KM practices that were implemented most frequently in the KM programs of U.S. federal agencies. This research provides the first empirical evidence to fill this gap by comparing the responses to the survey questions from each agency.

From a review of the literature, it has been determined that U.S. federal agencies are working to achieve a transformation to e-government by sharing knowledge within and across federal agencies. Government agencies are working together in communities of practice (CoP) to develop the interoperability technology necessary to transfer knowledge, both intraagency and cross-agency. The objective is to achieve a transition from a fixed bureaucratic culture to an open government of collaboration and consensus, which fosters the ability to share information across intraagency silos of operations, across agencies (cross-agency or interagency), and to share information vertically, between federal, state, and local public administrations with appropriate citizen privacy safeguards and transparent configuration management practice standards.

16.3.   Research Population

The research population of 16 cabinet-level departments and the 10 independent agencies of the U.S. federal government are listed in Table 16.1.

16.4.   Research Instrument

The KM practices research instrument, first developed for use by Statistics Canada, was used to determine the extent of KM practices implemented in the 26 federal departments and agencies and the type of practices most frequently employed. As mentioned previously, the survey was published in the book entitled *Measuring Knowledge Management in the Business Sector: First Steps* (2003) by the OECD and Statistics Canada. This survey was selected for our use, anticipating a possible future

Table 16.1: Research population.

U.S. federal cabinet-level departments	U.S. federal independent agencies
Agriculture	Agency for International Development
Commerce	Army Corps of Engineers
Defense	General Services Administration
Education	National Aeronautics and Space Administration
Energy	National Science Foundation
Environmental Protection Agency	Office of Management and Budget
Health and Human Services	Office of Personnel Management
Office of Homeland Security	Small Business Administration
Housing & Urban Development	Smithsonian Institute
Interior	Social Security Administration
Justice	
Labor	
State	
Transportation	
Treasury	
Veterans Administration	

comparison of similar questions included in the OECD KM Practices Survey. Prior to survey distribution, the authors presented helpful advice.

The decision was made to use an online survey, administered by a third-party service provider. The assumption was that (1) this would provide our research population with a user-friendly ability to quickly complete the survey and (2) it would also ensure that the research director was not directly involved in the process.

The first pilot test of the online survey indicated that it took too much time for respondents to remain focused and to fully answer the questions. To avoid abandonment of the survey, adjustments were made to redesign and streamline the survey presentation so that it could be completed within 10–15 min.

The survey was jointly sponsored by The George Washington University and the KM WG of the Federal CIO Council. The welcome letter from the sponsors to prospective respondents indicated that the survey was structured as a "blind" survey, without attribution to individuals. The letter also made the commitment to publish the results of the survey on the Web site of KM WG.

Table 16.2 summarizes the survey sections and types of questions. Section 4 collected limited participant demographic information since the survey was designated as a "blind" survey. No information was collected that might possibly connect survey answers with an individual respondent.

Note: All members of the KM WG participated in the study of KM practices — including KM practitioners in agencies other than the research population of 26 agencies — since the KM WG was one of the cosponsors of the study.

16.5. Validation and Reliability

The survey instrument was based on the previously validated studies by Statistics Canada, Denmark, France, Germany, and the OECD. The Web-based online survey was tested, and feedback was received from a Survey SIG (Special Interest Group) of members of the KM WG interested in taking the survey in order to provide feedback prior to the distribution. Feedback from these members indicated a concern for the time required to take the survey. It was decided that excess explanations of KM terms would be eliminated in order to streamline survey completion, since KM practitioner respondents would naturally be familiar with these terms.

The last two survey questions "Title Which Best Fits Your Work" and "Description of Your Role in the Agency" were made optional at the request of potential survey respondents. This was a difficult decision. However, it was felt that gaining the confidence of KM practitioner leadership in federal agencies to complete the survey honestly was important in order to eliminate the possibility of any concern that their answers might be recognized and tied to their names.

The survey was also tested by a group of faculty and university doctoral students enrolled in the discipline of knowledge management (KM), as well as KM thought leaders affiliated with the Institute for Knowledge and Innovation (IKI) of

Table 16.2: Survey construct.

Section	Description	Number of questions	Categories
1	KM practices in use	27	• Policies and Strategies (4) • Leadership (4) • Incentives (2) • Knowledge Capture (5) • Training and Mentoring (7) • Communications (5)
2	Perception of results from the use of KM practices	11	• Improved Workforce Efficiency • Improved Internal Customer Service Support • Increased Ability to Improve Services to External Customers • Increased Flexibility and Operations Innovation • Improved Workforce Skills and Knowledge • Prevented Duplicate Operations/Research • Improved Value of Organizational Memory/Intellectual Capital • Increased Ability to Capture Knowledge from External Sources • Improved Employee Satisfaction • Improved Operational Performance with Communities of Practice • Provided Evidence Organizational Reform and Transformation
3	Additional mixed questions	6	• Size of Federal Organization • Functional Area with Primary Responsibility for KM Practices • Length of Time KM Practices Have Been in Place • Measurement Methodology for KM Practices • Title Which Best Fits Your Work (Optional) • Description of Your Role in the Agency (Optional)
4	Demographic data		• Federal Agency Represented

The George Washington University (http://www.gwu.edu/~iki), in order to validate its content and face validity.

After collecting the data the Cronbach's alpha test was used to test the internal reliability of the KM practices. The overall alpha value for the KM practices is $\alpha = 0.941$, which reflects an excellent level of reliability.

16.6. Research Methodology

The rationale for a survey jointly sponsored by The George Washington University and the KM WG of the Federal CIO Council was to engage a self-selected population group of KM practitioners who would be knowledgeable about the subject matter, and who would be committed to respond to the survey to support their own interest in the research. In addition, the KM practitioners understood the meanings of the special terms of the language related to KM, and had "on the ground" experience to answer the questions easily and quickly. It was not necessary to provide explanations to the text in the questions or to provide a glossary of terms that would slow down the speed of collecting the online answers.

16.7. Research Procedures

A third-party survey service provider hosted and distributed the survey from its own Web site. There was no intervention by the research director, and protection of the anonymity of the respondents was guaranteed. The survey was designed to prevent respondents from skipping any questions and to provide a logical flow of pages designed for completion in less than 15 min. A "% completed" feature was provided after each question to show progress to the respondent. A provision was added so that after completing the survey, respondents had the capability of printing out a list of the questions, which included their own individual answers.

Procedures recommended by Statistics Canada in using the Survey SIG members to make calls to member respondents prior to the release of the survey were followed. Statistics Canada found that the response rate was high when the respondents were informed about the arrival date of the survey and the date required for its completion.

In addition, the recommendations of the central government office in Germany that piloted their KM practices survey to utilize a Likert scale were followed. The Canadian survey used a predictive scale that asked whether the respondent had implemented the KM practices within the past 24 months, or whether they considered implementation within the next 24 months. In January 2005, in a review of the survey prior to its distribution, Statistics Canada advised the use of a four-ratio Likert scale instead of a five-ratio scale. Using an even number of responses, with no middle neutral or undecided choice, was considered important in forcing the respondent to decide whether he or she leaned more toward the "agree" or "disagree" end of the scale for each item.

16.8. Findings

16.8.1. Demographics of Respondents

The survey was distributed in the first week of March 2005. It remained open for 6 weeks and was closed at the end of the first week in April. The online survey was distributed by e-mail to 326 KM practitioners, employees of U.S. federal agencies, and members of the KM WG of the Federal CIO Council.

After six weeks, the total count of survey responses received was 125, or 38% of the total of 326 KM practitioners. Of the 125 responses, 119 were fully exploitable, based on a minimum of missing data. The survey was purposely designed not to let the respondents opt out of the survey data collection process prior to completion.

Table 16.3 illustrates the number of survey respondents per agency. From the 26 federal agencies, 119 KM practitioners, members of the KM WG, responded to the KM practices survey. The World Bank was included in the survey as a benchmark public sector organization with a long and close affiliation with the KM WG.

Survey respondents, members of the KM WG, were from two groups of agencies: (1) cabinet-level departments or independent agencies large enough to warrant quarterly E-Government Scorecards from OMB for E-Government Transformation under the President's Management Agenda (OMB, 2002); and (2) KM practitioners of agencies *not rated by OMB* with quarterly scorecards indicating progress in e-government transformation. Both groups are included in the results of Table 16.3. Responding agencies are ranked in frequency order, indicating the number of responses per agency and the percentage of the total.

Table 16.4 indicates agency size. It also indicates that in our survey population of U.S. federal agencies, 42% of agencies are in the size range of 1,000–25,000 employees.

Table 16.5 indicates the longevity of KM program activity in agencies. It illustrates that in our survey population, 62.2% or more than half of the agencies had implementations of KM practices for a period of 2–4 years or less.

Table 16.6 summarizes the types of respondent titles and indicates that in our survey population, 34.2% of respondents incorporated the words KM in their titles; 7.9% were IT titles and 43.9% of the titles were in the "Other" category.

Table 16.7 summarizes the agency methods used to measure the effectiveness of KM practices and indicates that 20.2% of the organizational units with primary responsibility for KM programs, were KM units, 17.6% IT units, and 24.4% were grassroots efforts not formally supported by the organization.

Table 16.8 summarizes the frequency of use of KM practices measures and illustrates the frequency distribution of the types of methods used to measure the effectiveness of KM practices. Of the agencies, 23.5% had no formal measurement process, 16% used employee surveys, and 13.4% had no standardized measurement methods.

In conclusion, our survey population is comprised mainly of federal agencies with a population of between 1,000 and 25,000 employees in which the KM implementation indicated a longevity of less than 2–4 years. Thirty-four percent of

Table 16.3: Number of respondents per Agency.

	Government agency	Frequency	Percent
Department of Defense Civilian	DOD	13	10.9
Department of the Navy (incl. US Marine Corps)	US Navy	13	10.9
Department of Energy	DOE	11	9.2
Pension Benefit Guaranty Corporation	PBGC	9	7.6
Department of the Army	US Army	9	7.6
Department of Transportation	DOT	9	7.6
Department of Agriculture	USDA	8	6.7
United States Agency for International Development	USAID	7	5.9
Department of the Treasury	TREAS	6	5.0
General Services Administration	GSA	5	4.2
Army Corps of Engineers	USACE	5	4.2
Department of Veterans Affairs	VA	4	3.4
Department of the Air Force	USAF	3	2.5
World Bank	WB	2	1.7
Environmental Protection Agency	EPA	2	1.7
Department of Health and Human Services	HHS	2	1.7
Government Printing Office	GPO	2	1.7
National Aeronautics and Space Administration	NASA	1	0.8
Alcohol and Tobacco Tax and Trade Bureau	ATF-TTB	1	0.8
Government Accountability Office	GAO	1	0.8
Department of Commerce	DOC	1	0.8
Federal Deposit Insurance Corporation	FDIC	1	0.8
Federal Communications Commission	FCC	1	0.8
Federal Aviation Administration	FAA	1	0.8
Department of State	DOS	1	0.8
US Joint Forces Command	US JFC	1	0.8
Total	26	119	100.0

respondents had the word "knowledge management" in their title and 7.9% had "IT" titles. Twenty-four and one-half percent of the implementation of KM initiatives was a "grass roots" effort; and the KM unit had the responsibility for 20% of the implementation, while IT had the responsibility for 17% of the implementation. Twenty-three percent or almost one-quarter of the agencies had no formal KM measurements methods.

16.8.2. Status of KM practices in U.S. government

Twenty-seven questions were asked regarding the status of KM in various agencies. These 27 questions were grouped in six categories (policies and strategies, leadership,

Table 16.4: Size of federal agency.

	Frequency	Percent	Valid percent	Cumulative percent
1–499	12	10.1	10.1	10.1
500–999	9	7.6	7.6	17.6
1,000–4,999	24	20.2	20.2	37.8
5,000–24,999	26	21.8	21.8	59.7
25,000–99,999	20	16.8	16.8	76.5
100,000–124,999	4	3.4	3.4	79.8
>125,000	19	16.0	16.0	95.8
Don't know	5	4.2	4.2	100.0
Total	119	100.0	100.0	

Table 16.5: Longevity of agency KM initiatives.

	Frequency	Percent	Valid percent	Cumulative percent
<2 years	38	31.9	31.9	31.9
2–4 years	36	30.3	30.3	62.2
5–9 years	15	12.6	12.6	74.8
>10 years	8	6.7	6.7	81.5
Don't know!	22	18.5	18.5	100.0
Total	119	100.0	100.0	

Table 16.6: Representative titles of respondents.

	Frequency	Percent	Valid percent	Cumulative percent
CKO	4	3.4	3.5	3.5
Program Director KM	10	8.4	8.8	12.3
KM Architect	8	6.7	7.0	19.3
KM Champion	17	14.3	14.9	34.2
CIO, CTO	9	7.6	7.9	42.1
Business Process Analyst	8	6.7	7.0	49.1
Librarian — Content Manager	8	6.7	7.0	56.1
Other	50	42.0	43.9	100.0
Total	114	95.8	100.0	
Missing (optional)	5	4.2		
Total	119	100.0		

Table 16.7: Organization with primary responsibility for KM function.

	Frequency	Percent	Valid percent	Cumulative percent
Human resources	8	6.7	6.7	6.7
Information technology	21	17.6	17.6	24.4
KM unit	24	20.2	20.2	44.5
Library	2	1.7	1.7	46.2
Executive management	11	9.2	9.2	55.5
Grass-roots effort	29	24.4	24.4	79.8
Don't know	15	12.6	12.6	92.4
Other	9	7.6	7.6	100.0
Total	119	100.0	100.0	

Table 16.8: Frequency of methods used to measure KM practices.

	Frequency	Percent
No formal measurement system	56	23.5
Employee surveys	38	16.0
Not standardized	32	13.4
Balanced scorecard	23	9.7
Benchmarking	21	8.8
Anecdotal stories	20	8.4
Metrics for ROI	14	5.9
Baldridge criteria	11	4.6
ACSI	10	4.2
Don't know	6	2.5
Other	4	1.7
Value chain analysis	3	1.3
Total	238	100.0

incentives, knowledge capture, training and mentoring, and communication). For each question, the respondent was asked to select an answer between "Strongly disagree" and "Strongly agree" on a four-item Likert scale.

Policies and strategies your organization:

1. Has an effective written knowledge management policy or strategy;
2. Has an effective values system or culture intended to promote knowledge-sharing;
3. Has either policies or programs intended to improve workforce retention;
4. Uses either partnerships or strategic alliances to acquire knowledge.

Leadership in your organization, KM practices are:

5. Explicit criteria for assessing knowledge-sharing in the employee performance review
6. A responsibility of managers and executives
7. A responsibility of nonmanagement workers
8. A responsibility of a knowledge management officer or KM business unit

Incentives your organization specifically recognizes or rewards knowledge-sharing with:

9. Monetary incentives
10. Nonmonetary incentives

Knowledge capture your organization regularly:

11. Captures undocumented knowledge from employees prior to retirement
12. Captures explicit knowledge of best practices or lessons learned in knowledge repositories or portals accessible for possible reuse
13. Captures external knowledge obtained from research institutions, universities and industry sources and communicates it within the organization
14. Encourages workers to participate in *cross-department* teams or CoP.
15. Encourages workers to participate in *cross-agency* teams or CoP.

Training and mentoring your organization:

16. Provides formal training related to knowledge management practices
17. Provides informal training related to knowledge management practices
18. Provides formal mentoring practices within the organization
19. Provides informal mentoring practices within the organization
20. Encourages experienced workers to transfer their knowledge to new or less-experienced workers
21. Encourages workers to continue their education by providing funding for successfully completed work-related courses
22. Provides funding for courses of study in knowledge management

Communications in your organization, workers share knowledge and information by:

23. Accessing directories or expertise locators to find subject-matter experts
24. Accessing shared documents on a portal with the aid of a taxonomy or content management capability
25. Regularly submitting best practices or lessons learned to knowledge repositories or portals
26. Facilitating virtual knowledge-sharing via CoP or teams not physically located in the same place
27. Using storytelling as a mechanism to convey organizational meaning

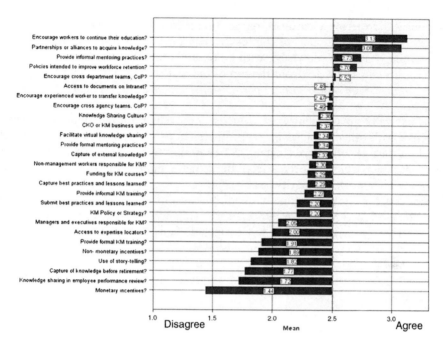

Figure 16.1: Ranking of the average score of each KM practices.

Figure 16.1 presents a ranking scale for the average score of each of the 27 KM practices. The scale displays a graphic representation of the average score of the 119 participants for each question. Since the 4-item scale uses the values between 1 and 4, we can consider the median value of the scale to be 2.5.

The top of the scale illustrates the *"high scores"* for *individual* questions relative to the implementation of KM practices. The "low scores" at the bottom of the scale are also centered on this median value.

Five practices scored above the median value of our instrument. The comments below relate to the meaning of the five highest scores. The possible rational for the *"low score"* questions relating to KM practices are also discussed — beginning with the lowest score from the bottom of the scale.

The *highest score* from the top of the scale is associated with the survey question *"Your organization encourages workers to continue their education by providing funding for successfully completed work-related courses."*

That this question should receive the highest score of the top five questions is unexpected, since government agencies often terminate funding for outside training at the first indication of a pending budget cut. Perhaps this response is due to the fact that the survey respondents are KM practitioners who recognize value in the development of the organization's human capital. The pay-back is immediate, and measurable, since by attending work-related courses, employees gain knowledge that they will be able to use immediately and if encouraged, will share the value of this new knowledge with their colleagues doing the same work. This is an important component to fostering a learning organization. Supervisors can be expected to check changes in the work products of employees. This practical investment measures well: educate one; share the knowledge with more; and multiply the gain.

The *second highest score* from the top of the scale is associated with the question *"Your organization uses either partnerships or strategic alliances to acquire knowledge."*

The nature of government work is increasingly reliant on the ability for agencies to partner with other agencies on work processes or policy measures that are vital to each of them. It often takes agency collaboration to solve the crux of a customer service problem which poorly affects the general public; or to forge together a solution to an important security issue that affects every agency; or to share costs and coordination for the development of joint solutions for lines of business (LoBs) related to the functions of the public sector. Alliances are expected to include not only other government agencies, but to include consultants and nonprofit groups from the private sector, as well as from academia.

The *third highest score* from the top of the scale is associated with the question *"Your organization provides informal mentoring practices within the organization."*

Informal employee mentoring in federal agencies is cost-effective, easy to measure, and often provides unexpected value. When a project is deemed "informal," it generally means that the agency plans to recruit existing employees to do the mentoring. First, this is cost-effective because this function can be created and directed in-house, with the human resources department or the training department, and perhaps with one outside consultant with expertise in designing mentoring programs who monitors the progress and provides a balanced approach to evaluation.

There are three beneficiaries of this type of learning and knowledge-sharing practice. Of course, the major benefit is to the selected employees who benefit from weekly meetings with executives to discuss how the organization works and to ferret out possible career changes (no promises) with an executive who has volunteered to be a mentor in the program. The executive benefits because most executives like to pay back to others the benefits they received as they moved through the ranks; and they like to talk about the accomplishments they have made to the organization over time. They also have the opportunity to listen to the insights and ideas of employees with whom they would normally not come into contact.

The most important beneficiary is the organization itself. Think of all the intellectual capital being shared — from executives at the top to up-and-coming employees eager to learn all they can. Also, the emergence of new knowledge or innovation may arise due to the interaction of these diverse audiences. Experience has proven that the organization's culture is markedly changed for the better by this type of in-house partnering and communication between employees with different departments, functions and status.

The *fourth highest score* from the top of the scale is associated with *"Your organization has either policies or programs intended to improve workforce retention."*

The main driver for the retention of key business knowledge is increasingly related to the forecast of a substantial number of government employees (baby boomers) expected to retire in the coming years.

We cannot predict the impact that this will have in terms of the loss of intellectual capital within the federal workforce. The fact that the U.S. government is aware of this and that it has placed it as one of its top priorities is good news. The implementation of mentoring practices and the transfer of knowledge through the establishment of CoP to resolve business problems held in common (discussed previously) is certainly a good way to retain and pass on the critical knowledge of these public sector knowledge workers who will soon leave the government.

Notwithstanding an expected loss of employees due to retirement, the retention of experienced employees is a problem at any time. As one of the preventions of this risk, agencies are required to develop and put in place a carefully prepared succession plan to determine which employee positions will need to be filled, and how time-critical this may be.

Another KM best practice option is to develop an agency "knowledge retention plan" to assess the individual contributions of experienced employees and to determine the risk to the agency if key employees were to depart suddenly. An exemplary example is the knowledge retention assessment and succession planning effort that has been carried out for many years by the Tennessee Valley Authority (TVA), a nuclear-powered electric utility managed by an agency of the federal government.

The *fifth score from the bottom up* is associated with the survey question "Your organization specifically recognizes or rewards knowledge sharing with non-monetary incentives for implementing KM practices."

The low score for this question was unexpected, since non-monetary awards are *frequently* given to individual employees or to employee teams engaged in specific KM projects.

"Non-mon" awards, as they are called, are an inexpensive token to give to those employees eager and willing to devote extra time added to their daily workload to establish a beachhead for KM in the agency. Most departments and supervisors have a minimum amount of discretionary funds at their disposal. Those participating in the introduction of KM might be provided with mugs, key chains, buttons, stickers, and wall plaques in recognition of their enthusiasm, especially if this is a "start-up" situation.

This kind of reach-out to employees gives them a chance to take their mugs with special mottos and insignia on them to meetings, for example. These items generate conversations from others, and promote bonding between members of the group.

In summary, in Figure 16.1 we have discussed the five highest scores of the individual responses to the 27 KM practices survey:

- Funding for continued employee education;
- Use of partnerships and strategic alliances to acquire knowledge;
- Use of internal mentoring practices;

- Policies and programs intended to improve workforce retention; and
- Encourages workers to participate in cross-department teams or CoP.

Figure 16.1 also aggregates the five lowest scores of responses to the KM practices survey, showing them at the bottom of the scale. Starting with the very lowest score, all five of the low scores are listed below. Your agency

- rewards knowledge-sharing with monetary incentives for implementing KM practices;
- provides explicit criteria for assessing knowledge-sharing in the employee performance review;
- captures undocumented knowledge from employees before retirement;
- shares knowledge and information by using storytelling as a mechanism to convey organizational meaning, and
- recognizes and rewards knowledge-sharing with non-monetary incentives for implementing KM practices.

A different view of the responses to the KM practices survey of U.S. federal agencies is presented in Figure 16.2.

Figure 16.2 depicts a *visual summary* of the results of the *aggregated* scores from the survey participants in each agency grouped into six topic dimensions representing agency Policies and Strategies; Leadership; Incentives; Training And Mentoring; and

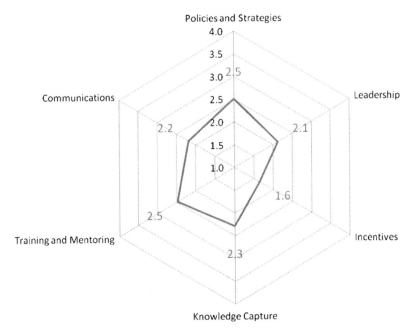

Figure 16.2: Average scores of the six dimensions of KM practices.

Communications. The six dimensions each pull together the results of the questions grouped within the topic as an overview finding.

This view of the data helps us to understand the relative strengths or weaknesses of each of the topic dimensions as they relate to each other. The relative strengths and weaknesses of each dimension can be compared.

The average use of the 27 KM practices shows us that the *Training and Mentoring* practices dimension appears high, with a score of 2.5, exactly at the median. This dimension combines the scores of both formal and informal training provided to agency employees; scores for both formal and informal mentoring activities; as well as the transfer of knowledge from experienced workers to new or less-experienced workers in the agencies that were studied. Funding is provided for continuing employee education; as well as for the study of KM itself.

Agencies with funding for outside or internal training are confident of the benefits of what educated workers can provide to continuously improve the business operations of the agency.

Excellent courses and conferences are available in the Washington DC area and require no outside travel costs. In addition, educational courses are available from the Office of Personnel Management (OPM), local universities such as The George Washington University (GWU), as well as courses especially designed for federal employees to learn government policy and practices through training courses prepared by consulting firms.

We see that the *Policy and Strategies* dimension is also scored at the median of 2.5. This dimension of KM practices determines whether the agency has committed to a written policy for knowledge management; whether it already has a culture ready to promote knowledge management; whether it has developed programs ready to improve the retention of an experienced workforce; and whether it has specifically established partnerships or strategic alliances in order to acquire knowledge.

Slightly behind these two dimensional views, the dimension for *Knowledge Capture* is ranked at 2.3, which includes the KM practices of capturing undocumented knowledge from employees prior to retirement; as well as capturing best practices and "lessons learned" from enterprise knowledge repositories or portals for reuse; capturing external knowledge from universities, research institutions, and various industry sources; and finally includes employee participation in either cross-department or cross-agency teams or CoP.

The dimension ranking for *Communications* is 2.2, and includes the KM practices for providing locators for subject-matter experts with the agency; use of a portal with a taxonomy or content management capability to access shared documents; regularly submitting best practices and "lessons learned" for access from a knowledge repository or portal; facilitating virtual knowledge-sharing via CoP or teams not physically located in the same place; and using storytelling as a mechanism to convey organizational meaning.

The *Leadership* dimension scores at the level of 2.1, and has set explicit criteria for assessing knowledge-sharing in the employee performance review; and KM practices are the combined responsibility of managers and executives or nonmanagement employees, or a CKO or KM business unit.

At the low end of this graphic is the score for the average use of *Incentives* as a KM Practice, at the level of 1.6. Incentives come in two types — monetary and nonmonetary. Monetary rewards for KM practices are not usually a part of federal agency culture. On the other hand, nonmonetary awards are continuously awarded, since this form of employee recognition carries only a minimum cost. This would include "thank you" mugs to recognize successful teamwork in CoP; wall plaque awards which are a favorite way to stretch out the recognition; and even mounting "Thank You" cards in a major hallway to those who have shared knowledge to benefit each other becomes an important way to provide open recognition of both the giver and the receiver.

The conclusion is that the median value of our measurement tool remains at 2.5. Overall we can see that the average score of each dimension is less or equal to the median value of the measurement tool. This indicates that KM practices implemented by U.S. federal agencies are still at a stage of infancy in terms of adoption. The KM maturity level is still low. More progress is required in order to excel; however, the distribution of scores are encouraging.

In summary, Figure 16.2 shows us that the six dimensions of KM practices adopted by U.S. federal agencies are clustered around the median value. Practices relating to the topic dimensions of Training and Mentoring, and Policies and Strategies are scored directly at the median value of 2.5. Close behind are the scores for Knowledge Capture, Communications, and Leadership, which still remain very reasonable. This shows that there is active movement in the implementation of KM practices, but there is still room for improvement. Finally, the scores related to Incentives remain low which is normal, based on the fact that nonmonetary incentives for KM practices are accepted in the culture of the federal government, but monetary rewards for sharing KM practices are unacceptable.

Figure 16.3 represents a ranking of the most common benefits resulting from the implementation of KM practices in U.S. federal agencies, as a perception of the KM practitioners who responded to the survey. The median value of these 11 practices is 2.5, ranked from *low* (at the top of the scale) to *high* (at the bottom of the scale).

These scores are fairly close. The two highest benefits represented improvements in workforce skills (shown at the bottom of the scale). The highest results in ranking order are (1) Improved workforce skills and/or knowledge (2.47); and (2) Improved workforce efficiency and/or productivity (2.37). Following closely are the scores for (3) Increased our ability to improve services to external customers (2.36) and (4) Improved internal customer support (2.34).

The next ranked score is for (5) Improved operational performance through the collaborative efforts of CoPs (2.31).

Benefits from the next four scores for the implementation of KM practices resulted in improved business operations through (6) Increased flexibility and innovation in business operations (2.23); (7) Improved the value of organizational memory and/or intellectual capital (2.23); (8) Increased ability to capture knowledge from other agencies, business enterprises, associations and universities; (2.13) and (9) Prevented duplicate or redundant operations and/or research (2.12).

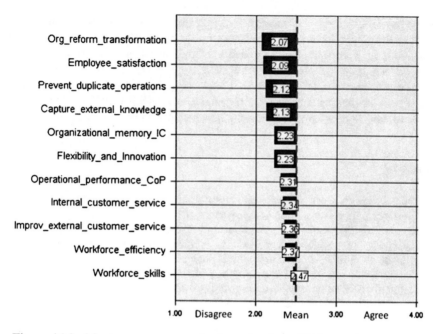

Figure 16.3: Most common perceived results from KM practices ranking.

Last on the list of benefits resulting from the implementation of KM practices are (10) Improved employee satisfaction (2.09); and (11) Provided evidence of organizational reform and transformation (2.07).

An indication of these results is important to receive. Improved employee satisfaction often contributes to agency reform and transformation. We look to the future to see more "evidence of the reform and transformation" of federal agencies through the results perceived from the implementation of KM practices.

16.9. Conclusions

KM programs, while not specifically mandated by the federal government, continue to achieve progress in collaboration between agencies led by the OMB reporting to the President, and by the GAO reporting to Congress. The focus of the leadership of these two agencies is to knit together the disparate initiatives of the business of government — aptly called the "gearbox" of society — for the benefit of all citizens.

After a decade of KM implementation, beginning in the late 1990s, many federal agencies have some type of KM initiative on its way. Based on our findings, while we see that KM may still be categorized at an infancy level, we are confident that it will of necessity reach a more mature stage, as the federal government copes with the retirement exodus of the "baby boomer" generation.

The result of our analysis reflects a strong emphasis on KM policies and strategies as well as on employee training and mentoring. Improving the use of our human capital is a core component of knowledge management, and a strong emphasis on this aspect is a good long-term strategy, since the U.S. government is faced with the potential retirement of a large number of federal employees within the next few years. An emphasis on sharing our best operational practices with other employees will be one way to pass on our knowledge to the new generations of the twenty-first century.

References

OMB. (2002). E-government strategy: Implementing the President's management agenda for E-Government. http://www.whitehouse,agency/OMB.

Organisation for Economic Co-operation and Development (OECD) (2002). Survey on knowledge management practices for ministries/departments/agencies of central government in OECD member countries. Public Management Service-Public Management Committee-JT00119787-PUMA/HRM/(2002)1.

Organisation for Economic Co-operation and Development (OECD). (2003). *Knowledge management: measuring knowledge management in the business sector-first steps*. Paris: Center for Educational Research and Statistics Canada.

Chapter 17

The Use of Organizational Knowledge in Professional Settings: A Case Study Analysis

Massimo Franco and Stefania Mariano

Abstract

In the last 20 years, debate concerning knowledge management (KM) initiatives in professional settings has become prominent in both academic and practitioners literature. In spite of an increased incidence of KM initiatives in organizational contexts, very few studies were conducted to better understand how individuals used the knowledge they retrieved to deal with present issues. Consequently, research that investigates the ways individuals use the knowledge to accomplish a work task and research that seeks to understand which factors are likely to influence the use of the retrieved knowledge have value. The purpose of this research is to address the following research question: "How do individuals in professional settings use the knowledge they retrieve to deal with present issues"? In this qualitative case study analysis, the process of knowledge retrieval was defined as "the process by which individuals retrieve knowledge from organizational memory with the purpose of making decisions on present issues" (Mariano & Casey, 2007, p. 315).

Findings showed that participants used both tacit and explicit knowledge. Participants used knowledge in several ways. The use of knowledge was influenced by the type of work to accomplish and the experience with such a knowledge. The relationship between type of decision to make and type of knowledge to use was highlighted. It was also found that employees generally had an attitude to ask other coworkers to get a validation of their work when using the retrieved knowledge.

In Search of Knowledge Management: Pursuing Primary Principles
Copyright © 2010 by Emerald Group Publishing Limited
All rights of reproduction in any form reserved
ISBN: 978-1-84950-673-1

17.1.   Introduction

> Sometimes what I will do, I will check with my personal network ... I will make a decision and come up with a solution and ... sometimes, not always, I will review that decision with somebody in my personal network, I will say 'what do you guys think?' (Employee of one organization practice)

According to Davenport and Prusak (2000), the first phase of the knowledge management (KM) debate dates back to 1998 with a chaotic and nonlinear growth. Seminal contribution to the KM debate was the work of Nonaka (1994). He was the first academic who referred to the knowledge creation process as "an upward spiral process, starting at the individual level, moving up to the collective (group) level, and then to the organizational level, sometimes reaching out to the inter organizational level" (Nonaka, 1994, p. 20). It is a common understanding that the KM debate defines the practical approach to the content of knowledge (Easterby-Smith & Lyles, 2003). "Much of the literature is practice, rather than theory driven, with many articles appearing in practitioner-oriented journals" (Scarbrough & Swan, 2003, p. 500). Within the literature, KM was defined and classified in different ways. A strong prescriptive element that, however, was recognized in all definitions was the concept of "managed learning" (Vera & Crossan, 2003, p. 124) and its positive impact on organizational performance (Barney, 1991; Stankosky & Baldanza, 2001). The critical role of knowledge in business performance was also documented by Scarbrough and Swan (2003). They stressed two main themes to relate to KM: (i) the management of knowledge for the pursuit of competitive advantage; and (ii) the importance of KM to store organizational knowledge. On the last theme, recent research — expanded upon the work of Nonaka (1994) — especially focused on information technology (IT) (Hayes & Walsham, 2003; Zack, 1999) by exploring the impact of those systems on organizational learning and memory (Olivera, 2000; Stein & Zwass, 1995; Franco & Mariano, 2007). Stankosky (2005) also recognized technology as one of the "four pillars" of his KM framework, which also included leadership, organization, and learning.

In the literature, the attention of researchers has been focused on KM initiatives such as knowledge acquisition (Shrivastava & Schneider, 1984; Stein, 1992), knowledge retention (Gioia & Poole, 1984; Nelson & Winter, 1982; Spender, 1996), and knowledge retrieval (Mariano & Casey, 2007). Moreover, research has investigated how social networks impact knowledge gathering and sharing (Cross, Parker, Prusak, & Borgatti, 2001; Cross & Sproull, 2004; Huber, 1982; Von Krogh, 1998).

17.2.   Research Methods and Data Collection

A case study of a single diversified high-technology research, engineering, and consulting company is analyzed (Creswell, 1998; Lincoln & Guba, 1985;

Stake, 1995, 2000; Yin, 2003). The research involved more than one subunit of analysis and thus it was considered as "embedded" (Yin, 2003). We used a constructivist perspective to explore the individuals' use of knowledge in a professional setting. The process was largely social and inductive (Creswell, 2003). Data were collected through individual semistructured interviews (Merriam, 2001), on-site observations (Creswell, 2003) and document analysis (Creswell, 2003; Merriam, 2001). Using these three data gathering methods provided data triangulation (Creswell, 2003; Yin, 2003) and accomplished the validity of the study.

The sample consisted of 15 consultants from five sections of one organization's division. We chose a sample of consultants who had to make day-to-day problem-solving decisions to accomplish their tasks. Participants were chosen on the recommendation of a "key informant", which in this study was the manager of each section. Sixty percent of the participants were males; 40 percent were females.

We also conducted on-site observations. An observation protocol (Creswell, 2003) was used to record descriptive field notes of the setting, behavior and activities of individuals at the research site, and reflective notes (Creswell, 2003) of the researcher's role in the observation process.

During the research process, data were also collected from public and private documents. We prepared researcher-generated documents (Merriam, 2001), i.e. statistical data from interviews and photos took during the on-site observations. We used a summary form to record data (Miles & Huberman, 1994).

17.3. Data Analysis

Data were analyzed through the use of Atlas.ti®, a qualitative data analysis software package. Data were open coded using key units of thoughts based on research questions, assumptions, and relevant literature on the topic. The coding scheme was updated on a continual basis. Comparative analysis was made to note emerging patterns and themes (Miles & Huberman, 1994). The analysis processes produced detailed descriptions about the type of knowledge retrieved and used, factors influencing the use of knowledge, the relationships between decisions to make and knowledge to use and the employee's attitude to ask other coworkers to get a validation of their work when using the retrieved knowledge.

We used member checks (Lincoln & Guba, 1985; Stake, 1995), peer debriefings (Creswell, 2003), and triangulation methods (Creswell, 1998, 2003; Stake, 1995, 2000; Yin, 2003) to cross-check data consistencies (Patton, 1987), improve the credibility of the study (Lincoln & Guba, 1985), and to enhance the accuracy of data analysis.

17.4. Findings

The case study analysis revealed that participants used both tacit and explicit knowledge in their day-to-day work. Type of work to accomplish, i.e. routine work or new work and the experience with the source of knowledge in terms of expertise and willingness to help influenced the processes of knowledge retrieval and usage:

> Probably I'll go to someone who has the most experience with it...I have also from my experience what people are easy to work with, what people are going to give me an answer that I can actually do something with ...

In this qualitative study it was found that the "experts" were those who have been within the organization longer, as a participant claimed:

> I can ask the senior people, so if I have a question about how we have dealt with similar projects in the past I can go to one of the more experienced people and I can say: 'well previously we had a similar experience and we did it in this way so help me to draw upon it.'

In the process of gathering knowledge, desire to learn (as a personal attitude) and desire to help (as other people's own attitude) were both critical factors (Figure 17.1). A participant claimed:

> The most important thing for my role is to make sure I ask questions. All the time. And asking the right questions ... so tacit knowledge is cool ... but you have to be able to extract it efficiently and quickly from these people 'cause they are really busy, and they don't want to sit down and explain it to you for two hours, what they are doing. You have to go and ask them very targeting questions, so you will get rapidly what you need to know so you are not bothering them more than you need to ...

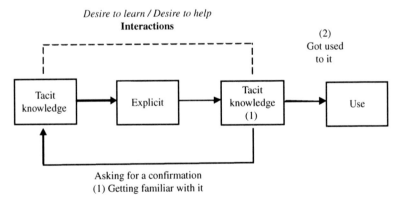

Figure 17.1: Using knowledge and asking for a confirmation.

In general, getting other people's tacit knowledge involved a process in which the interactions between two people allowed the conversion of tacit knowledge (of the person who originally had it) in explicit knowledge (in order to transfer it) and then in tacit knowledge again (of the person who got it).

Figure 17.2 shows a decision tree model (Miles & Huberman, 1994) to describe the task validation process that occurred when using the retrieved knowledge. This model was built considering participants' answers to interview questions about their day-to-day decisions, finding a source of knowledge and the number of people to contact to find the knowledge to use. From data analysis, it turned out that participants used and/or validated the knowledge they retrieved in four ways according to the following scheme: (1) retrieve it and use it; (2) use it and ask for a confirmation; (3) ask for it and use it; and (4) ask for it, use it and ask for a confirmation.

Asking coworkers to get a validation of the work to accomplish was essential when the knowledge was either not well known or not adequate to accomplish a certain task. In such a case participants would have asked someone either to get some

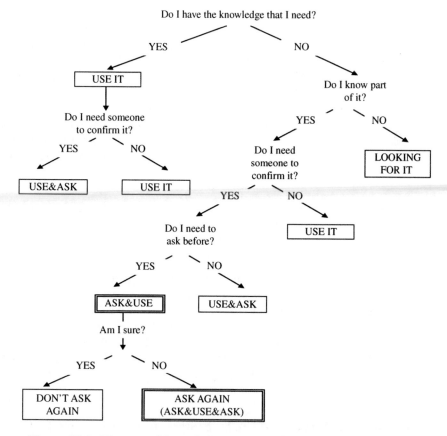

Figure 17.2: The use of knowledge and the need of a task validation.

knowledge (ask for it and use it): "*... they are somebody reliable that you can go to and ask for...helping me to make the decision*" or to confirm a decision already made (use it and ask for it): "*I will use my personal network to confirm my decision*".

In some cases, they would have asked someone to get it, then they would have used it, and finally they would have asked again to have the final confirmation of it (ask for it, use it, ask for a confirmation): "*sometimes what I will do, I will check with my personal network ... I will make a decision and come up with a solution and...sometimes, not always, I will review that decision with somebody in my personal network, I will say: what do you guys think?*" Otherwise, it would have meant participants already had the knowledge they needed: "*I will probably have some knowledge stored in my head. I will think!*" In such a case they would have used their own knowledge (use it) and, just if they needed it "*if I need to, if it's part of the adjustment*", they would have asked someone for a final confirmation (use it and ask for it): "*if I need to know something about a project that I have never done before I can go to whoever and say: 'Can you have a look at this?', and there is no problem.*" Depending on what participants already knew about the knowledge they needed, the sequence of actions would have been: "*use it — use and ask — ask and use — ask and use and ask.*"

If participants were looking for tacit knowledge of other people, the only two options would have been "ask for it and use it" or "ask for it, use it, and ask for a confirmation". Indeed, in the case of other people's tacit knowledge, the only way to get that knowledge would have been to ask directly someone who had such a knowledge.

Depending of the type of knowledge that is to be used, i.e. personal tacit knowledge, other people's own tacit knowledge, or explicit knowledge retrieved from information and communication technologies (ICTs) (e.g. Intranet, hard drives, and shared points), the need of a task validation was variable. A participant claimed:

> Usually I use my head, corporate Intranet if necessary and then personal network after I formed my initial decision. So I will use my personal network to confirm my decision.

Table 17.1 summarizes the relationship between type of used knowledge and type of decisions to make in terms of using and validating the work.

From data analysis, two types of learning processes were found: self-learning and learning from other people. Self-learning could be defined as learning by doing, learning from past projects, learning by reading, learning from past jobs, and learning from college. Learning from others implied interactions among people and was a process that involved senior employees most of the time, as a participant claimed:

> There are a lot of things that you have learned from other people, you know, from the more senior people.

Table 17.1: Relationship between type of decision to make and type of knowledge to use.

Type of decisions	Type of knowledge		
	My own tacit knowledge	Tacit knowledge of others	Explicit knowledge from ICT
Use it	√		√
Use and ask	√		√
Ask and use	√	√	√
Ask and use and ask	√	√	√
Total	4	2	4

Table 17.2: Learning style.

How did I learn?	
Learning style	Number of respondents mentioning item ($N = 15$)
Learning from other people	10
Learning by doing	13
Learning from past projects	8
Learning by reading	6
Learning from past jobs	5
Learning from college	1
Total	43

Table 17.2 summarizes the learning styles of participants of this study. Participants showed an attitude to learn in numerous ways. Learning by doing (87%) and learning from other people (67%) where the most mentioned learning types. By opposite, learning from college (7%) was the less mentioned learning type.

17.5. Discussion and Implications for Future Research

In this case study analysis (Yin, 2003) we discussed the use of knowledge in a professional setting. We collected qualitative data in the field (Crotty, 1998) and we provided empirical evidence on the process of knowledge usage.

Findings showed that the gap between what was known and what needed to be known affected the way to use the just acquired knowledge and influenced the need of a task validation (Cross & Sproull, 2004) from another person or coworker. Such a task validation also depended on the type of knowledge that was retrieved and the experience with the source of knowledge.

To retrieve other people's tacit knowledge, employees first asked for knowledge, then used it, and just in some cases they validated their own work by asking a confirmation from other people.

For individuals' own tacit and explicit knowledge the use of knowledge ranged from the simple use of it to the three step process "asking-using-validating."

In general, the validation process helped to get familiar with the knowledge just acquired in order to remove such a step when the individual became familiar with that knowledge. The desire to help and desire to learn motivated the interactions between knowledge source and knowledge recipient. These results offered additional ideas about the use of knowledge in the decision-making process and provided new insights on the relationship between knowledge seeker and knowledge source.

Getting familiar with such a knowledge involved two learning processes: self-learning (Simon, 1991), and learning from other people (Alavi, 2000) confirming that learning was a process of relating new information to previously learned information (Ormond, 1999) and that future learning was the result of cumulative learning and capabilities, often constrained and not easily malleable (DeFillippi & Ornstein, 2003).

Self-learning was involved when explicit knowledge needed to be acquired by informants. Usually such a process occurred either from the experience accumulated by doing the job (Kolb, 1984) or when the content of a repositories needed to be used to accomplish a task. In that case the individual had to interpret the explicit stored knowledge to get familiar with it order to best use it (Huber, 1991).

Finally learning from others meant to convert other people's tacit knowledge into explicit knowledge — through a process of interactions (Nonaka & Takeuchi, 1995). In turn, such a tacit knowledge would become tacit knowledge when acquired by the knowledge receiver. This result confirmed the spiral by Nonaka and Takeuchi (1995) about the learning conversion process and helped to better understand the process of knowledge creation (Alavi, 2000; Von Krogh, 1998; Von Krogh, Roos, & Klein, 1998) confirming that the process generally took place: (a) at the individual level through cognitive processes such as reflection and learning; and (2) at the group level through collaborative interactions within teams (Alavi & Tiwana, 2003).

This empirical study also offered additional ideas for consideration on the individual process of learning. Unlike most studies which affirmed that organizations learned by ingesting new members who had knowledge the organizations did not previously have (Simon, 1991; Vera & Crossan, 2003), in this research it was instead found that the process of learning generally took place through the learning of new employees from those who had been within the organization for a long time, the "experts." Such a process might be understood as a consequence of both the employee's professional position within the organization, and the type of work to accomplish (Allen, 1977), which in turn influenced the type of knowledge to need. These results confirmed the thesis of Allen (1977) who stated that the knowledge source selection was influenced by the characteristics of the task and contributed to the body of research on learning since it provided a means to better understand the influence of job position on the knowledge access.

This study had some limitations. First, this study did not focus on the process of knowledge storage but only on the process of knowledge retrieval and usage. Second, this study looked at the process of knowledge retrieval and usage during decision-making or problem-solving activities. Finally, this study collected data through individual interviews at the consultant level. It did not focus on other hierarchical levels, e.g. managerial level, which would have probably given different perspectives or results.

Future research should be conducted in other organizational settings to determine if similar factors influence the use of knowledge. Also, future studies should investigate the extent to which a better experience with the knowledge to use might influence the employees' preference to seek out their colleagues to validate their work.

References

Alavi, M. (2000). Managing organizational knowledge. In: R. W. Zmud (Ed.), *Framing the domains of IT management*. OH: Pinnaflex Educational Resources.

Alavi, M., & Tiwana, A. (2003). Knowledge management: The information technology dimension. In: M. Easterby-Smith & M. A. Lyles (Eds), *Handbook of organizational learning and knowledge management* (pp. 104–121). Malden, MA: Blackwell.

Allen, T. J. (1977). *Managing the flow of technology: Technology transfer and the dissemination of technological information within the R&D organization*. Cambridge, MA: MIT Press.

Barney, J. (1991). Firm resources and sustained competitive advantage. *Journal of Management, 17*(1), 99–120.

Creswell, J. W. (1998). *Qualitative inquiry and research design: Choosing among five traditions*. Thousand Oaks, CA: Sage.

Creswell, J. W. (2003). *Research design: Qualitative, quantitative, and mixed methods approaches*. Thousand Oaks, CA: Sage.

Cross, R., Parker, A., Prusak, L., & Borgatti, S. (2001). Knowing what we know: Supporting knowledge creation and sharing in social networks. *Organizational Dynamics, 30*(2), 100–120.

Cross, R., & Sproull, L. (2004). More than an answer: Information relationships for actionable knowledge. *Organization Science, 15*(4), 446–462.

Crotty, M. (1998). *The foundations of social research: Meaning and perspective in the research process*. London: Sage.

Davenport, T. H., & Prusak, L. (2000). *Working knowledge: How organizations manage what they know*. Boston, MA: Harvard Business School Press.

DeFillippi, R., & Ornstein, S. (2003). Psychological perspectives underlying theories of organizational learning. In: M. Easterby-Smith & M. A. Lyles (Eds), *Handbook of organizational learning and knowledge management* (pp. 19–37). Malden, MA: Blackwell.

Easterby-Smith, M., & Lyles, M. A. (2003). *Handbook of organizational learning and knowledge management*. Malden, MA: Blackwell.

Franco, M., & Mariano, S. (2007). Information technology repositories and knowledge management processes: A qualitative analysis. *VINE: the Journal of Information and Knowledge Management Systems, 37*(4), 440–451.

Gioia, D. A., & Poole, P. P. (1984). Script in organizational behavior. *Academy of Management Review, 9*, 449–459.

Hayes, N., & Walsham, G. (2003). Knowledge sharing and ICTs: A relational perspective. In: M. Easterby-Smith & M. A. Lyles (Eds), *Handbook of organizational learning and knowledge management* (pp. 54–77). Malden, MA: Blackwell.

Huber, G. P. (1982). Organizational information systems: Determinants of their performance and behavior. *Management Science, 28*, 669–718.

Huber, G. P. (1991). Organizational learning: The contributing processes and the literatures. *Organization Science, 2*(1), 88–115.

Kolb, D. A. (1984). *Experiential learning: Experience at the source of learning and development.* New Jersey, NJ: Prentice Hall.

Lincoln, Y. S., & Guba, E. G. (1985). *Naturalistic inquiry.* Newbury Park, CA: Sage.

Mariano, S., & Casey, A. (2007). The process of knowledge retrieval: A case study of an American high technology research, engineering and consulting company. *VINE: The Journal of Information and Knowledge Management Systems, 37*(3), 314–330.

Merriam, S. B. (2001). *Qualitative research and case study applications in education.* San Francisco, CA: Jossey-Bass.

Miles, M. B., & Huberman, A. M. (1994). *Qualitative data analysis: A sourcebook of new methods* (2nd ed.). Newbury Park, CA: Sage.

Nelson, R., & Winter, S. (1982). *An evolutionary theory of economic change.* Cambridge, MA: The Bellhop Press of Harvard University Press.

Nonaka, I. (1994). A dynamic theory of the organizational knowledge creation. *Organization Science, 5*(1), 14–37.

Nonaka, I., & Takeuchi, H. (1995). *The knowledge-creating company: How Japanese companies create the dynamics of innovation.* Oxford: Oxford University Press.

Olivera, F. (2000). Memory systems in organizations: An empirical investigation of mechanisms for knowledge collection, storage and access. *The Journal of Management Studies, 37*(6), 811–832.

Ormond, J. E. (1999). *Human Learning* (3rd ed.). Upper Saddle River, NJ: Merril/Prentice Hall.

Patton, M. Q. (1987). *How to use qualitative methods in evaluation.* Newbury Park, CA: Sage.

Scarbrough, H., & Swan, J. (2003). Discourses of knowledge management and the learning organization: Their production and consumption. In: M. Easterby-Smith & M. A. Lyles (Eds), *Handbook of organizational learning and knowledge management* (pp. 495–512). Malden, MA: Blackwell.

Shrivastava, P., & Schneider, S. (1984). Organizational frames of references. *Human Relations, 37*, 795–809.

Simon, H. A. (1991). Bounded rationality and organizational learning. *Organization Science, 2*(1), 125–134.

Spender, J. C. (1996). Organizational knowledge, learning and memory: Three concepts in search of a theory. *Journal of Organizational Change, 9*(1), 63–78.

Stake, R. E. (1995). *The art of case study research.* Thousand Oaks, CA: Sage.

Stake, R. E. (2000). Case studies. In: N. K. Denzin & Y. S. Lincoln (Eds), *Handbook of qualitative research* (2nd ed., pp. 435–454). Thousand Oaks, CA: Sage.

Stankosky, M. (2005). *Creating the discipline of knowledge management.* Burlington, MA: Elsevier.

Stankosky, M., & Baldanza, C. (2001). A system approach to engineering a knowledge management system. In: R. C. Barquin, A. Bennet & S. G. Remez (Eds), *Knowledge management: The catalyst for electronic government.* Vienna, VA: Management Concepts.

Stein, E. W. (1992). A method to identify candidates for knowledge acquisition. *Journal of Management Information Systems, 9*(2), 161–178.

Stein, E. W., & Zwass, V. (1995). Actualizing organizational memory with information systems. *Information Systems Research, 6*(2), 85–117.

Vera, D., & Crossan, M. (2003). Organizational learning and knowledge management: Toward an integrative framework. In: M. Easterby-Smith & M. A. Lyles (Eds), *Handbook of organizational learning and knowledge management* (pp. 122–141). Malden, MA: Blackwell.

Von Krogh, G. (1998). Care in knowledge creation. *California Management Review, 40*, 133–154.

Von Krogh, G., Roos, J., & Klein, D. (1998). *Knowing in firms: Understanding, managing and measuring knowledge.* London: Sage.

Yin, R. K. (2003). *Case study research: Design and methods.* Thousand Oaks, CA: Sage.

Zack, M. H. (1999). Managing codified knowledge. *Sloan Management Review, 40*(4), 45–58.

SECTION VI

KNOWLEDGE MANAGEMENT CASE STUDIES

> Empirical science is the key to one form of knowledge, the generalized knowledge that gives us power over nature; the key to wisdom however, is the knowledge of particulars. McWhinney, (1997).

Case studies are a critical tool for capturing, evaluating, synthesizing, organizing, distributing, and applying knowledge and wisdom. Understanding of how to use case studies to uncover valuable information and learn from others' experiences is fundamental to the practice of knowledge management (KM).

Case studies mean different things to different people. A case study is usually a description of an actual situation, which generally involves a decision, a problem, an issue, a challenge, or an opportunity. Case studies play an important role in organizational improvements. They contribute to the successful integration of the concrete with the abstract, the particular with the general, lessons learned with practices and practices with theoretical principles.

In this section, the authors present case studies to focus attention on KM practices in industry. They draw attention to strengths and weaknesses in implementing a KM system using two distinctly different approaches. The authors present a "system" perspective that defines a dynamic order of parts and processes in mutual interaction with each other (Von Bertallanfy, 1968), thus giving a view into the breath and depth of implementing a KM system within today's knowledge-based organizations.

References

McWhinney, I. (1997). *Textbook of family medicine*. New York: Oxford University Press.
Von Bertallanfy, L. (1968). *General system theory*. New York: George Braziller.

Chapter 18

NASA's Pioneering PBMA Knowledge Management System

J. Steven Newman and Stephen M. Wander

Abstract

Process-based mission assurance (PBMA) is an idea that grew to maturity during the mid-1990s reinvention of government initiatives in which many agencies including NASA were abandoning detailed policy and procedural requirements in lieu of performance-based contracts that proscribed only high-level assurance process requirements if any at all. The government oversight management emphasis was on sharing and using "industry best practices" and voluntary standards. PBMA grew up as a systematic attempt to codify and share those best practices across the aerospace industry "learning organiza-tion." (Newman, 1997) Thus the PBMA vision grew from formally documented case study reports into a multifunctional Web-based resource with the confluence of the strategic vision incorporated in the four-pillars framework (concepts evolving under Professor Michael Stankosky, in the graduate systems engineering curriculum at George Washington University) (Baldanza & Stankosky, 2000; Calabrese) and advances and evolution of Internet technology. Other important philosophical underpinnings are derived from Professor Marc Adleson, at George Mason University who emphasized that "work takes place in conversations." The authors extended the notion to "learning takes place in conversations," and "cultural change takes place in conversations." The PBMA-knowledge management system (KMS) intent has and continues to be the facilitation of "conversations"-communication and learning.

In Search of Knowledge Management: Pursuing Primary Principles
Copyright © 2010 by Emerald Group Publishing Limited
All rights of reproduction in any form reserved
ISBN: 978-1-84950-673-1

18.1. Introduction

The PBMA-KMS was developed and implemented by the NASA's Office of Safety and Mission Assurance (OSMA) with web-based infrastructure development beginning in 1998 and formal deployment on NASA Headquarters servers in April of 2000 as NASA's first fully operational agency-wide knowledge management system. The PBMA-KMS supported program management, engineering, and safety and mission assurance (SMA) communities. The initial collaborative functionality (work groups/communities of practice) was made available in October of 2000 followed by center rollouts and implementation and training workshops beginning in 2001. Other key milestones in PBMA-KMS evolution have included

- Information technology (IT) infrastructure shifted to Glenn Research Center with program management continuing from NASA Headquarters OSMA
- Support for Space Shuttle Columbia accident review teams (February–October 2003)
- Enhanced security work groups (ESWG) deployment in April 2004
- Knowledge Registry deployment in May 2004
- Secure Meeting deployment in August 2004
- Enterprise architecture certification in April 2005
- Redesigned into NASA Portal affinity August 2005

18.2. Concept Development/Implementation

18.2.1. Strategic Alignment

As managers in the NASA OSMA organization, the overall objective of the authors was to provide a knowledge management (KM) approach and structure, which would effectively and efficiently facilitate the implementation of the safety and mission assurance function across the agency. Consequently, a very important aspect of the initial conceptualization and development of the PBMA-KMS was that of obtaining senior level sponsorship, namely NASA's Chief Safety and Mission Assurance Officer (CSMO). The CSMO is also the associate administrator for the OSMA and a direct report to the NASA administrator. The OSMA is an important, independently funded, functional support organization with responsibilities that extend across all NASA centers, programs, facilities, and operations. In this context, it is important to note that the PBMA-KMS was neither directed or mandated (or for that matter even initially supported) by the chief information officer (CIO)/IT organizational infrastructure at NASA.

18.2.2. Systems Engineering (SE) Approach

PBMA-KMS was tactically implemented with a focus on the practical application of KM theory. A classical SE approach — defining top-level systems requirements, which are then translated into detailed functional requirements followed by design synthesis — was adopted for the development of this KM system. One of the first tasks in establishing top-level systems requirements was to develop an overarching knowledge architecture vision, which specifically identified and addressed the knowledge and information needs of the "business unit" in question, particularly as it relates to the primary work processes, products, and principal users and customers of the business unit. In our case the safety and mission assurance function is the business unit with the primary customers and principal stakeholders being the program and project management community within the agency. Consequently, the PBMA-KMS knowledge architecture or framework, as described in Section 18.3, was built around the traditional phased approach of a program/project development lifecycle. A complimentary step in this process was to identify and engage secondary stakeholders who, in this case, included the chief information officer (CIO), agency IT security, International Traffic in Arms Regulation (ITAR)/export control managers, human resource managers, the office of chief engineer, and appropriate training organizations and functions. The intent was to fully understand the requirements of these various external organizations and to develop, build, and operate the PBMA-KMS on the basis of "compliance by design."

18.2.3. Functional Requirements

The second step in the process was to translate the requirement set developed above into specific knowledge management system functional requirements. In particular, this related to the unique business unit content and functionality requirements of the PBMA-KMS. As to content this included SMA plans, policies, requirements, standards, work and work control processes, test and verification processes and consisted of both explicit (documentation, text, links) as well as tacit/corporate knowledge artifacts (video, storytelling, "best practices") and knowledge capture. Basic functionality requirements included document/data repository, basic libraries ("best practices," Lessons Learned, system failure case studies, program profiles), advanced search and discovery, secure collaborative environments (communities of practice/work groups), secure Web meetings, and knowledge registry/ expert finder.

18.2.4. Design Synthesis

Design synthesis for the PBMA-KMS involved the concepts of rapid prototype development of startup functionality including the assessment and, where appropriate, integration of commercial off-the-shelf (COTS) functional capabilities, and the assembly of startup content, which primarily involved populating the knowledge architecture with links, documents, text, video, etc. Appropriate beta-testing of the Web site was undertaken and was followed with an aggressive roll-out plan including the identification of "PBMA Champions" at each center coupled to briefings and site visits to all ten NASA centers.

18.3. Work-Centric Knowledge Architecture

The PBMA-KMS mission success management framework incorporates the "big picture" engineering management concepts of systems engineering, risk management, and KM. The PBMA-KMS philosophy is based on the foundation of systems thinking, coupled with the themes of recurrent risk management behavior, the reuse of knowledge, and an overarching safety and mission success perspective. PBMA-KMS represents an innovation in the application of safety, assurance, and risk management disciplines in that it consolidates and articulates assurance processes and activities within an integrated systems engineering context.

Thus the PBMA-KMS employs a program/project lifecycle framework consisting of eight elements (i.e., program management, concept development, acquisition, hardware (HW) design, software (SW) design, manufacturing, preoperations integration and test, and operations) familiar to program and project managers. Cross-referenced against each of the eight elements are the five categories of policies, plans, processes, program control and verification, and testing (see Table 18.1). Additional details regarding each category are provided later in this chapter. The resulting 8×5 matrix is intended to serve as a point of reference not only for planning and implementing new programs but also for conducting independent

Table 18.1: PBMA mission success management framework.

PBMA	Formulation			Implementation				
Project phase Elements	Program management	Concept development	Acq.	HW	SW	Mfg	Integ. test	Ops
Policies (rules & requirements)	1.1	2.1	3.1	4.1	5.1	6.1	7.1	8.1
Plans	1.2	2.2	3.2	4.2	5.2	6.2	7.2	8.2
Processes	1.3	2.3	3.3	4.3	5.3	6.3	7.3	8.3
Controls	1.4	2.4	3.4	4.4	5.4	6.4	7.4	8.4
Verification	1.5	2.5	3.5	4.5	5.5	6.5	7.5	8.5

Architecture: Systems engineering phase/activity vs. modified Deming (plan-do-check-act) elements.
Each cell contains video-nuggets, text, links.
Architecture: PBMA-KMS systems engineering knowledge architecture.

evaluations of existing programs as to their level of compliance with SMA requirements and standards and the application of "best practices."

18.4.   Information Technology

18.4.1.   IT Environment

The PBMA development team considered technology as an enabler, not a driver, but at the same time carefully evaluated the evolution of technology and sought to integrate best available COTS product functionality.

The PBMA-KMS infrastructure was designed to be flexible, agile, fully scalable, and in alignment and compliance with agency and external enterprise architecture (EA) requirements. The approach has been to not lock into a particular technology solution but, in fact, to allow users and content to drive IT requirements. The PBMA-KMS is compliant with NASA's current IT Standards (both security and architectural) and embodies a modular design that can be reconfigured to comply with evolving IT standards (e.g., Windows, SQL, Section 508), and is capable of being integrated within a "system of systems."

18.4.2.   IT Security

The PBMA-KMS evolved prior to the formal documentation of NASA IT security policies. As a result, implementation was challenged by a patchwork quilt of local center policies often at odds with each other. The reality of three agency CIOs within a 14-month period after the Columbia accident underscored the IT policy and leadership vacuum. In spite of these complications, the PBMA management team recognized the need to actively involve the CIO and security organizations as important stakeholders and developed long-term working relationships that became part of lifecycle KM program management and not just a one-time milestone to consider. PBMA-KMS conforms to the Glenn Research Center (GRC) IT Security requirements for an IT security plan, risk assessments, penetration tests, contingency plans, and disaster recovery plans (all plans signed and on file with GRC IT Security). Currently, GRC IT Security manages perimeter security from a technical standpoint, e.g., ESN, firewalls, and port management. The PBMA-KMS also employs a master IT Security Plan with subplans developed for each COTS application as required.

No other similar agency-level system exists that is capable of handling sensitive but unclassified (SBU) data. The ESWG environment is process aligned in accordance with NASA Procedural Requirement 1600. While other tools exist, PBMA ESWG represents a vetted agency-wide enterprise architected system which is currently certified by GRC IT Security as "SBU High."

18.4.3. IT Reliability

PBMA-KMS systems have maintained exceptional levels of system availability. In fact, all PBMA-KMS systems have had virtually 100% uptime since its inception, with the exception of scheduled outages and downtime. Indeed, it has been user/customer requirements that have driven this "standard" of operational uptime, a standard which has been primarily achieved through extensive design, hardware, and software redundancy.

18.4.4. Enterprise Architecture Certification

On April 7, 2005, the PBMA-KMS became the first KM system at NASA to become fully certified to enterprise architectural standards affirming and documenting; linkage with mission and customer requirements, management due diligence, rigorous resource planning, demonstrated use of metrics, implementation of an investment and cost recovery approach, implementation of risk management processes, compliance with IT security requirements, and alignment with the federal enterprise architectural (FEA) reference model.

18.5. Knowledge Base Content

18.5.1. Key Metrics of the Knowledge Base (As of Dec 2007)

- Over 210 best practices from 10 NASA locations
- 28 Lessons Learned resource links (NASA, DOD, DOE, other federal systems)
- 315 Video nuggets from 108 individuals
- Nine case studies
- Nine program profiles
- Over 800 links to various program/project management and SMA resources
- Over 8 million visitors during CY07

18.5.2. Best Practice Library

The best practice library contains NASA best practice assurance planning documents (e.g., quality assurance plans, risk management plans, software assurance plans, and system safety plans). This modality enables center and/or program/project knowledge to become NASA-wide organizational knowledge. Every NASA program or project manager, facility manager, hardware developer, software team, emergency response planner, or assurance manager benefits from ready access to a selection of proven program documents to abstract and build upon. The Best Practice mode contains a vast library of documents from across the Agency representing virtually every NASA center. Documents in this library encompass all of the life-cycle phases from the earliest concept development to operations and disposal. Currently, the best practice library contains over 200 plans, process and procedure documents, handbooks, manuals, requirement documents, tools and techniques, and more. The scope of the documents within this library is extensive, ranging from overall high level documents such as system safety and risk management plans, to lower level documents addressing topics such as fastener integrity requirements and radiological emergency procedures. The library also spans the range of program-/project-scale extending from the International Space Station (ISS) on one hand to single satellites and small instruments and experiments on the other. While this library continues to grow, the breadth and depth of documentation currently available offers immediate and wide-ranging utility for all PBMA-KMS users. Documents and links were provided by NASA Center Directors in response to a series of agency-wide call letters issued by the OSMA Associate Administrator. The intent of the PBMA management team was to leverage the center directors as peer reviewers, endorsing the documents as indeed "best practices." This also was an important strategic move because it allowed one to quickly truncate the inevitable questions and debate (e.g., "Who says this is a best practice?-"I don't agree with that document."). This also solidified the management team position that a KMS does not and should not answer specific user questions, rather it provides a framework and examples from which the user can provide their own assessment or develop their own plan, analysis, or document.

18.5.3.   *Video Nugget Library*

Video nuggets, first implemented in 2001, bring the PBMA content to life by capturing the reality and the passion of the experts. The PBMA-KMS video library, which populates the knowledge architecture shown in Table 18.1 provides context and personal experience perspective to assist organizational learning and as such video content is collocated with other related knowledge artifacts. However, the end user may also access video content separately or individually through search by speaker, title, and/or subject matter.

18.5.4.   *Program Profiles*

The program profiles (see Figure 18.1) represent a "fingertip benchmarking" capability, i.e., a window on how other NASA project managers have implemented assurance processes. Program profile mode provides access to descriptions of safety, mission assurance, and risk management processes employed on past and present NASA programs, based on NASA OSMA independent assessments. This functionality is designed to assist program/project managers and SMA professionals in observing how other programs have implemented assurance processes. It is

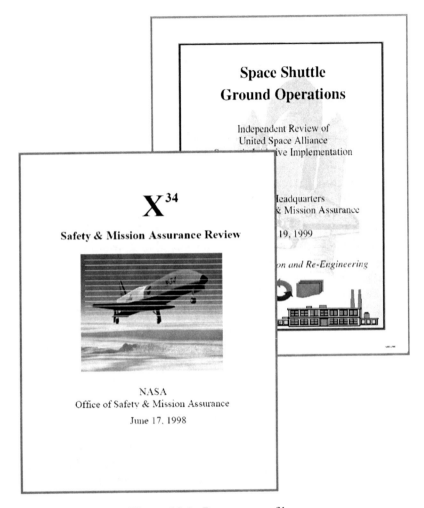

Figure 18.1: Program profiles.

possible to directly download the independent assessment reports in their entirety or select folders applicable to a specific area of interest (e.g. software or operations) for a given program.

18.5.5. *External Benchmarking Reports*

This section contains independent assessment reports (see Figure 18.2), which provide an external benchmarking of critical safety and mission assurance operations, functions, requirements, and work processes and procedures employed

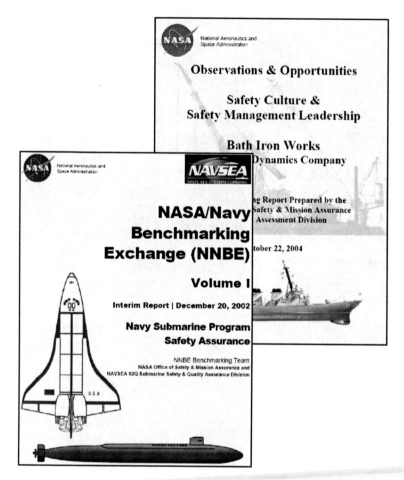

Figure 18.2: Benchmarking reports.

by other government agencies and private sector peers engaged in highly complex, high reliability operations. Most specifically these benchmarking activities have been used to provide insight and guidance for NASA's human space flight programs, namely the Space Shuttle, ISS, and Constellation programs. As a note of interest, Volume I of the NASA/Navy Benchmarking Exchange (NNBE) report was used extensively by the Columbia Accident Investigation Board during their deliberations and report preparation.

18.5.6. System Failure Case Studies

These knowledge artifacts (see Figure 18.3) use "storytelling" techniques, along with a systems engineering/mission assurance orientation, to stimulate thought and

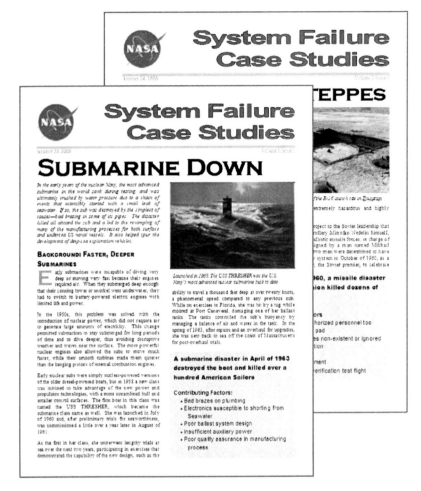

Figure 18.3: System failure case studies.

discussion within the ranks of high-reliability organizations. They are intended to promote an exchange of ideas among project personnel to examine and improve their own practices. In addition, they are intended to further develop and sustain technical excellence and help promote organizational learning, encourage systems thinking, enhance program/project team building, understand group dynamics and group decision-making, and provide recurrent training and new employee orientation.

18.6.   Communities of Practice (CoP)

The PBMA-KMS CoP functionality currently (end of 2007) supports *708* CoPs with over 12,500 members (see Figure 18.4). PBMA CoPs can be considered to fall within

Figure 18.4: CoP examples.

two general categories. First is the "work group" — project-oriented communities that typically follow a program/project lifecycle. The second category is discipline-oriented, sometimes referred to as a community of interest (COI), which is formed by groups of people joining across organizational boundaries and often outside traditional or formal channels of communication who share a concern, a set of problems, or a passion about a topic (see Figure 18.5).

CoPs *"repair the damage done by the organization chart."*

They deepen their knowledge and expertise in this area by interacting on an ongoing basis. CoPs share information, insight, and advice. They help each other solve problems. They create tools, standards, generic designs, manuals, and other documents. Best practices are compiled, shared, and knowledge transferred through CoPs. Focusing and cultivating this type of collaborative functionality in strategic areas is a practical way to manage knowledge as an asset, just as many public and private institutions systematically manage other critical assets. Primary CoP functionality includes document library, media library, database, calendar, polling, threaded discussions, real-time chat, mailing lists, and action tracking. Additional functionally includes single sign-on, full-text search, version control, check-in/check-out, relational databases, hierarchical calendars, layered security model, customizable communities, and RSS subscriptions. As previously discussed, PBMA-KMS CoPs provide secure, 128-bit encryption and are authorized to store SBU data.

WORKGROUPS BY CENTER   WORKGROUPS BY MISSION/OFFICE

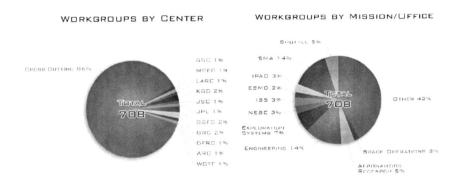

Figure 18.5: NASA CoP/WG distribution (2007).

18.7. Secure Web Meeting

Secure web meeting (SWM) provides a stable and secure real-time online remote meeting and conferencing capability within NASA infrastructure in full compliance with agency's directives (EA, IT Security). No other capability in the agency currently is certified to support this function. SWM supports up to 100 meetings per day. There are currently over 4400 registered users accomplishing their mission through secure virtual meeting interaction. This functionality is undergoing a major growth surge with 2194 user accounts created since the beginning of the 2007 calendar year. Of principal value is the ability to share presentations between multiple users and pass control of the meeting among attendees. In addition, participants can see and demonstrate applications and files without the need to have similar software on every attendee's PCs — as an example, advanced computer-aided design (CAD) and modeling simulators can be viewed by all attendees without the need for desktop software. There is also the ability to save transcripts and whiteboard within the presentation as well as built-in meeting scheduling and user invitation.

18.8. Knowledge Registry

The knowledge registry (KR) provides a permission-based, searchable database of registered NASA civil servant and contractor critical skills and their location and concentration across the agency. The KR is integrated with the NASA Competency Management System and can aid in quick identification of knowledgeable resources for mishap investigation board support, independent assessments/audit support, and other SMA activities. It is interesting to note the degree of complexity and institutional management hurdles associated with implementing this functionality. A number of issues emerged regarding privacy, access, union rules and member impact, use of information in re-organizations, mistrust of management, data field "ownership," and the standard "rice bowl" political issues existing within large organizations. While currently supporting SMA organizations the system is poised to support a broader program/project management, engineering, science and business management constituency.

18.9. Financial Metrics

What is the return on investment (ROI) on the email infrastructure at your company? Who last computed the ROI for the natural gas service provided to your business? What is the ROI for the electricity you spend to make a product? In time, as in the above examples, the question "What is the ROI for KM?" will go away. In the final analysis, it becomes a meaningless question because KM, like security and safety, becomes an essential and critical business service. Notwithstanding the authors' belief that KM ROI metrics are often a charade we recognize the need, from time-to-time, to "play the ROI game." Figure 18.6 represents a prime example of how to make the case for KM with line management and the enterprise CIO. The chart shows decreasing user cost with an increasing user base over time — the perfect IT investment dream.

18.10. Other Metrics

The quantitative metrics game has also been played often with dubious assumptions concerning "time saved" per visit or per return visit, assumed hourly rates, duration of visits, and number of visitors. In particular, collaborative tools are noted for their ability to save time and money by reducing travel, providing centralized work spaces and managing version control of group documents. We have all seen the laborious arithmetic gymnastics associated with these "cost savings analyses," which may appeal to certain accountants and managers. Instead, we submit that the chief executive officer (CEO) should look at what is happening within and across their organization using quantitative/qualitative "metric pictures" such as that presented in Figure 18.6. Here the message is qualitative — people are starting to integrate/communicate across organizational and geographic boundaries in a collaborative way — breaking down stovepipe behaviors so often apparent in dysfunctional organizations.

18.10.1. Activity Metrics

Sometimes, especially with a startup KMS, it is valid and useful to employ activity metrics. Examples from early PBMA-KMS development include

- Number of video nuggets on-line, number in approval/number in production
- Number of best practice documents on-line

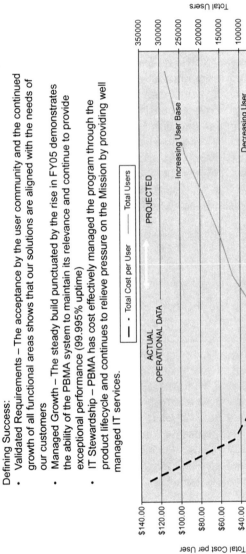

Defining Success:
- Validated Requirements – The acceptance by the user community and the continued growth of all functional areas shows that our solutions are aligned with the needs of our customers
- Managed Growth – The steady build punctuated by the rise in FY05 demonstrates the ability of the PBMA system to maintain its relevance and continue to provide exceptional performance (99.995% uptime)
- IT Stewardship – PBMA has cost effectively managed the program through the product lifecycle and continues to relieve pressure on the Mission by providing well managed IT services.

NASA ROI
Example

	FY00	FY01	FY02	FY03	FY04	FY05 (trended to EOY)	FY06 (projected)	FY07 (projected)	FY08 (projected)	FY09 (projected)	FY10 (projected)
Total Cost per User	$130.98	$46.94	$22.70	$27.90	$30.79	$14.46	$17.93	$11.43	$10.20	$10.21	$10.24
Total Users	3054	10652	26433	41430	53033	118488	150623	192423	237337	260703	285991

Figure 18.6: "Perfection" metric for IT investments.

- Number of active communities of practice
- Number of members
- Number of links to Lessons Learned case studies
- Number of documented testimonials
- Initial roll-out briefings and workshops conducted at X field centers
- Number of participants in roll-out events
- Anticipated time savings for functionality in development
- Implementing recognition (letters and certificates) for number of individuals supporting design, development, and implementation
- Number of strategic partnerships with NASA organizations, academic institutions, voluntary professional and standards organizations
- Number of conference presentations

18.11. Building a Knowledge-based Assurance Culture at NASA: Workshops and Champions

As mentioned previously, the PBMA-KMS early development phases included the establishment of "champions" at each facility/operating center across the organization or enterprise. The strategy also included formal, well-staffed, and well-funded roll-outs at each operating center/facility followed by hands-on training/workshops, which sought and facilitated customer/user feedback. In September 2001, the center PBMA-KMS champions assembled for the first workshop to discuss how best to develop and nurture communities of practice that span the NASA community. The workshop was designed to draw from the KM implementation experience of several leading U.S. corporations and addressed knowledge management theory and practice, approaches to building communities of practice, sponsorship and linkage to enterprise strategic goals, and lessons learned in identifying formal and informal communities. The workshops also provide a forum for discussion of center-specific strategies and issues for implementing a CoP. On May 29, 2001, a PBMA-KMS preview and workshop was held at NASA Glenn Research Center (GRC) in connection with NASA's 2001 Assurance Technology Conference. During this workshop, "champions" representing each of the NASA Centers were trained in PBMA-KMS concepts and operation. These champions played a prominent role in the initial center deployment activities that were completed between November 2001 and March 2002. Center champions have also been called upon to assist in developing an SMA functional discipline knowledge map for their center as well as identifying potential candidates for videotape interviews (i.e., video nuggets) capturing tacit knowledge residing in center-based subject matter experts (SMEs).

The initial deployment and evolution of the PBMA-KMS supported by workshops and center champions has been successful. However, it is acknowledged by the PBMA management team leaders that a more sustained and focused outreach and awareness training effort should have been employed to more effectively promote continued growth and organizational learning given the dynamic (e.g., people coming and going), evolving (e.g., organizational flux), and geographically distributed nature of the NASA enterprise.

18.12.   Future Directions

18.12.1.   User Interface Alternatives

Efforts are underway to expand user interface options allowing users to access the knowledge artifacts residing within the PBMA-KMS server environment. In effect, users will be able to effectively reshuffle the deck and have information delivered in a framework most suited to the work at hand. Under consideration are options to allow one to browse by engineering discipline and or system/subsystem element. Another option will be to establish a program/project milestone gate architecture.

18.12.2.   Wikis

Critical decision (CD) processes are key features in the engineering management/ systems engineering landscape. Program and project milestone reviews span the program/project lifecycle (i.e., concept development, design, build, test, operate, disposal), including many safety CD events. Early on in the program lifecycle, these events may determine critical design features; ultimately, CD forums make operational decisions, such as approving launch of the Space Shuttle, or approving the readiness of a nuclear submarine for sea trials. Many space program CD forums (most notably, NASA readiness reviews) rely almost exclusively on viewgraphs supplemented by verbal presentation as the primary communication methods. While arguably sufficient, over reliance on viewgraphs has been identified as a significant and fundamental weakness within the NASA communication culture.

Consequently, wiki technology implementation, within critical aerospace deliberative and decision-making processes, is proposed as a way to enhance safety and mission success for future space exploration endeavors. This technology can leverage a broader corporate knowledge-base in making critical decisions while maintaining traditional hierarchal organizational accountability. It is envisioned that initial implementation of CD Wikis will be focused on four critical NASA processes: (1) the Exploration Systems Mission Directorate risk management process, (2) the NASA program/project milestone reviews, (3) the OSMA's Safety & Mission Success Review (SMSR), and (4) the Environmental Management, Environmental Impact Statement (EIS) development, and associated public review processes. As proposed, CD Wikis would provide the necessary evolution of safety-critical communication and collaboration to support the next generation of space exploration.

18.12.3. Expanded Active Knowledge Sharing (AKS)

The "soft" element, but in many ways, the "end game" of KM is to accomplish knowledge transfer. As noted earlier, if one adheres to the notion that "work takes place in conversations," then one can certainly accept the extension that "learning and cultural change takes place in conversations," as well. The AKS aspect of the PBMA-KM Program is to facilitate and encourage dialogue within teams and work groups by distributing targeted knowledge bundles at periodic intervals to individuals and to program/project teams for group discussion. The PBMA-KMS management team is currently exploring a number of "push package" alternatives including email, video-nugget/document bundles created for the system failure case studies as seeds for group interaction and discussion. These initiatives are actively partnering with other organizational learning groups at NASA promoting the Pause and Learn concept, "after action debrief" (or "hot wash-up") sessions, knowledge-based risks, and knowledge sharing forums.

18.13. Awards and Recognition

The PBMA-KMS was recognized in 2003 with an eGov Pioneer Award, "Outstanding e-Government Best Practice application that has streamlined operations and improved government services." Other awards have included the 2004 NASA HQ Honor Award, the 2005 GRC Honor Award for "Outstanding support to Columbia Accident Investigation Board and NASA's Columbia Task Force" and the top NASA Agency Honor Award in 2005 for outstanding contributions to the Agency's mission.

18.14. Lessons Learned

Many of the Lessons learned can be traced to our initial developmental concepts; a practical and practiced application of KM theory, following basic systems engineering principles and practices, and adopting a continuous improvement/risk management philosophy. Just as the GWU proposed four-pillar KM model served as a good starting point for the PBMA-KMS journey, this model also provides an appropriate structure for examining lessons learned from the experiences in the overall development, implementation, and operation of the PBMA-KMS.

Leadership occurring at multiple, coordinated, management levels is indeed a necessary condition for success. As shown in this case study, leadership must exist at the enterprise or business unit top management level and include resource allocation as well as political "top-cover" or willingness to defend the project in the inevitable organizational political battles. At the implementation level, the program managers must be strong, resolute, thick skinned, and must adhere to an unflinching vision. The management/leadership team must be able to demonstrate the strategic alignment, articulate the value proposition for KM and cast the knowledge management initiative within the context of the work process and/or organizational mission.

- Develop a very top level or overarching knowledge management vision (K-vision)... a "going-in" knowledge architectural construct.
- Tie the K-vision to the corporate "knitting" or core competency of the business unit. The primary goal is to help people perform the core function more efficiently and effectively.
- Sell the K-vision to a powerful business unit sponsor with his/her own budget. "God bless the child that's got his own."
- "Mind the knitting" — keep focused on the core competency of the business unit.
- Develop appropriate metrics (i.e., activity and results-based) to manage the inevitable ROI questions.
- Involve management with implementation actions.
- Tie in to every available political toe-hold.

Organization involves identifying and addressing organizational policy requirements and constraints. The PBMA-KMS case study reflects the need to acquire a multitiered organizational perspective; engaging at the enterprise level, the business unit level, and, most importantly, the work process level in order to support development of the knowledge architecture.

- Use an existing distributed organizational structure as an advocate network.
- Forge partnerships with CIO/IT, security, and external affairs organizations. Find out what it takes to keep them happy. Build and operate the KMS on the basis of "compliance by design." Build the KMS within their constraints. Incorporate security measures as required — it actually enhances and strengthens the value of the KMS.
- Partner with a formal training organization.
- Partner with the formal systems engineering organization. Incorporate their needs and objectives — demonstrate synergy.

Technology was identified, used, and leveraged as it evolved to support a preexisting and well articulated goal and vision to disseminate "best practices" to the NASA community and promote communication and collaboration within program and project teams. In the broad and long-term vision of the authors, technology was always an important element but never the most important element. This case also demonstrates how one can succeed by integrating COTS behind a government "firewall fortress," retaining agility to bring innovative functionality while remaining in step with information security requirements.

- Use available organization IT infrastructure.
- Drive evolution of infrastructure to the extent possible.

- Create your own infrastructure when necessary to move beyond organizational inertia. (Note: Organization-managed IT infrastructures change slowly. Focus is on perceived "economies of scale" and standardization. The need to satisfy multiple, often disparate and unconnected customer requirements tends to slow everything down.)
- Use COTS hardware/software when it makes sense. COTS will almost always be way ahead of big, bureaucratic organizational technology.
- Remember that the www is the ultimate infrastructure.

Learning is manifest within the PBMA-KMS case study through the triple themes of content development (best practices, video nuggets), content organization (knowledge architecture), and content delivery (user interfaces and push packages). Further, the case reflects the need to extend content delivery to group discussions and team engagement with stories and case studies to achieve broader organizational learning.

- As in real estate-only three things matter — content, content, content/stay on top of content/keep it fresh and relevant
- Listen to your customers — give them functionality they need and want and use.
- Optimize access — keep as much as possible in the public domain
- Deliver product beyond the shell of the IT infrastructure. Implement KM content within formal and informal group discussions, and organizational decision forums

18.15. Conclusions

While numerous other KM initiatives were undertaken at NASA as either top-down, technology-driven (i.e., "build it and they will come") efforts or center-based, self-proclaimed KM-team pilot programs (i.e., here is your KM solution — use it), none have succeeded and none have endured as the PBMA. The PBMA case study demonstrates how a successful knowledge management program was implemented at NASA providing the right mix and balance of strategic vision, leadership, bottom-up alignment with business work processes, a theoretical framework (the four pillars), sensitivity to organizational and institutional stakeholder needs and constraints, and a measured adaptation of emergent Web-based technology.

FURTHER READING

Baldanza, C., & Stankosky, M., *Knowledge management: An evolutionary architecture toward enterprise engineering.* INCOSE, March 2000.

Calabrese, F., *A suggested framework of key elements defining effective enterprise-wide knowledge management programs*, Abstract of Dissertation, George Washington University.

Newman, J. S., D.Sc., NASA HQ, *The knowledge path to mission success: Overview of the NASA process based mission assurance knowledge management system*, Reliability and Maintainability Symposium (RAMS), January 28–31, 2002, Seattle, Washington.

Newman, J. S., D.Sc., *PBMA-KMS strategies for thriving KM Programs — KM myth-busting, space shuttles, & reindeer tracking.* TALES from the front lines of knowledge management. eGov 2005 Conference, April 21, 2005, Washington, DC.

Newman, J. S., D.Sc., *PBMA-KMS -NASA's IT systems and enterprise architecture: The present and the future.* Presentation to the NASA Small Business Solutions Conference, September 2, 2005, New York City.

Newman, J. S., D.Sc., & Wander, S. M., *The development of the PBMA-KMS — How we did it.* Presentation to GSA, December 2005, Washington, DC.

Newman, J. S., D.Sc., & Wander, S. M., *KM for improved decision-making and program management — a pioneering public sector KM case study.* eGov 2006 Conference, April 19, 2006, Washington, DC.

Newman, J. S., *Life cycle risk management elements for NASA programs, a program manager's guide to faster / better & cheaper, office of safety & mission assurance,* National Aeronautics & Space Administration, June 1997.

Stankosky, M. (Ed.) (2004). *Creating the discipline of knowledge management: The latest in university research.* Burlington, MA: Butterworth-Heinemann.

Wander, S. M., *The evolution of communities of practice in NASA's diverse business environment.* Session 2–6, Strategies to Integrate Communities of Practice into Business Operations, eGov 2006 Conference, April 21, 2006, Washington, DC.

Chapter 19

Driving Change Using Knowledge Management — Lessons Learned from an Unidentified Organization

Annie Green

Abstract

It has been said that organizations know a lot of things, but they don't always know what they know. Organizations know there is a wealth of information about the projects the workers are working on, but where it is, how to find it, where or who to call to get it, generally are obstacles that prevent sharing. This is not something new, but a problem many organizations face. Expertise is available, but organizations don't always capture it or know where to find it once it is captured. In most organizations, the most valuable asset is the collective skills and expertise of its staff. This "know-how" from staff that others can use when facing similar work experiences is "lost" and unavailable for reuse. In today's organizations, especially geographically disperse ones, it is more important than ever to establish effective lines of communication and share experiences amongst coworkers. This case study details practices and lessons learned experienced during a knowledge management journey in an unidentified[1] organization.

---

1. The journey discussed in this chapter is a true case study. The organization has requested not to be named — but the practices and lessons learned are very valuable and useful for other organizations.

19.1. An Opportunity to Leverage Knowledge

In 2002, the organization's workload significantly increases and its workforce/staffing levels remain constant. The increased workload led to the teaming of two large organizational units to provide better service to a larger base of customers. The managers of the two units entered into an agreement to share their experiences and knowledge in an effort to surmount the challenges that would accompany the increased workload.

Resulting from the new teaming approach are new and innovative ways of performing work. Capturing and sharing these new innovative work practices and lessons learned positions the organization to leverage valuable business operations knowledge to improve productivity and performance. This is the start of the organization's knowledge management journey.

19.2. The Journey (2002–2008) — Business Operations Improvement/KM Initiative

The organization begins its journey, using KM as its vehicle. Its direction is to proactively identify, codify, and capture valuable "promising practices"[2] and lessons learned that relate to its business operations and to establish a communications and collaboration platform to promote knowledge sharing. The organization has traveled through four phases of its KM initiative and is currently transcending into the fifth phase. Each phase's story is as follows:

- *Phase I — Build the knowledge repository*: Construct a centralized multimedia knowledge repository that provides users the ability to submit and search knowledge resources: promising practices, lessons learned, documents, personal profiles, and videos. Provide content management to ensure the relevancy, integrity, and quality of the knowledge resources.
- *Phase II — Institutionalize the use of the knowledge repository*: Establish the knowledge repository as a communication and collaboration tool and the cornerstone of business process improvement. The knowledge repository contains valuable knowledge that helps staff to work smarter and faster.
- *Phase III — Implement role-based communities of practice (CoPs)*: Coordinate CoP activities to generate content for the knowledge repository and implement business operations improvement projects that align with strategic goals and objectives.
- *Phase IV — Build a learning organization by sharing and managing knowledge throughout*: Define, establish, and implement support activities that institutionalize

---

2. "Promising practice" is a term adopted to represent good practices that have been identified, that once validated can be elevated to a "Best Practice."

a sharing culture, promote innovation, and institute efficient and effective practices for business processes and procedures.

- *Phase V — Sustain: knowledge integration, manage change, transform through training and measure for value and improvement*: Implement processes, procedures, guidelines, training, monitoring, and measurement tools to ensure KM activities are continuous and empowering to its users.

19.3. Phase I: Build the Knowledge Repository

In 2002, the organization's knowledge architect recognizes that staff are performing new innovative practices to handle their increased workloads. To prevent the loss of this business operations knowledge, the management makes a decision to interview staff to capture the new knowledge.

After the interviews, the management makes a decision to store the interview results and supporting documents in a central repository. Capturing and storing the new knowledge in a central repository makes it easy for staff to access, retrieve, learn from and leverage them in their work. A second decision was made to expand the interviews to include video interviews. The video interviews capture intellectual capital[3] that may have been missed during the pen-to-paper method used in the initial interviews. Yet another decision is made to capture personal profiles that identify the strengths of staff aligned with individual work activities. The centrally located multimedia knowledge repository is implemented with these knowledge resources: closed caption video's and their transcripts, interviews, and personal profiles.

The knowledge repository provides staff the ability to search for knowledge resources that identify new ways of performing work and obstacles to avoid. It facilitates the submission of promising practices, lessons learned, documents, personal profiles, and videos by staff. It provides staff the capability to share their knowledge and experiences in an explicit[4] or written format. The ability of staff to reuse the knowledge and/or experiences of other staff helps to validate its contribution to improve business operations. Validation of the knowledge contributions of staff establishes the knowledge and/or experiences as a candidate to include in standard operating procedures (SOPs). Inclusion of the validated new knowledge into SOPs makes this new knowledge available to the workforce and ensures its contribution to overall business performance.

The construction of the knowledge repository begins in October of 2002 and its completion occurs in July 2003. Development of the knowledge repository evolves through the following six activities.

---

3. Intellectual Capital (IC) is the total knowledge within an organization that may be converted into value, or used to produce a higher value asset.
4. Explicit Knowledge is that which is in a tangible or written form.

1. *Identified problem/opportunity*: Capture new promising practices and lessons learned from new innovative ways of doing work.
2. *Establish a steering committee*: Convene a steering committee of leadership and representative stakeholders to guide and support the KM initiative.
3. *Develop a proof of concept*: Construct a paper visual of the design and flow of the multimedia knowledge repository.
4. *Develop a prototype*: Construct an electronic "shell" version of the multi-media knowledge repository.
5. *Develop a multimedia knowledge repository*: Build the knowledge repository in four incremental modules:
   - *Search knowledge repository*: the ability to search the knowledge repository using evolving business taxonomy.[5]
   - *User submittal (self-service)*: the ability of the user to share new ideas, promising practices, lessons learned, and documents using an evolving taxonomy with others.
   - *Content management*: the ability to manage and control the submission and distribution of knowledge resources to and from the knowledge repository and maintain the quality and integrity of its content.
   - *Personal profiles (self-service)*: the ability of the user to submit their personal profiles aligned with functional areas using evolving taxonomy.
6. *Conduct focus groups*: Meet with staff to gauge staff satisfaction and to validate the topics and subtopics of the business taxonomy.

Work is occurring in tandem with the construction of the knowledge repository and staff requires access to the knowledge resources to be stored in the repository prior to its completion. Until the completion of the repository, the initial knowledge resources are made available in a folder on a shared hard drive. To accommodate the sharing of knowledge resources, the "search knowledge repository" function is developed first. The knowledge repository's initial implementation contains 100 documents and videos.

Metrics are established to monitor the usage of the repository. The number of hits (e.g., activities that occurred, such as opening a document, downloading a document), visits (the number of people who accessed portfolio), and areas of usage (e.g., the most frequently used activity, such as search or personal profile) are captured and reported weekly and monthly. Usage of the knowledge repository demonstrates a steady inclination to a weekly usage of about 20% of staff. To provide incentive to use the repository, the names of the most frequent users are identified and these users receive recognition of being pioneers and innovators in finding knowledge to improve their work.

By December 2003, usage begins to slow down and staff is saying they are not finding the information they are searching for and that the content is insufficient.

---

5. The classification of information in an ordered system that indicates natural relationships.

This presents the first obstacle. Staff is unaware of how the knowledge repository receives its content. Its content is generated by the organization's staff — the knowledge workers. The organization's knowledge workers are responsible for submitting content and assigning its taxonomy categories, either individually or as a group. This obstacle led the KM Steering Committee to re-direct the KM effort toward the institutionalization of the knowledge repository. The success of generating content in the repository requires the knowledge worker to think:

- When I discover a new practice that improves work, I will *share* this knowledge in the knowledge repository.
- When I discover an obstacle that impacts the successful completion of my work, I will *share* this knowledge in the knowledge repository.
- When I wonder if there is a better way of doing this work, I will *search* the knowledge repository for this knowledge.
- When I wonder if there are any known obstacles or problems that I can avoid, I will *search* the knowledge repository for this knowledge.

The goal is to change the culture such that staff understands that the content in the repository is generated by them. The success of the repository is dependent on the capture of innovative promising practices and lessons learned that the knowledge worker uncovers in their actual work.

19.4. Phase II: Institutionalize the Use of the Knowledge Repository

In 2004, the knowledge repository's focus shifts from development to institutionalization. The knowledge repository is to become a norm in performing work throughout the organization. To achieve this outcome, the following critical success factors are addressed.

Critical success factor for KM project:

1. *Define methodology*: Define the components and approach to the KM initiative.
2. *Define a road map:* Define the strategic alignment of knowledge to the mission and goals of the organization and expected outcomes.
3. *Define and procure labor and nonlabor resources*: Provide a level of effort estimation to perform work and appropriately staff/fund the effort.

Critical success factor for sharing:

1. *Establish a common living taxonomy that speaks the language of the worker*: Build a taxonomy that aligns with the topics and sub-topics that support the execution of work.
2. *Provide training in the use of the taxonomy to knowledge workers*: Terms and meanings may vary between the different organizational units and roles; train users to achieve a common understanding of terms and meanings.

3. *Establish communication mechanisms*: Communicate what is in the repository so that staff knows what is available.

Critical success factor for content generation:

1. *Build a knowledge foundation*: Determine what knowledge is needed and who needs what to ensure that the repository services the knowledge workers.
2. *Establish a content manager/coordinator*: Establish a worker, either as a role or a full time equivalent, who is responsible for the capture, storage and dissemination of content.
3. *Provide content management training*: Train the responsible worker, content manager/coordinator, in the task and activities that must be performed to ensure the capture, relevancy, integrity, and distribution of content.
4. *Provide knowledge repository training*: Train users in the use (i.e., search, submission and contribution) of the knowledge repository.
5. *Align content with work/taxonomy*: Ensure that all knowledge resources within the knowledge repository are aligned with a work activity and its related taxonomy category.
6. *Establish consistent and standard formats for knowledge resources*: Like knowledge resources within the knowledge repository should have a similar look and feel (e.g., interviews, transcripts, etc.).

The following five activities address the critical success factors: (1) define approach, (2) define road map, (3) establish a knowledge foundation, (4) establish roles and responsibilities, and (5) generate content in portfolio. The details for each of these activities are discussed.

19.5. Define Approach

An evaluation of the organization's KM initative identifies ten major components that need to be in place to increase the probability of its success. The ten KM components collectively form the KM methodology. The KM methodology is an integrated approach to the identification, creation, representation, capturing, dissemination, and adoption of knowledge within the organization. The ten critical KM components are:

1. *Opportunity for change*: Perform analysis, research, audits, assessments, evaluations, and mining of current business operations. Identify opportunities to improve business operations and ensure the strategic alignment of KM activities and outcomes.
2. *Knowledge repository*: Perform maintenance and administration of the knowledge repository.

3. *Content management*: Ensure generation, maintenance, and management of knowledge resources submitted and captured in the knowledge repository, to include quality, relevancy, and integrity of the content.
4. *Communication/awareness*: Keep staff and support departments informed and "in the know" about the availability of work related knowledge resources, the KM activities and projects of the communities of practice (CoPs).
5. *Metrics*: Capture and report performance measures to demonstrate return on investment (ROI) of KM activities and outcomes.
6. *Focus groups*: Conduct group sessions with staff to obtain feedback to gauge satisfaction with outputs and outcomes of KM activities.
7. *Training*: Refine and implement mechanisms and tools to accommodate the education of staff in new KM tools, processes, activities, and procedures. This includes methods of "just in time" training to effectively provide information at the point of use to strengthen the learning experience through immediate application.
8. *Rewards and recognition*: Provide support for the development of a recognition and incentive program.
9. *Systems enhancement/technology*: Develop, maintain, and administer a collaboration and communication platform and other software applications that support the execution or implementation of KM processes and activities.
10. *Communities of practice* (CoPs): Establish, institutionalize, and support CoPs and their contributions to business operations improvement.

19.6.   Define Road Map

Moving forward requires a clear view of the objectives and expected outcomes of the organization's KM initiative. The organization's KM goals are the efficient and effective execution of work and improvement in the productivity of their staff. Table 19.1 provides a view of the organization's KM business objectives and metrics to measure its KM outputs and outcomes.

Figure 19.1 depicts the relationship between the KM measures and the organization's business objectives of continuous improvement and teamwork/collaboration. The outcome, output, and system measures align with the following four KM objectives:

1. *Better decision making*: Provide accurate and timely information to improve business decisions.
2. *Shorten processing timeframes*: Share promising practices and lessons learned to improve the execution of activities and avoid known problems and redundancy.
3. *Employee satisfaction*: Provide accurate and timely information to perform work activities and meet customer service goals.
4. *Contact colleagues:* Provide a way to get in touch with the right people to get the right answer in a timely manner.

Table 19.1: KM business objectives and metrics.

The road map	
KM initiative	• Collect business operations knowledge — lessons learned and promising practices — from day-to-day work activities of staff to share with other staff to improve business operations.
Business objective	*Improved Business Operations through* • *Continuous Improvement* – improvements in day-to-day work activities through use of innovation • *Teamwork and Collaboration* – increased communication through improved teamwork
Key metrics	*Outcome measures* • *Communication use* — measure of the implementation of knowledge shared between team members and staff. • *Cultural change* — measure of sharing in the work environment. • *Knowledge use* — measure of the reuse of knowledge gained from the knowledge repository and CoPs. • *Process efficiency* — measure of the elapsed time to perform business activities based on knowledge gained from the knowledge repository and CoPs. • *Staff efficiency* — measure of elapsed time in decision-making to complete critical business activities based on knowledge gained from the knowledge repository and CoPs *Output measures* • *Communication quality* — measure of the relevancy and quality of knowledge shared from colleagues. • *Knowledge quality* — measure of the relevancy and quality of knowledge shared from the knowledge repository and CoPs. • *Staff contribution* — measure of the sharing of knowledge resources by staff. • *Staff collaboration* — measure of the interaction between team members and staff. *System measures* • *System usage* — measure of usage of knowledge repository as a tool for knowledge transfer.

----------Continuous Improvement------------------------------Teamwork/Collaboration--------------			
	Better Decision-Making	**Shorten Processing Timeframes**	**Employee Satisfaction**	**Collaboration with Colleagues**
Outcome Measures	Staff Efficiency Communication Use Knowledge Use	Process Efficiency Knowledge Use	Communication Use Knowledge Use	Communication Use Cultural Change
Output Measures	Communication Quality Knowledge Quality	Staff Contribution Knowledge Quality	Staff Contribution Staff Collaboration	Staff Collaboration
System Measures	System Usage	System Usage	System Usage	System Usage

Figure 19.1: KM measures align with business objectives.

The KM measures are quantitative[6] and qualitative[7] measures used to monitor KM's contribution to the organization's performance goals.

19.7. Establish a Knowledge Foundation

The building of a knowledge foundation identifies the what, when, how, why, where, and who that surrounds the organization's business operations. Understanding the knowledge that impacts business operations provides a direct view to the high and low leverage areas that contribute to operational performance.

Performing analyses, assessments, and evaluations provide a visual representation of an organization's key knowledge. The knowledge foundation is built from the results of the following activities:

- *Value chain analysis:* Analyze current business processes to identify the critical processes that ensure timely and effective business operations.
- *Workforce assessment*: Perform a value chain analysis to evaluate each business process and identify the key roles responsible for executing its activities.
- *Role-based process assessments*: Create and administer role-based surveys that align with the organization's operations manual (processes, activities, and procedures) for each key role. The assessment asks staff: (1) What works?

---

6. Quantitative performance measures are measures that can be expressed in terms of definite numbers or amounts.
7. Qualitative performance measures are descriptions of situations or conditions which cannot be recorded numerically.

(2) What does not work? (3) What are you doing differently from the operations manual? and (4) What are your recommendations for improvement?

- *Work-centered analysis:* Develop work-centered diagrams that identify the critical processes/activities that affect the work performed by each role. These diagrams define the "as is" work flow, from the organization's operations manual. Representative sample groups for each of the organization's key roles validate the diagrams.
- *Focus groups:* Conduct role-based focus groups to validate the process assessment and work-centered analysis results.
- *Gap analysis:* Align staff improvement suggestions with the following eight organizational gap areas to determine where disconnects occur within the operations of the organization. (Baldridge[8] quality standards serve as the guideline to identify and define the eight gap analysis (quality) areas.):
  1. *Leadership:* the decision-making processes of the organization.
  2. *Staff focus:* how the organization enables all staff to enhance their potential to attain the organization's objectives.
  3. *Organization structure:* the patterns of interrelationships among key components that can include the hierarchy and workflow.
  4. *Relationships:* building of collaborative relationships within and amongst groups.
  5. *Infrastructure:* specific mechanisms put in place to ensure business process flow through-out the enterprise. This includes technology, work processes and networks of people.
  6. *Information and analysis:* organization's ability to use information and data to improve its performance.
  7. *Customer focus:* identification and satisfaction of requirements, expectations and preferences of customers.
  8. *Policy/process/procedures:* systematic evaluation of policy, process and procedures to overcome fragmentation in information and workflow in business operations.

The analyses, evaluations, and assessments collectively identified the following opportunities for improvement to business operations.

- Capture new practices
- Share innovative practices
- Facilitate consistent work activities/practices

---

8. The Baldridge criteria for performance excellence provide a systems perspective for understanding performance management. They reflect validated, leading-edge management practices against which an organization can measure itself. With their acceptance nationally and internationally as the model for performance excellence, the criteria represent a common language for communication among organizations for sharing best practices. The criteria is also the basis for the Malcolm Baldridge National Quality Award process.

- Connect work practices and standard operating procedures
- Provide awareness of known obstacles or problems
- Reduce redundant activities-multiple people performing the same task.

In addition, it was determined that the organization's staff would benefit as follows:

- Information is available and accessible to make better decisions.
- Information to perform work is obtained faster.
- The organization's staff knows more through increased transparency.
- Capability to identify ways to get in touch with the right people to get the right answer at the right time.
- New ways to perform work that improve operational effectiveness.
- Acceleration of innovation through sharing practices.

19.8. Establish Roles and Responsibilities

The assignment of KM roles and responsibilities is fundamental to the execution of the KM activities. These roles and their subsequent responsibilities support a continuum of information and knowledge to and from the knowledge workers. The KM team is composed of or is a subset of the following nine roles. These roles ensure parallel and sequential processing of KM activities.

1. Chief knowledge strategist architect/KM SME
2. Knowledge officer/community of practice (CoP) coordinator
3. Solutions architect: interface and content modeler integrator
4. Solutions architect: data and information integrator
5. Knowledge engineer/business analyst/trainer
6. Communications coordinator/trainer
7. Content manager
8. KM developer
9. KM administrator

Table 19.2 defines the KM roles and their primary KM activities/responsibilities. Each role has one or more primary responsibilities. All roles play a significant part in the integration of the KM components to produce a streamlined process. These roles are scalable based on project constraints such as scope, funding, and timeframes. The alignment of the KM roles to their primary responsibilities (see "Define Approach" section for description of KM components) provides a basis for trade-offs when prioritizing tasks and deliverables.

Table 19.2: KM roles aligned with KM components.

KM methodology component	KM role
Opportunity for change	• Chief Knowledge Strategist Architect/ KM SME • Knowledge Engineer/Business Analyst/Trainer
Portfolio: Knowledge repository	• KM Developer • Knowledge Engineer/Business Analyst/Trainer
Content management	• Solutions Architect – Interface and Content Modeler Integrator • Content Manager
Communication/awareness	• Knowledge Officer/Community of Practice (CoP) Coordinator • Communication Coordinator/Trainer
Metrics	• Solutions Architect — Data and Information Integrator • Chief Knowledge Strategist Architect/ KM SME
Focus groups	• Knowledge Engineer/Business Analyst/Trainer
Training	• Knowledge Engineer/Business Analyst/Trainer • Knowledge Officer/ CoP Coordinator
Rewards and recognition	• Chief Knowledge Strategist Architect/ KM SME
Systems enhancement/ technology	• KM Developer • KM Administrator • Solutions Architect — Data & Information Integrator • Solutions Architect — Interface and Content Modeler Integrator
Communities of Practice (CoP)	• Knowledge Officer/CoP Coordinator • KM Administrator
KM methodology development and refinement *(**Note:** this is a global requirement to ensure the development, capturing, documenting and maintenance of the methodology that drives the KM components).*	• Chief Knowledge Strategist Architect/ KM SME

19.9. Generate Content in the Knowledge Repository

The sustainment of knowledge in the knowledge repository is of high importance. A continuum of content is critical. The organization establishes a content manager position to be responsible for the generation of content for the repository. The content manager

- identifies critical knowledge to document and store,
- secures experts to interview and video capture the results of the interviews, and
- schedules video capture of operational knowledge such as session report-outs at training conferences and highlights of new software applications.

The new content generated by the content manager is successful in increasing the usage of the knowledge repository. However, the increase in usage uncovers obstacles caused by the limited capability of the system's Web-based development environment — *MS Access Database*[9] and *.Net code*.[10] Given the limitations of the development environment, the steering committee makes a decision to transfer the knowledge repository to a portal[11] platform.

The identification of a portal platform is already in progress. The organization's information technology (IT) department had already begun an initiative to purchase portal technology to accommodate a business requirement to expand its communication and collaboration platform. In 2005, a selection of the Plumtree portal[12] is made. Migration of the knowledge repository to a portal version begins immediately after its implementation.

19.10. Phase III: Implement Role-Based Communities of Practice

Although this phase is focused on implementing CoPs, there are multiple KM activities being performed to ensure the success of the CoPs. These activities are: (1) start-up CoPs, (2) measure contributions of CoP projects, (3) establish CoP workspaces, (4) revitalize CoPs, (5) integrate the knowledge repository into portal, (6) measure the contribution of the portal, and (7) manage impact of change on staff. The following discussion provides the details for each of the seven activities.

---

9. Access Database is an end-user tool that allows the collection, tracking and reporting of information with ease of use. (www.microsoft.com).

10. The .Net framework is Microsoft's comprehensive and consistent programming model for building applications that have visual user experiences, seamless and secure communication, and the ability to model a range of business processes (www.microsoft.com/net/).

11. Portal is a site that provides a single function via a web page or site. Portals function as a point of access to information.

12. Plumtree Portal is now the BEAOracle WebLogic 2.0 portal (www.oracle.com).

19.11. Start-Up CoPs

Using information and knowledge from the results of the workforce assessment and focus groups in phase II, the organization's management makes a decision to establish role-based CoPs. The purpose of the CoPs is to identify and implement business operations improvement projects and maintain a portal workspace for sharing and bringing together members of the community to promote camaraderie. Each CoP aligns its business operations projects with operational goals and objectives, business activities defined in the operations manual, and milestones defined in operational work plans. The CoPs are the first step in empowering the organization's staff to improve the way they work.

The CoPs use the results from the focus groups to identify and execute projects. At start up, the CoPs jointly have 137 volunteers, or 23% of staff who are core members. The CoP core members occupy active roles in sustaining the CoPs. The remaining 77% of staff in key roles have access to the CoP's portal workspace. Access to the CoP portal workspace allows all staff to benefit from the efforts of the community core members. The CoPs are open to all staff to become active members at any time. The CoPs implement 41 business operation improvement projects. Of the 41 projects, approximately fifty percent are successful with varying degrees of contribution to business operations improvements.

19.12. Measure Contributions of CoP Projects

The basic measurement for a CoP project is process efficiency. Process efficiency is the measure of the elapsed time to finalize a milestone. Each major work activity in the organization's processes has an associated milestone and milestone execution is a component of the organizations project work plans. CoP project leaders associate each CoP project with a specific milestone. The relationship between the CoP project and the activity milestone establishes the process efficiency measurement that is used to provide an estimate of a CoP project's contribution to business operations improvement.

The process of determining if there are changes in the elapsed time to finalize a milestone requires collecting, analyzing and summarizing operational milestone data. These tasks are accomplished through the creation of a prototype scorecard to capture milestone data and provide a visual display of improvement measures. The initial capture of the process efficiency measures is a tedious and manual process that prevents the timely capture and monitoring of the measures. The untimely capture of the process efficiency measures impacts the decision-making process necessary to manage the successful implementation of the CoP improvement projects. To improve the timeliness of capturing and reporting process efficiency information, a decision is made to add a task to the project schedule to investigate tools that accommodate the capture, reporting, and monitoring of the process efficiency measures.

19.13. Establish CoP Workspaces

The portal takes a front seat as the communications and collaboration platform for the CoPs and the entire organization's workforce. Personalized workspaces are developed for each CoP, where its members can share documents, link to information, and take advantage of other communications and collaboration capabilities of the portal. Unfortunately, the portal (as another new tool for the staff to learn) suffers from a steep learning curve and the lack of user training. This leads to a high level of user dissatisfaction with the portal. Given these obstacles, the team re-directs efforts to develop basic user portal training that instructs staff in the use of portal workspaces and the overall portal. Resources are re-assigned to develop the basic user portal training which requires significant time to develop. The re-assignment of resources impacts support to the CoPs and the CoPs become sluggish in operations which brings to the forefront a budding risk that CoP members may become dis-engaged. To mitigate the risk of dis-engagement of CoP members, resources supporting the CoP's focus on methods and techniques to manage the risk of a potential decrease in staff participation in the CoPs.

19.14. Revitalize CoP

In an effort to sustain the momentum of the CoPs, resources supporting the CoPs attend a CoP training course, knowledge management: building and sustaining communities of practice (CoP), at American Productivity and Quality Center (APQC[13]). The objective for attending the course is to identify loop holes in the CoP process. The result of the APQC training is the identification of revitalization sessions to re-engage CoP members. The CoPs need nurturing-attention, feedback, and support. Periodically, a CoP must revitalize its members to the true value of the communities.

Revitalization sessions for CoPs are to:

- educate community members about the CoP and its purpose,
- show community members how to become more involved,
- identify and recruit new members with new ideas,
- provide an opportunity for community members to meet face-to-face,
- promote communication and transparency among members,
- provide an open forum for members to share their ideas and experiences, including success stories,
- provide an opportunity for community members to evaluate CoP processes and provide feedback, and

---

13. APQC is a member-based nonprofit that provides benchmarking and best-practice research for approximately 500 organizations worldwide in all industries (www.apqc.org).

- identify business processes that might need realignment to better support CoP activity.

The CoP revitalization sessions are successful in re-engaging members in the CoPs. The sessions promote open communication amongst members and sharing of ideas. The revitalization sessions

- re-emphasize the purpose of CoPs and their role within the organization,
- present summaries of CoP projects by project leaders along with discussions of opportunities where members can become more involved in the community, and
- provide informative testimonials by staff members currently or previously involved with CoP, projects These "first hand" experiences enable community members to get a closer look into the operations and work of the CoPs.

The revitalization sessions render some immediate results, whereby

- several community members volunteer to take on new roles within their respective CoPs,
- CoP members participate in small brainstorming or feedback sessions that enable CoP community members to discuss ways in which the CoPs can better work for them. These sessions are effective with CoP members identifying such items as: routine meetings, guest speakers, leadership topics, and other ways they can bond together as a team to help sustain their participation in the CoPs.

19.15.   Integrate the Knowledge Repository into Portal

The integration of the knowledge repository (intranet version) into the organization's portal occurs in tandem with implementing the CoPs. The knowledge repository (portal version) continues to offer the same features as the intranet version. The user interface is user friendly and provides a streamline way to navigate its features.

The portal version of the knowledge repository provides:

1. *Find it*: the capability to search the knowledge repository to retrieve information.
2. *Share it*: the capability to share documents, promising practices, lessons learned, and personal profiles.
3. *In the spotlight*: a central spot which highlights special activities and/or events that occur within the organization.
4. *View profiles*: the capability to locate staff that has skills and expertise necessary to support others in their work.
5. *Quick links*: the capability to access knowledge outside of the knowledge repository.
6. *Feedback*: the capability to provide comments, suggestions, and recommendations.

To jump start the use of the portal version of the knowledge repository, the following items accompany its release:

1. *A user manual:* Provides step-by-step instructions on how to use its features.
2. *Brown-bag training sessions:* *A* series of small learning sessions during lunch, to demonstrate its use.

After its release, in July 2006, the content manager announces the new content in the knowledge repository to attract staff. This new content kicks off a new interest in the knowledge repository. The integration of the knowledge repository into the portal is a success. However, this success did not come without lessons learned. The expectation was that the knowledge repository being part of the portal would lessen the impact of introducing two systems at the same time. The knowledge repository's integration into the portal platform surfaces confusion surrounding the difference between the knowledge repository and the portal. The introduction of two tools at the same time and no clear definition that distinguishes how to use either in the organization's business operations was a definite lesson learned. Information was prepared and distributed to the users to help minimize the confusion on the use of the portal versus the knowledge repository. This information is a viable work-around, but training, which is in development and has a high priority in the KM initiative, is paramount to the successful use of these tools.

19.16. Measure the Contribution of the Portal

The portal as a KM tool introduces another measurement item. ROI[14] of the portal is necessary to determine the value from a communication and collaboration platform. The purpose of this measurement is to understand the total cost of ownership of the portal and its benefits. The following measures are the basis of the portal ROI calculation.

Portal cost
1. Hardware purchased for portal deployment
2. Software and licensing for portal development and use
3. Services to initially deploy the portal
4. Annual services required to maintain the portal

IT savings
5. Network traffic and storage costs
6. Web-publishing costs
7. Delivering e-business services
8. Web-enabling existing applications

---

14. Return on investment (ROI) is a performance measure used to evaluate the efficiency of an investment.

9. Regulatory compliance costs
10. Internationalization costs

Employee self-service
11. Increased user productivity by providing capability to find information on their own
12. Reduction in training costs
13. Reduction in corporate communication costs
14. Reduction in travel costs
15. Improved user effectiveness by readily providing required information to do their job

Partner, customer self-service
16. Improved customer support by providing a resource center for customers and partners to get support for them

To satisfy the portal ROI requirement, a decision was made to develop a portal ROI calculation prototype. The purpose of the prototype is to provide a clear view of the measures and indicators that evolve into the ROI calculation (portal savings — portal cost) (Figure 19.2). The measurement structure is in place and once again the effort to capture the operational data encounters an obstacle. The capture and alignment of operational data takes a lower priority to other higher priority activities within the IT

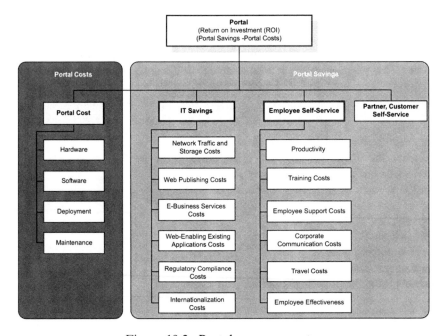

Figure 19.2: Portal measurements.

department and management delays the capture of the measurements. This is a manageable and perhaps beneficial obstacle. Delaying this activity allows time to train the users, which could reduce the impact of the learning curve on the portal ROI results.

19.17. Manage the Impact of Change on Staff

Institutionalizing the CoPs, the knowledge repository and the portal introduces lots of change to the staff. Managing this change is essential to obtaining buy-in and adoption of these new activities. A staff member with a background in organizational development (OD) as a "change agent" joins the KM project. The OD expert brings the component that is critical to managing the impact of a changing work environment on staff. The OD expert seeks to correlate the obstacles of the KM initiative to results from the following assessments:

- Gallup Q12[15] (measures employee engagement): Uses this assessment to measure a direct link between employee engagement and high productivity using critical indicators within the organization.
- Gallup's StrengthsFinder[16] (assesses individual's strengths/talents): Uses this assessment to help staff identify and understand their innate talents. Employees are more productive when they use their innate talents to do their work.
- American Customer Service Index (ACSI)[17] customer service survey (measures customer satisfaction): Results of this survey are used to identify ways to improve customer service and to compare this organization customer service ratings to other entities.

Awareness of the above attributes as they relate to staff helps surmount barriers in the success of approaching individuals and engaging them in sharing as staff is core to the success of this KM initiative.

19.18. Phase IV: Building a Learning Organization by Sharing and Managing Knowledge throughout BOD

In the fall of 2006, all ten KM components from phase II are in motion. Phase IV enters into a state of learning. Focus is on tracking, monitoring,

---

15. Gallup Q12 are 12 questions that measure employee engagement and link to relevant business outcomes, including retention, productivity, profitability, customer engagement, and safety (www.gallup.com).
16. Gallup StrengthsFinder is an online assessment that helps people uncover their talents (www.strengths.gallup.com).
17. ACSI measures satisfaction and enables benchmarking and predictive analyses using data obtained from interviews with customers (www.theasci.org).

adjusting, and sustaining KM activities to ensure the organization's goals and objectives are met. As portal awareness and usage increases, so does the need to make sure that everyone has the knowledge to successfully use the portal. Ongoing portal survey results continue to indicate that training on the portal is essential.

Although users view the knowledge repository as a valuable tool, results of surveys and focus groups continue to indicate that its search function needs improvement and some of its functionality needs updating. Additionally, there is a "hole" in the metrics component — the structure exists, but the measurement data is lacking.

The activities of this phase are: (1) provide portal training, (2) uncover the impact of change on staff, (3) modernize the knowledge repository, (4) establish KM business intelligence, and (5) re-design community workspaces. The following paragraphs provide the details for each of these five activities.

19.19.   Provide Portal Training

The basic portal user training is enhanced to accommodate the users' portal needs. The enhancement is to change the emphasis of the training to teach "how to" use the portal from the user's experience. The previous portal training was organized around portal capabilities. The kick-off of the new basic portal training occurs in January 2007. The training sessions are successful. Through the sessions, users are able to

- gain general knowledge about the portal,
- learn how to access the portal,
- become familiar with and learn how to use portlets,
- gain an understanding of how to use "My Pages" (personalized workspace),
- learn how to participate in portal projects,
- learn how to work together on assignments, and
- learn how to participate in portal communities and work in virtual groups.

To supplement the training, portal "job aids" were created that enable users to easily find the "know-how" to navigate and perform specific functions on the portal. The job aids provide staff with "just-in-time" information, such as understanding common icons, how to set up a personalized view of their work activities and guidance on using standard functions (announcements, calendar, tasks, documents, and discussions). The portal job aids are easy to use and provide general information along with detailed "step-by-step" instructions. The portal job aids are a frequent request from the organization's staff.

19.20.   Uncover the Impact of Change on Staff

By 2008, the expectation is that a significant amount of the organization's staff is sharing their knowledge. With all this support, sharing is easier. Some of the knowledge repository content areas are empty and the Content Manager is generating most of its content. Potential users say they like the knowledge repository, but just do not have time for it, and the the "culture" wall — *Change* becomes a major obstacle to sharing. With the KM efforts, sharing is easy and encouraged by all. The knowledge repository is for staff to share knowledge and it has areas where staff can share and look up information. However, the organization is not achieving its sharing goals. The question of "Why staff is not sharing?" is examined. The first hurdle is formalizing the process of sharing. Formalized sharing is intimidating when people are use to exchanging ideas informally in casual conversations and settings. The second hurdle is that the desire to access knowledge is seen as valuable, however, the additional effort of loading data is not seen as value-adding for the individual contributor. The organization faces a cultural dilemma – everyone wants knowledge, but no-one wants to contribute knowledge. Given this dilemma, how does the organization achieve the expected outcome that staff shares documents, promising practices, lessons learned, and personal profiles?

When introducing KM, the user needs to see the value it brings to them, especially when it requires additional effort. When change occurs and the value to the individual user is not sufficiently addressed, resistance becomes the biggest barrier to business operations improvement. Change implies uncertainty and the discomfort of not knowing what may potentially happen. The change may require new skills and abilities that are beyond current capabilities. This builds a resistance to try something new, because comfort is with the existing order of how work is done.

The organization uses various methods through its OD area to stay abreast of the impact of change on its staff. To supplement the organization's current assessment information, approval to administer a loss of effectiveness (LOE)[18] index assessment to CoP members is requested. The LOE index identifies behaviors, perceptions, and attitudes that emerge in organizations as a response to change and that ultimately impact overall effectiveness. The tool enables organizations to plan, anticipate symptoms, and adapt effectively to the impact of change. The LOE index results supplement information from other assessments with more granularities. Visibility or awareness of the symptoms or indicators resulting from change helps organizational leaders to better plan and manage the impact of change.

---

18. The LOE index is an assessment tool of Victoria Grady, LLC, an organizational change management consultant.

Between February 2008 and April 2008, the LOE index is administered to members of three CoPs. The LOE Index results for all three sets of employees identify

- high level of anxiety: indicates low morale
- high level of "rejection of environment": indicates conflict
- high level of frustration: indicates a loss of productivity

The results of the LOE index led to a recommendation to prepare a plan of action to address the morale, conflict, and loss of productivity issues impacting the effectiveness of the staff. In addition, a recommendation is put forth that a stronger relationship be established between the organizational develop-ment and leadership programs. These relationships help to form a more holistic approach to monitoring and controlling the "change health"[19] of the organization's staff.

19.21. Modernize the Knowledge Repository

In the spring of 2008, the knowledge repository begins to undergo a moderniza-tion and enhancement effort to improve its taxonomy and search capability. This effort is to re-establish the knowledge repository as the place to find innovative promising practices and lessons learned that target business operations improvement.

19.22. Establish KM Business Intelligence

Another prominent activity taking place in the spring of 2008 is the capture and structuring of key enterprise data to analyze, track, and monitor the performance of KM activities and outcomes. The process efficiency performance report (PEPR) prototype developed in phase III re-surfaces in the KM work plan.

Creating the PEPR scorecard using the Cognos 7.3[20] business intelligence (BI) tool should significantly improve the contribution of the tool in measuring process efficiency of CoP projects. An evaluation of the Cognos BI tool is performed and an implementation strategy is prepared.

The organization launches a study to identify its "best fit" BI tool solution. The six leading BI tools are evaluated and researched to identify a common list of

---

19. "Change health" is a term established by Victoria Grady, LLC that describes how staff of an organization is adapting to a changing work environment.
20. Cognos 7.3 is a business intelligence and performance management tool offered by IBM (see www.cognos.com).

capabilities. Each of the six leading tools was evaluated for strengths and weaknesses against the list of BI capabilities below.

1. *Information delivery services*: Make available information from multiple sources and deliver it through multiple channels in the most commonly used formats: e-mail, Web pages, Excel, PDF, word-processing, etc. to the right people at the right time.
2. *Analysis services*: Enables the end user to extract, transform and integrate data from multiple sources for time-based studies. Additionally, allows the end user to customize business metrics and use predictive techniques to anticipate future events.
3. *Integration services*: Provide standardized features to get external connectivity, application integration, and developer tools and platforms.
4. *Extract, transform, & load* (ETL) *services*: Access, parse, validate, standardize, organize, and consolidate data in various forms from various internal and/or external sources. Stores the data where it can be used conveniently to support analysis, decision-making, and other business needs. Includes the management of metadata (overall definitions of data structures) and a list of extractable data sources.
5. *Collaboration services*: Connect with others to facilitate a joint effort of multiple individuals or work groups to share and communicate to accomplish work (use of groupware and real-time communication between individuals).
6. *Management services*: Direct and control the BI platform, infrastructure, and repository. Includes installing, supporting, and updating application servers; assuring system and data integrity; responding to disruptions and other problems; scheduling and following up on application-related activities; and extending BI to other organizational and computer system environments.

The organization's BI initiative takes a global approach to its tool selection and includes representatives from all business units who have a stake in the selection. The search for an organization's "best fit" BI tool continues into the next phase of this KM journey.

19.23. Re-Design Community Workspaces

Survey results from portal workspace users indicate they are not satisfied with their workspaces. In the spring of 2008, the organization launches an initiative to redesign its portal community workspaces. The portal communities are getting a new look that delivers more content, structure, and functionality that aligns with business operations. The initial workspace designs did not incorporate input from the users. The new approach to re-designing the workspaces includes requirements gathering workshops. The workshops allow community managers and users to determine their workspace needs: what they want to see and don't want to see and how the information should be organized so that it is most useful. Prior to implementing the new approach, an investigation is performed to uncover global and common needs. Using the global and common needs, a KM portal community prototype is developed that provides a standard and consistent look to the workspaces. The prototype is the starting point to create an initial workspace in a requirements gathering workshop. Prior to the workshop, participants receive preliminary documents and checklists to review and complete that provoke thought and better prepare them for the workshop activities. The workshop facilitator also encourages the workshop participants to take a look at existing workspaces. Reviewing existing workspaces allows them to get some ideas about content and organization to incorporate in the design of their workspace. Upon completion of requirements gathering, development of the final workspace commences. The community manager and members receive training to empower them to be stewards of their community structure and content after the community workspace is implemented.

The workspace redesigns are successful and portal usage as a tool in performing day-to-day work activities is increasing.

19.24.   Future Direction — Phase V — Sustain: Knowledge Integration, Managing Change, Transforming through Training, and Measuring for Value and Improvement

The KM initiative enters into a critical stage of its journey. Its execution faces a challenging balance such that it must sustain the momentum of some components while it builds the momentum in others. This balance requires further refinement of the KM methodology to identify the activities, roles, and responsibilities that are necessary to ensure continuous progress. In essence, Phase V "brings knowledge together" (Figure 19.3) along with managing change and transformation using training and learning.

The KM methodology is the map to integrate KM activities. During phase V, the activities to evolve the methodology are given in Table 19.3.

The expected outcome of Phase V is a mature KM infrastructure that is sustaining its growth and renewal through knowledge integration, change management, and transformation.

19.25.   Lessons Learned

There are many KM initiatives and each tends to have methodologies that are specific to its own interest. Currently, there is no consistent and standard methodology to effectively and efficiently implement KM within an organization. Most KM initiatives start with a disadvantage because of the lack of a consistent and standard methodology to follow. There have been many KM initiatives and this project leverages their successes and failures to evolve a KM methodology. This KM project began as a small grassroots project to capture and leverage new practices

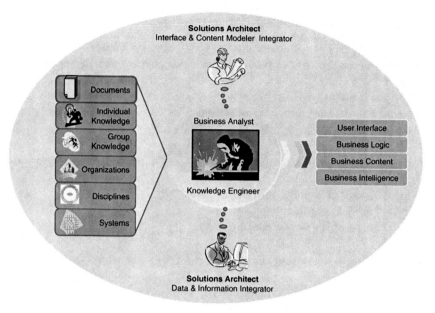

Figure 19.3: Bringing knowledge together.

being introduced because of this its commitment to improve business operations. The outcome of this initiative has been progressive and the lessons learned summarized in the four categories (leadership, organization, technology, and learning) are deemed to be very valuable to other organizations.

1. *Leadership* in this case study occurs from the start. Leadership extends from the top to the operational level. The organization's leadership commits to allocating resources and engaging staff. The main lesson learned is there needs to be a champion leader for the KM effort that exists at the enterprise level. KM leadership at the enterprise level establishes an advocate to support strategic alignment of KM with the organization's value chain, as well as articulate its value proposition. Enterprise leadership ensures the KM initiative has the integration of organizational units that must work together to ensure resources, funding, and communications. The lessons learned in leadership are:

- Be intentional about planning. Know the knowledge you need to capture and manage.
- Develop a KM strategic plan that evolves from and aligns with the organization's vision/mission through to the tactical level. Identify activities that are performed to ensure a successful KM infrastructure implementation.
- Know from the beginning what your expected outcomes are and how they are to be measured. Develop and define appropriate metrics (to include security and operational measures) to capture, track, monitor, and measure performance.

Table 19.3: Activities to evolve the KM methodology in Phase V.

Opportunity for change — Stay abreast of what's driving change
- Define, document, and implement organizational change management process and procedures
- Identify inconsistent work activities/practices, disconnect between work practices and standard operating procedures, obstacles or problems, redundant activities, and new industry opportunities

The knowledge repository — Generate and capture innovative practices and lessons learned
- Provide Training in use and purpose of tool
- Establish a robust search capability
- Link content to business processes/activities

Content management — Ensure the quality, integrity, and relevancy of resources captured and shared
- Define, document, and implement content management process and procedures
- Establish consistent and standard formats for resources
- Refine BOD taxonomy to ensure that it speaks the language of the worker to facilitate ease of searching
- Provide training in use of taxonomy to knowledge workers
- Develop and implement a knowledge map
- Identify knowledge nuggets (interviews and videos)

Communication — Keep everyone in the know
- Continue the development and dissemination of marketing materials (announcements, posters, flyers, pamphlets, trinkets…etc.)
- Continue the maintenance and dissemination of job aids
- Continue the writing and submission of KM articles and status to BOD Online (KM Corner)

Focus groups — Share experiences, feedback, and opinions
- Conduct periodic focus groups to get feedback on KM activities
- Capture suggestions and ideas for operational improvements that align with current process and procedures
- Administer surveys and conduct periodic focus groups to validate survey results

Training — Reduce the impact of change
- Conduct basic and advance portal training
- Conduct CoP role-based training
- Conduct The knowledge repository training
- Conduct community manager/administrator training
- Develop and Implement portal project management training
- Develop and Implement Learning Games

Table 19.3: (*Continued*)

- Develop and implement computer-based training (CBT)
- Develop and implement content manager training
- Develop and implement taxonomy use training

Metrics — Learn from change
- Measure Process Efficiency
- Measure Staff Efficiency
- Measure ROI of KM Communication & Collaboration Platform
- Measure Cultural Change
- Measure Impact of Change
- Measure Process Effectiveness

Rewards and recognition — Highlight the contributions of workers
- Develop a Recognition Plan
- Monitor and Track Recognition Methods
- Relate Recognition to Employee Satisfaction

Technology — Provide tools that help everyone work smarter and faster
- Maintain and enhance portal communication and collaboration platform
- Develop and implement a performance dashboard to monitor and track progress.

Communities of Practice (CoPs) — Bring people together
- Establish a Knowledge Administrator to provide on-going support
- Maintain a repeatable CoP Stand Up Process and procedures
- Empower the CoPs to be self-governing

- Construct the metrics map from the vision, goals, and objectives through to the tactics, processes, and activities.
- Identify the roles and responsibilities of all stakeholders that will have an impact on the success of the KM effort.
- Establish a steering committee that represents all stakeholders and that meets on a routine and frequent basis.
- Involve leadership early in resolution of obstacles and issues that impact implementation.
- Monitor and manage the strategic plan — don't lose sight of the vision. Update the vision if change is justified and don't forget to communicate the changes down to the implementation level.
2. *Organization* in this case study is at a disadvantage from the start. The knowledge workers and leadership are in line with moving forward. The lack of a KM Strategic Plan, KM competent resources, and a KM methodology or map to follow presents major obstacles to the execution of the KM vision. Even in light of these obstacles, the achievements in establishing a methodology, knowledge

repository, portal, training, focus groups, taxonomy, communities of practice (CoPs) etc., of this effort are outstanding. If the destination of the journey is foreseeable given the obstacles existing from the start, imagine the time savings if the obstacles are minimized or eliminated. The lessons learned in organization are:

- Plan time upfront to establish key KM processes and procedures. This not only improves the competence of the implementers, it also lessens the stress on the knowledge worker.
- Start with a pilot and then refine and leverage the results of the pilot.
- Take an incremental approach and incorporate change as needed.
- Practice what KM preaches. During execution, dedicate resources to capturing and documenting the KM processes, procedures, and guidelines that are being practiced. This is the KM methodology baseline, which also requires process improvement over time.
- Establish partnerships and keep open communications with the IT, security, and external affairs organizations. Work together to build a complimentary relationship that jointly supports the vision of the organization.
- Partner with a formal training organization. KM introduces new ways of working and employees and staff must be trained in methods that minimize learning curves.
- Partner with a formal organizational development organization. KM introduces change and the impact of change can be more traumatic than the change itself. Always be cognizant of the impact of the initiative on the knowledge worker.
- Ensure transparency by communicating, communicating, communicating. This builds trust and helps to transform a skeptical culture.
- Listen to the knowledge worker. Give them the functionality they need, want, and will use.

3. *Technology* in this case study evolves from prototypes to operational applications. Prototyping helps to capture requirements and supports the development of tools that service the needs of the users. The challenge in the technology component is the actual technology tools that facilitate the capture, sharing, and dissemination of knowledge. Although KM is not a new concept, the implementation of a KM infrastructure within organizations is relatively new. Thus, there are limited resources that are familiar enough with the discipline to develop and design the necessary solutions. The lessons learned in technology are:

- Always be mindful that technology enables and supports business functions. Know that technology it is not a complete solution.
- Define, design, and implement an approach to capture, disseminate, and use the knowledge.
- Partner with a formal systems engineering organization. Have a clear view of where technology is to be inserted.
- Develop a concept of the expected outcomes. Define the whole picture. This provides a clear picture of the business requirements.

- Map the business requirements to the capabilities to ensure the tool can produce the expected outcomes.
- Be knowledgeable about the functions of a tool and how these functions support business operations before implementing the tool. Improper roll-out of a tool can taint the expected outcome. Sometimes there is only one chance to get buy-in on a solution. Improper implementation can cause re-work, and the same solution has to be re-introduced differently.
- Evaluate your technology to identify high and low leverage capabilities. Implement them one at a time to ensure successful adoption by the organization.
- Start with a pilot and then refine and leverage the results of the pilot.
- Take an incremental approach.

4. *Learning*[21] by . It requires and collective interpretation of new that to collective action and involves taking as experimentation. has a qualitative existence in this case study. Throughout this effort, capturing measures has been prominent. Although the intent has been to capture measures and indicators upfront and monitor them throughout the project, the actual capture has been tedious and slow. The next major hurdle for this case study is to establish a quantitative baseline of measurement to monitor and learn the value contribution of the KM infrastructure to the performance of the organization. The lessons learned in learning are:

- Develop your measurement plan in the strategic planning phase.
- Ensure all measures support strategic direction.
- Identify the sources of the metrics upfront. Know what you are measuring.
- Model the knowledge needed to determine if goals are met and/or to make decisions that support future growth, renewal and direction.
- Get feedback. Don't forget to engage the knowledge worker. Remember that qualitative measures also uncover significant knowledge.
- Remember to use the knowledge learned to improve performance. Don't forget to share what's learned.
- Remember that KM is not an overnight epiphany. It takes time to provide a KM solution and the solution be adopted by the culture.

19.26. Conclusion

KM is an enabler of transformation and this organization is using it to transform into an organization that has a sharing culture. This organization recognizes the value buried in the minds of individuals as intellectual capital and is working to leverage this

---

21. The context of "learning" in lessons learned is organizational learning. Organizational learning involves the use of an organizations collective capability of its staff to create new or improved business and operational processes, procedures, products and services. Organizational learning is more than the sum of the information held by employees. It requires systematic integration and collective interpretation of new knowledge that leads to collective action and involves risk taking as experimentation.

knowledge in a broader way as organizational assets that positively affect organizational performance. This KM initiative is a very rewarding journey and although the organization has not reached its destination, they are confident in their direction to achieve a sharing culture that contributes to operational performance improvements.

Six years later, this organization knows so much more than it would have known without its KM initiative. A quick summary below of their journey depicts they are on the road to success. This organization has

1. a knowledge foundation that aligns with organizational performance,
2. a communication and collaboration platform that enhances the working environment of staff to help them work smarter and faster,
3. a road map to reach their KM objectives and goals,
4. the definition of a high-level KM methodology that can be leveraged, expanded, and implemented in future phases,
5. a "change agent" to help minimize the impact of change on the organization's most valuable asset — its staff,
6. formal CoPs that empower the knowledge worker to contribute to individual and organizational performance,
7. enhanced training on KM tools and job aids to improve the use of the tools,
8. a baseline of the "change health" of members of three CoPs,
9. the start of business intelligence to create KM scorecards, dashboards, and professional reports that support the visualization of performance trends and patterns,
10. a path to identify and subsequently measure KM's contributions to gauge success, and
11. a maturing KM infrastructure to sustain its growth and renewal through knowledge integration, change management, and transformation.

Significant outcomes of this organization's KM initiative are contributing to improvements in business operations and to helping this organization handle its workload in a timely manner. Staff

1. performs timelier work activities due to better decision-making,
2. benefits from improved business operations through sharing innovative ideas and practices and known obstacles and problems,
3. contributes to the identification of inconsistent and redundant work activities and practices,
4. helps to bridge disconnects between work practices and standard operating procedures,
5. benefits from improved communication and collaboration through better ways to get in touch with the right people to get the right answer at the right time,
6. experiences reduced learning curves when new to the organization, and
7. retains valuable knowledge of key employees who are eligible to retire.

This organization is on the right path to achieving its KM goals and objectives.

Author Biographies

Dr. Aurilla Aurélie Bechina ARNTZEN is a Professor at the college University of Buskerud, Norway. She is an adjunct Professor at the college University of Hedmark in Norway and visiting Professor at Bangkok University in Thailand. She received her Ph.D in Automation, from Institute National des Sciences Appliquées (INSA) of Strasbourg, France. Dr. Arntzen has several years of teaching and research IT experience with several well-known International institutions in Australia, Thailand, Sweden, Germany, Norway and France. Her academic interests are broad ranging from real-time systems development to the conception of knowledge systems. As an independent consultant, she works with customers in France, Germany, Sweden and Norway in Project management, training, business process improvement, and information and knowledge management systems. She has participated in and co-led several European projects. Dr. Arntzen serves as an expert evaluator for the European commission and the Norwegian research council, is an author and co-author of several technical and scientific publications, and is the Director for International Relations at the South–East Asian Branch of the Institute for Knowledge and Innovation (iKi-SEA) http://iki.bu.ac.th

Dr. Vittal S. ANANTATMULA's current research is focused on integrating knowledge management and project management, which includes knowledge management effectiveness, project management performance, and leadership. Dr. Anantatmula is an Associate Professor and Director of Graduate Programs in Project Management, College of Business, Western Carolina University. He has publications in journals such as Journal of Knowledge Management, International Journal of Knowledge Management, Journal of Information and Knowledge Management Systems (VINE), International Journal of Knowledge and Learning, and Project Management Journal, co-authored a book, Project Planning Techniques with Praviz Rad, and presented numerous papers in prestigious and international conferences. Prior to joining Western Carolina University, Dr. Anantatmula was on the faculty at the George Washington University teaching and directing a graduate degree program. For several years, he has worked in the petroleum and power industries as an electrical engineer and project manager. As a independent consultant, he has worked with the World Bank, Arthur Andersen, and other international consulting firms. Dr. Anantatmula holds a B.E. (Electrical Engineering) from Andhra University, MBA from IIM-MDI, MS and D.Sc. in Engineering Management from the George Washington University. He is a certified Project Management Professional and Certified Cost Engineer.

Dr. Francesco A. CALABRESE is Founder/President/CEO of the Enterprise Excellence Management Group, Int'l. Inc. (ExMG), a leadership and enterprise strategies consulting firm. He is an Adjunct Professor in The George Washington University, School of Engineering and Applied Science, specializing at the Graduate level in the fields of: Transformational Enterprise Change, Leadership, Knowledge Management, Systems Engineering, Decision Support Systems and Technology Impact Analyses; and also serves as Managing Director of GWU's Institute for Knowledge and Innovation. He has had extensive writings in project and information management methods/tools/techniques; technical reports in geodetic, cartographic, engineering and intelligence systems; authored technical manuals in engineering and guided missiles subject areas; and has recently been publishing in the KM field on cultural behavior influences, system implementation structures, and holistic models and frameworks.

A major portion of his 50 plus professional years have been spent in project management and enterprise leadership/mentoring roles. The spectrum embraces government military and civilian service assignments; large corporate full P&L responsibilities for a global 52 site, 2,500 person staff; and individual/small business technical and mentoring consultant/advisor engagements.

Dr. Calabrese holds degrees in Civil Engineering, Management, and Systems Engineering. He is a Fellow of the American Society for Engineering Management; a Charter Member of Epsilon Mu Eta, the Engineering Management Honor Society; a Member of Chi Epsilon, the Civil Engineering National Honor Society; and a member of the Order of the Engineer. He is a graduate of Dartmouth University's Executive Program "Beyond the Bottom Line"; attended two winter sessions at the Jungian Institute on the "Psychology of Human Behavior"; and was a Certified Nuclear Weapons Analyst and the US Army's Program Manager and Technology Representative for Mapping and Geodesy during the '60's change management era in moving from ground, sea and air to satellite based technology and processes for acquisition and production of cartographic and geospatial intelligence materials and products.

Dr. Vincent M. RIBIÈRE is Assistant Professor at the Graduate School of Bangkok University. He is also the Managing Director of the South Asian branch of the Institute for Knowledge and Innovation (IKI) of Thailand hosted by Bangkok University (http://iki.bu.ac.th) and the Director for Asian activities at the Institute for Knowledge and Innovation at the George Washington University, in Washington, DC, USA (http://www.gwu.edu/~iki). Prior to his current position, Dr. Ribière taught for 10 years at American University (Washington, DC) and at the New York Institute of Technology (NYIT) in New York and in the Kingdom of Bahrain. He received his Doctorate of Science in Knowledge Management from the George Washington University, and a Ph.D. in Management Sciences from the Paul Cézanne University, in Aix en Provence, France. Vincent teaches, conducts research and consults in the area of knowledge management and information systems. Over the past years, he presented various research papers at different international conferences on knowledge management, organizational culture, information systems and quality as well as publishing in various refereed journals and books. vince@vincentribiere.com

Aleša Saša SITAR, M.Sc., is a Teaching Assistant in the Department of Management and Organization at the Faculty of Economics, University of Ljubljana in Slovenia. She teaches and conducts research in the area of management, organization theory, corporate culture, organizational learning, and knowledge management. Over the past years, she has written and presented various research papers at different international conferences in organizational learning and knowledge management.

Dr. Elsa RHOADS was a Management and Information Technology Consultant in Chicago, where she earned a Master's degree in Public Administration from Roosevelt University, and served as an Adjunct Professor, prior to being recruited to join a U.S. federal agency in Washington D.C. She earned a Doctor of Science degree from The School of Engineering and Applied Science at The George Washington University. Her empirical research compared the relationship between knowledge management practices in U.S. federal agencies towards the achievement of presidential mandates for the "transformation" of federal agencies to electronic government – first, to improve the government's services to citizens, and after the events of "9/11/2001", to provide cross-agency collaboration and the sharing of knowledge to prevent future terrorist attacks. She was a charter member of the Federal Knowledge Management Working Group in 2000, and served as Co-Chair and Board member.

Dr. Kevin J. O'SULLIVAN is an Associate Professor of Management specializing in Knowledge Management and Information Systems at New York Institute of Technology. He also holds the posts of Associate Dean and Chair of the Management and Marketing Department. He has over sixteen years of experience IT and KM experience in multinational firms and consulting both in the private and public sector in American, Middle Eastern, European and Far Eastern cultures. Dr. O'Sullivan has delivered professional seminars to global Fortune 100 organizations on subjects such as global collaboration, knowledge management, information security and multinational information systems. His research interests include knowledge management, intellectual capital, and security and information visualization. He has been published in journals such as the Journal of Knowledge Management, The Journal of Information and Knowledge Management and the International Journal of Knowledge Management among others and has published many book chapters, proceedings and papers as well as presenting at and chairing international academic conferences. Dr. O'Sullivan is the author of Strategic Knowledge Management in Multinational Organizations (2007) and the forthcoming Strategic Intellectual Capital Management in Multinational Organizations: Sustainability and Successful Implications (2009).

Juan Pablo GIRALDO is a Senior IT Architect at IBM Global Business Services. He has over nineteen years of experience as a Systems Engineer, IT Architect and IT Manager leading the successful design, development and deployment of complex solutions. Since 2003, he has led the Systems Engineering and Architecture Governance activity for large telecommunication clients. He has managed numerous initiatives that foster the creation and reuse of knowledge assets, the development of formal and informal communities of practice, and mentoring the use of collaboration technologies. Dr. Giraldo is also coauthor of two process patents filed by IBM in 2004 and 2007. He can be reached at giraldo@us.ibm.com or jpg703@gmail.com

Jeffery GRABOWSKI serves as vice president, Emerging Technologies at Xerox. As a knowledgeable information technology executive, Grabowski has experience in all levels of technology deployment, with a demonstrated track record in developing and implementing global, enterprise-scale solutions. Grabowski leads a Xerox Global Services team that has extensive experience using innovative technologies to help manage clients' document content and infrastructure assets. In his current role, Grabowski is responsible for identifying, assessing and piloting emerging technologies for platforms used to deliver Xerox Global Services' offerings. Grabowski works closely with Xerox's research centers, technology development groups and customer delivery teams to ensure consistent, high-quality execution of all service offerings. Prior to joining Xerox, Grabowski served as chief technology officer for Datrose Technology Services, a business-process outsourcing firm that provides back-office outsourcing services to Fortune 500 companies. He was also a senior vice president and chief technology officer for VisualPlex Corp., an e-commerce venture in partnership with Bausch & Lomb, Oracle and Enterprise Technology Partners. Grabowski holds a bachelor of science degree in economics and computer science from the University of Rochester in Rochester, NY. He is certified in supply chain management by the American Production and Inventory Control Society (APICS).

Gabriele McLAUGHLIN In her role as Innovation Architect at Xerox Corporation, McLaughlin advised Fortune 100 research teams and Chief Engineers on strategies and techniques to validate industry needs for emerging technologies. Her particular contributions include shortening the transfer and adoption cycle of new research for value creation, digital transformation, and the Enterprise of the Future. McLaughlin moderated the Thought Leadership Program for Xerox Global Services. She is a frequent guest speaker at national events and has authored numerous strategic white papers for innovation focused corporations.

As Director of National Knowledge Practice and Xerox Intellectual Asset Management at Xerox Connect, Inc. (a wholly owned Xerox subsidiary), McLaughlin was responsible for building and leading the KM consultancy and establishing the organizational framework for consistent regional adoption and delivery of Knowledge and Intellectual Asset Management. Previously, McLaughlin held senior-level positions building, expanding, and managing the consulting capabilities for Xerox Federal Systems, Xerox International Technology Deployment, and Xerox Industry Consulting and Systems Integration. McLaughlin studied English and Economics at the undergraduate level in Europe and holds a MS for Information Systems Management from The American University in Washington DC.

She is a doctoral candidate at the School of Engineering and Applied Science at The George Washington University and a research scholar at GWU Institute for Knowledge and Innovation. Her upcoming dissertation focuses on the innovation of knowledge processes in rapidly changing business structures. As adjunct faculty at the School of Engineering and Applied Science, she teaches the graduate-level Knowledge Management curriculum.

Dr. Rudy GARRITY is a manager, consultant, and educator with executive-level experience in the public and private sectors. He writes and teaches on a variety of topics directed toward organizational leadership, strategy, and performance improvement. Dr. Garrity is president of Garrity Associates, Inc., founder of the American Learnership Forum, and author of a new book entitled: *Learnership 2009: The REJUVINATION OF AMERICA through Total Learning, Knowing, and Leading as a Mindful Way-of-Being*. He holds a D.P.A. and M.P.A. in Public Administration from USC, and an MBA and BBA from Monmouth University in N.J.

Dr. Annie GREEN has a Doctor of Science from the School of Engineering and Applied Sciences (SEAS) at George Washington University and a Masters in Information Systems from the George Mason University. She is a Associate Professorial Lecturer at George Washington University. Dr. Green has over twenty years of experience in Information Technology (IT) and Knowledge Management (KM) in the private and public sector. She currently leads a major Knowledge Management effort as a consultant for Keane Federal Systems with the Pension Benefits Guaranty Corporation. Dr. Green has delivered presentations at professional seminars and international academic conferences on subjects such as systems engineering, requirements engineering, intangible asset valuation and knowledge management. She is the author of "Framework of Intangible Asset Valuation Areas: The Sources of Intangibles within an Organization" (2008), has published in journals such as the Journal of Intellectual Capital and Vine, as well as authored a chapter in the "Creating the Discipline of Knowledge Management" (2005) book. Dr. Green was the Knowledge Valuation Portfolio Editor for Vine Journal and is an Associate Fellow of the Institute of Knowledge and Innovation (IKI). Her research interests include systems engineering, knowledge management, and intangible asset valuation. anegreen@seedfirstllc.com

Dr. Philippe VAN BERTEN received a Ph.D. in Management Science from "Telecommunication & Management-Paris" (former National Institute of Telecommunication-INT), a Master degree in Management from the CNAM-Paris and a Master degree in Science from the University of Aix-Marseilles. He has been working for fifteen years in the Bank & Insurance sector both in France and the United States as well as an Agent of the International Trade in the Wine sector. He is an Assistant Professor of Marketing at the University of Pittsburgh, PA-USA. His main research focus is on Systemic Modeling contribution to the Customer Knowledge Management in Marketing.

Dr. Linda J. VANDERGRIFF is a Senior Engineering Specialist at a non-profit Federally Funded Research and Development Corporation. At the Aerospace Institute, she teaches specialty courses on "Architecture Frameworks" and "Complexity, Uncertainty, and Decision Making." She received a BS from the University of Tennessee in Engineering Physics, MS and postgraduate work in Electro-optical Systems Engineering from Southeastern Institute of Technology, and a Doctorate of Science in Engineering Management from George Washington University. Her dissertation focused on decision support framework for Intelligence Age Agile Enterprises. She continues to be an active contributor to the Knowledge Management Community of Practice at George Washington University. She has extensive experience in general and photonics domain-specific system engineering and architecting and in complexity theory engineering implications. Her 30+ years of engineering experience include work to support the Strategic Defense Initiative as a Chief Engineer, Project Lead on a reconnaissance and surveillance system, various experiences in enterprise management, architecting, system engineering, electro-optics development and testing, multi/hyper/ultra spectral intelligence solutions, knowledge management application characterization, and complexity theory, performance/capability simulation. She is co-author of the National Science Foundation Scientific and Technological Education in Photonics (STEP) 8 Course curriculum on the Nature and Properties of Light. (1999). Currently, she serves on the National Science Foundation Visiting Committee to oversee Photonics Technician Training development.

Dr. Alfredo Fedrico Revilak de LA VEGA, has a Doctor of Science from the School of Engineering and Applied Sciences at George Washington University (2006) (Concentration: Innovation and Knowledge Management in Government), He also has a Masters in Computer Science from the University of Arizona (2001) and a Bachelors in Computer Engineering from The Instituto Tecnológico Autónomo de México (ITAM). He worked as Information Technology Manager and Consultant for the largest Financial Institutions in Mexico (Bancomer, Banamex and the CNBV). He has been full time and part time Professor for ITAM University since 1990, teaching Information Technology (IT) and Knowledge Management (KM) related courses. Alfredo Revilak has participated in KM projects at the World Bank, the World Health Organization (PAHO) and the General Service Administration (GSA) in the

US. Currently, Dr. Revilak is a consultant for Keane Federal Systems, supporting the ongoing KM platform at the Pension Benefit Guarantee Corporation (PBGC).

Lieutenant Colonel Anthony P. BURGESS graduated from the United States Military Academy at West Point, NY in 1990 and was commissioned a second lieutenant of Infantry. Burgess holds a masters degree in leader development and counseling from Long Island University and a doctorate of science in knowledge management from the George Washington University where he focused his research on leadership within informal social systems and, specifically, the core group phenomenon in communities of practice. In addition to co-founding the *Company Command* and *Platoon Leader* professional forums for the U.S. Army, Burgess has co-authored two books: *Taking the Guidon: Exceptional Leadership at the Company Level* (2001) and *Company Command: Unleashing the Power of the Army Profession* (2005). He is the Director of the Center for the Advancement of Leader Development and Organizational Learning at West Point, New York.

Massimo FRANCO is Professor of Organization and Human Resources Management at University of Molise. He serves as the Chairman of the Business Management Studies within the Undergraduate and Graduate Programs. He is also Associate Director of the Department of Economics, Management and Social Sciences (SEGeS) of the University of Molise and a member of the Evaluation Board of the University of Sannio-Benevento. Franco teaches courses on organizational studies, organizational behaviour and team dynamics. His research interests and publications focus on new forms of organizations, team based organizations, teamwork and teambuilding, human resource management and competences. mfranco@unimol.it

Dr. Stefania MARIANO received her PhD in Management from Molise University in 2006 and her MBA with honours in Business Management from Molise University in 2002. She was visiting scholar at the Department of Management Science of the George Washington University (USA) and visiting researcher at IKI – Institute of Knowledge and Innovation at GWU (USA). She was associated as an intern with the KM practice of SAIC (McLean, Virginia, USA) and worked at the Department of HR of M. Demajo

Group (Malta). She has a consolidate experience in national and international research projects. She taught classes in Strategic Management, Organizational Behaviour, and KM. Her research interests are: knowledge management and organizational learning, organizational memory, knowledge retrieval. She is an Assistant Professor of Management at NYIT – New York Institute of Technology. smariano@nyit.edu

Dr. J. Steven NEWMAN is Vice President, Technology Application of ARES Corporation. He has a distinguished 32 years of service in the government with the National Aeronautics and Space Administration (NASA) and the Federal Aviation Administration (FAA). At ARES Dr. Newman manages programs related to the Space Exploration Mission Directorate integrated knowledge management and risk management program. In this role Dr. Newman is spearheading NASA implementation of wiki technology to assist more effective communication and collaboration. Dr. Newman is also responsible for implementing risk management strategies for the NASA Headquarters Constellation Program as well as knowledge management support to the Office of Safety & Mission Assurance and the NASA Safety Center. Dr. Newman serves as a member of the Missile Defense Agency, senior Readiness Review Team providing independent evaluation of safety and mission assurance issues. He serves on the Board of the International Space Safety Foundation and as a Senior Research Fellow, George Washington University, Institute for Knowledge & Innovation Management. Prior to joining ARES Corporation Newman served as Government, Senior Executive, as Director of the Review and Assessment Division of the NASA Office of Safety & Mission Assurance. In the mid 1990's Newman led the design, development, and implementation of NASA's first operational, multi-functional knowledge management system (KMS). The PBMA-KMS also served as the web-based information hub for two investigation teams – the NASA-led Columbia Task Force, as well as the Columbia Accident Investigation Board. The PBMA-KMS received OMB, 2003 e-Gov Pioneer Award for an "outstanding E-Government best practice application that streamlined operations and improved government services." Dr. Newman also served as Chief Environmental Engineer in the NASA Office of Space Flight, Special Assistant to the Space Shuttle Program Director, Chief Environmental Engineer in the Office of Space Flight, Titan IV Program Manager, and Manager of OSHA and Industrial Safety during his fourteen-year tenure at NASA. Newman is a Fellow of the International Association for the Advancement of Space Safety (IAASS). Previously, Dr. Newman served twelve years at the Federal Aviation Administration, directing over 45 flight test programs. Dr. Newman holds a Bachelor of Science in Electrical Engineering, a Master of Science in Environmental Engineering from Northwestern University, and a Doctorate of Science in Systems Engineering from The George Washington University.

Stephen M. WANDER, NASA (retired) is an Aerospace Engineering Consultant. Mr. Wander most recently served as the Programmatic Audit and Review Manager at NASA Headquarters responsible for the development and implementation of a comprehensive independent compliance verification process to assure the effective implementation of safety and mission assurance requirements across the Agency's program/project community. He was also the co-author/developer of the web-based Process Based Mission Assurance Knowledge Management System (http://pbma.nasa.gov). Mr. Wander has over 39 years of research and development experience in aerospace science and engineering, energy, and environmental management with NASA, the Energy Research and Development Administration (ERDA)/Department of Energy (DOE), and the United States Air Force. He holds a Bachelor of Mechanical Engineering degree from The Ohio State University and a Master of Engineering Administration degree from George Washington University. He has received numerous awards and honors including NASA Exceptional Performance Award, NASA Special Accomplishment Award, NASA Sustained Superior Performance Award, and the IR100 Award. Mr. Wander is a Professorial Lecturer at George Washington University in the School of Engineering and Applied Sciences. He teaches graduate courses in engineering management, decision-making and problem-solving – core courses for both the master and doctoral degree programs-and undergraduate courses in probability, statistics, and statistical inference methods in the Systems Engineering and Engineering Management Department.

Linda Larson KEMP is a consultant with over thirty years of technical and leadership experience in strategic planning, business process reengineering, performance measurement, knowledge management and portal systems, knowledge engineering and expert systems, information engineering, software engineering, systems analysis, interface design, object-oriented development, methodology development, and project management. She has a BBA, an MCIS, and a Certificate in Artificial Intelligence from the University of Denver and is a doctoral candidate in Knowledge Management at the George Washington University. Her current area of interest and study is the intersection between knowledge management and enterprise risk management.

Vladimir TIKHOMIROV, is a Professor, Ph.D. in Industry Economics and Management. Doctor of Science (Economics).
President of the Moscow State University of Economics, Statistics and Informatics.
President of the Euro-Asian Association of Distance Learning.
President of the Association of Economic Higher Schools.
President of the International Academy of Open Education.
Chief Editor and founder of E-learning World Magazine.
Chairman of Expert Board of the State Duma Education and Science Committee.

Natalia TIKHOMIROVA, Professor, PhD in Economics.
Rector of the Moscow State University of Economics, Statistics and Informatics.
Russian envoy in the European Organization for Quality. Head of working group on e-learning, distance education and new educational technologies at the Committee of the State Duma. Her current research is in the field of the knowledge and quality management, e-learning. The editor of the journal "Economics, Statistics and Informatics" (Russia).

Valentina MAKSIMOVA, Professor, PhD in Economics.
The Head of Economics and Investment Department of the Moscow State University of Economics, Statistics and Informatics. Her research fields are Economics, Intellectual Capital, Knowledge Economy, Investments in Human Capital., Investments. She has published textbooks on Microeconomics and Investment.

Yury TELNOV, Professor, Doctor of Science in Economics.
Vice-rector of the Moscow State University of Economics, Statistics and Informatics. He is a regular speaker in conferences on reengineering and knowledge management. His current research is in the field of knowledge management, learning organization, competence modeling.

Dr. Juan A. ROMÁN works at the National Aeronautics and Space Administration's (NASA) Goddard Space Flight Center as Assistant Director of Engineering in the Applied Engineering and Technology Directorate. In this capacity, he is responsible for overall leadership, direction, management, planning, and implementation of the Directorate's business development activities in Earth Science, Space Science, and Exploration Systems that are strategically important to Goddard. He provides leadership and strategic direction to teams of scientists and engineers developing new scientific mission concepts and proposals. Dr. Román is recognized as an expert in project management, including engineering concept development, process integration, and mission implementation, taking into consideration schedule, cost, and performance requirements.

In addition to his work at NASA, Dr. Román is a faculty member at the Johns Hopkins University, Carey Business School in the Master of Science in Information Technology and Telecommunication Systems for Business (MSITS) program. His research interest focuses on Knowledge Management (KM) covering a wide range of KM strategies, techniques, and technologies that organizations can introduce to improve efficiency, effectiveness, and competitiveness.

Dr. Román has a BS with honors in Mechanical Engineering from the University of Puerto Rico, a MS in Engineering Management with a minor in Systems Engineering from the University of Maryland, and a DSc in Systems Engineering and Engineering Management from The George Washington University.

Subject Index